D1276095

THE EURODOLLAR

Contributors:

Edward M. Bernstein
Head, E M B (Ltd.),
Washington, D.C.

Sir George Bolton, K.C.M.G.
Chairman, Bank of London & South America Limited,
London, England

Otmar Emminger
Vice-President,
Der Deutschen Bundesbank,
Frankfurt, West Germany

Alberto Ferrari
Managing Director,
Banca Nazionale del Lavoro,
Rome, Italy

Gabriel Ferras
General Manager,
Bank for International Settlements,
Basle, Switzerland

Milton Friedman
Professor of Economics,
University of Chicago,
Chicago, Illinois

Robert L. Genillard
General Partner,
White, Weld & Co.,
Geneva, Switzerland

Milton Gilbert
Economic Adviser,
Bank for International Settlements,
Basle, Switzerland
and Warren McClam

Yoshizane Iwasa
Chairman of the Board and President,
The Fuji Bank Limited,
Tokyo, Japan

Charles P. Kindleberger
Professor of Economics,
Massachusetts Institute of Technology, Cambridge,
Massachusetts

Fred H. Klopstock
Manager, International Research Department,
Federal Reserve Bank of New York, New York, New York

Andre de Lattre
Le Sous-Gouverneur,
Banque de France,
Paris, France

W. Earle McLaughlin
Chairman and President,
The Royal Bank of Canada,
Montreal, Canada

THE EURODOLLAR

Frank E. Morris
President
Federal Reserve Bank of Boston,
Boston, Massachusetts
and Jane S. Little

Charles J. Scanlon
Former President,
Federal Reserve Bank of Chicago,
Chicago, Illinois; now Vice-President,
General Motors Corporation,
New York, New York

E. Stopper
President, Banque Nationale Suisse,
Zurich, Switzerland

Alexander K. Swoboda
Professor of International Economics,
Graduate Institute of International Studies,
Geneva, Switzerland

Franz Heinrich Ulrich
Managing Director, Deutsche Bank AG,
Dusseldorf, West Germany

The Bank of England Quarterly Bulletin
The Bank of England,
London, England

Edited by
Herbert V. Prochnow

RAND McNALLY & COMPANY · Chicago

THE GRADUATE SCHOOL
OF BANKING
at the
UNIVERSITY OF WISCONSIN

Sponsored by the
CENTRAL STATES CONFERENCE
OF BANKERS ASSOCIATIONS

Series in Economic Issues

The Five-Year Outlook for Interest Rates

The One-Bank Holding Company

The Eurodollar

Printed in U.S.A. by Rand McNally & Company
Library of Congress Catalogue Card Number: 74-137217

Foreword

The Graduate School of Banking at the University of Wisconsin was organized in 1945 to offer bankers an opportunity for advanced study and research in banking, economics, and monetary problems. Forty-seven students attended the first annual two-week session on the university campus, conducted in cooperation with the Wisconsin Bankers Association. The sponsorship of the School was shortly assumed by the Central States Conference, consisting of the bankers associations of sixteen midwestern states. Attendance at the School increased rapidly and since 1959 has exceeded 1,000 every year. To date, about 7,000 bankers in the United States, as well as a number from abroad, have graduated from the School, which requires attendance at three two-week summer sessions plus satisfactory completion of certain comprehensive problems.

In an effort to broaden its area of influence and service beyond the annual campus session, The Graduate School of Banking at the University of Wisconsin has undertaken a program of publishing occasional papers. This book, The Eurodollar, *is the third in the series. The first,* The Five-Year Outlook for Interest Rates, *was published in August, 1968; the second,* The One-Bank Holding Company, *was published in May, 1969.*

Preface

During the past decade the Eurodollar market has grown from obscurity to a position of prominence in world and national financial affairs. Its sudden and astounding rise is without precedent in modern financial history. The most recent estimates place the volume of funds in the market at about $45 billion. With growth has come change and evolution in structure, operation and capabilities. Even more important, bankers, businessmen, central banks, and governments have become increasingly involved with Eurodollar transactions.

The market has become extremely flexible and effective in mobilizing short-term liquid funds on an international scale, and its advantages and efficiencies are well established. One result is that the flows of funds to and from the market have assumed large proportions. In order to serve their customers, bankers use the market on a daily basis as an alternative source of funds, equivalent in many ways to federal funds or certificates of deposit. Businessmen have discovered that the Eurodollar market and the related Eurobond market are useful sources of financing for their foreign and domestic business operations. Consequently, developments in the Eurodollar market have an impact on domestic liquidity, credit, interest rates, and the balance of payments. Even central banks and governments have made extensive use of the market, on occasion, to offset capital flows and other balance-of-payment developments.

The rapid growth of the market, however, has raised some difficult issues and problems which affect monetary policy, the balance of payments, and the stability of the international financial system. The ability of banks, businesses, and individuals to use the Eurodollar market, when confronted by differences in credit availability and interest rates in domestic money markets and the Eurodollar market, has led to a growing interdependence between world money markets. It has become increasingly difficult for one country to pursue an independent monetary policy if this should be seriously at odds with that of its neighbors or with the conditions prevailing in the Eurodollar market. Although restrictions have been imposed, the market operates outside the direct reach of the regulatory authorities in many important respects. In view of the explosive growth of the Eurodollar market, its evolutionary character, and its present importance for banking and the whole international financial system, the third book in this series published by the Graduate School of Banking is devoted to this significant subject.

At the outset it became evident that a single comprehensive viewpoint of the market was neither possible nor desirable. The market has come to mean many things to different people, and it was concluded that the text should reflect this diversity of opinion. To present the history of the early development of the market, we invited Sir George Bolton, Chairman of Bank of London & South America Limited, London, who was instrumental in the development of the market. For an examination of the size, structure, and mechanics of the market and its use by U.S. banks, we turned to the Federal Reserve System, from which we invited Mr. Charles J. Scanlon, until recently President of the Federal Reserve Bank of Chicago; Mr. Frank E. Morris, President of the Federal Reserve Bank of Boston; and Mr. Fred H. Klopstock, Manager of International Research of the Federal Reserve Bank of New York. For an assessment of the impact of the market upon the U.S. balance of payments, we invited Mr. Edward M. Bernstein, Head of E M B (Ltd.), Washington, and an influential student of international monetary affairs since the Bretton Woods Conference in 1944 at which The International Monetary Fund Agreements were worked out.

The Eurodollar market poses many problems for the central banks and the monetary authorities. For a review and analysis of these and the restrictions on Eurodollar transactions which have resulted, we invited Dr. Otmar Emminger, Vice President, Der Deutschen Bundesbank, the German central bank; Dr. Gabriel Ferras, Managing Director of the Bank for International Settlements, Basle, Switzerland; and Dr. Milton Gilbert, Economic Adviser of the Bank for International Settlements.

The Eurodollar and Eurobond markets are international markets in the true sense of the term. Consequently, we decided to include an examination of the experience and problems that Canada, five leading European countries, and Japan have experienced with the Eurodollar market. We invited Mr. W. Earle McLaughlin, Chairman and President of The Royal Bank of Canada, Montreal; Mr. Andre de Lattre, Le Sous Gouverneur, Banque de France, Paris; Mr. Franz Heinrich Ulrich, Managing Director, Deutsche Bank AG, Dusseldorf, West Germany; Mr. Alberto Ferrari, Managing Director of the Banca Nazionale del Lavoro, Rome; Mr. Yoshizane Iwasa, Chairman of the Board and President, The Fuji Bank Limited, Tokyo; and Dr. E. Stopper, President, Banque Nationale Suisse, Zurich to contribute the view of the Eurodollar market as seen from the perspective of their various countries. Similarly, for the view from London we obtained permission from the Bank of England to include an article which appeared in a recent Bank of England *Quarterly Bulletin.* Mr. Robert Genillard, General Partner of White, Weld Co., Geneva, Switzerland, one of the leading factors in the Eurobond market, prepared the chapter on this market.

The academic community has also developed some useful viewpoints and commentary on the Eurodollar market and, in an effort to include these, we turned to several distinguished monetary scholars. Dr. Milton Friedman of the University of Chicago kindly allowed us to include an article which originally was published by the Morgan Guaranty Trust Company. Dr. Charles P. Kindleberger of the Massachusetts Institute of Technology and Dr. Alexander K. Swoboda of the Graduate Institute of International Studies, Geneva, Switzerland, have also presented their viewpoints.

The editor is indebted to William J. Korsvik, Vice-President, The First National Bank of Chicago, for his helpfulness in the organization and preparation of the first two books in this series, and to John M. Davis, Jr., Assistant Vice-President of the Bank, for similar assistance with this book on the Eurodollar. Both Mr. Korsvik and Mr. Davis have made important contributions in making these books possible. The result, we believe, is a timely, balanced, readable review of the Eurodollar market, a development which is likely to continue to play a significant role in monetary and international financial affairs in years to come.

Herbert V. Prochnow
Editor

October, 1970

Table of Contents

THE EURODOLLAR

I

SIR GEORGE BOLTON, K.C.M.G.

Sir George was born in 1900 and attended Leyton County High School. He started his career with the Société Générale de Paris in London and, in 1920, joined the merchant banking firm of Helbert Wagg & Co. Ltd., in whose employ he served for twelve years. At the invitation of the late Montagu Norman, Sir George joined the Bank of England to assist in the management of the Exchange Equalization Account. Only two years later he assumed sole charge of the Bank's exchange operations.

Playing a major role in the administration of the wartime exchange control, he was appointed Adviser to the Governor of the Bank of England in 1942 and was elected to the Court of the Bank and appointed an Executive Director in 1948.

An adviser to the U.K. Delegation to the Bretton Woods Conference in 1944, Sir George was appointed the first U.K. Director of the IMF when it commenced operation two years later. He continued in this capacity until 1952, when he became the U.K. Alternate Governor of the Fund. In 1949 he also became a Director of the Bank for International Settlements in Basle.

Sir George retired from the Bank of England on February 29, 1968. He is presently Chairman of the Bank of London and South America Limited, Chairman of Intercontinental Banking Services Limited, and Chairman of the Commonwealth Development Finance Co. Ltd.

Background and Emergence of the Eurodollar Market

"*Si Dieu n'existait pas, il faudrait l'inventer.*" It has been said that if the Eurocurrency market did not exist it would have had to be invented. Unlike in Voltaire's definition of God, the market did in fact evolve and in response to real needs. Indeed, it would be misleading to suggest that what has become a unique source of international finance for a capital-hungry world was the outcome of some economic freak or monetary accident, or that the owners of unconverted foreign currencies discovered by chance how to place them profitably. It is precisely because the market meets the needs of both borrowers and lenders that it has developed so strongly and is now far from being the transient phenomenon it was once held to be.

TRADITIONAL MARKETS

The traditional money-market organization, persisting up to about 1958, was regulated by central banks and governments through a variety of mechanisms, the most important being in the highly sophisticated financial centers of London and New York. The most efficient machinery then devised included a money market which mobilized and offset the cash resources and claims of the local banking community, with the central bank using the market to help in controlling the liquidity of the deposit banks in relation to the general economic needs of the community. The existence of short-term government bonds, treasury bills, and commercial bills in volume was an essential element in enabling money markets to function at a profit and to provide the liquidity guarantee demanded by the commercial banks.

Probably the most efficient and highly articulated system could be found in London where, under the supervision of the Bank of England, the money market operated principally in evening out the daily movement of cash between banks, the net money position being invested in treasury bills, commercial bills, and short-term government bonds. Something of the same kind of machinery was available in New York; the total figures were larger than in London, but the operation of the market was much more dependent upon decisions of both a technical and a policy nature reached in Washington between the U.S. Treasury and the Federal Reserve Board. The money market in New York was also much more involved in supplying short-term credit to the New York stock exchange than was the case in London, and there were few organizations that acted as principals. Both London and New York have developed and maintain organizations and techniques that enable the dollar and sterling systems to operate a daily clearing, not only of the domestic but of all the international movements in their currencies.

Over the years, but largely as a result of the stresses brought about by wartime expenditure and postwar inflationary financing, both New York and London have tended to lose the character of free markets and to become less flexible, both in their structure and in their day-to-day operations. In the U.S.A. all interest rates are subject to mandatory control and the treasury-bill rate is more or less determined from day to day by the decisions of the committee in charge of open-market operations. In London, the firms in the money market are supervised by the Bank of England; the clearing banks have established fixed rates of interest affecting depositors and borrowers over a very wide range. There is also, however, a variety of banking and quasi-banking companies which operate independently of any agreements that fix rates of interest. Until recently most of the European centers operated their domestic monetary markets where they existed, largely in relation to the ultimate clearing centers of New York and London. The key to the short-term money rates on the Continent was the rediscount rate in the Federal Reserve centers and the bank rate in London.

FRAMEWORK FOR INTERNATIONAL MONEY MARKET

Foreign-exchange markets were active in all financial centers and, in many instances, provided the channel through which local cash surpluses in domestic currency and foreign exchange could be placed. They represented the means of access to the two main markets, New York and London, where short-term funds could be invested or deposited in practically any volume. The London foreign-exchange market was supervised by the Bank of England, which was obliged at all times to intervene in order to ensure an orderly market and to maintain the international value of sterling within the established margins of fluctuation. In New York, the market was less highly organized, largely because the international value of the U.S. dollar was ultimately controlled by the purchase and sale of gold at fixed prices and therefore required a somewhat less sophisticated exchange market. Until 1968 anyway, this facility was available only to central banks and comparable monetary authorities who had been given permission by the Secretary of the Treasury to buy and sell gold at the official price through the agency of the Federal Reserve Bank. In London, there existed an international gold market available only to authorized bullion dealers and nonresidents which was a bridge between the U.S. gold reserves and the world at large and was subject to intervention by the Bank of England. The Bank of England, however, took no official responsibility for maintaining a fixed price for gold. Nevertheless, apart from the flurry in October 1960, the price did not vary significantly from the notional gold parity of sterling and there had been very substantial transactions with central banks through the agency of the London bullion market. The combination of gold markets in Europe and earmarking in the U.S.A., and of money markets and foreign-exchange markets, seemingly provided the technical foundation of the international currency system and ensured that the machine worked efficiently.

NEED FOR NEW TECHNIQUES

These arrangements broadly satisfied the needs of both the domestic and foreign banking communities included in the two major international currency areas, namely, the dollar and sterling systems, and led to the establishment of the essential banking mechanisms for financing domestic and foreign trade and investment. The procedures had been inherited from the gold standard days and had been gradually reconciled with current needs during the long period of monetary inflation that began after the depression of the 1930s, a process greatly accelerated during and after the Second World War. The policies of the two central banks, the Federal Reserve System and the Bank of England, although not coordinated, had tended to be taken into account by each party. It was assumed that the markets and the facilities available, plus the control exercised through the New York rediscount rate and the London bank rate, along with open-market money operations and gold transactions, sufficed for all practical needs.

That both markets were subject to growing internal rigidities arising from increasing control which made them less capable of carrying out a comprehensive international function either was overlooked or was tolerated on the assumption that other centers would have no alternative but to accept the situations in the two major markets. While pre-1939 monetary techniques and procedures survived the war and were reinforced by the Bretton Woods Agreements, they had proved to be increasingly deficient in meeting the monetary consequences of the political burdens accepted by the British and U.S. governments in connection with the postwar situation. These burdens included large-scale rearmament—the automatic consequence of the cold war—combined with growing welfare expenditure for domestic political reasons. In the case of the U.S.A., aid to weaker countries (substantially for the purpose of implementing foreign policy) was a further cause of the economy being strained to the breaking point.

The consequences of decisions in the political sphere were felt progressively in the economic field, and they subsequently had their effects on the solidity of the reserve currencies. Non-American holders enjoyed a large and growing supply of dollars from the time of the Korean conflict while sterling holdings remained substantially at the immediate postwar figure. Strong reserve situations had been built up in countries such as Germany, the Benelux group, Italy, and France, which had been less affected than Britain and the United States by both the domestic and the international pressures that dictated U.S. and British policies. In addition, the local cash surpluses on the Continent tended to become more difficult to place as they increased in volume and found no outlet in local markets.

Despite the assumed flexibility of the New York and London money markets, strains became manifest as a result of this growing volume of foreign exchange, and a loose organization developed and began operating at rates of interest freely established without central bank supervision or control. In many dollar-surplus countries, dollars tended to remain in private hands; in fact, many European central banks, under pressure from the Federal Reserve not to demand gold, at times did everything possible to avoid buying surplus dollars from their domestic banks.

These developments, which became noticeable in the early 1950s, greatly increased the activity of foreign-exchange markets and brought about a growth of forward-exchange operations largely as a corollary of surplus funds endeavoring to move from one center to another with the minimum of exchange risk. In the course of the development of this embryonic international money market, interest rates for sterling and dollar deposits tended to fluctuate with the volume of supply and demand, the level of forward exchange rates, and the rates of interest current outside the official New York or London markets. While the official domestic money-market rates played a determining part in setting the general level of interest rates in the international market, it is significant that the movement of money did not flow through old established channels. It is clear that, because of the official regulations in the U.S.A. and the accepted practices among the clearing banks in London, the various participants in these two domestic money markets were precluded from dealing in the international market. Their place was filled by a mixture of overseas banks, the offices of foreign banks and, to some extent, the larger industrial corporations in the U.S.A. and Continental Europe who were anxious to participate in the exchange of surplus cash resources among themselves without the intervention of domestic banks.

There has been a tendency in recent years for financial journalists and economic commentators to suggest that there is a technical way out of monetary and exchange difficulties through the use by central banks of forward-exchange markets. There is no doubt that gerrymandering the forward exchange is a technical device that can be used to some advantage by central banks from time to time. If, however, the central banks lend their names permanently to forward-exchange operations in any of the leading currencies using the largest domestic banks as agents, they will vastly increase the scope of these markets and, incidentally, will make much easier than need be the path of the speculator and the hedging of fixed assets in countries with a weak currency.

Most banks impose limits on their activities in foreign-currency deposits and forward-exchange operations and on the volume of transactions with each individual bank. A central bank, by definition, has no such limitation in its own market. While transactions between central banks may have limitations, if all central banks were to engage in this kind of operation the velocity of foreign-exchange turnover could substantially increase and the volume of transactions could be magnified out of all proportion to business and financial needs.

An even greater danger could occur, in the event of there being an alarm about the financial position of any one country. If the outstanding volume of transactions in foreign exchange had greatly increased internationally as the result of the wider market following central bank operations, the point could be reached when leads and lags could make nonsense of balance-of-payments statistics. It is to be hoped, therefore, that whatever the central banks may do in this field, they will not regard forward-exchange rate intervention as an alternative to some simple, though painful, reforms of the monetary and budgetary policies of their own governments. Intra–central bank swaps to provide resources to help support weak currencies are nothing more than short-term loans, the forward contract providing a guarantee against loss.

Central bank cooperation, under the stress of balance of payments and gold and exchange difficulties, has been making great strides in recent years. So far, the central banks have been concentrating on maintaining the present official pattern of rates of exchange. Some of the techniques that are being used, however, do no more than buy time. With the danger, already mentioned, of difficulties developing among the banks of any one country and causing a chain reaction internationally, it would appear very necessary that the central banks, in concentrating on exchange problems, should act with the greatest prudence. The confidence that exists among members of the international banking system is as strong as each individual link in the chain. The central banking community, while carrying out its responsibilities for the soundness and value of national currencies, should not overlook the fact that the currency in a modern state cannot exist independently of the domestic and foreign banking system, and that no banking system in the Western world can be treated in isolation from any other.

The importance of the central banks' experiment in controlling foreign-exchange markets reveals the growing remoteness from the original concept of providing money and a credit base to enable trade in the widest sense to be financed and settled. Their increased awareness of the dangers to all communities of violent inflation with its concomitant of social unrest and panic movements of money across the exchanges has persuaded the monetary authorities to restrict commercial banking activities at home and abroad without consideration to the long-term consequences. As a result, monetary authorities in many countries may incur the hostility of trade and industry. In such circumstances the maintenance of an international money market operating broadly under the rules of demand and supply becomes a matter of great importance to the world of free enterprise.

EMERGENCE OF EUROCURRENCY MARKET

The real antecedents of the international money market—known colloquially as the Eurocurrency market—can be traced back to 1933: sterling and the dollar had both been driven off the gold and gold exchange standards. In 1936 came the Tripartite Monetary Agreement, designed to restrict the fluctuations of the French franc, the U.S. dollar, and sterling by central bank cooperation in the exchange markets. This agreement was the first successful attempt after the events of 1931–33 to organize cooperation between monetary authorities, and it helped eventually to clarify postwar thinking on monetary arrangements. The Bretton Woods Conference of 1944 set up the International Monetary Fund and the International Bank for Reconstruction and Development to restore the monetary world that we had previously known. But the breakdown of the international payments system, an inevitable consequence of the world depression which, it is often forgotten, only terminated with the massive mobilization of human and material resources for military purposes beginning in 1939, brought into being in the 1930s barter trade, clearing agreements, and similar unorthodox experiments organized to keep trade going. Many of these methods depended upon the use of a third currency as a measure of value, and finance organizations began to be utilized to break away from classic methods of financing foreign trade.

The final transition from established orthodox banking techniques began in 1957, when the impending decline of the sterling system became clearly visible following the decision by the British authorities to impose restrictions on certain types of foreign investment and trade financing together with a bank rate of 7 per cent and a credit squeeze. Eurodollar transactions in London and Switzerland began to assume significant proportions. The liberalization in 1958 of exchange controls by a large number of central bank authorities gave to British and Swiss commercial banks the freedom to accept foreign-currency deposits at more favorable rates of interest than were obtainable in New York. This was followed by progressive measures taken by the American monetary authorities to limit access by foreigners to the New York market; today, fresh dollar resources needed to finance third parties can in practice be found only in the European market. In the early days, the main activity between banks was in comparatively short-term fixed deposits, and it became possible to arrange overnight money and callable deposits. The market now provides medium-term facilities to industry, term deposits, and has moved into the short end of the capital market.

For a long time there was thought to be some special mystique surrounding the Eurodollar, and a certain amount of confusion has arisen over what is meant by this term. Although any currency can be denominated a Eurocurrency, it is convenient to talk in terms of Eurodollars because the U.S. dollar is the main channel of communication and calculation between the other currencies. Eurodollars, therefore, are in reality claims on the U.S. Treasury whose ownership temporarily changes hands at rates of interest above those permitted in the U.S.A. Eurodollars have no separate rate of exchange and Eurocurrency rates of interest are the rates at which deposits are lent and borrowed in European and other markets. While both lender and borrower are frequently domiciled outside the U.S.A., American corporations of all kinds and the foreign branches of American banks use the market extensively. In all cases, when a Eurodollar deposit is made or repaid, a transfer of funds takes place either in or between banks in the U.S.A.; in other words, the market is an extension of the American banking system, since all settlements take place in the U.S.A.; however, the American authorities cannot control directly the operations that take place.

When these activities first developed it was thought that the limits established by practically every bank on every other bank regarding forward-exchange contracts would ultimately restrict the market. It was also felt that making deposits for periods varying from one day to one year between banks would have some natural limitation and the market would reach saturation in a relatively short time. However, this has not occurred for a variety of reasons, notably because the composition of the market now includes institutions whose credit rating in some cases could not be measured by traditional or practical standards. For example, the leading British local government authorities, as a result of credit squeezes and high money rates, were left in a position where recourse to the London market represented only a remote hope and not a reality. To meet their growing liabilities, the various local government treasurers, who had been in the habit of taking local short-term money, were in a position (if they paid high enough rates) to take deposits from seven days up to one year or more. There is no doubt whatever that some of the short-term liabilities of the British local authorities have a foreign-exchange origin. Similarly, the British hire-purchase finance companies, when they became associated with or controlled by the clearing banks, also found that their credit standing was such that they could compete for this kind of money, and very large sums have been deposited with them through the operations of the international money market. The market was also broadened by the Canadian Chartered Banks and the London and European offices of the leading United States banks, the latter being anxious to accept deposits partly through a desire to have a position in this market and partly to keep up the deposit figures of each bank as a whole. It is perhaps a paradox that the cash liquidity of many of the large American banks is dependent upon the supply of funds in the Eurocurrency market.

A situation has now been reached where hundreds of the leading banks of the world are engaged in depositing money with each other, without security, at rates of interest affected but not determined by the margins of the official money rates prevalent in the New York and London markets. This has been accomplished entirely as a result of international needs, the enterprise of the banks, the confidence they have in each other, and the fact that the main domestic money markets have become too subject to domestic requirements and political direction. There seemed little doubt that, through the passage of time and in the absence of any change in the procedures of the official money markets, this international market would affect domestic money rates. One can now see the extent to which it has done so. It is scarcely accurate to describe these activities as hot-money movements. They do not represent speculation; in fact, if there appears to be too much money on current account in short-term international circulation, government policies over the postwar period are mainly if not entirely responsible.

THE MARKET'S PROBLEMS

The international money market has attracted comment and criticism, partly because, traditionally, any banking operation not conforming to a set of precepts laid down by established authority and hallowed by custom raises questions. Since international money market operations do not conform to precedent and are not subject to direct control, the suspicion arises that unsound practices will develop and that the resources available will be used unwisely. However, it is difficult to see why anyone should think that regulation by exchange control, taxation, or even central banking authority makes a banker more cautious in his handling of other people's money.

There have indeed been several crises on which the market's critics will seize to illustrate their point. There was the Japanese crisis of 1963, which was overcome largely by the action of the Bank of Japan with the support of the international banks. This was followed by the Italian Stock Exchange collapse which severely shook international confidence and set off a flight of capital from Italy. The assistance given to Italy by foreign central banks, as well as her Eurodollar borrowings during this period, exceeded $750 million, and these funds were employed to increase domestic liquidity and to finance external transactions in order to reduce the claim on official reserves. Then again, there was the vegetable oil affair in New York, and a number of other bankruptcies, one example being the Intra Bank of Beirut which would have endangered a market that was not basically sound.

Another severe test began in the autumn of 1965 with the sterling crisis. Starting with a massive outflow of funds from London, the crisis brought about pressures on international interest rates that have since been rising rapidly, partly as a direct result of monetary techniques but largely—so far as Britain was concerned—because of a loss of confidence. Close on the heels of the sterling crisis came a growing shortage of cash resources in the U.S.A. and, in August 1966, the American banking system was on the verge of seizing up. What then seemed startlingly high interest rates were paid by the European branches of American banks, who drew $2 to $3 billion out of Europe. Although the situation became less tense, crisis level was again reached in 1969. Once more the market showed its resilience and powers of survival.

An international money market has been created which is more efficient in terms of the speed and the sophistication of its transactions than were the classic money markets. It has shown its strength by withstanding, without apparent ill effect, a series of crises. By tapping previously unused liquid reserves of various sorts and origins, the market has made a contribution to the financing of international trade as well as to the financing of domestic operations. Despite the dangerous meddling and interference of governments in the workings of a highly sophisticated mechanism (which they may seek to curb to satisfy their desire for overriding control of all economic activity), the ceaseless ingenuity of the financial world will continue to provide essential facilities even under the most unfavorable circumstances.

II

CHARLES J. SCANLON

Mr. Scanlon, former President of the Federal Reserve Bank of Chicago, is a Chicagoan by birth. He attended Northwestern University's School of Commerce and is a graduate of the Stonier Graduate School of Banking.

Mr. Scanlon began his career with the Federal Reserve Bank as a young man. Eventually, he served as Chief Examiner for the Seventh Federal Reserve District, was elected First Vice-President of the bank in 1959 and was named President in 1962.

As President of the Federal Reserve Bank, Mr. Scanlon was a member of the Federal Open Market Committee, and served as Chairman of the Investment Committee of the Federal Reserve Retirement System. In 1969–70 Mr. Scanlon was Chairman of the Conference of Presidents of the Federal Reserve Banks and has been a member of numerous System committees.

During 1961 Mr. Scanlon served as a banking consultant to the Republic of Liberia. He has been a frequent lecturer at the Graduate School of Banking, University of Wisconsin, and is the author of numerous articles on bank supervision and monetary policy.

He is the recipient of honorary degrees from North Central College in Illinois and from Western Michigan University.

Mr. Scanlon has recently left the Federal Reserve Bank of Chicago to assume duties as Vice President of General Motors Corporation's pension fund investments.

Definitions and Mechanics of Eurodollar Transactions

DEFINITION OF EURODOLLARS

Eurodollars are U.S. dollar-denominated deposits at commercial banks outside the United States. Eurodollars are not money in the sense that the term is commonly understood. Eurodollars derive all their money-characteristics from the U.S. dollar. Perhaps the only characteristic Eurodollars share with other monies somewhat independently of the dollar is their ability to serve as a store of value. But even in this respect their function is closely tied to the United States dollar. While Eurodollar deposits may, at times, offer an investment return greater than that available on ordinary dollar assets of comparable maturity and security, they still share with the dollar the fortunes (and misfortunes) of changes in the relative purchasing power.

Thus, generally speaking, the only difference between *Eurodollars* and *dollars on deposit* at American banks is the geographic location of the bank at which the dollar-denominated claim is held. Here, too, the term is somewhat a misnomer because such deposit need not be held in a European bank; as

---

Joseph G. Kvasnicka, Assistant Vice-President and Economist with the Federal Reserve Bank of Chicago, has collaborated closely and has been of great assistance in the preparation of this article.

the term is now used, it applies to deposits anywhere in the world outside the United States. Also, unlike the U.S. dollars held by foreigners, Eurodollars are not direct claims on the resources of the United States. They are only claims on foreign banks, and it remains for these banks to provide the dollars from their reserves when the claims are exercised.

MECHANICS OF ESTABLISHING EURODOLLAR DEPOSITS

In the present setting, a dollar-denominated deposit at a bank abroad may be established for a variety of reasons and in many ways. All of these, however, have several characteristics in common. First, considerations of profit, convenience, or safety invariably underlie the process. An individual or a corporation may want to use dollar-denominated deposit facilities in order to improve profits or because the form or location of the deposit is more convenient. He may feel more secure in holding a dollar claim on a bank not under the direct jurisdiction of the U.S. authorities (as would be the case if the funds were held in a U.S. bank).

Second, the transactions leading to the establishment of a Eurodollar deposit invariably involve both an American and a foreign bank at some stage of the process. Although some Eurodollar deposits result from the deposit of U.S. currency in foreign banks, these are relatively rare. Moreover, since foreign banks normally maintain only small amounts of foreign currencies on hand, most of the currency received is promptly shipped to the United States for credit to their accounts with U.S. banks.

A typical sequence of transactions by which a Eurodollar deposit comes into existence is illustrated by the following hypothetical example: Company W, an exporter in Frankfurt, Germany, receives a $1,000,000 payment for goods shipped to the United States in the form of a credit to its demand-deposit account at Bank A in Chicago. The funds will be needed later to make payments for imports from the United States. The company, therefore, wishes to maintain the funds in dollars, preferably in a form that yields a return.

After surveying the financial markets, the treasurer of the company decides to place the funds with Bank Alpha in Frankfurt as a dollar-denominated time deposit. A check is drawn on his account at Bank A in favor of Bank Alpha. (To simplify the matter, we assume Bank A in Chicago and Bank Alpha in Frankfurt maintain correspondent relationships and have working balances with each other.) The check is sent to Bank A and cleared, with the following changes taking place in the balance sheets of the two banks:

BANK A (CHICAGO)

Assets	Liabilities
	−$1,000,000 demand deposit account of Company W +$1,000,000 demand deposit account of Bank Alpha

BANK ALPHA (FRANKFURT)

Assets	Liabilities
+$1,000,000 demand deposit balances at Bank A	+$1,000,000 time deposit of Company W

The $1,000,000 time-deposit liability of Bank Alpha to Company W is a Eurodollar deposit.

Since banks in Germany are required to maintain reserves against their liabilities in the form of deposits with the German Federal Bank, some further adjustments in the balance sheet of Bank Alpha would follow. Assume, for purposes of illustration, that Bank Alpha meets its reserve requirement by selling part of the dollar deposit it holds at Bank A to the German Federal Bank and depositing the marks obtained to its reserve account. With the reserve requirements currently at 7.25 per cent and an exchange rate of 3.66 marks per dollar, the balance sheet of Bank Alpha would change as follows:

BANK ALPHA

Assets	Liabilities
−$72,500 demand deposit balances at Bank A +DM 265,350 reserve balances at the German Federal Bank	

Since the German Federal Bank maintains an account with the U.S. Federal Reserve System, it would probably send the check issued by Bank Alpha to the Federal Reserve Bank of New York for crediting to its account. The Federal Reserve Bank of New York collects the funds from Bank A, with the following changes occuring in the Chicago bank's balance sheet:

BANK A (CHICAGO)

Assets	Liabilities
−$72,500 balances at the Federal Reserve[1]	−$72,500 demand deposit balances of Bank Alpha

Once these transactions have been completed, the amount of Eurodollars outstanding would have been increased by $1,000,000. What was formerly a demand deposit of a German corporation in an American bank, is now a dollar-denominated time deposit at a bank abroad.

The dollar-denominated liability of Bank Alpha—the Eurodollar deposit—is backed up by $927,500 demand deposit of Bank Alpha in Bank A in Chicago and by DM 265,350 (i.e., $72,500, if expressed in dollar terms) at the German Federal Bank. Only the latter backing is required by law; the former represents excess liquidity that Bank Alpha can invest in earning assets. We shall return to this point in subsequent discussion.

[1] The net reserve loss of Bank A would be only $59,812 because the bank is no longer required to maintain 17½ per cent legal reserve requirement (i.e., $12,688) against $72,500 in demand deposits it lost.

This example illustrates a case where a Eurodollar deposit is initiated by a foreign entity holding dollar balances in the United States. A dollar-denominated deposit abroad could also originate with an American resident transferring deposits abroad to take advantage of the higher interest rates paid by foreign banks on dollar deposits.

But the process by which a Eurodollar deposit can be established is not completely dependent upon prior holdings of dollars by the private sectors in the U.S. or abroad. Any holder of convertible currencies such as German marks, Swiss francs, and others, can acquire dollars simply by exchanging his holding of foreign currencies for dollars in the foreign-exchange markets. In most instances, a private holder of U.S. dollar deposits is the other party to the transaction. If, however, the demand for dollars exceeds the supply in a particular national market, the price of dollars, in terms of that country's currency, rises. This, in accordance with international agreements, necessitates intervention by the monetary authority of that country in order to maintain the exchange rate within the agreed upon limits. The authority must draw upon the country's official reserve of dollars and sell dollars into the market in exchange for the country's own currency. If the country does not hold dollar reserves, it must sell gold or use its international credit facilities to acquire dollars to supply to the market. Once the dollars have been placed in the market, the holder can deposit them with a non-U.S. bank and Eurodollars have thereby come into existence.

The central banks have not confined their role in creating Eurodollar deposits to the passive posture just described. Some central banks have placed funds as dollar-denominated deposits at foreign commercial banks simply to maximize the earnings on their holdings of reserves. Other foreign central banks have on occasion used the Eurodollar market to control the liquidity position of the commercial banks in their countries. For example, large amounts of funds flowed into Germany in the spring of 1969 as a result of rumors that the German mark would be revalued. This caused both a rapid and undesired increase in the liquidity of the German banking system and a sharp decline in the availability of funds in the Eurodollar market. The German Federal Bank wanted funds to be cycled back into an international market so as to reduce the excessive liquidity of the German banks and, therefore, offered to provide forward cover for funds placed in the Eurodollar market at an attractive rate. German commercial banks responded to the offer and channeled a large amount of funds into the Eurodollar market.

MECHANICS OF DEALING IN EURODOLLARS

A Eurodollar deposit, once it is created, usually passes through a chain of transactions. The deposit may be loaned and reloaned among banks, borrowed by commercial firms, converted into other currencies, redeposited in foreign commercial banks, and rechannelled back into the market—all within a matter of minutes.

The readiness and speed with which the Eurodollar deposits move reflects the high degree of organization of the market. The *market* refers to the well-established channels of communication between commercial banks abroad through which transactions are conducted quickly and efficiently, serving the needs of both the banks and their customers. The market has no specific location. Its physical dimension is essentially a network of international telecommunication media, linking all major financial centers in Europe. The vital element of the market, of course, is the array of well-informed and versatile traders.

Since the beginning, London has been the major center for trading in Eurodollars. Trading in Eurodollars was an outgrowth of trading in foreign exchange in which London had long had an important role. The key participants in the London market include British banks authorized to deal in foreign currencies, branches of foreign banks, and foreign currency brokers. These brokers serve as intermediaries between banks having funds to sell and those wanting to purchase. In the "trading room" at each of these institutions, a number of traders remain in almost continuous contact by direct telephone lines with other traders in the City and at banks and brokerage houses on the Continent. They receive and give quotes at which they are willing to sell or purchase funds of various maturities. The dealers adjust their quotes almost continuously in response to conditions in the market, their own needs, and the anticipated needs of their customers. The spread between the *bid-ask* quotation is usually from ⅛ to ½ per cent, annual-rate basis. In giving a quotation, the trader may not know whether the inquirer wants to sell or to buy funds and must be prepared to stand by his quote when "hit" on either side. A number of dealers can be contacted within a matter of minutes and a deal concluded at the most advantageous rate.

The brokers' sole function is to bring together buyers and sellers of funds in the most efficient manner. They serve as clearing centers, eliminating the need for individual banks to contact all other banks in the market individually to determine the best deal available at any moment. The brokers maintain large staffs of traders and have a broad knowledge of conditions in the market both locally and abroad. They can usually close deals at rates that are advantageous to both sellers and purchasers. The brokers in London—currently, nine operate there—do not maintain an "inventory" but charge 1/32 of 1 per cent (on annual-rate basis) to both the sellers and buyers they bring together.

The Eurodollar market provides facilities for short-term investment of funds that otherwise would probably remain idle for lack of suitable investment instruments. Banks with a close linkage to the market are able to offer investment facilities closely tailored to the needs of depositors. Given the broadness of the market, borrowers can be found whose needs coincide with those of the lenders.

MECHANICS OF INTERBANK EURODOLLAR TRANSACTIONS

A large portion of the trading among banks consists of "passing on" deposits in the amount and maturity received. For example, in the hypothetical illustration used previously, Bank Alpha in Frankfurt, Germany, received a three-month time deposit of $1,000,000 from Company W and, after satisfying legal reserve requirements with the German Federal Bank, it held $927,500 as a demand deposit in Bank A in Chicago.

Bank Alpha, of course, pays interest to Company W on its deposit but earns no interest on the demand deposit held at Bank A. Clearly, Bank Alpha would want to invest the non-earning deposit it has at Bank A. It has a number of alternatives. It could, for example, lend the dollars to one of its customers to finance an international transaction requiring payment in dollars. Or, it could convert the dollars into German marks and loan them to a local customer. Another possibility is to sell (i.e., redeposit) the dollars in the Eurodollar market.

Let us assume that, after examining the potential return offered by any one of these alternatives, the bank decides to follow the last one. It contacts a Eurodollar broker in London and inquires about the possibility of placing a deposit in London at the going rates. Assume further that the broker has a customer—Bank Beta in London—that approached him a few minutes earlier with a request for a Eurodollar deposit. He would so advise Bank Alpha without revealing the identity of the prospective customer beyond indicating that it was "a merchant bank in the class with such-and-such known bank." This information is important to Bank Alpha because loans (i.e., deposits) in the Eurodollar market are made unsecured on the basis of the name and reputation of the recipient. For that reason, banks lending in the interbank Eurodollar market usually establish specific limits as to how much their traders can place with other banks in the market.

If Bank Alpha is satisfied as to the standing of the would-be borrower and accepts his bid, the broker then reveals the borrower's identity and the broker's role in the transaction is thereby completed. The trader at Bank Alpha then calls Bank Beta to obtain instructions on delivery of the funds. Confirmations of the transactions are forwarded through mail by both the seller and the recipient of the funds, stating the amount, date due, and the contracted rate of interest.

Bank Beta would instruct Bank Alpha to place the funds with Bank Beta's correspondent, Bank B in New York, two days hence.[2] Bank Alpha then wires its correspondent, Bank A in Chicago, instructions to transfer the funds to Bank B in New York for credit to Bank Beta. The transfer of funds from the account of Bank Alpha at Bank A to the account of Bank Beta at Bank B would probably be handled by a wire transfer. Bank B could use the Federal Reserve wire transfer facilities to reduce the reserve account of Bank A at the Federal Reserve Bank of Chicago and to increase the reserve account of Bank B at the Federal Reserve Bank of New York. The following changes would take place in the balance sheets of the banks involved.[3]

BANK A (CHICAGO)

ASSETS	LIABILITIES
—$927,500 reserve balances at the Federal Reserve	—$927,500 demand deposit account of Bank Alpha

[2] As is customary in all "spot" foreign exchange transactions, the transactions in Eurodollars are for delivery two days later. That is, funds sold are "good" after two full business days have elapsed.

[3] For illustrative purposes it is assumed that the deposit is "sold" in its original amount. In the day-to-day transactions it is more likely that the bank would combine other dollar deposits it received during that day into a *round lot,* say of $1 million or more. Transactions in the Eurodollar market are usually carried out in such round lots of $1 million or more, with $10–50 million lots fairly common.

BANK ALPHA (FRANKFURT)

Assets	Liabilities
−$927,500 demand deposits at Bank A +$927,500 time deposit at Bank Beta	

BANK BETA (LONDON)

Assets	Liabilities
+$927,500 demand deposit in Bank B (New York)	+$927,500 time deposit of Bank Alpha

BANK B (NEW YORK)

Assets	Liabilities
+$927,500 reserve balances at the Federal Reserve	+$927,500 demand deposit account of Bank Beta (London)

MECHANICS OF EURODOLLAR LENDING

One of the most typical uses of Eurodollars is in the financing of international trade. To continue the preceding illustration, we assume that Bank Beta acquired the Eurodollar deposit in order to accommodate a Eurodollar loan request by one of its customers. This customer, Company X in Japan, must make a payment to an Australian exporter, Company Y, in U.S. dollars to be credited to Y's account at Bank C in New York.

Pursuant to instructions from Company X, Bank Beta wires its correspondent in New York, Bank B, to effect the transfer. The balance sheet of Bank Beta changes as follows:

BANK BETA (LONDON)

Assets	Liabilities
+$927,500 loans to Company X in Japan −$927,500 demand deposit balances at Bank B in New York	

In New York, a following set of transactions takes place: Upon the receipt of the cable, Bank B issues an *officer's check*—a check drawn by a bank on itself—in favor of Bank C. The check is presented to Bank C and the next day, through the New York Clearing House facilities, to the Federal Reserve where the reserve account of Bank B is debited and that of Bank C is credited with the appropriate amounts.

On the first day the banks' balance sheets change as follows:

BANK B (NEW YORK)

Assets	Liabilities
	+$927,500 officer's check payable to Bank C −$927,500 demand deposit account of Bank Beta

BANK C (NEW YORK)

Assets	Liabilities
+$927,500 cash items in process of collection	+$927,500 demand deposit of Company Y

On the next day, the following changes take place:

BANK B (NEW YORK)

Assets	Liabilities
−$927,500 reserve balances at the Federal Reserve	−$927,500 officer's check

BANK C (NEW YORK)

Assets	Liabilities
−$927,500 cash items in the process of collection +$927,500 reserve balances at the Federal Reserve	

In this example the maturity of the deposit Bank B obtained from Bank A coincided with the maturity of the loan. The bank, in the jargon of the market, was able to "marry" its liability with a claim. Not all loans are made on this basis. Some Eurodollar loans are made for longer maturities, at times up to five years. Such loans are customarily made with a provision that the rate can be adjusted every three months according to the prevailing rate on three-month Eurodollar deposits, plus ½ to ¾ of 1 per cent *add on.* This arrangement enables the lending banks to extend loans for longer terms than three months—the most prevalent maturity in the Eurodollar market. When an outstanding dollar liability matures, the lending bank purchases in the market, at the going rate, another Eurodollar deposit to replace the maturing one.

MECHANICS OF EURODOLLAR SWAPS

Eurodollars are often borrowed and swapped (i.e., exchanged) into other currencies. This is done frequently by commercial banks abroad (foreign exchange regulations of individual countries permitting) to adjust their day-to-day liquidity position or to obtain loanable funds in their own currencies. It is done also by commercial firms to meet their credit needs and, at times, by local government units.

The purpose, of course, is to obtain funds at the lowest possible cost. However, in addition to the relative interest rate at which funds can be obtained in the various markets, the borrower must also consider the *spot*-exchange rates at which dollars can be converted into local currency and the *forward*-exchange rate at which funds in the local currency can be exchanged back into dollars at the time the Eurodollar loan comes due.

With constantly changing conditions in all these markets, situations often arise when it is economical to engage in these swap transactions. But these conditions do not usually persist very long in markets that are relatively free of foreign-exchange controls. As soon as the various market rates are favorable for swaps, such transactions ensue and this causes the rates to move in the direction where the advantage of exchanging one currency for another currency is eliminated.

These transactions provide close linkage between the various convertible currencies and cause the pressures in one national money market to be transmitted to others. An important side effect of this international financial mechanism is the interdependence of interest-rate structures among countries. The Eurodollar market, an important "transmission medium," has contributed greatly to the development of this close linkage of national money and credit markets.

To illustrate the transactions in swapping, we assume that Company Y requested payment in dollars from Company X, anticipating a need to make payment in dollars to a Brazilian exporter three months hence. By obtaining dollars now, the company protects itself against the risk of changes in exchange rates three months later. However, the company does not want to hold an idle demand deposit at Bank C in New York on which no interest is paid, so it invests the funds through the Company's British subsidiary as a three-month Eurodollar deposit at Bank Gamma, a London clearing bank. The company treasurer instructs the subsidiary to issue a check on the Company's account at Bank C in New York in favor of Bank Gamma and deposit it at Bank Gamma. Bank Gamma then sends the check to the Edge-Act subsidiary of a Detroit bank, Bank D International in New York, its U.S. correspondent, to be credited to its account.

Bank D International would present the check to Bank C in New York for payment, and the already familiar changes would take place in the balance sheets of Banks C and D. After the check has cleared, the balance sheet of Bank Gamma would be changed as follows:

BANK GAMMA (LONDON)

ASSETS	LIABILITIES
+\$927,500 due from Bank D International	+\$927,500 time deposit due to Company Y

British banks are not subject to statutory reserve requirements but are expected to maintain a *liquidity ratio* against demand-deposit liabilities of at least 28 per cent in the form of vault cash, deposits at the Bank of England, call loans to the discount market, or short-term government securities. Therefore, Bank Gamma would put aside a portion of the deposit as a *liquidity reserve.* Assuming that the bank maintains a customary liquidity ratio of about 30 per cent, it could convert into sterling $277,500 and invest the proceeds in an asset that fulfills the liquidity requirements, say United Kingdom Treasury bills. If the dollar/sterling exchange rate is £1 = $2.407, the bank's balance sheet would change as follows:

BANK GAMMA (LONDON)

Assets	Liabilities
−$277,500 due from Bank D International	
+£115,300 U.K. Treasury Bills	

Bank Gamma now has $650,000 on deposit at Bank D International that is available for investment. Now assume that Bank Gamma is approached by Company Z in England with a request for a Eurodollar swap loan. Before approaching the bank, the treasurer of Company K probably did the following set of calculations: He needs £270,000 for three months. At 10 per cent annual-rate interest charge (the going rate for such loans in the local market), a sterling loan would cost him £6,750 so that, at the end of the three-months period, he would have to pay his bank £276,750 (principal plus interest).

Alternatively, he could obtain a Eurodollar loan, say, at 9½ per cent annual rate, and convert dollars into pound sterling at the rate currently prevailing in the market of £1 = $2.407. He would need to borrow $650,000 that, after conversion, would give him £270,000. After three months he would have to repay $665,438 (principal plus $15,438 in interest, disregarding any transaction costs associated with conversion). At the current sterling/dollar rate the loan would cost him £6,414, £336 less than if he borrowed sterling.

In order for this transaction to be attractive, however, the borrower must be sure that when the loan matures he can purchase dollars for pounds at about the same rate at which he purchased pounds for dollars. The advantage of borrowing Eurodollars would be wiped out if the pound/dollar rate moved to the lower limit allowed under international agreements, i.e., £1 = $2.380. The treasurer would then need £279,595 to repay the principal and interest—£2,845 more than if he had borrowed sterling.

To ensure against such a decline in the exchange rate, he can "hedge" his loan in the forward foreign-exchange market. In that market, foreign-exchange dealers contract to buy or sell foreign currencies for future delivery at specified rates of exchange. The rates at which they offer such contracts are posted as forward rates.

Forward rates of various currencies may be higher or lower than the spot rates, depending on relative interest rates in the different countries and the market's estimates of future movements in rates.

The treasurer could protect his company against the possibility of an unfavorable change in the sterling/dollar exchange rate by buying *90-day forward dollars*—a contract specifying delivery to him of dollars for sterling three months hence.

The forward-exchange rate specified in the contract, i.e., the rate at which the exchange is to be effected three months hence, would of course be an integral part of his calculations. For example, if the forward dollars were selling at a premium of, say, 2 per cent (annual-rate basis) over the spot dollars in the current market, i.e., £1 = $2.395 ninety days forward, the cost of the loan (including principal and interest) would be

£277,844—£1,094 more than he would have to pay for a sterling loan.

Assume, however, that at the time the loan is being negotiated, 90-day forward dollars can be purchased at a 2 per cent (annual rate) discount from the spot rate, i.e., at £1 = $2.419. The treasurer could enter into contract to purchase the $665,438 he will need to repay the principal and interest on his Eurodollar loan for a fixed amount, £275,088, three months hence. The total cost of his Eurodollar loan (disregarding transaction costs of conversion and forward contract) would be £1,587 lower than if he had borrowed sterling.

With this information in hand, the treasurer approached Bank Gamma for a $650,000 Eurodollar loan. Once the Eurodollar funds were obtained, they were immediately converted by Bank Gamma into sterling through the London foreign-exchange market on behalf of its customer. Bank Gamma simply sold the dollar-demand deposit it held at Bank D in New York to another London bank, Bank Delta, in exchange for an equivalent amount of sterling balances.

Bank Gamma wires instructions to Bank D to transfer the balance to the account of Bank Delta at, say, Bank E in New York. After the transactions have cleared, the balance sheet of Bank Gamma would change as follows:

BANK GAMMA (LONDON)

Assets	Liabilities
−$650,000 demand deposit account at Bank D International	+£270,000 demand deposit of Company Z
+£270,000 balances at Bank Delta	
+$650,000 loan to Company Z	

Company Z may now disburse its sterling balances at Bank Gamma.

MECHANICS OF EURODOLLAR "CREATION"

The "creation" of Eurodollar deposits by the banks participating in the market remains a source of controversy among academicians and market participants. On the one hand, the market participants have maintained that they do not "create" Eurodollars—they merely receive dollars as deposits and, after satisfying necessary reserve requirements, simply pass on or lend the remainder to those willing to pay for the use of such funds. They are, of course, correct in this view.

On the other hand, many observers of the market point out that it is precisely this "passing on" of funds from banks to commercial users and back to banks, ad infinitum, that leaves in its wake a sequence of dollar-denominated liabilities of banks to their customers that may aggregate much more than the amount that is being passed on. They, too, are correct in this observation.

In the foregoing examples, as the $1,000,000 deposit was moved to banks Alpha, Beta, Gamma and Delta, and between banks A, B, C, D, and E, each bank merely lent out the deposit it received from others. Yet, each receiving bank incurred a dollar-denominated liability to the previous owner of the deposit. At the end of the chain of transactions traced so far we have:

1. $1,000,000 dollar-denominated liability of Bank Alpha to Company W;
2. $927,500 dollar-denominated liability of Bank Beta to Bank Alpha;
3. $927,500 dollar-denominated liability of Bank Gamma to Company Y;
4. $650,000 dollar-denominated liability of Bank E to Bank Delta;

—a total of $3,505,000 of dollar-denominated liabilities arising from what was originally a $1,000,000 demand deposit at Bank A in Chicago. In accordance with our definition of Eurodollars we would exclude the $650,000 liability of Bank E to Bank Delta, since it is not a dollar-denominated liability of a *non-U.S.* bank. Following the convention adopted by the Bank for International Settlements that compiles most of the widely used statistics on the Eurodollar market, we would also exclude the interbank liabilities, i.e., the $927,500 liability of Bank Beta to Bank Alpha. After these adjustments we have a total of 1,927,500 Eurodollars outstanding, based on the $1,000,000 foreign deposit in the U.S. banking system, and backed up by $650,000 demand deposits in the United States. Clearly, Eurodollars have been "created" as a result of the sequence of transactions described in our examples.

In theory, the "creation" of Eurodollar deposits is somewhat analogous to the familiar process of deposit expansion in the U.S. or in any other fractional-reserve banking system. The overall expansion of deposits that can take place following the injection of new reserves into the system is determined by the reserve-requirement ratio and can be illustrated as follows:

$$\text{change in deposits} = \text{change in reserves} \times \frac{1}{\text{percentage reserve requirement}}$$

Assuming there are no leakages (such as the withdrawal of funds in the form of currency) and that 10 per cent of deposits are held as reserves, $1,000,000 additional deposits after the process of redepositing has fully absorbed the additional reserves will leave:

$$\text{change in deposits} = \$1{,}000{,}000 \times \frac{1}{.10} = \$10{,}000{,}000$$

In adapting the formula to the Eurodollar market, the *change in Eurodollar deposits* can be substituted for *change in deposits; change in "primary" Eurodollar deposits* (i.e., U.S. demand deposits that are "converted" into Eurodollar deposits, such as the deposit of Company W in Bank Alpha) for *change in reserves;* and the *reserve requirements* in various countries participating in the market for *percentage reserve requirement.*

The result is a formula that provides a theoretical base for determining the expansionary potential of the Eurodollar market.

In a practical application, however, there are certain differences between a national system and an international system such as the Eurodollar market. In the Eurodollar system only a very small portion (if any) of the dollar-deposits received by banks in the Eurodollar market is absorbed as reserves. While banks in most countries are required to maintain reserves against their deposit liabilities, however denominated, these need not be held in dollars. Banks receiving dollar deposits can usually pass them on in the original amount either to other banks or to nonbank users. The back up for the dollar-denominated liability is provided by the dollar-denominated claim, and any required reserves can be provided in the banks' own domestic currency.

Furthermore, while in a national system the reserve base is under close control of the monetary authorities, the "reserve base" in the Eurodollar market can be expanded almost at will by the participants themselves. In the Eurodollar market, banks, corporations, and individuals in countries not subject to foreign-exchange controls can convert their own currency into dollars and, subsequently, into Eurodollars, thereby increasing the "reserve base" on which the expansion of Eurodollars can take place.[4]

These differences suggest that the expansionary potential of the Eurodollar system is larger than that of a national system. However, certain other differences militate against realization of this potential at all times. In a national system,

[4] Some observers prefer to analyze the expansionary potential of the Eurodollar market from a *global credit* viewpoint rather than, as is being done here, from a *dollar-asset* viewpoint. In the former type of analysis the expansionary potential would not be significantly affected by the two factors discussed above because, in both instances, one form of "credit" (i.e., foreign currencies) is merely being substituted for another (i.e., dollars). A net global-credit expansion occurs only to the extent that otherwise idle funds are utilized via the Eurodollar market.

the expansion takes place because the funds received at each stage by nonbank recipients necessarily remain as deposits somewhere within the banking system. The recipients of funds in the lending and redepositing chain that underlies the creation of deposits have no choice but to channel funds back into the banking system unless they wish to hold currency.

In the Eurodollar market, the ultimate nonbank recipient of funds, unlike his counterpart in a national system, has alternatives: He may maintain the funds in a U.S. bank, redeposit them in a bank abroad, or convert them into other currencies.

In general, his decision depends upon economic incentives (for example, the interest paid on dollar time deposits abroad being higher than that paid on dollar time deposits in the U.S.) and the existing foreign-exchange regulations in his country. If at any one stage of the expansionary process the dollar proceeds of a Eurodollar loan are received by a recipient who does not want to or who, because of regulations, cannot redeposit them in a bank participating in the Eurodollar market, the redepositing expansionary chain is interrupted and the expansionary potential cannot be realized.

MECHANICS OF U.S. BANKS' BORROWING OF EURODOLLARS

During the tight monetary conditions in this country in recent years, a number of U.S. commercial banks, particularly those with branches abroad, turned to the Eurodollar market to obtain funds to accommodate loan customers. The foreign branches of these banks bid for Eurodollars in the interbank market abroad and transfer the funds to their home office.

To illustrate the mechanics of such transfer, assume that Bank Delta, which has a $650,000 demand deposit at Bank E in New York "sells" the deposit through a London broker to a London branch of Bank F in Chicago. The branch requests that the deposit be transferred to the account of the Edge-Act subsidiary of Bank F—Bank F International in New York. The following changes take place in the balance sheets of the relevant banks:

LONDON BRANCH OF BANK F

Assets	Liabilities
+$650,000 due from head office	+$650,000 due to Bank Delta

BANK DELTA (LONDON)

Assets	Liabilities
−$650,000 demand deposit at Bank E	
+$650,000 due from London branch of Bank F	

Upon receiving cable instructions from Bank Delta, Bank E issues an officer check payable through the New York Clearing House to the New York subsidiary of Bank F. Upon presentation, the balance sheets of the banks change as follows:

BANK E (NEW YORK)

Assets	Liabilities
	−$650,000 demand deposit account of Bank Delta
	+$650,000 officer's check outstanding

NEW YORK SUBSIDIARY OF BANK F

Assets	Liabilities
+$650,000 cash items in process of collection	+$650,000 due to head office

The subsidiary wires its head office and the following changes occur on the balance sheet of the head office:

BANK F (CHICAGO)

Assets	Liabilities
+$650,000 due from New York subsidiary	+$650,000 due to London Branch

The next day the check is cleared and the following changes take place in the balance sheets of the banks involved:

BANK E (NEW YORK)

Assets	Liabilities
−$650,000 reserve balances at the Federal Reserve	−$650,000 officer's check outstanding to the subsidiary of Bank F

SUBSIDIARY OF BANK F (NEW YORK)

Assets	Liabilities
−$650,000 cash items in process of collection +$650,000 reserve balances at the Federal Reserve	
−$650,000 reserve balances at the Federal Reserve	−$650,000 due to head office

BANK F (CHICAGO)

Assets	Liabilities
−$650,000 due from New York subsidiary +$650,000 reserve balances at the Federal Reserve	

Bank F has increased its total reserves and, therefore, its ability to extend loans and acquire other earning assets. Bank E's reserves have declined.

The net loss of reserves of Bank E was $536,250 because the demand-deposit liability which Bank E had to Bank Delta has been taken off its books, freeing $113,750 of reserves that the bank was required to maintain against that liability. The net reserve gain to Bank F would depend upon the bank's position in respect to its total borrowing of Eurodollars. Such borrowing is currently subject to statutory reserve requirement of 10 per cent on the amount in excess of the daily average of such borrowing outstanding during May 1969. If the amount borrowed brought the bank's total above this average by the full amount, Bank F's net gain of reserves would be $585,000 (i.e., $650,000 minus $65,000 the bank has to put aside as required reserves). If, on the other hand, the amount borrowed left the bank's total outstanding below its May average, the net gain of reserves would be $650,000.

Thus, as a result of the $650,000 borrowed by one U.S. bank in the Eurodollar market, total reserves in the U.S. banking system remained unchanged, but the required reserves have been reduced (or excess reserves increased) by a minimum of $48,750 and possibly by as much as $113,750 given the current reserve requirements.

MECHANICS OF EURODOLLAR EXTINCTION

All the hypothetical transactions described here, from the initial deposit by Company W of $1,000,000 in Bank Alpha in Frankfurt, Germany, to the borrowing of the $650,000 in Eurodollars by the London branch of Bank F in Chicago, could be completed in the market in no more than 10 to 15 minutes. The chain of Eurodollar transactions as described here would come to a standstill with the acquisition and transfer of funds to the head office by the London branch of Bank F. The final book entries recorded at each stage of the transaction would remain on the books of the institutions that participated in the process until about two days before the stated maturity date of the final deposit. At that time action will be initiated to reverse the transactions: Bank F will repay its subsidiary in New York, who in turn will repay the correspondent of Bank Delta, Bank E in New York. Company Z takes delivery on its forward contract to purchase dollars and repays dollars to Bank Gamma by transferring the balance to Bank Gamma's account at Bank D International. Bank Gamma will use the balance to make the payment to the Brazilian exporter on behalf of Company Y. Company X repays the dollar loan to Bank Beta, which repays Bank Alpha, which in turn makes the dollar balance available to Company W for its payment to an American exporter. With that repayment, the superstructure of dollar-denominated deposits would be extinguished.

In our example, it was the return of dollar deposits to the United States banking system that, in the first instance, brought the expansionary process to a standstill and, eventually, reduced the amount of Eurodollars outstanding. Absorption of dollars by central monetary authorities abroad would have essentially the same impact. For example, if, as a result of swapping the proceeds of a Eurodollar loan into another currency, the monetary authority in that country obtained the deposit as a result of its intervention in the exchange market, the process of redepositing would cease unless, of course, the authorities themselves were to become depositors in the Eurodollar market.

EPILOGUE

In this chapter we have attempted to illustrate the mechanics of Eurodollar transactions by tracing a single deposit as it moved through various transactions in the market. This tends to oversimplify the operations of the market. In practice, a myriad of transactions take place concurrently in the market for Eurodollars.

The technique of tracing individual transactions has its pitfalls. By focusing on the "trees," the view of the "forest" may tend to be obscured. The Eurodollar market should be viewed as a whole, against the background of the developments that led to its emergence and within the framework of forces that continually reshape it.

III

FRANK E. MORRIS and JANE S. LITTLE

Mr. Morris, President of the Federal Reserve Bank of Boston, has a long and distinguished career in economics in both the private sector and public service. He received his B.A. degree from Wayne University, and earned his Master's and Ph.D. degrees in economics from the University of Michigan, where he later taught.

Mr. Morris served as staff economist with the U.S. Office of Price Stabilization and the Central Intelligence Agency before being named Research Director of the Investment Bankers Association of America. He was appointed Assistant to the Secretary of the Treasury for Debt Management by President Kennedy in 1961.

Mr. Morris joined the Boston firm of Loomis, Sayles and Company, Inc. in 1963 as Vice-President and Economist, and was later named Vice-President for Institutional Policy and Development. He serves as a Trustee of The New England Economic Research Foundation and as a Director of the International Center of New England, Inc.

Mrs. Little is an Assistant Economist at the Federal Reserve Bank of Boston, specializing in international economics. She earned her undergraduate degree from Wellesley College in 1964, and received her M.A. and M.A.L.D., with a concentration in economics and Asian affairs, from the Fletcher School of Law and Diplomacy. She writes on economic and public policy subjects.

The Eurodollar Market Today: Size, Scope, and Participants

From its unnoticed birth about a dozen years ago, the Eurodollar market has become the major channel for international short-term capital movements and, more generally, one of the largest money markets anywhere in the world. Its growing importance is reflected in the decisions of six of the powerful Group of 10 monetary authorities—France, Italy, Belgium, the Netherlands, Canada, and the United States—to limit the access of their banks to the Eurodollar market during 1969. The European and Canadian authorities were reacting to an unwelcome loss of official reserves and a rise in domestic interest rates caused, in part, by their residents converting domestic currency to dollars to obtain the high Eurodollar yields. Later in the year, the Federal Reserve Board amended Regulations D and M in order to raise the cost of borrowing additional Eurodollars to banks in the United States. It made these changes primarily because of pressures from uncomfortable European central bankers. In addition, some observers

This paper has benefitted greatly from the comments of Mr. Fred H. Klopstock, Manager, International Research Department, Federal Reserve Bank of New York, and Mr. Carl H. Stem, Economist, Division of International Finance, Board of Governors of the Federal Reserve System.

were concerned that these borrowings were subverting the United States's own battle against inflation. Of course, the high U.S. interest rates would have resulted in unsettling international capital flows in 1969 with or without the Eurodollar market. However, this well-organized but generally unregulated market holds a large pool of highly interest-sensitive funds which move with ease across national borders. For these reasons, it greatly complicates the problem of shielding domestic economies from outside influences.

An indication of the organization and speed with which funds move in the Eurodollar market was the startling ability of U.S. banks to increase their Eurodollar borrowings from their foreign branches by $3 billion during three short weeks in June 1969. This spectacular increase in the liabilities of U.S. banks to their foreign branches was not accomplished without strain, since the three-month deposit rate leaped from 9.6 to 12.6 per cent during this period. It demonstrated, however, that an unprecedented volume of funds—a volume equivalent to all the demand deposits in Belgium's banking system—could be raised within this market almost overnight.

THE SIZE AND GROWTH OF THE MARKET

As of the beginning of 1970, the net size of the Eurodollar market is estimated to stand above $40 billion. Unfortunately, any estimate on the size of the Eurodollar market must be rather inexact because few totally satisfactory data sources are available. One difficulty is that the large number of interbank deposits raises the problem of double counting—a problem which is aggravated by the lack of distinction between banks and nonbanks in some national data. However, the Bank of England, the Bank of Canada, and the Bank for International Settlements (BIS) have published data series since 1964 which make some approximations possible.

According to a BIS estimate, the net size of the Eurodollar market, measured by the outstanding dollar assets or liabilities of reporting banks from eight European countries[1] (excluding interbank deposits), was $37.5 billion at the end of 1968. Because the Canadian chartered banks are important intermediaries in this market, perhaps second only to the London institutions, it seems important to incorporate their U.S. dollar assets and liabilities vis-à-vis non-Europeans into the BIS data. The inclusion of Canadian Eurodollar activities not reflected in the BIS figure raises the estimated size of the market to about $42 billion at the end of 1969.

Although rapid growth has always been characteristic of this market, the rate of increase apparently jumped sharply in 1968 and again in 1969. While according to the BIS the Eurodollar market grew at an average rate of 25 per cent a year between 1964 and 1967, it expanded 43 per cent in 1968 and 50 per cent in 1969. Primarily responsible for these spurts in the market's growth rate were the tight credit conditions in the United States and the resulting increase in Eurodollar borrowings by U.S. banks. In addition, during 1969 the already intense demand pressures were aggravated by heavy borrowings made by French and Italian banks complying with official instructions to reduce their net foreign asset positions and by speculators anticipating a revaluation of the German mark.[2]

Some perspective on the estimated size of the Eurodollar market might be gained by comparing it with the volume of investments in various sectors of the New York money market, the leading national and international financial center of the world. At the end of 1969 outstanding assets in the major types of money market instruments available in New York

[1] Belgium-Luxembourg, France, Germany, Italy, The Netherlands, Sweden, Switzerland, and the United Kingdom.

[2] This causal connection between currency crises and an increase in the demand for Eurodollars will be discussed in more detail below.

totaled as follows: bankers' acceptances, $5.4 billion; commercial and finance company paper, $31.6 billion; large commercial bank loans to brokers and dealers for purchasing or carrying securities, $5.1 billion; large commercial bank sales of Federal Funds, $4.6 billion; large negotiable certificates of deposit (CD) at large commercial banks, $10.9 billion; and, finally, U.S. Treasury bills outstanding, $80.6 billion. On the basis of this rather impressionistic sketch, the Eurodollar market clearly has not yet acquired the stature of the New York money market as a whole. On the other hand, it appears that investors can now expect the Eurodollar market to supply and absorb large amounts of money with as little price variation as the individual sectors of the New York market show under similar circumstances.[3]

Moreover, using data on U.S. bank short-term liabilities to foreigners, it is possible to separate its international sector from the New York money market as a whole. At the end of December 1969 these liabilities amounted to $39.9 billion, just slightly less than our estimate of the Eurodollar market. Since some $2 billion included in this figure represent working and contingency balances which cannot strictly be considered money market investments, however, it seems clear that the Eurodollar market now stands as the foremost international exchange for short-term funds in the world.

When the net volume of dollar-denominated liabilities of the BIS European banks is compared with the volume of domestic currency deposits held by banks in the same eight countries,

[3] Perhaps it should be pointed out here, however, that the only secondary market for Eurodollar investments is that for London CDs; thus, Eurodollar investors must generally rely on the wide spectrum of available maturities, which run from call to one year and beyond, to provide a substitute for the liquidity which New York's secondary markets ensure. For instance, at the end of November 1969, 42.9 per cent of the Eurodollar deposits with foreign branches of U.S. banks had a maturity of less than 30 days, with these deposits earning interest rates of about 9.5–11.5 per cent. In New York, of course, banks are prohibited from paying any interest at all on deposits made for under 30 days.

Eurodollar deposits actually dwarf the domestic currency deposits of several individual countries, as can be seen from Table III.1. These foreign currency deposits equaled just less

TABLE III.1
EUROPEAN DOMESTIC CURRENCY DEPOSITS AND EURODOLLAR DEPOSITS
(1964 and 1968)

	December 1964	December 1968	Change
	(BILLIONS OF DOLLARS)		(PER CENT)
Belgium			
Demand deposits	1.7	2.5	47.1
Time deposits*	1.4	2.7	92.9
Total	3.1	5.2	67.7
France			
Demand deposits	14.1	20.0	41.8
Time deposits	3.1	9.2	196.8
Total	17.2	29.2	69.8
Germany			
Demand deposits	9.9	13.9	40.4
Time deposits	25.6	49.1	91.8
Total	35.5	63.0	77.5
Italy			
Demand deposits	13.0	24.1	85.4
Savings deposits	14.9	25.2	69.1
Total	27.9	49.3	76.7
Netherlands			
Demand deposits	2.3	3.5	52.2
Time and savings deposits*	1.5	3.0	100.0
Total	3.8	6.5	71.1

TABLE III.1—(Continued)

	December 1964	December 1968	Change
	(Billions of Dollars)		(Per Cent)
Sweden			
Demand deposits	1.0	1.7	70.0
Time and savings deposits	4.1	6.2	51.2
Total	5.1	7.9	54.9
Switzerland			
Demand deposits	3.4	4.4	29.4
Time and savings deposits	7.0	10.5	50.0
Total	10.4	14.9	43.3
United Kingdom			
Domestic currency deposits†	25.0	32.1	28.4
Total demand deposits‡	45.4	70.1	54.4
Total time deposits‡	57.6	105.9	83.9
TOTAL	128.0	208.1	62.6
EURODOLLAR DEPOSITS §	9.0	25.0	177.8

* Including foreign currency deposits.
† Excluding deposits at Scottish and Northern Ireland banks.
‡ Excluding the United Kingdom.
§ BIS estimate of net Euro-dollar liabilities, excluding interbank deposits.

Source: International Monetary Fund, *International Financial Statistics*, and the Bank for International Settlements, *Annual Reports.*

than one-eighth of Europe's local currency deposits as a whole. Eurodollar deposits have also grown almost three times as fast as the domestic currency deposits since 1964. The difference in the two rates reflects in part the high degree of competition—national and international—rampant in the largely unregulated Eurodollar market. Since Eurodollar lenders and borrowers can reach beyond national borders, central bank interest-rate ceilings and restrictive cartel arangements generally have not applied to Eurodollar deposits; thus, the sophisticated and valued customers who operate in the Eurodollar market have typically been able to obtain higher rates for dollar balances than for domestic currency deposits.

Theoretically, of course, the Eurodollar market should have a raison d'être as long as rates on Eurodollar deposits are higher than those available in the United States and rates on Eurodollar loans are lower than the cost of alternative ways of obtaining dollars—either from U.S. lenders or via the foreign-exchange market. It is not necessary that Eurodollar deposit rates be higher than those on domestic currency alternatives outside of the United States. Obviously, however, whenever these gaps occur, the market supply will grow more rapidly than otherwise.[4] Although this differential has often existed in the past, during the last two years returns on Eurodollar assets (whether covered against exchange risks or not) have become increasingly attractive in comparison to alternative investments in domestic currency markets.[5] This broadening in rate differentials was largely due to the unusually strong Eurodollar demand from U.S. banks seeking funds to replace time deposits lost during recent periods of tight money.

GEOGRAPHY OF EURODOLLARS

In addition to being one of the world's largest markets for short-term funds, the Eurodollar market is also characterized

[4] To meet these conditions, the banks which choose to enter this very competitive but profitable market clearly must be able to work with narrower margins between Eurodollar deposit and loan rates than they would find acceptable for any sizable portion of their domestic loan business. In fact, Eurobanks find that they can operate with these reduced margins because most placements in the predominantly wholesale Eurodollar market are large scale and low risk. Usually involving prime customers only, Eurodollar transactions can be executed in a matter of minutes or hours and are considered practically costless additions to normal banking and foreign-exchange business.

[5] For an excellent description of the recent widening of the gaps between interest rates on Eurodollar and domestic currency deposits, see "Euro-dollars: A Changing Market," *Federal Reserve Bulletin*, October 1969.

by a high degree of freedom, flexibility, and institutional organization. Because of these attributes and the widespread international demand for dollar assets, the market aids the rapid transfer of capital from surplus areas to areas where shortages are most acute. The previously mentioned statistics published by the Bank of England, the Bank of Canada, and the Bank for International Settlements also indicate the typical direction of such Eurodollar flows between various centers. Chart III.1, which is based on a similar chart prepared by Klaus Friedrich[6] for the year 1966, shows the net positions of important sectors of market participants as of the end of 1969. The arrows point from the areas holding net bank claims to the areas holding the corresponding net liabilities. Although the figures represent levels, they indicate the areas which have supplied and the areas which have absorbed Eurodollars on a cumulative basis over time.

The statistics readily reveal London's role as the major intermediary in the Eurodollar system. U.K. banks are large net lenders to the United States and, to a smaller extent, to their own residents as well.[7] The U.K. claims on the United States are very largely advances to their head offices made by the American branches in London. American overseas banks accounted for close to 75 per cent of all the external foreign currency assets of U.K. banks in September 1969. This proportion had risen from about 65 per cent at the end of 1968. Particularly during the last two years, a great part of these American branch assets was undoubtedly returned to their head offices to help cushion their loss of liquidity.

More generally, U.S. borrowers in toto are also obtaining

[6] Klaus Friedrich, *The Euro-dollar System* (Ithaca, N.Y.: Program on Comparative Economic Development, Cornell University, 1968).

[7] This net lender position does not imply, of course, that the funds lent out were received from U.K. residents. In fact, the funds lent by the intermediating U.K. banks generally originate in Canada, Western Europe, and elsewhere.

CHART III.1
APPROXIMATE NET EURODOLLAR POSITIONS, DECEMBER 1968
(Billions of U.S. Dollars)

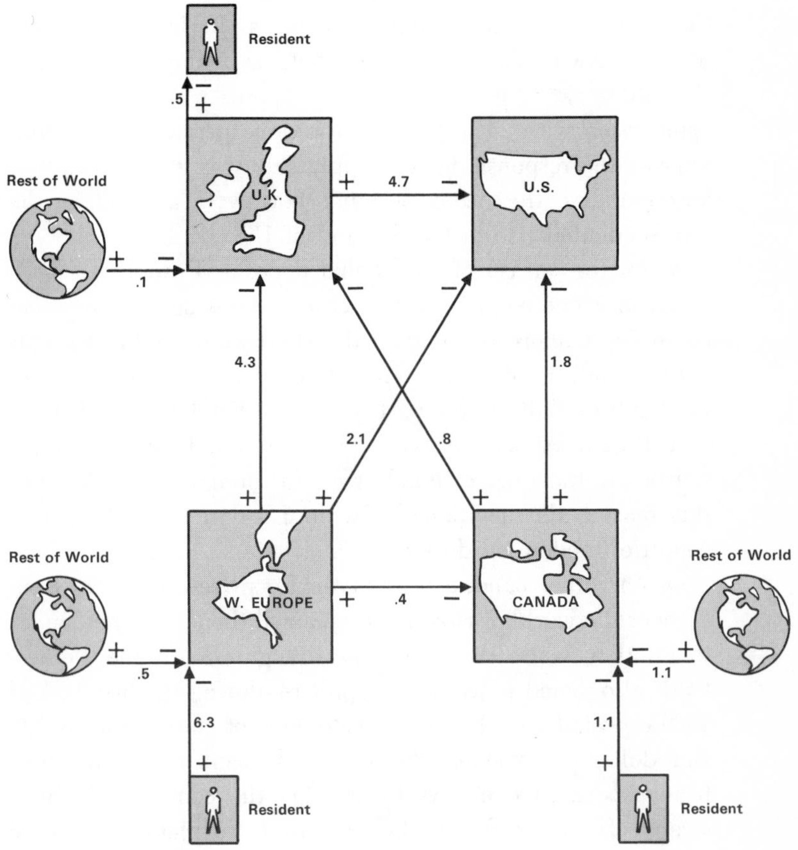

Source: Bank for International Settlements, Bank of Canada, and Bank of England. The diagram is based on a similar chart prepared for 1966 by Klaus Friedrich, *The Euro-dollar System* (Ithaca, N.Y.: Cornell University, 1968).

an increasing share of all U.K. banks' Eurodollar loans to nonresidents. Between December 1968 and September 1969, the U.S. borrowers' share rose from 48 to 58 per cent, again reflecting the monetary tensions felt by U.S. banks during the last year. It would, however, be a mistake to conclude that the appetite of the U.S. banks has been fed at the expense of the total starvation of other borrowers. In fact, the dollar loans of U.K. banks to borrowers outside of the United States actually grew 33 per cent in the first nine months of 1969 in comparison with 24 per cent in the same period in 1968. Obviously, the response on the supply side was great enough to accommodate the needs of other borrowers as well as the unprecedented rise in the demand of U.S. banks.

As for the sources of U.K. dollar deposits, Europe is a large and consistent net lender to London. Looking at individual countries in more detail than the chart allows indicates that Switzerland, France, and Italy have generally invested net most substantially in the past. In early 1969, however, French and Italian banks were instructed to eliminate or reduce drastically their net external assets in foreign currencies. For this reason, the net dollar flow to London from these two countries moderated during 1969.

On the other hand, as a reservoir for private balances from all over the world, Switzerland remained the largest net lender to London, while West Germany, Belgium, and the Netherlands also joined in as major suppliers—during the first half of 1969 especially. In the case of Germany, of course, the sizable Eurodollar placements reflected Bundesbank efforts to offset heavy speculative inflows by offering the commercial banks swaps of dollars for marks, as will be explained in more detail below.

Not surprisingly given the rate patterns, from the end of 1968 none of the West European countries except Spain and West Germany have been net borrowers from London. The dramatic reversal of the German banks' earlier net-asset position occurred after the revaluation of the mark when they were drained of speculative deposits and turned to the Eurodollar market to ease their strained liquidity position. While Japan was, as usual, a heavy net borrower at the end of 1969, it began to lend Eurodollars in significant amounts for the first time last year. With the Japanese authorities encouraging a capital outflow to stop an unwelcome growth in official reserves, Japanese banks reduced their net liability position vis-à-vis London from $1.5 billion at the end of 1968 to $1.1 billion at the end of 1969.

As the diagram again indicates, Canada is a second major intermediary in the Eurodollar market, although it still channels a diminishing portion of its funds through the United Kingdom. Canada's sizable claims on the United States are largely "street loans" to brokers and dealers on Wall Street. Despite the fact that the Canadian banks are net borrowers vis-à-vis Europe and "the rest of the world," these positions do not balance Canada's lending to the United States and Britain; thus, the Canadian banks turn to their own residents for deposits to help finance their growing loans to the United States. In fact, the chartered banks were so successful in persuading Canadian residents to hold U.S. dollar deposits acquired through the spot sale and forward purchase of Canadian dollars that at mid-1969 the Canadian government felt compelled to ask these banks not to accept any additional "swapped deposits." In the few preceding months, such swapped deposits had more than doubled, permitting a sizable increase in the Canadian banks' net foreign assets and a drop of $80 million in Canadian official reserves.[8]

While Western Europe is also a direct net lender to the United States, by far the larger portion of its funds flows through London and Canada. Like London and Canada, Europe has been a net borrower from the underdeveloped world,

[8] "Euro-dollars: A Changing Market."

especially the Middle East. These deposits from the developing countries undoubtedly reflect a scarcity of domestic short-term investment opportunities as well as a wish to be beyond the reach of domestic regulations and currency crises. European banks also appear to receive Eurodollar deposits from their own residents on an increasingly large scale, although part of the estimated $7.8 billion net assets of European residents shown in the diagram represents conversions of domestic currencies to dollars by the banks themselves.

To summarize the information on the chart, given existing constraints on capital flows, the United States and Europe appear to be at opposite ends of the system. Europe lends to all major blocs, while the United States borrows from all blocs. London and Canada function primarily as intermediaries.

Unfortunately, however, since the Eurodollar market seems to be growing as rapidly in geographic scope as it is in size, the chart does not even hint at two potentially important new developments. While the banks which make the market for Eurodollar deposits used to be concentrated in Western Europe and Canada, the explosion of new U.S. branch openings in the Bahamas suggests that this area may soon become a significant new Eurodollar channel. Almost entirely within the past year, more than 20 U.S. banks have opened "Nassau shells" for the specific purpose of collecting Eurodollar balances for head office use. Because it is much less expensive to establish a "shell" conducting no local business in the Bahamas than a branch in London, where a full-service bank is required, this new location has been particularly attractive to medium-sized banks which have not found it possible to venture abroad in the past. By the end of December 1969, these Nassau shells had acquired well over $1 billion in total liabilities.[9]

[9] Andrew F. Brimmer, Member of the Board of Governors of the Federal Reserve System, "Capital Outflows and the U.S. Balance of Payments: A Review and Outlook," an address delivered to a meeting of Bankers, Businessmen, and the Board of Directors of the Federal Reserve Bank of Dallas, Dallas, Texas, February 11, 1970.

A similar development is the emergence of the "Asia-dollar market," with Singapore at its center. In an effort to stimulate this $150 million market, the Singapore government has waived its customary tax on interest payments for Asia-dollar transactions.[10] Apparently the participating bankers hope to attract dollar balances owned by U.S. corporations, Asian governments—particularly the Japanese, and the overseas Chinese. According to the original plan, the banks intend to use these dollars, which often end up in the European sector of the market now, to provide medium-term funds for regional development projects. Although local currencies may often be borrowed at 5 to 7 per cent from development agencies, it is believed that the current Asia-dollar rates of 10 to 12 per cent are not excessive for the hard currency component of a development loan.

MARKET PARTICIPANTS

With the Eurodollar market expanding both in volume and geographic scope, it is also attracting an increasingly varied group of participants.

The Institutions Which Make the Market

Undoubtedly, banks choose to enter this market because Eurodollar transactions, which are generally large scale and low risk, can be very profitable indeed—despite the narrow margins between deposit and loan rates. Then, too, many banks are loathe to risk losing the domestic business of the prime-name customers who operate in the market to competitors who are able to serve them in the Eurodollar arena. This second consideration has apparently persuaded several U.S. banks to establish foreign branches when the possibility of obtaining

[10] William D. Hartley, "Fledgling 'Asia Dollar' Market Has Deposits but Faces Problem of Finding Borrowers," *The Wall Street Journal,* December 29, 1969.

Eurodollar funds for head-office use did not alone seem to justify the expense. Generally, of course, the U.S. banks' prime motive for jumping into the Eurodollar market has been to attract funds not subject to Regulation Q for loans to their head offices.

Just looking at the city of London gives some indication of the diversity of institutions which create this market. In the first rank come the very active 29 branches of U.S. banks.[11] Other foreign banks located in London, such as the Japanese, are also heavily involved in the Eurodollar market. Then the British overseas banks, which were among the most active early participants, have continued to add wholesale Eurodollar business to their traditional retail activities. Including fringe banks which deal in Eurodollars from time to time, perhaps 200 London banks, employing some 1,500 people on Eurodollar work, participate in the market.[12]

Eurobanks can also be broadly grouped according to their areas of specialization. As one of the few safeguards they like to maintain in this high-speed market, many banks emphasize a particular type of Eurodollar business. For instance, some banks prefer to deal primarily with other banks and keep their contact with commercial and industrial borrowers to a minimum. They thus reduce their risk, and yet perform a useful service by bringing together the major international banks, who have loanable funds but limited knowledge of local markets, and the large number of smaller banks which want dollar deposits for end-use loans. Other banks, however, prefer to make final loans to nonbank customers only. They thereby minimize the distance between themselves and the last,

[11] U.S. banks have been in this dominant position only since 1966, however. Originally, overseas banks like the Bank of London & South America Limited developed the market most actively.

[12] "The Euro-dollar Market—What it Means for London," *The Banker*, August 1969.

possibly weakest, link in the often long chains of intermediated loans.

In addition to the Eurobanks, two other specialized groups of institutional participants are the merchant banks, which maintain the secondary market for London's Eurodollar CDs, and the Eurodollar brokers. Since the First National City Bank began to issue negotiable Eurodollar CDs in 1966, more than 50 London banks have followed its example, and Eurodollar CDs outstanding now amount to about $3.5 billion. The original success of this negotiable instrument must be credited in large part to the deliberate, simultaneous development of a secondary market. As for the Eurodollar brokers, they have traditionally served to screen the prestigious participants who may know each other too well. While some banks prefer to handle Eurodollar negotiations directly, believing they gain a better feel of the market in this way, others prefer to work through brokers despite the fee. This practice permits a bank to maintain its anonymity and, for instance, avoid responsibility for the insult of refusing to make a loan. Recently, the brokers have also served as a link between the growing number of less-well known participants who seek to enter the market.

The Eurobank's Customers

As for the Eurobank's customers, the available data unfortunately do not permit a very precise discussion of the sources and uses of Eurodollars by type of participant or by function. A few generalizations may be made, however.

Eurodollar depositors. From the beginning, central banks have been among the major sources of funds. It is important, however, to distinguish between the two senses in which monetary officials are frequently described as suppliers of Eurodollars. First, under our present international monetary system, central banks have agreed to prevent their exchange rates from moving more than 1 per cent above or below par by absorbing or supplying dollars in the foreign-exchange market; thus, when private investors decide to hold or purchase dollars specifically for placement in the Eurodollar market, their decisions will either reduce central bank dollar gains below the level they would otherwise have reached, or they will actually force the central banks to sell dollars from their official reserve stocks. In these cases, central banks are often viewed as residual suppliers of funds to the Eurodollar market; they are not, however, acting on their own initiative but are merely responding to the initiatives of private investors.

As a recent example, during 1969, despite a liquidity deficit of $7.1 billion, the United States had an official settlements surplus of $2.7 billion.[13] The difference between the two figures indicates that private foreigners wanted to increase their dollar assets by an even greater amount than the unusually large liquidity deficit placed at their disposal. Given the simultaneous $9.4 billion increase in U.S. banks' short-term liabilities to foreign commercial banks, it would appear that these decisions reflected the attractions of the Eurodollar market almost entirely. Since most monetary authorities were discouraging this flood of private capital into the market, the difference also provides a *very* rough measure of the funds that central banks might be said to have "supplied" in a residual sense to the Eurodollar market during 1969.

It should be re-emphasized, however, that the central banks are forced to "supply" funds for the Eurodollar market in such cases only because private foreigners *choose* to hold Eurodollar assets rather than U.S. money market assets or assets denominated in other currencies. For the same reasons, U.S. balance-of-payments deficits cannot be described as a "source

[13] While the liquidity balance is measured by the change in U.S. reserve assets and liquid liabilities to foreigners, both official and private, the official settlements balance is measured by the change in U.S. reserve assets plus certain liquid and nonliquid liabilities to foreign official monetary institutions.

of funds for the Eurodollar market" in any literal sense. Although U.S. deficits place dollars in foreign hands, a foreigner's decision to hold dollars for liquidity and transactions or investment purposes, and his second separate decision to place these dollars in a bank outside of the United States, are not dependent upon a particular U.S. payments position.

In a second sense, however, central banks can and frequently do take the initiative in supplying funds to the Eurodollar market. In fact, when the Eurodollar market first developed, central banks were probably the most important depositors. According to an estimate made by the late Oscar Altman of the International Monetary Fund, as of 1962, over two-thirds of all Eurodollars were owned by central banks and official agencies. By 1967, however, Mr. Altman was suggesting that only one-third of the Eurodollar deposits were owned by these institutions.[14] The explanation for the decrease seems to be two-fold: first, foreign official dollar holdings have been increasing less than nonofficial dollar holdings; and second, after Regulation Q was amended in 1962 to exempt foreign official deposits from its ceilings, the Eurodollar rates no longer looked so attractive in comparison to deposits at banks in the United States.

Nevertheless, central banks and official agencies still play important roles in channeling funds to the Eurodollar market for domestic and international policy reasons. Many central banks take advantage of the Eurodollar market in their efforts either to expand or to reduce domestic liquidity. The German, Italian, Swiss, and Dutch monetary authorities in particular have frequently used dollar swaps to prevent an unwelcome expansion of domestic credit. By providing their commercial banks with spot dollars in exchange for domestic currency and offering to buy the dollars forward at a higher price than the market rate, these central banks have increased the incentive

[14] Oscar L. Altman, "Euro-dollars," *Finance and Development,* March 1967.

for commercial banks to invest their cash reserves in the Eurodollar market instead of in domestic currency loans.[15] Following the opposite policy goal, central banks have sometimes deposited dollars with their commercial banks without making swaps specifically in order to expand domestic liquidity. The Italian policy of 1961 presents a good example.[16]

In addition, European monetary authorities, including the BIS and often in cooperation with the Federal Reserve System, may pour dollars into the market to maintain orderly conditions. During the fall of 1967, for example, the German, Swiss, Dutch, and Belgian central banks and the BIS, drawing in small part on swap lines with the United States, channeled $1.4 billion into the market to prevent Eurodollar rates from flaring too high in response to the sterling crisis. Generally, international financial crises tend to put a strain on the Eurodollar market as speculators try to borrow dollars to buy the currencies which appear to be strongest at the same time that Eurodollar investors are moving funds into other currencies. Apparently the former group chooses to borrow Eurodollars to avoid domestic-exchange controls and to reduce the cost of their gamble, since Eurodollars are often less expensive than domestic currency loans.

Foreign commercial banks make up a second major group of Eurodollar depositors when they accept domestic currency liabilities and convert the corresponding excess reserves to dollar form. Perhaps even more than the central banks they find the flexibility of the Eurodollar market, with its great

---

[15] The authorities' action results in raising the banks' return in Eurodollar investments because this return must be calculated—when the forward dollar is at a discount—by subtracting from the interest earned the loss incurred by selling dollars forward at less than their spot value to cover the exchange risk. When the forward dollar is at a premium, of course, the profit gained by selling dollars forward at more than their spot rate is added to the interest earned.

[16] See Francesco Masera, "International Movements of Bank Funds and Monetary Policy in Italy," *Banca Nazionale del Lavoro Quarterly Review,* December 1966.

convenience, diversity of maturities, low risk and good yields, very attractive. Particularly in countries where money market facilities are inadequate, the commercial banks have welcomed the additional investment opportunities.

In Switzerland, where the commercial banks receive large volumes of sometimes highly volatile funds from all over the world, the Treasury bill and commercial paper markets are not large enough to absorb the flows. Instead, the Swiss banks turn to the Eurodollar market to find the requisite liquid assets. In addition, European commercial banks also appreciate the extra scope which the Eurodollar market provides for adjusting the ratio of the average maturity of their liabilities to the average maturity of their assets. If they can lend Eurodollars at call, having borrowed them for 90 days, they feel justified in employing a larger proportion of their other resources in a less liquid form.[17] Moreover, when banks face an atmosphere of high domestic liquidity and low interest rates, they can transfer their excess funds in dollar form to a nation in a more expansionary phase. The use of the dollar greatly facilitates this type of transfer, since many lenders who are willing to accept a foreign liability in dollars might not be willing to accept a liability in another currency.

A third important group of suppliers is composed of nonbanks, such as insurance companies, large multinational corporations and, most recently, international mutual funds. In addition to questions of safety, convenience, and rate differentials, these depositors are influenced by the range of Eurodollar maturities which permits them to put their money to work when it is available for only very brief periods. In taking advantage of this possibility, corporations like Standard Oil of New Jersey, Shell, Unilever, and Volkswagen carry on an im-

[17] Paul Einzig, *The Euro-dollar System: Practice and Theory of International Interest Rates* (New York: St. Martin's Press, 1964).

pressive daily business with the market.[18] A growing number of firms seem to find it convenient and profitable to deposit their working balances, or the proceeds of Eurobond issues floated in advance of need, in the Eurodollar market.

Until 1965, U.S. resident companies were depositing substantial quantities of dollars in Canada and Europe. In response to the voluntary balance-of-payments program, however, a large part of these funds was repatriated.[19] Since then, the majority of Eurodollars have been placed in the market by foreign residents (including the subsidiaries of American companies abroad). At the end of 1968, U.S. residents owned only about 15 per cent of the outstanding Eurodollar deposits. Recently, however, the stepped-up outflow of deposits held by U.S. residents has aroused concern because of the unfavorable impact on the U.S. balance of payments. Although some commentators have blamed a much larger share of last year's deterioration in the U.S. liquidity deficit on this flood of funds to the Eurodollar market, according to BIS estimate (based on U.S. payments statistics rather than data from the European reporting banks) this outflow amounted to about $2 billion during 1969. Since recorded, U.S. resident deposits at European reporting banks rose only $.6 billion in 1969 in comparison with $1.5 billion in 1968, the BIS concludes that much of last year's outflow reached Europe in "roundabout" ways.

Eurodollar borrowers. When the market first developed, most Eurodollar loans were made to borrowers who used them to finance international trade.[20] Trade was considered to be

[18] "The Money-Machine Magic of Euro-dollars," *Business Week,* February 21, 1970.

[19] The liabilities of U.K. and Canadian banks to U.S. residents dropped by almost one-third between December 1964 and December 1965, for example.

[20] G. Carroll Martenson, *The Euro-dollar Market* (Boston: Bankers Publishing Company, 1964). See also Fred H. Klopstock, "The International Money Market: Structure, Scope and Instruments," *Journal of Finance,* May 1965.

the Eurodollar's "natural purpose," and even countries such as France, which have restricted the borrowing of Eurodollars for domestic reasons, have usually not tried to discourage this use. At present, a substantial amount (one-quarter in 1967, according to some authorities)[21] of world trade is still financed by Eurodollars.

Since the early days of the market, however, commercial banks have found many other investment opportunities for Eurodollar balances. These investments may, of course, include loans in dollars or in some other currency bought with dollars. Although Eurodollar loans are no longer necessarily linked to activities with an international flavor, many outlets continue to bear this character. For instance, the Norwegian shipping industry has significant ties with the Eurodollar market,[22] and many multinational corporations, especially those in petroleum, chemicals and minerals, frequently seek large quantities of Eurodollars. Within this second category are the loans which finance the foreign operations of U.S. corporations. These loans have permitted U.S. firms to continue their overseas expansion despite controls on capital exports from the United States.

Elsewhere, too, the Eurodollar market has made it possible for investors to expand abroad while living within measures designed to protect their countries' balance of payments. A large part of new British direct investment overseas has been financed by U.K. banks from their foreign-currency deposits, for instance.[23] Since the ceiling on foreign-security holdings has been raised, British pension funds and other institutional investors have also recently used Eurodollar loans to purchase additional assets of this kind. Borrowing Eurodollars can be

---

[21] Peter Oppenheimer, "Short-Term Capital Flows," *The Banker,* August 1967.

[22] Martenson, *The Euro-dollar Market.*

[23] "An Inventory of U.K. External Assets and Liabilities: End-1968," *Bank of England Quarterly Bulletin,* December 1969.

a welcome alternative to buying earmarked dollars from the dwindling pool of investment funds repatriated by U.K. residents who have sold foreign securities.[24]

On the other hand, some Eurodollar investments finance purely domestic transactions. Currently, in fact, the major outlet of these funds is the large volume of loans made to U.S. banks which borrow Eurodollars to adjust their reserve positions. One of the great merits of the Eurodollar market from the point of view of the American banks is that balances acquired by their foreign branches are not subject to Regulation Q; thus, during periods of monetary stringency, institutions with foreign branches can bid in the Eurodollar market for funds with which to cushion Federal Reserve pressure and live up to loan commitments.

Until September 1969, another advantage in borrowing Eurodollars was that these funds were not subject to reserve requirements or FDIC insurance fees. Since that time the Federal Reserve Board has imposed a 10 per cent marginal reserve requirement on any increase in U.S. bank Eurodollar borrowings from their foreign branches above the levels reached during May 1969.[25] The Board's regulations also deliberately leave a large base entirely free of reserves. Since the reserve requirements went into effect, U.S. banks appear to have moderated their demand for Eurodollars slightly, but they also have avoided (at least thus far) the automatic reduction their reserve-free base would suffer if their liabilities to their foreign branches fall below the May 1969 figures.

[24] With each sale, one-quarter of the proceeds must be surrendered to the Bank of England at the official rate of exchange. See "The Future of the U.K. Dollar Premium," *International Currency Review*, January 1970.

[25] This marginal reserve requirement was established through amendments to the Federal Reserve Board's Regulation M, which became effective on September 4, 1969. Another amendment to Regulation D also set reserve requirements for borrowings from foreign banks (as distinct from foreign branches of U.S. banks). See *U.S. Code,* Title 12, Chapter II, Subchapter A, Parts 204 and 213.

While the U.S. banks' share of outstanding Eurodollar borrowings has stopped its precipitous climb from about 20 per cent at the end of 1968 to about 40 per cent in June and September 1969, it still accounted for 35 per cent of these investments at the end of 1969. At present, U.S. bank borrowings undoubtedly continue to constitute the single most important use of Eurodollar funds.

In addition to these mammoth U.S. bank liabilities to their foreign branches, other loans to U.S. borrowers include the Canadian "street loans" and loans to resident nonbank corporations. The latter first became worthy of BIS mention in 1968 and almost certainly grew further with tightening U.S. monetary conditions last year.

Loans to British local authorities are important examples of borrowings made to finance domestic needs in other countries. Many Eurobanks located in Britain have at times solicited Eurodollar funds specifically for the purpose of converting them on a covered basis into pounds for local authority loans. Italian and Japanese banks are also prime illustrations of institutions which lend Eurodollars for domestic purposes whenever borrowing dollars and converting, covered, to domestic currency becomes less costly than borrowing domestic funds directly. In some years, such as 1964, Italian banks have placed the major part of their foreign-currency deposits in loans to domestic business firms.[26] In Japan, as much as one-half of the large quantity of Eurodollars borrowed abroad by Japanese banks has at times been used for local financing.[27]

More generally, Eurodollar loans made for domestic purposes may merely reflect commercial bank determination to make loans in the face of restrictive monetary policy, although the central banks may, of course, take offsetting action. Such

---

[26] Klopstock, "The International Money Market."

[27] Martenson, *The Eurodollar Market*; Einzig, *The Euro-dollar System.*

loans may also occur, however, with official acquiescence because the monetary authorities are more willing to permit an increase in the domestic money supply which is accompanied by an inflow of capital and official reserve assets than they would be without such advantageous offsets.[28] Still a third explanation for this development may be that in countries where investors traditionally prefer highly liquid assets, the Eurodollar market provides their industries with access to lower cost intermediate-term credit than is available from the domestic banking system.[29] At present, medium-term credit with commitments for five or even seven years is considered the most dynamic sector of the market.[30]

Finally, in contrast to their important role as suppliers of Eurodollar funds, central banks—with the exception of several Communist states and the Belgian Treasury—seldom borrow in the Eurodollar market. The Belgian Treasury often turns to the Eurodollar market because of the Belgian National Bank's firm ceiling on its advances to the government.

Clearly, the Eurodollar market has now developed a sustainable momentum. As it continues its rapid expansion in size and geographic scope, borrowers and lenders constantly discover new ways to take advantage of its broadening facilities. As the market comes to serve a growing number and diversity of participants and purposes, the stronger and more direct become the links between national capital markets. While this development has long-run economic, and perhaps even political, advantages, it also poses policy problems for

[28] See Masera, "International Movements of Bank Funds . . . in Italy," for a description of the Italian policy between November 1962 and August 1963.

[29] Klopstock, "The International Money Market."

[30] Such credit actually takes the form of a series of 90–180 day notes. See "The Money-Machine Magic of Euro-dollars."

"sovereign" monetary authorities—even in the largest economy in the world.

IV

FRED H. KLOPSTOCK

Mr. Klopstock, Manager of the International Research Department, Federal Reserve Bank of New York, received his Ph.D. degree from the University of Berlin in 1936. In 1942 he joined the Federal Reserve Bank of New York as an economist and became Chief of its Balance of Payments Division in 1951.

In 1945, Mr. Klopstock served in various capacities with the U.S. Strategic Bombing service; in 1946–47, with the Allied Commission in Austria; in 1950, with the United States High Commission for Germany; and in 1949 and again in 1950–51, as a consultant for the State Department.

Mr. Klopstock is the author of numerous papers published in professional journals, including several studies of the Eurodollar Market. Among these are "The Market for Dollar Deposits in Europe" (together with Alan R. Holmes), Monthly Review, *Federal Reserve Bank of New York, November 1960; "The International Money Market: Structure, Scope and Instruments,"* Journal of Finance, *May 1965; "The Eurodollar Market: Some Unresolved Problems,"* Essays in International Finance, *No. 65, Department of Economics, Princeton University; and "Eurodollars in the Liquidity and Reserve Management of U.S. Banks,"* Monthly Review, *Federal Reserve Bank of New York, July 1968.*

Use of Eurodollars by U.S. Banks

United States banks played a major role in the genesis of the Eurodollar market and, soon after its emergence in the late 1950s, became active market participants through their London, Frankfurt, and Paris branches. In the market's early days, U.S. banks were among the major intermediaries who engaged in making a market in Eurodollars—accepting deposits and redepositing them with other banks, and thereby earning a small spread on the operation. At the same time, these United States banks, through their branches, took advantage of the market to recapture some of the time deposits that had been withdrawn from their head offices whenever rates paid for dollar deposits abroad rose above the maximum interest rates that banks in the United States were permitted to pay for time deposits under Regulation Q of the Board of Governors of the Federal Reserve System.

This chapter expresses the personal views of the author and carries no implications as to the views of the Federal Reserve Bank of New York.

DOMESTIC USE OF EURODOLLARS

Early in the 1960s, one or two major American banks began to use the market systematically for the purpose of supplementing their liquidity and reserve positions. But such usage remained quite limited until 1966, when the banks came under substantial reserve pressure. In drawing funds from the market for domestic use, United States banks benefited greatly from the fact that balances obtained by them from their branches were (until 1969) not subject to member bank reserve requirements. Moreover, they were and continue to be exempt from the fees of the Federal Deposit Insurance Corporation. In addition, the foreign branches may, unlike their head offices, pay interest on overnight and call deposits and on time deposits with maturities of less than 30 days. Nor are they subject to Regulation Q rate ceilings. Thus, United States banks could gain access through the overseas-branch route to sizable amounts of funds that they were precluded by various regulations from attracting directly from foreign depositors.

With their position in the market resting on firm foundations, the branches gradually expanded their dollar operations by employing Eurodollars for lending to their customers abroad, primarily the affiliates of companies who were on the books of their head offices. In the early years of the market, the demand for financing by corporate customers abroad remained rather modest. This changed radically following the imposition of the voluntary restraints on foreign direct investment and bank lending to foreigners adopted in response to President Johnson's 1965 program to improve the nation's balance of payments. As American corporations became subject to restraint on the funds that they could transfer to their affiliates abroad, they turned increasingly to the overseas branches of United States and foreign banks for the financing of their short- and medium-term needs. The branches in turn fell back on the Eurodollar market for obtaining the necessary resources. Their need for sizable additional funds was further increased as a result of the Federal Reserve's Voluntary Credit Restraint Program which greatly impaired the ability of American banks to extend loans to foreign borrowers out of head office funds.

At the end of March 1970, the Eurodollar deposit liabilities of the overseas branches of American banks were close to $25 billion. More than half of these funds were redeposited with head offices, and substantial additional funds were used by the branches to extend loans to corporations in the United States. Of the funds employed abroad, the major portion was redeposited with foreign banks, while most of the remainder was used for customer loans.

American banks without overseas branches also make use of Eurodollars by borrowing from foreign banks. Under these arrangements, the bank would negotiate (typically with the assistance of a money broker) a loan from a European or Canadian bank for a fixed maturity, paying interest somewhat above the going rate for Eurodollar deposits. Such interbank loans would show on the borrowing bank's statement not as a deposit, but as notes payable and, as such, were exempt from Regulation Q ceilings and, until 1969, also from member bank reserve requirements. The aggregate amount of such borrowings has remained relatively modest because some of the principal inland banks making use of direct borrowings established branches in London and the Bahamas through which they acquired Eurodollars for use at head offices.

Continuous Borrowing for Expanding Credit Base

The intensive use of Eurodollars by a small number of large American banks for augmenting their liquidity and reserve positions should be viewed in a broad and longer term perspective. During World War II, the share held by the large-money market banks (particularly those in New York) in total deposits at all commercial banks had suffered a sharp decline.

This share declined further, but not quite as rapidly, in the 1946–59 period, and remained almost stationary, although at a somewhat higher level, in subsequent years.

Meanwhile, opportunities for profitable employment of funds increasingly outpaced available resources. Consequently, the East Coast banks, together with leading money market banks elsewhere, notably in Chicago and San Francisco, began in the early 1960's to search for new methods to attract additional resources. Many spectacular examples of financial innovations can be cited. Among them have been the development of the negotiable certificate of time deposit, the consumer-investment certificate, the flotation of unsecured notes and debentures, and the systematic and continuous use of Federal funds as a source of reserves rather than merely as an item to meet temporary day-to-day reserve deficiencies. Thus, the large banks' use of Eurodollars for domestic credit operations must be regarded as part of a steadily evolving mechanism designed by large and aggressive banks for the purpose of expanding their assets more rapidly than permitted by the actual growth of their deposit and capital resources.

Large-scale use of Eurodollars by major American banks to meet their liquidity and reserve requirements and thus to sustain their credit operations did not begin until the summer of 1966. In the immediately preceding years, it is true, one or two major New York banks recognized the usefulness of the market as a supplementary source of funds for head office operations, but actual use of the market for this purpose was rather modest. Before 1964, head office liabilities to their branches remained substantially below $1 billion. Liabilities passed the $2 billion mark only in the spring of 1966, when the large money market banks faced rapidly rising loan demands and thus found themselves under mounting pressure to add to their available funds. In the late summer of that year, rates for commercial paper and bankers acceptances and, in the fall, rates for treasury bills rose well above the 5½ per cent ceiling provided by the Federal Reserve Board's Regulation Q for time deposits. Yet the Board refused to lift the ceiling. Its evident intent was to use Regulation Q as a device to price the large money banks out of the national market for certificates of time deposits (CD) and thus to force them to reduce the rate of their lending to large business borrowers.

As their CD rates became increasingly noncompetitive during the summer and fall of 1966, the large money market banks suffered very heavy time-deposit losses. Eurodollar acquisitions served to replace a large part of the time-deposit decline. Thus, the banks during this particular period reached out for Eurodollars primarily in defense against the Federal Reserve's resort to Regulation Q as a monetary-policy weapon.

As money market conditions eased toward the end of 1966 and during the early part of 1967, Eurodollar takings rapidly declined but, by the summer of 1967, the banks again began to add to their Eurodollar takings. Evidently, the large money market banks, having become familiar with the market's potentialities, were using it as a normal, rather than marginal, source of funds whenever Eurodollar rates appeared attractive relative to rates in domestic money markets. Meanwhile, several additional banks had in the course of the year opened, or were about to open, branches in London, often for the specific purpose of gaining access to the Eurodollar market.

In 1968, as money-market conditions tightened, Eurodollar acquisitions of the overseas branches for head-office accounts quickened, and total borrowings reached more than $7.4 billion by November. In that month, money-market rates had again passed Regulation Q ceilings which had been held at 6.25 per cent for minimum maturities of 180 days since April 1968. Again the large New York and Chicago banks began to suffer severe CD losses precisely at a time when they were exposed to extraordinarily heavy demands for business loans from their large corporate customers. And again the Eurodollar market provided the major vehicle by which the banks were able to replace large parts of their CD losses. Thus, the large banks with access to the Eurodollar market through their branches were able in 1969 to sustain their lending activities despite heavy time-deposit attrition. Moreover, they were in a position to delay, if not to avoid, to some extent at least, the necessity of making large sales of marketable assets and other costly adjustments to their portfolio.

The 1969 surge of Eurodollar takings differed from that witnessed three years earlier in that the Eurodollar market in 1969 was only one of several major avenues used by American banks to attract nondeposit types of funds with which to offset the heavy attrition of certificates of deposit. Other sources were commercial paper sales by bank subsidiaries and one-bank holding companies and the sale of participations in loans or pools of loans to nonbank customers.

Yet, despite these and other devices which made it possible for banks to obtain funds without regard to interest-rate ceilings and reserve requirements, the rise in Eurodollar acquisitions for domestic use was much more massive in the more recent period, as was the time-deposit decline. Altogether, Eurodollar borrowings by weekly reporting member banks from their branches during the 12 months beginning in December 1968 rose by $8 billion, offsetting much of the CD attrition of about $13 billion during the same period. During the four weeks beginning May 28, 1969, Eurodollar takings shot up by no less than $3.4 billion, providing the banks with ready proof that, at a price, the Eurodollar market could supply them in short order with very impressive amounts of funds. However, the price that had to be paid to mobilize such large amounts of funds proved to be exceedingly high. Rates for three-month Eurodollars which had hovered around 9 per cent through most of the spring advanced to 12.5 per cent. But banks proved quite willing to pay whatever the market price happened to be for what their money-desk managers considered "last resort" money. This was confirmed when, in the fall of 1969, United States bank liabilities to overseas branches became subject to a 10 per cent marginal reserve requirement on borrowings from their branches in excess of those in May 1969. Even though this requirement made borrowings in excess of the reserve-exempt base substantially more expensive, United States banks did not materially reduce their takings from their branches until the closing weeks of the year.

Eurodollar Transactions as an Alternative to Federal Funds Purchases

As American banks expanded their role in the market and became increasingly familiar with market processes, several of them discovered that they could reap sizable benefits by taking advantage of certain techniques used in settling Eurodollar transactions. One such type of operation has become known as Thursday-Friday transactions, inasmuch as they involve borrowings of Eurodollar balances for value dates on Thursday and the repayment of the borrowing on the following day. Banks have engaged in these transactions in huge volume in order to obtain balances that can serve as Federal funds at rates below the going Federal funds rate. Eurodollar transactions are generally settled between New York banks through clearing house checks. A check received by a Eurodollar-borrowing United States bank on Thursday becomes a good balance in its Federal Reserve account only on Friday. However, the check issued by a bank on Friday in repayment of the borrowing does not clear until Monday, and its Federal Reserve account is only debited on that day. Thus the borrowing bank can, because of the check-clearing delay, obtain Federal funds for three days, i.e., Friday, Saturday and Sunday, even though it borrows dollars for only one day. Of course, as more and more banks became aware of the profit opportunities inherent in such transactions, the overnight rate for Thursday-value dates began to reflect this advantage.

Another type of transaction yielding relatively low-cost Federal funds took advantage of accounting techniques which involved the use of so-called *bills payable* or *London checks* in the settlement of overnight Eurodollar deposits. In the mid-1960s, a few United States banks discovered that by using such checks they could achieve substantial reductions of deposits subject to reserve requirements. The practice spread slowly and by the end of 1968 was used on a large scale by many American banks with overseas branches. In July 1969, however, an amendment of the Federal Reserve Board's Regulation D ruled out the practice.

Operations involving the use of bills payable and London checks comprised both deposits in the Eurodollar markets and repayments of such deposits. When a London branch of a United States bank made a Eurodollar deposit in a foreign bank (or in another branch of a U.S. bank), it would request its head office to issue a cashier's check for deposit in the foreign bank's correspondent bank in New York. Under Federal Reserve regulations, officers' checks must be added to gross-demand deposits subject to reserve requirements, but the banks engaging in such transactions considered such checks as not subject to reserves either because they were issued in settlement of what in essence were Federal funds transactions or on behalf of their London offices. On the following day, the correspondent bank or the head office of the borrowing branch would repay the overnight deposit with its own clearing-house check. As with all clearing-house checks received, the head office of the London branch having the account for which this check would be received would book it in an account designated as "Cash Items in the Process of Collection." Under Federal Reserve regulations, items in this account may be deducted from deposits subject to reserve requirements. Since, as we have pointed out, gross deposits were not increased when the bills payable or London check was issued, but were reduced when the repayment check was received, banks could reduce their deposits subject to reserve requirements by having their branches make overnight dollar deposits with other banks.

Similar reserve savings could be achieved by a branch borrowing overnight Eurodollars. The check received by the head office of the borrowing branch was deducted from deposits subject to reserve requirements, but the check issued in repayment was not credited to official checks outstanding. The net effect of these accounting techniques was to reduce the effective rates on overnight Eurodollars to levels below the Federal-funds rate. It thus became profitable for United States banks not only to turn on a large scale to the use of overnight Eurodollars in lieu of Federal funds, but to place overnight deposits for the specific purpose of reducing deposits subject to reserve requirement and thereby making unnecessary the purchase of a corresponding amount of Federal funds. A partial indication of the very large reserve savings is provided by the fact that on June 30, 1969, overnight deposits in the foreign branches of United States banks were as much as $2.4 billion. But there are no figures available on aggregate overnight deposits made by the branches for the purpose of reducing their reserve requirements.

An incidental effect of these operations was to escalate overnight rates in the Eurodollar market and to create a reverse maturity gap in the market as European banks borrowed long and lent short to take advantage of the premium that could be earned on overnight placements.

An amendment of the Federal Reserve Board's Regulation D, which became effective July 31, 1969, aimed at putting an end to the cost savings generated by overnight purchases and sales of Eurodollars. The amendment required that checks issued by or on behalf of a foreign branch against its account with its head office be included in gross-demand deposits like other officers' checks.

Eurodollars Loans to United States Residents

For the most part, overseas branch loans of Eurodollars to residents of the United States have been made to facilitate the borrowers' compliance with the Commerce Department's quota restrictions on foreign direct investment. Direct investments financed with foreign borrowings were not required to be charged against these quotas. As these quota restrictions were gradually tightened in the years subsequent to their adoption in 1965 (and made mandatory in 1968), corporations which wished to step up their foreign investments had a strong incentive to borrow abroad. While most of these borrowings took the form of bond issues in the Eurobond market, substantial funds were also borrowed from the branches of U.S. banks (and also from foreign banks), not only by foreign affiliates of U.S. corporations but also by their parent companies. In addition, during the 1966 period of tight money, and again in 1968 and 1969, a significant amount of branch loans to U.S. corporations served to finance general corporate needs for funds and, on occasion, to provide funds for takeover bids and mergers. Moreover, a few banks sold domestic loans, or participations in such loans, to their foreign branches and thus were able to improve their liquidity or to obtain funds for additional loans. Loans to American corporations to meet their needs in the United States and sales of the banks' domestic loans to foreign branches have become less common since the Federal Reserve Board imposed, in August 1969, a 10 per cent marginal-reserve requirement on credit extended by branches to United States residents. Branch loans extended to enable borrowers to comply with quota requirements of the Commerce Department's Office of Foreign Direct Investments are exempt from this requirement.

USE OF EURODOLLARS FOR U.S. BANKS' FOREIGN OPERATIONS

Eurodollars obtained by the overseas branches of United States banks have been employed abroad for a variety of purposes. Conceptually, these may be separated into four main categories: (a) deposits with other banks; (b) loans to foreign customers; (c) acquisitions of head-office loans to foreigners, usually under repurchase agreements; and (d) deposits with other branches.

Deposits with Other Banks

Deposits with other banks far outweigh any other category in the aggregate balance sheets of overseas branches of United States banks except claims on head offices. These deposits serve several objectives. Perhaps the most important is to extend reciprocal facilities to those banks that habitually supply substantial deposits to the same branch. Whenever such banks in turn need additional dollar balances for their own operations, the respective branch typically stands ready to make funds available to them. Another major motive for branch deposits in foreign banks is to take advantage of interest-arbitrage opportunities. These usually involve borrowings and redeposits in the form of dollars, but some of the more sophisticated branches have been quite willing to swap substantial amounts of dollars for third currencies which they then place in foreign-currency deposit markets. Or, they have accepted foreign-currency deposits, swapped them for dollars, and placed the dollars with other banks.

In their interest-arbitrage operations, the branches of United States banks have been able to take advantage of the fact that, traditionally, they are able to obtain deposits at rates slightly below the going-market rate. This has been possible because many suppliers have regarded the branches as preferred names, primarily because of the unsurpassed strength of their head offices and the fact that these offices are located in the country in whose currency the deposit is made. Moreover, the branches of large United States banks are normally in a position to absorb very large amounts at a moment's notice.

Finally, branches redeposit dollars with foreign banks because of liquidity considerations. While in theory the branches can always fall back on balances with their head offices, the latters' own requirements may make it inconvenient for them to satisfy the branches' unexpected needs for funds. For this reason, branches employ redeposits in foreign banks as a supplementary means to strengthen their liquidity position.

Loans to Foreign Customers

Following adoption of the Voluntary Foreign Credit Restraint Program, the foreign branches have taken over a substantial part of the new foreign lending which would ordinarily have been handled by their head offices. The Eurodollar market has been the single most important source of funds for such lending. A large and, for many branches, predominant part of their dollar loans to foreigners has always been to the overseas affiliates of United States corporations. The affiliates' demand for loan facilities increased substantially after their parent companies became subject to quota restrictions on their direct investments. Beginning in 1968, when a moratorium was imposed on new corporate-capital outflows from the U.S. to almost all Western European countries, this demand intensified.

Eurodollar credit facilities comprise several types of loans and are used to satisfy a large variety of borrowing requirements. Short-term loans are usually extended as lines of credit under which banks stand ready to lend up to a specified amount of Eurodollars at the time they are actually needed by the borrower. Such loans are usually for seasonal and other short-term requirements. The interest rate on such loans is usually based on the interbank deposit rate quoted at the time the line is being utilized. Such drawings are subject to the availability of funds as determined by the lender.

Many borrowers prefer revolving loan commitments to lines of credit because the former represent a definite assurance of credit facilities while the latter are subject to cancellation. Eurodollar revolving commitments are established for one to five years and obligate the branch to lend to the borrower up to a specified amount of Eurodollars in the form of short-term advances. These arrangements require a commitment fee; the actual interest rate charged on each borrowing corresponds to the prevailing rate level in the market at the time the advance is made. In many cases such arrangements constitute no more than standby facilities to be used in case of future need.

Finally, United States branches have used Eurodollars to extend medium-term loans in the one- to five-year maturity range. The underlying loan agreements usually call for periodic rate adjustments and, like their counterparts in the United States, provide for amortization schedules related to anticipated cash flows of the borrower.

American banks without branches frequently introduce their customers in need of Eurodollar financing to their banking friends abroad. If the borrower is not well-known, the United States bank may be required to commit itself to support the borrower's obligation with a guarantee in the form of a letter of credit.

Sales of Head-Office Loans

United States banks have made intensive use of Eurodollars for the financing of sales to their overseas branches of head-office loans. The major purpose of these loan sales has been to enable the head office to finance the foreign-credit needs of their domestic customers as well as the needs of foreign customers even if such loans would carry their aggregate foreign claims above the quota ceiling of the Voluntary Foreign Credit

Restraint Program. For the most part, these sales have been made on a permanent basis, though usually subject to repurchase agreement prior to or at maturity. In some cases, however, foreign credits have been shifted off head-office books prior to reporting dates under the Restraint Program and reacquired a few days after the month-end. In addition, many United States banks without branches have sold their foreign customers' notes to foreign banks, typically under a commitment in form of a letter of credit to repurchase the notes at a later date. The foreign banks are financing these loan purchases largely with Eurodollars.

Deposits with Other Branches

A few major United States banks have shifted Eurodollar acquisitions of their branches from areas abroad where lending opportunities are limited to other areas where the branches of the same parent are unable to find an adequate deposit base but have attractive lending opportunities. In some cases, dollar (and foreign-currency) deposits are passed on, under head-office instructions, by branches with deposit sources in excess of their needs directly to branches in deficit areas. However, some of the banks use their London branches as gathering and redistribution points for dollars obtained by branches elsewhere. The London branches then pass these dollars on to branches in other areas in response to head-office instructions.

CONCLUSION

The large United States banks with overseas branches have shown a remarkable degree of ingenuity and imagination in making use of the borrowing and lending opportunities that offered themselves as the Eurodollar market emerged and expanded. The banks' determined and successful effort to tap the market as a source of huge amounts of funds for financing their operations in the United States has helped them to greatly reduce the disintermediatory impact of Regulation Q interest-rate ceilings. The banks' rapidly increasing use of the market to supplement the resources of their overseas branches for the latter's own operations has made a major contribution to the increasingly important position of the branches in foreign banking systems. Indeed, the intensive use of the Euro-dollar market by some of the major commercial banks in the United States has added a new and significant dimension to their role in both domestic and international banking.

V

GABRIEL FERRAS

Dr. Gabriel Ferras, French banker and international civil servant, was born in Bois-Colombes, near Paris, in 1913. A graduate of the Ecole Libre des Sciences Politiques, Paris, and recipient of a Doctor of Laws from Paris University, he entered the Bank of France in 1938. After the war Dr. Ferras was entrusted with important functions at the Organization for European Economic Cooperation (OEEC) and, from 1950 to 1953, he was Alternate Representative for France in the European Payments Union (EPU). In April 1953 he was sent to the United States as Alternate Executive Director of the Managing Board of the International Monetary Fund (IMF). Shortly afterwards he was appointed Deputy Director of the Exchange Restrictions Department and then Director of the European Department.

Since May 1963 Dr. Ferras has been General Manager of the Bank for International Settlements, Basle, the "central banks' bank," where Governors of the leading central banks meet regularly to discuss important monetary problems. He has thus been closely associated with major decisions in the monetary field during recent years. As the chief of the Bank's operating staff, he is responsible not only for the Bank's technical operations but also for the work of economic and monetary analysis and forecasting that is carried out by the Bank, some of which is published in its Annual Reports.

Central Banks and the Eurodollar Market

INTRODUCTION

The Eurodollar market is a market created, organized and run by commercial banks, mainly those situated in London and other European financial centers. Its growth has not been sponsored by central banks, nor have central banks had a guiding role in it. There has not been any common approach to the market on the part of the central banks in those countries where it is located, nor any attempt by them to make uniform such of their regulatory practices as are relevant to the market.

Nevertheless, it is obvious that the market could not exist if the central banks of the countries mainly concerned did not allow their commercial banks some considerable freedom to operate in dollars. More than that, the growth of the market over the past decade or so, and the fact that it has reached its present size, is undoubtedly connected with certain long-standing features of the ways in which central banks regulate the activities of their commercial banks. One of these features is the decline in the international use of sterling that resulted from the restrictions introduced in 1957 on sterling financing by U.K. banks of transactions between third countries. Another is the fact that banks in the United States may not pay interest on deposits made for periods of up to 30 days, all of which are classified as demand deposits, and the way in which U.S. authorities have operated the limits on rates payable by U.S. banks on longer-term deposits. More recently, there have been the limits placed by the Federal Reserve System, within the framework of the U.S. balance-of-payments restraint program, on foreign lending by banks in the United States. Yet another way in which central-bank policies may be said to have favored the growth of the market arises from the fact that in most European countries foreign-currency deposits are not subject to reserve requirements, whereas banks in the United States must hold reserves with the Federal Reserve System against all their dollar deposits.

Apart from certain basic features of their regulatory practices which have contributed to the growth of the market, central banks have reacted in various ways to the market as it has grown. First, some of them have made direct use of its banking facilities in the same way as other participants, i.e., through the depositing of dollar reserves in the market or, more rarely, through central-bank borrowing in the market. Second, certain central banks and the Bank for International Settlements (BIS) have from time to time acted to smooth out temporary disturbances in the market, either through the temporary placing of central-bank funds in the market or through measures aimed at discouraging temporary withdrawals of commercial-bank funds from the market. Third, central-bank policies and conditions in the Eurodollar market have often reacted on one another. In some cases central banks have sought to isolate conditions in their own economies from the effects of the market or, at any rate, to limit such effects. In other cases, they have allowed or encouraged the use of the market's resources within their own spheres of influence. The effects of these central-bank policies have sometimes been most important from the point of view of domestic monetary conditions, while at other times their main consequences have been felt on the balance of payments and the level of monetary reserves.

In view of the dominant role of commercial banks in the market, it is not surprising that central-bank measures designed to influence relations between their own economies and the Eurodollar market have to a large extent consisted of actions taken (or, in some cases, not taken) to regulate the foreign operations of their commercial banks. Furthermore, the authorities are able to exercise a wide measure of control over the foreign operations of the banks even in the absence of exchange-control legislation.

DIRECT USE OF THE MARKET BY CENTRAL BANKS

So far as concerns what may be called the ordinary banking operations carried out by central banks in the Eurodollar market, no precise information about their scope, either on the lending or the borrowing side, is available. It is known, however, that quite a few central banks, for whom the income earned on external reserves is an important consideration, have for a number of years now employed a part of their dollar holdings in the market for reasons of yield. And some other central banks have placed funds in the market for what are best described as political reasons, because they prefer not to hold balances with banks in the United States. A comparison of Western countries' exchange reserves with the size of their short-term dollar assets held with banks in the United States suggests that in late 1969 the total of dollar reserves employed directly in the market by Western monetary authorities may have been about $2 billion. In addition, Eastern European dollar balances held with commercial banks in the main Western European countries amounted at that time to about $800 million.

Also under this heading may be mentioned the employment of central-bank dollars in the market by the BIS. Leaving aside its occasional interventions in the market for the purpose of smoothing out temporary disturbances (to which reference will be made later), the BIS normally employs in the Eurodollar market some part of the central-bank funds entrusted to it. While the amounts involved vary in accordance with circumstances, they have had a natural tendency to go up gradually as the size of the Bank's total operations has increased and it may be said that their volume increased quite markedly in the first half of 1969 with the sharp rise in the yields obtainable on Eurodollar deposits.

In connection with central-bank employment of funds in the Eurodollar market it is of interest to note that the total volume is not insignificant despite the fact that since October 1962 the rates of interest payable by U.S. banks on central-bank deposits have been exempt from the Regulation Q ceilings. No doubt one important reason for this is the fact, already referred to, that banks in the United States may not pay interest at all on deposits for periods of up to 30 days.

On the borrowing side, little is known about central-bank participation in the Eurodollar market. It is safe to say, however, that Western monetary authorities have taken much less out of the market than they have put into it. On the other hand, Eastern European takings from the market (or, more precisely, these countries' borrowings from the commercial banks of the principal Western European countries) amounted in late 1969 to about $1 billion, which was somewhat more than the total of their dollar deposits with these same banks at that time. These borrowings are not always central-bank borrowings, however, and include funds taken up by governmental foreign-trade banks.

TEMPORARY CENTRAL-BANK ACTION TO INFLUENCE THE MARKET

A second type of central-bank impact on the market has resulted from actions taken by certain European central banks and by the BIS with the aim of easing temporary disturbances in the market. This has particularly been the case at year-ends, when the commercial banks in certain Western European countries withdraw funds from the market, partly for window-dressing purposes and partly to meet seasonal liquidity needs. The best example of such action is the regular rechannelling to the market of the dollars withdrawn from it at year-ends by the Swiss commercial banks. For a number of years this rechannelling took place via the BIS—the dollars first being swapped by the Swiss banks with the Swiss National Bank against francs, then swapped by the National Bank with the BIS against gold, and then returned to the market by the BIS. Since 1966, the Swiss National Bank itself has also made temporary deposits of dollars in the market.

In addition to individual central banks acting to replace temporary withdrawals of dollars from the market, there have been instances of concerted action being taken by a number of central banks and the BIS in order to relieve temporary stringency in the market. These moves may be considered as exceptions to the general statement that there has been no concerted central-bank approach to the market. Such concerted action occurred, for instance, towards the end of 1966 in the face of a sudden rise in the one-month Eurodollar rate from 6½ to 7⅜ per cent at end-November of that year. As part of a joint effort, the Swiss National Bank made substantial direct investments in the market; the BIS placed in the market funds received from the Swiss National Bank and the Netherlands Bank, as well as $200 million drawn on its swap line with the Federal Reserve Bank of New York; and the

German and Italian authorities took action to reduce end-year repatriation of funds by their banks. The German action consisted of temporarily reducing the reserves required to be held by German commercial banks at the Deutsche Bundesbank; in the Italian effort, the central bank temporarily increased its short-term accommodation to the banks. As a consequence of these various steps, the one-month Eurodollar deposit rate had, by mid-December 1966, fallen to about the level at which it had been standing before the end-November rise.

INTERACTION OF CENTRAL-BANK POLICIES AND EURODOLLAR DEVELOPMENTS

This aspect of relations between central banks and the Eurodollar market may conveniently be discussed under a number of headings. First, one may distinguish two kinds of situation: that in which central banks were seeking to limit inflows of funds from, or to bring about outflows of funds to, other markets, including the Eurodollar market; and that in which central banks allowed or encouraged the use of the Eurodollar market's resources by their banks or, what comes to much the same thing, encouraged or enforced the withdrawal by their banks of funds previously placed in the market.

Broadly speaking, these two types of situation may be distinguished according to whether the effects of the central-bank actions were more important from the viewpoint of domestic liquidity or from that of the balance-of-payments and reserve situation of their countries. In some cases, however, both effects were important. Second, it is useful to treat separately the events of 1969, since during that year the impact of some central-bank policies on the market was much greater than ever before, and the reactions of other central banks to conditions in the market more generalized.

Domestic Liquidity Effects

This kind of situation existed in Italy from late 1959 to late 1962 and again for a period of two to three years, beginning in late 1963. Concerning the first of these episodes, towards the end of the 1950s Italian banks had been accepting foreign-currency deposits from nonresidents for relending to residents at rates below those charged for similar loans in lire. By late 1959, the banks had run up net foreign-currency liabilities to nonresidents totaling about $350 million and, in November of that year, the Italian authorities decided to discourage this inflow of liquidity from the rest of the world. At that date they began offering the banks facilities for obtaining dollars by means of swaps with the Italian Exchange Office on terms more favorable than those obtainable in the market, and this was followed in 1960 by an instruction to the banks to bring their foreign-currency positions vis-à-vis nonresidents into balance. Between November 1959 and September 1962, about $950 million was made available to the banks out of Italy's dollar reserves—mostly through the swap facilities mentioned above but also to some extent through deposits of dollars by the Italian Exchange Office with Italian commercial banks. As a result, over this period of nearly three years the Italian banks' net exchange position vis-à-vis nonresidents shifted from liabilities of $350 million to assets of nearly $200 million, while at the same time the banks were enabled to increase their net foreign-currency lending to resident customers by about $400 million. Thus, something over half of the dollars made available by the authorities were transferred abroad for employment, probably mostly in the Eurodollar market.

The second Italian episode followed a period from late 1962 until August 1963 during which the banks again made use of the market's resources, this time on a much larger scale. By the end of August 1963 their net exchange liabilities to nonresidents had reached about $1 billion and, in the following month, the authorities issued instructions to the banks not to increase their foreign borrowing any further and to try progressively to eliminate it. On this occasion, too, help was given by means of preferential swap facilities offered by the Italian Exchange Office. As a result, between end-August 1963 and the end of 1965 the banks' net exchange position vis-à-vis nonresidents turned round by over $1 billion, to a small net asset position of about $100 million; over the same period their swaps with the Exchange Office (which had decreased considerably during the 1962–63 monetary stringency) rose by about $1.3 billion to a level of about $1.5 billion. In this way, the funds taken out of the market in 1962–63 were returned to it over the course of the following two years or so. While this process was begun in late 1963, when Italy was still in external deficit, it is probable that at a later stage, when the balance of payments had turned into substantial surplus, one consideration in the minds of the Italian authorities was the desire to avoid, in the interests of international stability, an undue piling-up of monetary reserves. In late 1965, by which time most of the Italian banks had worked off their earlier foreign borrowing, the Exchange Office limited its preferential swap facilities to those banks which were not yet back in balance.

During much of the 1960s Germany, too, was taking measures designed both to avoid adding to its external surplus and domestic liquidity through inflows of short-term funds and to offset part of its foreign-exchange receipts by encouraging the banks to build up their foreign positions.

To discourage inflows of funds, the German authorities made use on a number of occasions of differential, and higher, reserve requirements on bank liabilities to nonresidents. These requirements were in force, either on all or part of such liabilities, from May 1957 to March 1959, from January 1960 to January 1962, from April 1964 to January 1967, from December 1968 to October 1969, and again from April 1970. These higher rates of reserve requirement applied both to Deutsche mark and foreign-currency liabilities to nonresidents. Another technique used by the German authorities was to forbid the payment of interest on deposits received by German banks from nonresidents. From the end of World War II (except for a brief period from mid-1959 to mid-1960) until very recently, following the October 1969 revaluation of the Deutsche mark, German banks were not allowed to pay interest on nonresident sight and time deposits. Between May 1962 and March 1964, however, the payment of interest on nonresident time deposits was allowed in certain cases.

While it is not possible to say how much effect these measures had on the development of German banks' liabilities to nonresidents (which, by the end of 1967, had risen to $2.2 billion as compared with $750 million in mid-1957), it may be that to some extent they restricted the German banks' participation in the Eurodollar market. On the other hand, the German authorities have also taken measures designed to encourage the banks to re-export a part of the country's foreign-exchange receipts, and which tended to promote the employment of funds in the Eurodollar market by German banks. One way this was done was to free the banks from all reserve requirements on any of their foreign liabilities that they offset by acquiring assets, excluding loans to nonresident customers. In other words, they were required to hold reserves at the Bundesbank only against that part of their foreign liabilities that exceeded the total of their balances with banks and their investments in foreign money-market paper. This measure was introduced in May 1961 and remained in force until the end of 1966.

The German authorities have also made use of the technique of preferential swaps between the central bank and the commercial banks for the purpose of encouraging outflows or, in some cases, of discouraging reflows of exchange through the banks, in particular at times when movements of funds were taking place in expectation of a revaluation of the Deutsche mark. Such swap facilities were first introduced by the Bundesbank in October 1958 with the intention of helping the banks to develop their foreign business after the removal of exchange restrictions; from then on until early 1963, such facilities were constantly available to the banks. Their importance in the development of the short-term foreign assets of the German banks can be seen from the following figures: in September 1958, the month immediately before the introduction of the facilities, the total short-term claims of German banks on nonresidents, excluding credits—i.e., the total of their balances with foreign banks and their investments in foreign money-market paper—amounted to the equivalent of $260 million. By the end of January 1962, at which time the total of DM/dollar swaps outstanding between the Bundesbank and the commercial banks had reached just over $1 billion, the banks' total short-term foreign assets had reached the equivalent of $1.5 billion. As conditions in Germany changed during 1962, these swaps were gradually run off and by early 1963 they had been entirely eliminated.

Swaps between the Bundesbank and the German commercial banks became important again in the troubled period that followed the devaluation of the pound in November 1967. In order to reduce the inflow of funds to Germany, the Bundesbank reintroduced preferential swap facilities towards the end of November 1967; by March 1968, when the gold crisis reached its climax, the total outstanding had reached just over $850 million. After being totally eliminated by the end of June 1968, such swaps were again used during the successive inflows of funds to Germany that occurred between September 1968 and the temporary setting free of the DM-exchange rate at the end of September 1969. Little information has been made available as to the amounts involved, but it is known that at the end of 1968 the total of such swaps outstanding was $1.9 billion, while on September 29, 1969, immediately before the setting free of the Deutsche mark, it amounted to slightly less than $1.5 billion.

It may be added that at moments of great speculative fever the German authorities have not found the swap technique an effective way of limiting inflows of funds. Indeed, during the April/May 1969 crisis the authorities suspended the swap facilities because experience showed that they were being abused and were not serving to decrease the net inflow of funds. What happened was that, given the difference between the Bundesbank's swap rates and those of the market, it was profitable for banks to borrow dollars abroad, covering the transaction in the forward-exchange market, convert the dollars into Deutsche marks, make a DM/dollar swap with the Bundesbank at the preferential rate, and invest the dollars abroad. In this way the banks could make a profit corresponding to the difference between the cost of forward cover in the market and its cost at the Bundesbank.

Another country whose monetary authorities have taken action to avoid inflows of short-term funds, or to offset them once they had occurred, is Switzerland. In August 1960, by agreement with the Swiss National Bank, the Swiss banks undertook not to pay interest on Swiss franc deposits received from nonresidents after June 30, 1960 and even to apply a service charge, at an annual rate of 1 per cent, on all nonresidents' Swiss-franc deposits with a maturity of less than six months. This agreement was renewed annually until 1964, when it was replaced by a new one under which banks paid no interest on nonresident Swiss-franc deposits received after December 31, 1963. This agreement lapsed in March 1967. This Swiss measure, in contrast to the somewhat similar one introduced in Germany in 1960, applied only to nonresident deposits made in Swiss francs. Two consequences for the Euromarket followed from this. One was that nonresidents wishing to deposit funds in Switzerland were given an incentive to place them in currencies other than the Swiss franc; the result was that the Swiss banks' participation in the Eurodollar market was given a stimulus. The other consequence was to encourage the growth of a Euromarket in Swiss francs.

Another measure used by the Swiss authorities was the introduction in March 1964 of the rule that any increase in the banks' gross Swiss-franc liabilities to nonresidents above the end-1963 level had either to be converted into foreign currency and employed abroad or to be deposited on noninterest-bearing accounts at the Swiss National Bank. This, too, gave a fillip to the Swiss banks' employment of funds in the Eurodollar market.

Balance-of-Payments/Reserve Effects

As well as taking actions to prevent, limit or offset inflows of funds from the Eurodollar market, central banks have on a number of occasions allowed or encouraged the use of the market's resources by their commercial banks. In most of these cases an important effect of such inflows has been to finance balance-of-payments deficits.

In Japan there were three periods during the 1960s when balance-of-payments deficits were to an important extent financed by bank borrowing, or withdrawals of funds, from abroad. The first period, which covered the year 1961 and the first half of 1962, saw an overall external deficit of $1,095 million, $440 million of which was covered by an increase in the banks' net foreign-exchange liabilities to nonresidents. During the second period, which lasted from mid-1963 to mid-1964, $310 million out of an overall payments deficit of $680 million was financed in this way. The third such period covered the year 1967 and the first quarter of 1968. The overall payments deficit for these 15 months was $815 million, of which bank net borrowings of exchange from nonresidents covered $645 million. While details concerning the sources from which the

Japanese banks obtained foreign funds are not available for all three periods, during the third episode the main source was clearly the Eurodollar market, since during this period the Japanese banks obtained a net amount of $475 million from sources outside the United States.

In Italy, from late 1962 until August 1963, the banks were allowed to use the market's resources under circumstances in which it was certain, as in fact happened, that they would have substantial recourse to it. In November 1962 they were dispensed from the obligation to maintain a balanced position in foreign currencies vis-à-vis nonresidents. The removal of this restriction came at a time when Italy's balance of payments had turned from surplus into deficit and when, as a consequence, the internal liquidity situation was getting tighter. At the end of September 1962, shortly before the ban on foreign borrowing was lifted, the banks had net exchange claims on nonresidents of a little less than $200 million; 11 months later, at the end of August 1963, their position had turned round dramatically, to net liabilities of rather over $1 billion. The effect of this borrowing on Italy's reserves can be seen from the following figures: During the 12-month period from October 1962 to September 1963 there was an overall deficit of roughly $1 billion; however, owing to the banks' foreign borrowing, net official assets actually increased over these 12 months by nearly $250 million. A not insignificant part ot the dollars borrowed by the banks during this period was used to increase their net lending in foreign currencies to resident customers. Indeed, one reason why the authorities had allowed the banks to start borrowing abroad again towards the end of 1962 was to facilitate their meeting the growing demand for foreign-currency credits from their domestic clientèle.

Another example of Eurodollar funds flowing into a country at a time of tightening monetary conditions and a balance-of-payments deficit is provided by the United Kingdom during the period from the end of 1963 to March 1965. Between these two dates the net foreign-exchange liabilities of British banks to nonresidents increased by about $800 million, in round figures from $50 to $850 million. A considerable part of these borrowings were used by the banks for making sterling loans to UK local authorities. Unlike the Italian situation in 1962–63, this inflow through the banks occurred without any change in the regulations governing the banks' foreign positions; nor, for these 15 months as a whole, did it cover more than one third of the overall payments deficit.

In the first quarter of 1965, however, the net inflow (which amounted to $400 million) more than covered the overall payments deficit and it is certain that during this period it was made possible by the Bank of England's intervention in the forward market. Indirectly, therefore, the U.K. authorities acted in a sense that encouraged the banks to make use of the market's resources during the first quarter of 1965, though that was not, of course, the purpose of their intervention in the forward-exchange market. From the second quarter of 1965 onwards, the banks' net exchange liabilities to nonresidents began to decline and by about the middle of 1966 their position was in balance.

By far the principal user of the Eurodollar market in recent years has been the U.S. banking system. Owing to the fact that foreign branches of U.S. banks are not subject to Regulation Q and that, until recently, the home offices of U.S. banks did not have to keep compulsory reserves against funds obtained from their foreign branches, banks in the United States have been led to borrow from the Eurodollar market via their foreign branches at times when U.S. monetary conditions have been sufficiently tight so that it was difficult for them under the existing Regulation Q ceilings to compete for deposits at home. The 1969 inflow of funds to the U.S. banking system will be dealt with subsequently. But even before that, U.S. banks had been making increasing use of the market through their foreign branches.

The first period in which U.S. bank liabilities to their foreign branches began to rise quite rapidly was in 1966, during which year they rose from $1.3 to just over $4 billion. During the third quarter of 1966 alone, when U.S. monetary conditions were very tight, U.S. banks borrowed $1.5 billion from their foreign branches. As a consequence of these borrowings, for the year 1966 as a whole the net reserve position of the United States (i.e., the change in reserve assets and in liquid official liabilities) showed a surplus of about $1 billion despite the fact that there was a balance-of-payments deficit on the liquidity basis of nearly $1.4 billion.

During the first three quarters of 1968, when the monetary situation in the United States was again tight, U.S. banks once more borrowed in the Eurodollar market, this time on an even more substantial scale. Their liabilities to foreign branches went up from $4.1 billion in early January to just over $7.5 billion in mid-September. And this time the effect on the balance of payments was, of course, more pronounced than in 1966, the net reserve position showing a surplus of $3.4 billion for the first nine months of 1968 concurrently with a moderate deficit of just over $0.6 billion on the "liquidity" balance of payments.

Developments in 1969

Coming now to the events of 1969, the first seven months of last year was the period of fastest growth, not to say the most hectic period, in the history of the Eurodollar market. It was also the period in which central-bank policies influenced the market more strongly than ever before. It may be estimated that in the course of the first half of 1969 the net size of the Eurodollar market increased by $8.5 billion, from $25 to $33.4 billion. Over the same period the rate for three-month Eurodollar deposits showed an unprecedented rise from about 7.5 per cent per annum at the end of 1968 to 12.5 per cent in mid-June 1969. By far the biggest influence on the market during this period was United States monetary policy. The U.S. authorities had begun again to tighten policy towards the end of 1968 and, as this policy was implemented in the first half of 1969, U.S. money-market rates of interest went above the Regulation Q ceilings for the banks' deposit rates. As the authorities chose not to adjust these ceilings (which had last been raised in April 1968) to the new situation, U.S. commercial banks began to experience a very large run-off of their certificates of deposit. To compensate for this, they embarked on a new and massive intake of funds from the Eurodollar market through their foreign branches, their liabilities to which rose by about $8.4 billion during the first seven months of 1969.

This large-scale recourse of U.S. banks to the Eurodollar market had a very pronounced effect on the U.S. balance-of-payments results for the first half of 1969, of the same kind as in 1966 and 1968 but on a far larger scale. Thus, parallel with an unadjusted liquidity deficit of just over $5 billion for January–June 1969, there was an improvement of $2.6 billion in the net-reserve position. It should be added, however, that part of the funds collected by U.S. banks from their foreign branches during this period came from the United States in the first place, thus making the liquidity deficit larger than it otherwise would have been.

The tensions to which U.S. recourse to the market gave rise were aggravated by quite substantial withdrawals of French and Italian bank funds from the market. During the six months October 1968–March 1969, the foreign-exchange position of the French banks vis-à-vis nonresidents decreased by about $1.5 billion, from net assets of $1.1 billion to net liabilities of $0.4 billion. This occurred to a large extent as a result of official action taken to mobilize the banks' foreign assets in the face of the large payments deficit, but also to some extent in reaction to the tightening of the monetary situation in France. In the Italian move, the banks were instructed in late March

1969 to bring their overall foreign position, which at that time showed net assets of about $750 million, into balance by mid-year. This instruction, which as in the French case was designed primarily to help finance the payments deficit that had emerged, resulted in a decline of $600 million in the banks' net-exchange assets vis-à-vis nonresidents between end-March and end-July 1969.

Thus, during the first half of 1969, U.S. monetary policy was causing the Eurodollar market to expand at an unprecedented rate, while at the same time putting strong pressures on Eurodollar interest rates. These pressures were intensified by the withdrawal of French and Italian bank funds from the market.

The conditions that prevailed in the Eurodollar market during the first half of 1969 and, in particular, the steep rise in interest rates produced unwelcome effects in a number of European countries. Defensive measures were therefore taken by the authorities to stem or reverse the conversion of domestic currency for employment in the market—a phenomenon which in some cases was already affecting official reserves. There were widespread increases in European central banks' discount and other lending rates and in many cases direct controls over the banks' foreign operations were exercised. Mention has already been made of the enforced reduction in the French and Italian banks' foreign positions; these measures may be seen as having been to some extent, though not mainly, a reaction to Eurodollar developments. In addition, somewhat similar measures were taken by Denmark in February, by Belgium in April, and by The Netherlands in July.

That it was not only European countries that were being inconvenienced by the turn of events in the market was shown in June 1969 when the U.S. authorities announced several measures designed to limit the recourse of their banks to the market. First, banks were obliged to add to their demand deposits subject to reserve requirements checks issued by them on behalf of their foreign branches. Second, a 10 per cent reserve requirement was introduced on (a) borrowings by U.S. banks from their foreign branches in excess of the average level of such borrowings during the four weeks ending May 28; (b) assets held by foreign branches which were acquired from their domestic offices in excess of the average level during the four weeks ending May 28; and (c) loans by foreign branches to U.S. residents in excess either of the amounts outstanding on June 25 or of the average amounts outstanding over the four weeks ending May 28. Third, borrowings by U.S. banks from foreign banks were made subject to a 10 per cent reserve requirement.

If the American banks' borrowing from their branches in Europe were to fall below the level recorded during the base period, their reserve-free quotas would be reduced correspondingly. This would have the effect, should they later step up their borrowings from foreign branches again, of increasing the cost of these borrowings and, other things being equal, would normally discourage them from letting the volume of their liabilities to foreign branches fall below the figures for last May. It seems safe to assume that balance-of-payments considerations had some bearing on this arrangement.

Since end-July 1969, U.S. bank borrowing from the Eurodollar market has no longer been on an upward trend. The total of the U.S. banks' liabilities to their foreign branches, which at that date had reached almost $14.5 billion, has since fluctuated between a high point of about $15 billion in mid-November 1969 and a low point of $13 billion at the end of the year. With U.S. demands on the market no longer so large, the growth of the market appears to have slowed down considerably from the very high rate observed in the first half of 1969. Despite this de-escalation, despite official measures to encourage the Japanese banks to reduce their borrowings in the market and to employ funds there, and despite the huge outflow of funds from Germany since October 1969, Eurodollar interest rates have remained very high except in comparison with their mid-1969 peaks. It can be said, however, that early in 1970 the Eurodollar market presented less of a problem for the monetary authorities than it had done a year earlier.

CONCLUSION

The most important aspect of the relations between central banks and the Eurodollar market lies in the extent to which the market affects the ability of central banks to carry out monetary policies that are appropriate to conditions in their own economies. In a general way it can be said that the development of the Eurodollar market has diminished the freedom of central banks to use the conventional instruments of monetary policy for domestic purposes. The measures that central banks have taken at various times to try to isolate their financial circuits and their economies from the influence of the market are a clear indication of this. At the same time, the effects of these measures suggest that up to a certain point each country is reasonably well-equipped to deal with the problems that may arise for it in this field. Experience also shows, however, that in certain circumstances one or another central bank may be led to allow or encourage the use of the market's resources by its banking system. And, more particularly, the experience of 1969 shows that this can happen on a scale that causes major repercussions in national money markets and on the conduct of central-bank policies.

VI

OTMAR EMMINGER

Dr. Emminger was born on March 2, 1911, in Augsburg, Germany. He studied law and economics at the Universities of Berlin, Munich, and Edinburgh and at the London School of Economics.

In 1950 Dr. Emminger joined Die Deutsche Bundesbank (until 1957 called the Bank Deutscher Länder). Three years later he became a member of its Board of Governors. Since 1958 he has also been a member of the Central Bank Council of Der Deutschen Bundesbank. On January 1, 1970, Dr. Emminger was appointed Vice-President of Der Deutschen Bundesbank and Vice-Chairman of the Central Bank Council.

While serving on the board of the Bundesbank, Dr. Emminger represented the Federal Republic of Germany on the Executive Board of the International Monetary Fund (IMF) from 1953 to 1959. He has served as Vice-President of the Monetary Committee of the European Economic Community (Common Market) since 1958 and, from 1964 through 1967, he was chairman of the Deputies of the Group of Ten.

For a number of years, Dr. Emminger has represented the Federal Republic in the Economic Policy Committee of the Organization of Economic Cooperation and Development (OECD) and in its Working Party No. 3. Since 1969, he has served as Chairman of this Working Party.

The Euromarket: A Source of Stability or Instability?

In August 1969, the London *Economist* commented in an article as follows: "Over $37 billion of Euro-currency loans are outstanding at this moment, a huge pool of convertible international liquidity, subject to (virtually) no central bank controls of any sort. Both central and commercial bankers alike, in quiet moments, are appalled by the dimensions of the monster they have created. . . ." Less dramatically, the President of the Swiss Central Bank, Dr. Stopper, in a speech in the spring of 1969 called the Euromoney market "a vulnerable part of the international currency front"—a remark that at the time was considered a remarkable understatement by some of his central bank colleagues.

On the other side, there are some who enthuse about the vast potentialities of this international money market which links national money markets, evens out national liquidity shortages and surpluses and, over time—so they assume—should lead to a harmonization of interest rates in the participating countries.[1]

[1] While it is true that the interest-rate induced transfer of short-term bank liquidity between various countries has a tendency to diminish interest-rate differentials between participating countries, it is rather surprising that in spite of the growth of

A "monster" the Eurocurrency market certainly is, if one considers its phenomenal growth over the last decade and its present gigantic size. The $45 billion odd of Eurocurrency deposits at the end of 1969 surpassed the entire currency reserves of Western European countries. Before trying to appraise whether it is a benevolent or malevolent monster, I want to clarify a few points concerning the nature of the problem.

THE NATURE OF THE PROBLEM

First, the following analysis is strictly limited to the Euro*money* market, of which the Euro*dollar* market is by far the most important component (about four fifths of the total). Thus I leave completely aside the Euro*capital* (or Eurobond) market. Although the two markets may overlap at the margins, they ordinarily deal with very different kinds of funds, and for different purposes. Movements in the short-term Euromoney markets usually have little to do with the channelling of capital funds to their most productive uses. The Euromoney market is essentially an international pool of *bank liquidity* (although large corporations may also deposit surplus liquid funds there or replenish their short-term working funds). The shoving to and fro over national frontiers of such liquid Eurofunds is usually determined not by relative shortages and yields of productive capital in the participating countries, but by changes in relative national *liquidity* positions and short-term interest rate relations and is thus very much related to monetary-policy actions that influence such changes in bank liquidity and short-term rates. Of course, Eurobanks use part of the Euromoney they have attracted for the financing of

the Euromoney market, these differentials are still far from having disappeared. Thus to this day (February 1970) we see, for example, official rediscount rates (and corresponding market rates) as far apart as 8 per cent in Great Britain and 3¾ per cent in Switzerland coexisting side by side. Similarly, up to the spring of 1969 the German rediscount rate was still at 3 per cent when most international short-term rates were double or more (the Eurodollar rate in London being at that time about 8½ per cent.

foreign trade and similar transactions (perhaps at slightly lower rates of interest than they otherwise could), but this is not characteristic of the functions which the market has assumed after its enormous growth.

Second, the Euromoney market to some extent may only have magnified and highlighted certain tendencies which would exist without it. Thus, the international mobility of short-term funds, which is so characteristic of Euromoney, has been really due to the widespread liberalization of short-term money movements in the wake of currency convertibility since the end of the 1950s. Large movements of short-term funds would therefore have to be expected nowadays even without the existence of the Eurocurrency market. The tightening or relaxing of credit conditions in such an important country as the United States, for example, would always set large amounts of banking funds in motion, whether the Euromarket existed or not. The same is true of speculative movements into, or out of, suspected currencies.

How far has the emergence of the Eurocurrency market added to the potential for such international movements of volatile funds? There is no doubt in my mind that it has added a whole new dimension. This is due to a number of factors. Some countries, e.g., Eastern countries, would not deposit their liquid funds at all in, say, the U.S., but they do make them available in the anonymous Euromarket from where the funds can go anywhere. Many banks would probably have narrower quantitative limits for depositing surplus liquidity in a single foreign country than they require for deposits in the large international market.

A major reason for the attraction of additional funds is the fact that Euromoney banks in places like London are exempt from regulations (e.g., on interest-rate ceilings, liquidity ratios, etc.) and minimum-reserve requirements. They can therefore—and also because they are strictly wholesale dealers in money—

quote narrower margins between credit and debit interest rates and thus sometimes offer more favorable terms to depositors and borrowers alike. Moreover, the vast opportunities of this international market for bank liquidity have led to an interpenetration of the participating banking systems on both sides of the Atlantic and to the setting up of branches for the express purpose of participating in this international money market, thus again enlarging its world-wide ramifications and also its pull on liquid funds.

With the Euromoney market being essentially a wholesale market and outside national boundaries, banks are often prepared to pay considerably higher interest rates for marginal funds from this market, rates which they would not be prepared to pay at home (or may not be permitted to pay, as in the case of U.S. banks) for the same kind of funds over the whole range of their depositors. As a consequence, a tightening of credit in one important market (e.g., the U.S. market) may be transmitted in magnified form to the interest rates in the Euromoney market (as we witnessed in 1969) and from there to other countries, thus again increasing the pull of the Euromarket on short-term funds from all over the world. Altogether, both the available amounts and their mobility have been enormously increased through the emergence of this wide and flexible market. While it is true that most of the problems connected with the Euromarket would in principle also exist without it, as long as free movement of short-term funds over the frontiers exists, nevertheless the Euromarket has given them added weight and importance.

Third, I shall deal with the subject strictly from the viewpoint of monetary authorities. It is in the nature of things that, e.g., commercial bankers would in some respects look at the Euromarket with different feelings. For them, it represents mainly a large extension of their business opportunities and, for American banks in particular, a field where they are not (or at least less) hampered by regulations.[2] For these banks, the Eurodollar market constitutes a huge reservoir of bank liquidity outside their own central banks, which they can tap for needed liquidity (e.g., in order to escape the rigors of domestic monetary policy) or where they can invest liquid surplus funds at advantageous rates. For international corporations, too, it not only offers favorable borrowing and depositing facilities in general, but, in particular circumstances, may also serve as an escape hatch from national money squeezes.

DANGERS TO INTERNATIONAL STABILITY

What, then, are the problems and dangers connected with the Eurocurrency market, from the point of view of international monetary stability?

The following points merit examination:

1. The risk of breakdown in cases of default of final borrowers or of transfer difficulties.
2. The furtherance of international inflation through uncontrolled credit expansion in the Euromarket.
3. The undue recourse to the Euromarket in order to cover up balance-of-payments deficits, with the risk of delaying a more basic adjustment.
4. The strain on national currency reserves through large swings in short-term money flows and, in particular, the financing of huge speculative flows which tend to magnify enormously every currency crisis.
5. The impairment of national monetary policies by the Euromarket's providing a source of bank liquidity outside central banks.

[2] This is entirely true of branches of American banks operating as Eurobanks in European markets, although since the autumn of 1969 the banks' head offices in the U.S. have been subjected to reserve requirements on additional borrowings from Eurobanks, including their own branches abroad.

6. The partial transfer of the U.S. money market abroad, thus making it possible to elude U.S. regulations.

Risk of Breakdown

In nearly all national credit systems, banks and other credit institutions are subject to an elaborate system of rules and regulations and to continuous supervision by some banking authority. To guarantee the liquidity of the system, central banks act as "lenders of last resort" on national levels. Nothing of the sort exists in the huge Eurocurrency market, at least not in its major market place, i.e., London. There the only rule seems to be that the Euro-operations should be kept separate as much as possible from the domestic credit system based on sterling. London has become the center of the Euromarket, not only because of its historical tradition as an international money center but even more because, in Great Britain, the whole non-sterling banking business has from the beginning been treated as a sort of *extraterritorial market.*[3]

Certainly there are risks in the fact that short-term Euro-funds are sometimes re-lent for medium-term loans (*maturity transformation*) or that a lender or intermediary often does not know anything about the end use of its money, or that in an on-lending chain the funds are sometimes converted from one currency into another. As against these risks, there are relieving factors on the other side: e.g., that the participants in the Euromarket are generally only banks or corporations with the highest credit rating, and that about three fifths of the Eurodollar deposits are held with European branches of large U.S. banks so that their dollar liquidity is beyond doubt. As concerns national transfer difficulties, not

[3] By contrast, in a country like Germany, all foreign deposits and loans, whether in German or non-German currency, are subject to the same rules and regulations, including reserve requirements on bank liabilities to nonresidents.

even the foreign-exchange crisis of France in 1968–69 has impaired the free transferability of short-term foreign claims on French banks. Thus, while some risks exist, they should not be dramatized. Much depends, of course, on the attitude which central banks would assume in the case of transfer difficulties or other crises.

There is one contingency where the Euromoney market may really become a monster which could shatter international financial equilibrium: namely, a general loss of confidence in the U.S. dollar. The fact that most of the Eurodeposits are denominated in U.S. dollars would, quite certainly, lead to a complete collapse of the Euromarket in case of a general flight from the dollar. This contingency is altogether too terrifying to visualize in earnest.

Now and again it has been suggested that some of the above-mentioned risks and dangers might be lessened by a collective supervision of the Euromarket through a group of major central banks, acting, for example, through the Bank for International Settlements (BIS). Discussions among central bank experts have shown that such possibilities scarcely exist in practice. Supervision of the Euromoney market can only be exercised through the central bank responsible for the market place in which the individual Eurobank operates, or else through each and every central bank regulating the access to the international market by its own banks and corporations. If a better control of the Euromarket were deemed necessary, the major responsibility would rest with the United States, whose currency is mainly used, and Great Britain, where the bulk of the market is situated.

Occasionally, and especially at year-ends, a helping hand has been given to the Euromarket by some central banks which—either directly or via the Bank for International Settlements—channelled short-term liquidity into the market in order to ease a temporary liquidity squeeze there.

The Market as a Source of Inflation

The Euromoney market has always been suspected of furthering inflation by an overexpansion of credit. This has, for instance, been the view of an expert such as Dr. Holtrop, well-known former president of the Dutch Central Bank. Some experts even attribute to the Euromoney market "an enormous inflation potential."[4] In my view, three different aspects need to be distinguished here.

First, there can be no doubt that the world-wide pull on (otherwise idle) cash reserves exerted by the Euromarket and, in general, its extreme flexibility in employing funds may lead to an increase in the velocity of money or, to put it differently, to more credit being extended on a given monetary base.

Second, when a commercial bank of one country puts part of its liquidity reserve in the Euromarket, it usually continues to count it as part of its liquidity, while a bank in another country may borrow the same amount from the Euro-intermediary and treat it as an addition to its cash reserve. This is an expansionary effect which, of course, could also come about by direct interbank lending of cash reserves between various countries, without the interposition of a Eurobank; however, the expansionary effect will be furthered by the fact that dollar deposits in the Euromarket enjoy a particularly high liquidity. Through the Euromarket, bank money in the U.S. may become "high-powered money" in Europe or Japan.

Third, the Eurocurrency market may create credit like any national banking system. How far it is able to do so is highly controversial. Milton Friedman[5] has attributed to

[4] Robert A. Mundell, "A Plan for a European Currency." Paper presented at the American Management Association Conference, New York City, December 10–12, 1969.

[5] Milton Friedman, "The Euro-Dollar Market: Some First Principles," reprinted on pp. 273–293 (Chapter XVI).

the Eurodollar market the same faculty of multiple-credit creation that exists for the American banking system at home. To him, the major source of Eurodollars has been "a bookkeeper's pen," as it is of the liabilities of U.S. banks. As against this, Fred H. Klopstock[6] of the Federal Reserve Bank of New York has argued that, in contrast to a national banking system, Eurobanks, as a group, "cannot count on recapturing more than a relatively small fraction of their loan proceeds." He therefore puts the Eurobanks' capacity for multiple-credit creation rather low. (In an article of March 1968, he estimated the credit creation multiplier as lying in the approximate range of 0.5 to 0.9.)

On the other side, if—as in the recent past—a lot of Eurodollars are channelled back to the United States, this may lead to a contractionary effect on the countries parting with dollars while not expanding the money base in the U.S. It *may*, because much depends on where the funds come from and how their outflow is being financed. It is somewhat doubtful, however, whether a strongly restrictive monetary policy in the U.S. would not have exerted a similar effect even without the interposition of the Euromarket. The same would be true of a reversal of U.S. monetary policy which would lead to a reflow of funds from the U.S. to Europe.

To sum up: *The potential expansionary (or inflationary) credit effect of international money movements may be greatly magnified by the existence of the Euromarket.* But it is certainly not beyond the power of the monetary authorities to counteract this effect if they so desire.

The Balance-of-Payments Effects of the Euromarket

The Euromoney market constitutes a huge pool of inter-

[6] Fred H. Klopstock, "Money Creation in the Euro-Dollar Market—A Note on Professor Friedman's Views," *Monthly Review*, Federal Reserve Bank of New York, January 1970, pp. 12–15.

national liquidity, but on a nonofficial basis. Its effects on a country's foreign-exchange position may cut both ways. On the one side, it may be used as an additional source of reserves to relieve a strain on a country's balance of payments. On the other side, it can, by helping to finance large disequilibrating foreign-exchange movements, augment the strain on a country's external position.

Is the existence of such a big potential supplement to currency reserves good or bad? As in the case of international liquidity in general, this depends on the use countries make of this additional reserve pool.

Was it to the advantage of Italy (and of European stability in general) when in 1963 the Italian balance-of-payments deficit was financed to the tune of over $1 billion by recourse of the Italian banking system to the Euromarket? This prevented the deficit from both becoming visible in Italy's foreign exchange reserves and exerting a contractionary effect on the liquidity of the Italian banking system. Only when the central bank finally stopped the recourse to the Euromarket did the self-healing forces of the shrinkage of domestic liquidity begin to play in the direction of a better domestic and external equilibrium of the Italian economy.

Has it been to the advantage of the United States and the world at large that the basic balance-of-payments deficit of the U.S. in 1969 was covered by attracting about $8 billion of short-term funds via the Euromoney market? Of course, this has provided the United States with the short-lived satisfaction of having had, in 1969, a surplus in the balance of official-reserve settlements to the tune of $2.7 billion, while the balance on liquidity basis was in the red with the highest amount ever recorded, namely, $7.2 billion. It has also been instrumental in giving the U.S. dollar an appearance of strength in the foreign-exchange markets throughout most of 1969. It is difficult to judge whether these positive elements outweigh the negative ones, namely, that the "real" balance-of-payments position of the United States has been concealed, that the U.S. has burdened itself with a large amount of volatile foreign debt, and that, when the time comes for a relaxation of U.S. monetary policy, there may be very large re-flows of short-term money from the United States to the Euromarket which may swamp European money markets and exacerbate the U.S. balance-of-payments position. Finally, it is at least arguable whether a monetary tightness in the United States on the order of that of 1969 would not in any case—regardless of the existence of the Euromarket—have led to somewhat similar, although certainly less massive movements of short-term funds to the United States.

A more general question has been raised: Should we count on the Euromoney pool as a permanent addition to international reserves? There have in the past been suggestions (e.g., by Dr. Baffi, Director General of the Bank of Italy) to the effect that the vastly expanded Euromarket may suffice to satisfy the future reserve needs of the industrial countries so that any additional provision of official reserves might be redundant. But the Euromarket would be a very unreliable source of reserves for monetary authorities. Except in the few countries where the central bank has full control over every bank's foreign position (as happens to be the case in Italy), monetary authorities can never be sure of whether and to what extent they can tap the Euromoney pool for currency reserves when needed. They cannot, therefore, count on such a recourse in the same way they can depend on their own reserves, or on official unconditional credit lines. In my opinion, more recent experience would rather lead to the opposite conclusion, i.e., *that the growth of the Euromarket, far from alleviating the problem of official reserves, has actually aggravated it.* This question will be discussed subsequently.

A Source of Speculative and Other Destabilizing Short-Term Flows

It is self-evident that with the enlargement of the international pool of short-term funds, destabilizing short-term movements, when they occur, may assume much larger proportions. This is true of movements due to interest-rate differentials; it is even more true of speculative movements based on exchange-rate hunches and the like. The huge foreign-exchange inflows at the occasion of the various speculative Deutsche mark crises—which reached a high point at the beginning of May 1969 when, within a period of about ten days, more than $4 billion were converted into DMarks—cannot be otherwise explained than that a large part of them were financed through the Euromarket. This Euromarket-fed speculation on the DMark led, as a counterpart, to sharp pressures on the vulnerable currencies. Again, the French experience in 1968 has shown that, in view of the volatility of short-term banking funds, every country has to consider a large part of the foreign short-term claims on its banks as a potential mortgage on its official reserves.

Whatever the precise role of the Euromoney market may have been in all this, the result of the experience since 1967 has been unequivocal: Everywhere an increased demand for official reserves has been making itself felt. This is not only because of the enormous growth in regular turnover and the fluctuations of foreign trade and payments, but also because of the need for a shield against the increased volatility of greatly expanded short-term capital flows.

Interference with National Monetary Policies

Just as the Euromoney pool has a potential two-way effect on the balance of payments and external reserves, it may, depending on circumstances, equally well aid domestic monetary policy, or disturb and even undermine it. The stringency and high-interest rates in the Euromarket in 1969 proved to be a boon to the monetary authorities of Switzerland. By attracting the surplus liquidity of the Swiss banks (which were temporarily heavily swollen by speculative inflows), the remunerative London Euromarket was instrumental in sparing Switzerland a liquidity inflation at home. It is very likely that without this diversion of Swiss banking funds to high-interest investments in the London market, the Swiss policy of quantitative credit ceilings for the domestic economy, introduced in the autumn of 1969, would not have had much chance of success. On the other side, this same situation in the Euromarket has led to repeated complaints from some other countries (e.g., Belgium) because they felt that the pull of the Euromarket not only deprived them of official reserves but imposed upon them an interest-rate level which did not entirely suit their domestic policy intentions.

Occasionally the effect of the Euromarket on a domestic monetary situation has changed within a matter of months from a "stabilizing" to a "destabilizing" influence. Thus, the Federal Reserve in the first months of 1969 repeatedly proclaimed that the Eurodollar inflows "provided a needed safety valve for American banks—which enabled the Federal Reserve to pursue a more vigorous policy of monetary restraint than it otherwise would be able to do." By July 1969 it had become clear, however, that these same inflows "were ceasing to be a safety valve and were becoming an obvious escape route around a national policy of credit restraint" (Governor A. F. Brimmer of the Federal Reserve Board). And the then Chairman of the Federal Reserve Board, William McChesney Martin, Jr., even expressed concern "that excessive Eurodollar borrowings would have disruptive effects in financial markets, both domestic and foreign."

If such effects are deemed possible on the domestic monetary situation of the United States (beside whose domestic credit volume of $450 billion any conceivable Eurodollar flows appear marginal), what can smaller European countries expect? Indeed, *one of the major problems of European monetary policy is whether, and how, central banks will be able to maintain control over their banks' liquidity situation and over their national money volume with such a huge pool of international liquidity hovering before their door.*

Some European central banks have drawn from this situation one conclusion: *They consider changes in the net foreign position of their banks as an important element in the domestic liquidity supply.* Committed, by law, to regulate domestic liquidity, these central banks have laid down rules for, or control directly, their banks' short-term foreign positions. For years this has been done quite systematically in Italy. Over the last two to three years, the Netherlands, Belgium, France, and others have also come to a similar conclusion. In Germany, the destabilizing money inflows into German banks during the currency crises of 1969 were, at least in part, warded off by temporarily imposing a 100 per cent reserve requirement on all additional foreign deposits with German banks.

To influence the short-term foreign loans and borrowings of commercial banks is, however, not a sufficient or final solution to the potential conflict between national monetary policy and short-term international money flows. It still leaves the door open to such flows via nonbanks. It has been one of the recent experiences in Germany that while imposition of the special minimum reserve requirements reduced the unwanted inflow into banks to relatively small proportions, the foreign funds flowing directly to German corporations and, in particular, to German subsidiaries of foreign corporations took on correspondingly larger proportions.

A further stage in this tug-of-war between national monetary policies and the potentially countervailing influences of the Euromoney pool looms ahead: i.e., the time when the United States will relax its monetary policy and, as a consequence, interest-rates in the Euromarket will go down. This may undermine restrictive monetary policies in those European countries where the inflationary boom is still going strong.

This undercutting of domestic monetary policies through money flows from abroad cannot, of course, be laid entirely at the door of the Euromarket. It is mainly the consequence of freedom of international money movements as such—magnified, however, by the enormous size of the funds concentrated in the Europool. European central banks will have to learn to live with this "monster" at their door. It is certainly an exaggeration to claim that European central banks are in the process of "becoming satellite banks not only of the U.S. Federal Reserve, but even of the big U.S. commercial banks" (Professor R. A. Mundell). But it is true that they will have to give up the hope that they will ever be able to have full control of their domestic money volume and other monetary aggregates.

The Partial Transfer of the U.S. Money System Abroad

The possible interference of international money flows with domestic monetary policies, while of crucial importance for European countries, at first sight seems to have only marginal significance for the huge United States economy. Nevertheless, the statements of leading Federal Reserve officials, quoted previously, show that the problem may no longer be negligible even for the U.S. It may become less so once present American rules and guidelines which limit the investing abroad of bank and corporate funds are abolished. Why, indeed, should corporate finance managers in the U.S. be content with a 6 or 7 per cent interest rate on liquid dollar funds if they can have 1 or 2 per cent more in a London branch of a big American bank? Why should they go without any interest on call deposits if they can get a handy one on a dollar deposit in London?

Already in 1969, some $2 to $3 billion of American non-bank funds seem to have found their way into the Euromarket, only to be re-cycled back to the United States by the American banks. It is not at all certain whether such American funds deposited in the Euromarket will in future always be re-cycled back to the United States. There is a distinct possibility that a significant part of the American monetary and banking system may be shifted to the Euromarket in London or elsewhere in order to escape domestic interest-rate regulations and reserve requirements, thereby earning more money. This would in some ways parallel a similar movement in American industry, i.e., the transfer abroad of important American export bases throught direct investment abroad, in order to escape high wages at home.

The Eurodollar market has, to be sure, very much enlarged the international role of the U.S. dollar as a trading and "vehicle" currency. It has also increased the impact of American monetary policy on monetary developments and policies in other countries. The price, however, has been that even the United States is no longer full master over its national monetary policy, with more and more foreign escape routes being opened up. This, of course, is an experience with which smaller countries have been confronted for quite some time.

SUMMARY

To sum up: The Euromoney market has brought with it a number of advantages. A broad and flexible international market in itself carries some presumption of being a useful thing. The advantages, however, are more in the realm of widened opportunities for commercial banking. In a more general sense, some countries may benefit from the fact that the Euromarket provides them with a large money market which they lack within their own boundaries (e.g., Switzerland). However, *from the point of view of the stability of the international system, the negative aspects probably outweigh the positive ones.* For what is the use of an evening out of national liquidity positions or of short-term interest rates if what is required is very often the reverse? It is undeniable that stabilization policies and the adjustment of balance-of-payment disequilibria very often necessitate national liquidity and interest-rate policies which may vary from country to country and may even be contradictory.

Thus, the huge international pool of liquidity which at a moment's notice is ready to flow hither and thither may, more often than not, undercut national stabilization or adjustment policies. Also, the balance-of-payments effect of such short-term money flows is likely to be more often destabilizing than stabilizing, because these flows conceal the real "underlying" balance-of-payments deficit and blunt the automatic adjustment process, and because they are apt to inflate minor speculative flurries into major currency crises. The mere "recycling" of short-term funds from one central bank to another does not seem to solve the real problems involved. Thus, *the Euromoney market has made monetary management much more difficult and complicated in both the domestic and the external field.*

Probably there is also something to the fear that the Euromarket, by attracting cash reserves from all over the world and activating them, may contribute to inflationary credit expansion on an international scale. However, it does not appear to be beyond the power of the monetary authorities to keep these inflationary forces under control, provided the major countries pull in the same direction.

As against these major disadvantages, the danger of a breakdown from ordinary lending risks, or even the danger of a chain-reaction from a national transfer crisis, appear to be of minor significance.

Altogether, the concentration of such huge amounts of short-term funds in one big international market would seem to require some supervision and control on a world-wide scale. Nothing of the sort is, however, in sight. So each central bank is left to battle this "monster" as best it can.

VII

EDWARD M. BERNSTEIN

Mr. Bernstein is a graduate of the University of Chicago and Harvard University. He was associate professor and professor of economics at the University of North Carolina from 1930 to 1940 and visiting professor of economics at Harvard University in the summer of 1957.

From 1940 to 1946, Mr. Bernstein was with the Treasury Department, holding various posts from principal economist to Assistant to the Secretary of the Treasury. In 1946 he became director of research and statistics at the International Monetary Fund. Since 1958 he has been head of EMB (Ltd.), Research Economists.

Mr. Bernstein has served on a number of U.S. Government missions and committees. He was executive secretary and chief technical adviser of the U.S. delegation at the Bretton Woods Conference, 1944. He was staff director of the report to the President on a Trade and Tariff Policy in the National Interest, 1953. Mr. Bernstein was chairman of the Review Committee for Balance of Payments Statistics, whose report was published in 1965. From 1965 to 1968, he was a member of the U.S. Treasury's Advisory Committee on International Monetary Arrangements (Dillon Committee).

Mr. Bernstein is the author of Money and the Economic System *and numerous papers on monetary policy, the international monetary system, and balance-of-payments problems.*

Eurodollars: Capital Flows and the U.S. Balance of Payments

EURODOLLAR TRANSACTIONS

The Eurodollar market—that is, the deposits with and loans of banking institutions in Europe denominated in U.S. dollars—is the largest international money market in the world. At the end of 1969, the short-term dollar liabilities (deposits) of the banks of eight European countries to nonresidents amounted to over $37 billion. About two-thirds of these Eurodollar deposits ($24.7 billion) were in foreign branches of U.S. banks, mainly located in London. An international money market of this size is certain to have great effects on international money flows and on the world pattern of payments.

The significance of the Eurodollar market for the U.S. balance of payments does not arise from the fact that the deposits and loans are denominated in dollars. That is merely a convenience for international banking in a world in which the dollar is the principal currency used in international trade and investment. What is significant for the world pattern of payments is that Eurodollar deposits originating in some countries are used to make loans to borrowers in other countries. As this indicates, the Eurodollar market affects the U.S. balance of payments directly only as U.S. residents are depositors and borrowers of Eurodollars.

For example, if a Swiss bank makes a Eurodollar deposit and an equivalent Eurodollar loan is made to an Italian firm, this has no direct effect on the U.S. balance of payments, even though the deposit is with and the loan is made by a London branch of an American bank. The United States does not enter into the transactions; the dollar is simply used as a convenient unit of account. The Swiss bank may acquire the dollars it deposits by buying them in the exchange market with Swiss francs it does not need for domestic loans and investments. The Italian firm may sell the dollars for lire it needs for its business outlays. Neither U.S. receipts nor U.S. payments are directly affected by the Eurodollar transactions.

The situation is not essentially different if the Eurodollars are identifiably derived from and used in international trade. Suppose that a German firm acquires dollars in payment for its exports and deposits them in the Eurodollar market. Suppose that a Japanese firm borrows the Eurodollars to pay for its imports. The fact that some German export receipts have been used for making Eurodollar deposits and that some Japanese imports have been financed by Eurodollar loans will not directly affect the U.S. balance of payments. Germany's balance of payments will show the receipt from exports and the corresponding payment for capital outflow—the Eurodollar deposit. Japan's balance of payments will show the payment for imports and the corresponding receipt from capital inflow—the Eurodollar loan. Neither transaction will be shown in the U.S. balance of payments.

Even if Germany's exports were to the United States and Japan's imports were from the United States, the fact that the export receipt was deposited in the Eurodollar market and that the import payment was financed by a Eurodollar loan would not directly affect the U.S. balance of payments. It would be precisely the same if the German exporter sold the dollars to the Bundesbank and the Japanese importer bought the dollars from the Bank of Japan. Indirectly, however, these and similar operations of the Eurodollar market may affect the U.S. balance of payments and its reserve position, depending on what would have happened to world trade and investment in the absence of the Eurodollar market.

The U.S. balance of payments is directly affected only where the deposit is from a U.S. resident or the loan is to a U.S. resident. Thus, if a U.S. corporation makes a Eurodollar deposit, the balance of payments will show a capital outflow without offsetting receipts. When a U.S. corporation borrows in the Eurodollar market, that is a capital inflow, disregarding the possibility that it is used for a payment (e.g., direct investment) that might not otherwise be made. When a U.S. bank borrows in the Eurodollar market, including the liabilities of a head office to a foreign branch, that is a capital inflow in the official reserve balance but not in the liquidity balance.

The view that the Eurodollar market is possible only because the United States has a balance-of-payments deficit is not correct. If U.S. payments were precisely balanced, without any flow to or from the Eurodollar market involving residents of this country, Eurodollar deposits would be created by purchases of dollars with foreign currencies and Eurodollar loans would be made to other foreigners. Even if the United States had a surplus, there would still be a Eurodollar market, although more of the Eurodollar deposits would probably be derived from U.S. banks and firms and more of the Eurodollar loans would be made to foreigners. That is not to deny that the U.S. payments position has a considerable effect on the Eurodollar market, but the effect is the consequence of U.S. policies rather than of the precise state of the balance of payments.

The size and the direction of the flow of funds into and out of the Eurodollar market are, however, affected by the pattern of international payments because the credit situation and the monetary policy of a country are determined in large part by its payments position. When the United States has a payments deficit and Europe has a payments surplus, the monetary situation is automatically eased in Europe and automatically tightened in the United States. Furthermore, monetary policy may be tightened in the deficit country and eased in the surplus country because of the payments position. Thus, the flow of Eurodollars should ordinarily be from countries with a strong balance of payments to countries with a weak balance of payments.

The Eurodollar market came into existence primarily because of the convenience of having a truly international money market in London and other European financial centers. Given the diversity of national sources and uses of funds in such a market, there is an obvious convenience in denominating the transactions in dollars because of the wide use of dollars in international payments and because of the breadth of the spot and forward foreign-exchange markets in dollars. The growth of the Eurodollar market has been stimulated by the interest-rate limitations placed on U.S. banks in bidding for time deposits under Regulation Q and by the controls imposed on transfer of U.S. funds for direct investment and on foreign lending by U.S. banks and other financial institutions. Most important, the very high interest rates offered by U.S. banks have resulted in an enormous increase of Eurodollar deposits that have been transferred to this country.

IMPACT ON WORLD TRADE AND INVESTMENT

Until 1965, the United States was the principal source of international bank credit. U.S. banks financed not only the international transactions of the United States but some of the transactions of foreign countries with each other. At the end of 1964, short-term and long-term claims on foreigners reported by U.S. banks amounted to $12,242 million of which $1,135 million were collections outstanding for their own account and that of their customers. At the end of 1969, short-term and long-term claims on foreigners reported by U.S. banks amounted to $12,806 million of which $1,952 million were in collections outstanding. Thus, in the five years since the program for restraining bank lending to foreigners was begun, total claims on foreigners increased by $564 million and, excluding collections outstanding, they fell by $253 million. In the meantime, U.S. banks greatly increased their liabilities to foreigners. Far from providing bank credit for the world economy, the United States became a net absorber of such credit from other countries.

The need for bank credit for international transactions in the past five years was met by the Eurodollar market. Eurodollar deposits in London increased from $4.4 billion at the end of 1964 to $25.6 billion at the end of 1969. Of this increase, $4.1 billion came from the United States and Canada, $11.8 billion from Western Europe, and $5.4 billion from all other countries. These deposits were lent to residents of many countries, although mainly of the United States. From the end of 1964 to the end of 1969, claims of London banks in dollars on residents of the United States increased from $1.2 billion to $13.3 billion. Claims in dollars on residents of other countries increased from $2.5 billion to $11.9 billion in the same period. There was a similar growth of Eurodollar deposits and loans in other European financial centers, although in the aggregate these other markets are about half as large as that of London. Of course, not all of the Eurodollars were used to finance international trade and investment. In fact, most of the U.S. borrowing was by banks to acquire funds to meet the demand for loans in this country.

There is no way of determining what would have happened if the Eurodollar market had not expanded on such a scale. National money markets in the principal European countries would have taken over more of the task of financing international trade and investment. It is doubtful, however, whether foreign banks would have been willing or able to increase their

TABLE VII.1

FOREIGN CLAIMS AND LIABILITIES IN DOLLARS OF LONDON BANKS, 1964–69

	Million Dollars, End of Year					
	1964	1965	1966	1967	1968	1969
U.K. liabilities, total (deposits)	*4,379*	*5,300*	*7,636*	*9,689*	*15,379*	*25,639*
United States	535	529	952	1,385	2,568	2,894
Canada	739	468	543	768	1,174	2,510
Western Europe	2,005	2,853	4,211	5,191	8,186	13,781
Other countries	1,100	1,450	1,930	2,345	3,451	6,454
U.K. claims, total (loans)	*3,674*	*4,547*	*7,311*	*9,206*	*14,978*	*25,212*
United States	1,210	1,596	3,466	4,066	7,243	13,291
Canada	42	112	188	276	418	554
Japan	375	465	624	991	1,589	1,423
Western Europe	1,680	1,795	2,349	2,539	3,698	6,317
Other countries	367	579	684	1,334	2,030	3,627

Source: *Quarterly Bulletin* of the Bank of England, March 1970, p. 101. The difference between U.K. liabilities and U.K. claims is equal to Eurodollars used in the United Kingdom.

international lending in national currencies to the same extent as was done through the Eurodollar market. U.S. banks might have been able to acquire foreign funds, either through dollar deposits in this country or through borrowing in foreign currencies, but far less than they did through the Eurodollar market.

The four principal ways in which the U.S. balance of payments has been affected by the growth of the Eurodollar market can be summarized as follows:

First, U.S. imports would have remained much the same, as they are financed through bank credit in this country or through trade credit. It is conceivable, however, that with the impairment of the U.S. reserve position, other measures would have had to be taken to limit U.S. imports. On the other hand, U.S. exports would have been somewhat less, as they are partly financed through borrowing of other countries in the Eurodollar market.

Second, net transfers in connection with U.S. foreign direct investment would have been greater, even if the direct-investment control had been made more restrictive. The borrowing by U.S. corporations for financing direct investment has been mainly through foreign-bond issues, but there was also considerable borrowing from the Eurodollar market.

Third, less U.S. funds would have gone abroad in response to higher interest rates. Although some of these funds came from the proceeds of foreign-bond issues of U.S. corporations, a considerable amount came directly from the United States and indirectly through Canada and other countries. Most of these funds, however, were returned by U.S. banks from the Eurodollar market.

Fourth, some of the foreign funds that went into Eurodollar deposits would probably have come to the United States. This certainly would have been much less than U.S. banks were able to acquire in the Eurodollar market, particularly at the lower interest rates in this country and with the need to keep reserves against foreign time deposits placed directly in the United States.

In evaluating the broad impact of the Eurodollar market on the world pattern of payments, it should be emphasized that the flow of funds has generally been from surplus countries to deficit countries. In a few instances large sums were transferred to the Eurodollar market from countries whose currencies were under speculative pressure, but the same capital flight would have taken place if the funds had to be placed elsewhere. There were also transfers from some countries in excess of what their monetary authorities regarded as desirable in the light of their payments and reserve position. This occurred because the restrictive monetary policy in the United States was determined more by the need to restrain inflation than to protect the reserves. Clearly, the flow of Eurodollars contributed to the increase in U.S. reserve assets and the decrease in U.S. reserve liabilities in 1968 and 1969. How this is accounted for in the U.S. balance of payments depends on the concepts used in defining the surplus or deficit.

U.S. BALANCE OF PAYMENTS CONCEPTS

The effect of the Eurodollar market on the U.S. balance of payments depends primarily on how these financial transactions are classified. All transactions by U.S. residents with nonresidents, including foreign affiliates of U.S. corporations and foreign branches of U.S. banks, are properly part of the balance of payments. The major difficulty is not in identifying the transactions, although this is a problem too, but in distinguishing between those that are capital flows and those that are settlement items—that is, a means of financing the payments surplus or deficit. The economic distinction between financial transactions that are capital flows and those that are settlement items is by no means absolute. That is particularly true for the United States because dollars are held as reserves, working balances, and short-term investments, not only by central banks but by commercial banks, business firms, and individuals in all parts of the world.

The United States shows the balance of payments in two forms. The official reserve balance measures the surplus (or deficit) by the increase (or decrease) in reserves of gold, Special Drawing Rights, foreign exchange, and the U.S. position in the International Monetary Fund plus the decrease (or increase) in liabilities to foreign central banks, the Bank for International Settlements, and the European Fund. In the official reserve balance, the distinction between financial transactions that are capital flows and those that are settlement items is made on the basis of whether they are with monetary authorities or with other foreigners and international institutions. The principle is that financial transactions with foreigners other than monetary authorities are undertaken in response to market forces, particularly relative interest rates. They are, therefore, capital flows, whether they are to or from the United States, and whether they give rise to short-term or long-term, liquid or nonliquid assets and liabilities. On the other hand, financial transactions of monetary authorities are undertaken in order to settle the surplus or deficit, and it is not relevant whether the change in official dollar holdings is in one form or another.

The alternative method, the liquidity balance, measures the surplus (or deficit) by the increase (or decrease) in official reserve assets and by the decrease (or increase) in short-term and liquid liabilities to all foreigners and international institutions. The difference between the liquidity balance and the official reserve balance is entirely in the method of accounting changes in U.S. liabilities. In the official reserve balance, only liabilities to foreign monetary authorities are classified as settlement items, and no distinction is made between liquid and nonliquid liabilities. In the liquidity balance, all liabilities that are not short-term and liquid are classified as capital inflow, even if they are claims of foreign monetary authorities.

TABLE VII.2

RECONCILIATION OF U.S. BALANCE OF PAYMENTS ON TWO BASES, 1964–69

	Million Dollars					
	1964	1965	1966	1967	1968	1969
Balance on a liquidity basis	*−2,800*	*−1,335*	*−1,357*	*−3,544*	*168*	*−7,058*
Add as capital inflow, increase of:						
Liquid liabilities to commercial banks	1,454	116	2,697	1,272	3,382	9,272
Liquid liabilities to other foreigners	343	306	212	414	374	−437
Liquid liabilities to intern'l organiz'ns	−243	−291	−525	−214	55	−63
Deduct as settlement items, increase of:						
Nonliquid liabilities of U.S. Government	169	123	−32	452	1,806	−162
Nonliquid liabilities of U.S. banks, etc.	149	−38	793	894	535	−836
Balance on official reserve basis	*−1,564*	*−1,289*	*266*	*−3,418*	*1,638*	*2,712*

SOURCE: *Survey of Current Business*, June 1969, p. 31, and March 1970, p. 38.

Thus, the liquidity balance depends on the deliberate or accidental decision of foreign central banks, with or without the persuasion of the U.S. Government, to hold long-term rather than short-term certificates of deposit, to buy or sell U.S. Agency securities rather than Treasury securities, and to buy or sell nonmarketable Treasury securities rather than ordinary Treasury bills, notes, and bonds. Similarly, liabilities to other foreigners and international institutions are regarded as capital inflow if they are long-term, and settlement items if they are short-term and liquid. It should be noted that while private foreign claims on U.S. banks and the U.S. money market are classified as settlement items, private U.S. claims on foreign banks and money markets are classified as capital outflow. For this reason, there is an asymmetry in the liquidity balance so that an equilibrium position does not require a "zero" balance but is consistent with a very considerable deficit.

Depending on money-market conditions in the United States and abroad and the efforts made by the Treasury to get foreign central banks to hold nonliquid claims, the difference between these two methods of presenting the balance of payments is not ordinarily very large. For example, between 1964 and 1968, the official reserve balance averaged $915 million a year more than the liquidity balance. In 1969, however, the official reserve balance showed a surplus of $2.7 billion while the liquidity balance showed a deficit of $7.1 billion. The sudden and enormous increase in the difference between the two balances ($9.8 billion) was due to an inflow of $8.8 billion in foreign short-term and liquid private funds, mainly Eurodollars transferred by foreign branches of U.S. banks, and a decrease of $1 billion in nonliquid liabilities to foreign official institutions through the cashing in of nonmarketable Treasury bonds and notes and of long-term CDs.

What is striking about the balance of payments in 1969

TABLE VII.3

EURODOLLAR TRANSACTIONS IN THE U.S. BALANCE OF PAYMENTS

	Liquidity Basis	Official Reserve Basis
1. Transfer of funds to Eurodollar bank by U.S. corporation	Capital outflow	Capital outflow
2. Transfer of funds from U.S. bank to Eurodollar bank by foreign resident	No effect	Capital outflow
3. Borrowing by U.S. corporation from Eurodollar bank	Capital inflow	Capital inflow
4. Borrowing by U.S. bank from Eurodollar bank, including transfers from foreign branches	No effect	Capital inflow
5. Deposit of Eurodollar bank with U.S. bank	No effect	Capital inflow

is not merely the unusually large difference between the official reserve surplus and the liquidity deficit. Equally noteworthy is the increase of $7.2 billion in the liquidity deficit in a year in which the balance on goods, services and ordinary remittances, U.S. private-capital outflow, and U.S. Government grants and credits was down by only $211 million. The asymmetrical and illogical accounting of the liquidity balance added another $7 billion to the deficit. This is because the liquidity deficit ignores the numerous ways in which the relation of U.S. banks and business to the Eurodollar market affected the private-capital inflow from abroad, the cashing in of nonliquid foreign official holdings of dollars, and the unrecorded outflow of funds from the United States (errors and omissions).

EURODOLLAR TRANSACTIONS IN THE BALANCE OF PAYMENTS

The manner in which a Eurodollar transaction involving a resident of the United States enters directly into the balance of payments depends on whether it is the official reserve balance or the liquidity balance. There is generally no difference between the accounting unless a U.S. bank is engaged in the transaction. All Eurodollar transfers to or from the United States are a capital flow in the official reserve balance. On the other hand, the transfer of funds by foreigners (including foreign branches of U.S. banks) to or from a U.S. bank is a settlement item in the liquidity balance; however, a transfer of Eurodollars to or from any other U.S. resident is a capital flow. There is no good reason for this distinction as can be seen in an analysis of the economic aspects of Eurodollar transactions.

When a U.S. corporation transfers funds from the United States to the Eurodollar market because interest rates are higher there, this is a capital outflow in the official reserve balance and in the liquidity balance. If the same funds are then returned by a U.S. bank from its foreign branch, that is a capital inflow in the official reserve balance but not in the liquidity balance. Thus, a circular flow of U.S. funds to the Eurodollar market and back has no effect on the official reserve balance but it does increase the deficit in the liquidity balance.

When a U.S. bank transfers funds from a foreign branch and uses the money to make a loan to an American corporation, that is a capital inflow in the official reserve balance but not in the liquidity balance. If the U.S. bank refers the American corporation to its London branch to borrow the same amount of Eurodollars, that is a capital inflow in both the liquidity balance and the official reserve balance. Thus, the borrowing of a U.S. corporation from the same ultimate source of the funds, the Eurodollar market, is a capital inflow in the official reserve balance but is not a capital inflow in the liquidity balance if a U.S. bank is the intermediary in first acquiring the funds abroad.

When a U.S. bank transfers funds from its London branch to its head office and uses the funds to make a loan to a foreign corporation, the two transactions have no net effect on the official reserve balance. The transfer of Eurodollars by the U.S. bank is a capital inflow that is matched by the loan to the foreign corporation, which is a capital outflow. The same two transactions would have an adverse effect on the liquidity balance: the transfer of Eurodollars by the U.S. bank is not a capital inflow, but the loan to the foreign corporation is a capital outflow. If the U.S. bank were to send the foreign corporation to borrow the same amount from its London branch, transferring less Eurodollars to its head office, the transaction would have no effect on either the liquidity balance or the official reserve balance. Thus, a loan of the same funds to the same foreign corporation would have the same effect on the official reserve balance, regardless of where it is made, but different effects on the liquidity balance, depending on whether the U.S. bank made the loan at its head office or at its foreign branch.

In these illustrations, the treatment of Eurodollar transactions is more consistent from an economic point of view in the official reserve balance than in the liquidity balance. It is possible, however, to cite an example in which the liquidity balance would reflect more accurately the economic significance of a Eurodollar transaction than would the official reserve balance. Thus, if a foreign central bank were to withdraw funds from the U.S. money market and place the same funds in the Eurodollar market, it would not affect either the liquidity balance or the official reserve balance. If a U.S. bank then transfers the Eurodollars from its London branch to its head office, it would be a capital inflow in the official reserve balance but not in the liquidity balance. In this case, the liquidity balance is more logical in treating the two transactions as offsetting.

IMPACT ON THE OFFICIAL RESERVE BALANCE

There are large U.S. payments of interest on Eurodollar borrowings and considerable U.S. receipts of interest from Eurodollar deposits. These current account transactions are shown in the same way in the liquidity balance and the official reserve balance. The difference between the two methods of presenting the U.S. balance of payments is confined to the treatment of foreign capital inflow and particularly to the Eurodollar transactions of U.S. banks. The enormous deficit on a liquidity basis in 1969 is directly and indirectly due to the asymmetrical classification of the inflow and outflow of Eurodollars. The large surplus in the official reserve balance is due to the Eurodollar borrowing of U.S. banks and business firms which greatly exceeded U.S. payments for the recorded and unrecorded outflow of funds to acquire Eurodollar deposits. It is these Eurodollar flows that must be analyzed in order to

TABLE VII.4
EURODOLLAR CAPITAL FLOWS IN THE U.S. OFFICIAL RESERVE BALANCE, 1968–69

	Million Dollars	
	1968	1969
Receipts as derived from foreign data	*3,739*	*7,115*
Liabilities of U.S. residents to U.K. banks*	3,178	6,048
Allowance for liabilities to other Eurodollar markets†	561	1,067
Payments as derived from foreign data	*1,869*	*1,721*
Claims of U.S. residents on U.K. banks*	1,183	326
Claims of Canadian residents on U.K. banks*	406	1,137
Allowance for claims on other Eurodollar markets†	280	258
Receipts as shown in U.S. data	*3,389*	*7,203*
Demand and time deposits of foreign commercial banks‡	2,742	7,203
Short-term liabilities of other U.S. residents to U.K.§	117	−82
Short-term liabilities of other U.S. residents to other Europe§	530	95
Payments as shown in U.S. data	*1,310*	*2,607*
Short-term claims of U.S. residents on U.K.§	448	−262
Short-term claims of U.S. residents on other Europe§	220	−94
Errors and omissions (total)§	642	2,963

* *Quarterly Bulletin* of the Bank of England, March 1970, p. 101.
† 15 per cent of the total.
‡ U.S. Treasury Bulletin, March 1970, p. 94.
§ *Survey of Current Business*, March 1970, p. 44 (lines 55 and 40) for U.K., pp. 44–45 (lines 55 and 40) for other Europe, and p. 36 (line 60) for errors and omissions.

understand their full impact on the U.S. balance of payments.

It is very difficult to estimate with accuracy the Eurodollar transactions that enter into the capital movements in the official reserve balance. The data reported by banks are accurate. On the other hand, the data reported by corporations have many omissions, and attribution of the changes in corporate claims and liabilities to Eurodollar transactions is, at best, tenuous. This is not true, of course, of the large multinational corporations, whose reports are full and accurate. Finally, it should be noted that most individuals do not have an obligation to report their foreign financial transactions at all. The gap in some of the U.S. balance-of-payments data related to the Eurodollar market is broadly indicated by the $3 billion of net errors and omissions in 1969.

Considerable help in estimating the Eurodollar receipts and payments of the United States can be secured from the liabilities and claims in dollars of U.K. banks published in the *Quarterly Bulletin* of the Bank of England. There are two difficulties in estimating the Eurodollar component of the U.S. balance of payments from these data. One is that Eurodollar deposits in London are only two-thirds of total Eurodollar deposits, although they are about 85 per cent of the Eurodollar deposits in foreign branches of U.S. banks. An allowance for the difference can be made without too much margin of error. The other difficulty is that Eurodollar deposits of U.S. residents may be held through banks in other countries and thus not reported as liabilities of U.K. banks to U.S. residents. A considerable amount of such deposits are made through Canadian banks and banks in the Bahamas and Bermuda. One way of allowing for this would be to regard the Eurodollar deposits of Canada as being held for the account of U.S. residents. While this overestimates the actual Eurodollar deposits of Americans by way of Canada, it is not an excessive allowance for Eurodollar deposits held by Americans through other countries.

The U.S. data conform reasonably well to the data reported by the Bank of England, as adjusted, on the receipts side. That is because nearly all of the inflow of Eurodollars is represented by deposits of foreign banks in the United States. There is much more difficulty in reconciling the data on the payments side. Even attributing all of the increase in U.S. short-term claims on the United Kingdom and "other Europe" to Eurodollar deposits would leave the amount short in 1968 and very short in 1969 of the increase shown in the Bank of England data. It should be noted that the recorded increase of short-term claims was relatively large in 1968 and negative in 1969. That is because the multinational corporations that issued securities abroad placed some of the proceeds in the Eurodollar market in 1968 and withdrew these funds to finance direct investment in 1969. The only way of reconciling the incomplete U.S. data with the data reported by London banks is to attribute much of the errors and omissions in the U.S. balance of payments in 1968 and most of them in 1969 to unreported transfers of funds to acquire Eurodollar deposits.

Whatever the defects in the data, it is reasonable to conclude that the excess of Eurodollar receipts over Eurodollar payments in the capital accounts of the official reserve balance was on the order of $2 billion in 1968 and $5 billion in 1969. This is the reason why the official reserve balance was in surplus in 1968 and in even greater surplus in 1969. Despite the $3 billion increase in net receipts from Eurodollar transactions, the increase in the official reserve balance in 1969 was only $1.1 billion because the huge inflow of Eurodollars decreased the availability of foreign funds for investment in the United States in other forms.

IMPACT ON THE LIQUIDITY BALANCE

While the direct effects of the Eurodollar transactions were highly favorable in the official reserve balance, they were very unfavorable in the liquidity balance. Only a very small part of the Eurodollar receipts (borrowing by U.S. corporations) is included in the liquidity balance as capital inflow. On the other hand, all of the outflow of funds to the Eurodollar market is included as payments in the liquidity balance as well as the official reserve balance. This one-sided treatment of Eurodollar transactions in the liquidity balance inevitably results in an exaggerated deficit under ordinary circumstances and a greatly exaggerated deficit in the special circumstances of 1969.

The artificiality of this aspect of the liquidity balance was recognized in an article in the *Survey of Current Business:*

> If the transfer of dollar funds by U.S. residents from U.S. banks to foreign banks (whether properly reported or not) and by the latter back to U.S. banks is induced by conditions in domestic U.S. capital markets, including [interest rate] regulations. . . it does not reflect the usual types of international capital movements. . . . In these circular movements of U.S. funds, the role of the foreign banks (including the U.S. branch banks abroad) is merely that of a transit channel. Therefore, one may question whether the outflow and return flow of funds should be considered international transactions in substance as well as in form.[1]

This is a recognition of one major defect in the liquidity balance; but the inflow of Eurodollars in 1969 distorted the liquidity balance in various other ways.

The liquidity balance deteriorated by $7.2 billion in 1969 compared with 1968. This occurred even though the surplus on goods, services and ordinary remittances fell by only $448 million; recorded U.S. private capital outflow was reduced by $147 million; and U.S. Government grants and credits were down by $90 million. On all these transactions, which are accounted in the same way on both a liquidity basis and an

[1] *Survey of Current Business,* June 1969, p. 24.

TABLE VII.5

SUMMARY OF THE LIQUIDITY BALANCE OF PAYMENTS, 1968–69

	MILLION DOLLARS		
	1968	1969	CHANGE
Liquidity balance	*168*	*−7,058*	*−7,226*
Balance on goods, services and ordinary remittances	1,357	909	−448
U.S. private capital outflow	−5,157	−5,009	+147
U.S. Government grants and credits	−3,955	−3,865	+90
Foreign capital inflow	8,564	3,870	−4,694
Errors and omissions, net	−642	−2,963	−2,321

TABLE VII.6

FOREIGN CAPITAL INFLOW IN THE LIQUIDITY BALANCE OF PAYMENTS, 1968–69

	MILLION DOLLARS		
	1968	1969	CHANGE
Foreign capital inflow	*8,564*	*3,870*	*−4,694*
Direct investments	319	749	+430
U.S. securities other than Treasury issues	4,360	3,032	−1,328
Long-term liabilities reported by U.S. banks	590	−675	−1,265
Other liabilities reported by U.S. private residents	1,423	641	−782
Nonmarketable liabilities of U.S. Government	1,872	123	−1,749

SOURCE FOR TABLES: *Survey of Current Business*, March 1970, p. 36.

official reserve basis, the balance of payments was less favorable by only $211 million in 1969 than in 1968. This modest decline occurred primarily because of the increase of $1.4 billion in private payments on foreign investments in the United States, mainly reflecting larger Eurodollar borrowing and higher interest rates. The huge increase in the liquidity deficit in 1969 was almost entirely due to an increase of $2.3 billion in unrecorded payments and a decrease of $4.7 billion in foreign capital inflow as defined in the liquidity balance.

Obviously, the large increase in errors and omissions distorted the liquidity balance in 1969. It is also true that the large inflow of Eurodollars and the resulting surplus in the official reserve balance caused a sharp reduction of foreign capital inflow. Because they were hard-pressed for dollars, foreign official agencies liquidated $365 million of their holdings of certain nonmarketable medium-term U.S. Government securities instead of buying $1,510 million, as they did in 1968. In addition, foreign official agencies reduced by $836 million their long-term deposits and CDs in contrast to an increase of $535 million in 1968. In all, the shift from the acquisition to the cashing in of certain nonliquid liabilities by foreign official agencies resulted in a reduction of $3,339 million in so-called foreign capital inflow in the liquidity balance.

Apart from the action of foreign official agencies, private foreign capital inflow (except foreign direct investment) was sharply reduced in 1969. New issues of securities by U.S. corporations fell from $2,129 million in 1968 to $1,026 million in 1969. Other liabilities reported by U.S. private residents, some of which were loans from the Eurodollar market, were down from $1,423 million in 1968 to $641 million in 1969. There are a number of reasons for this decline of nearly $1.9 billion in such private borrowing. U.S. corporations may have been well-supplied with funds from previous bond issues and credits. They may not have been willing to pay the very high interest rates in the Eurodollar and Eurobond markets. The major reason for the reduction of foreign private capital inflow, however, was that the Eurodollar borrowing of U.S. banks absorbed a much larger part of the funds available for foreign lending and investing in this country. The only type of foreign investment that increased in 1969 was direct investment, and that was due to several takeovers involving special factors.

The liquidity balance in 1969 did not properly show the change that occurred in the U.S. payments position. That is because of its artificial definition of foreign capital inflow. The fact is that foreigners have many ways of investing their funds in the U.S. assets, and they choose those assets that offer the best return. If Eurodollar deposits pay very high interest rates, more of the foreign investment will go into this form and less into other forms. If Eurodollar borrowing by U.S. banks is excluded from capital inflow, there will inevitably be an increase in the liquidity deficit because other private capital inflow will fall. And if the inflow of Eurodollars is large enough to result in a surplus in the official reserve balance, foreign monetary authorities will reduce their holdings of nonliquid dollar assets, and the increase in the liquidity deficit will be enormous, as happened in 1969.

EURODOLLARS AND THE U.S. PAYMENTS PROBLEM

In the past five years, the United States has been passing through a period of war and inflation that has resulted in a serious deterioration of its long-term payments position. In three of these years (1966, 1968, and 1969), the United States had a surplus on an official reserve basis as a result of the large inflow of Eurodollars when monetary policy was tight. The liquidity balance was in deficit throughout this period except in 1968, when there was a small surplus because of large special transactions with foreign official agencies which were classified as capital inflow on the grounds that the resulting liabilities were not liquid. Which of these alternative methods of presenting the balance of payments can be said to reflect more accurately the international payments position of the United States?

No single figure, whether a surplus or a deficit, can show the international payments position in a meaningful way, regardless of how it is calculated. The international payments position of the United States is the result of many complex domestic and international forces. The only way to determine its strength or weakness is by a thorough analysis of every major account. All that the balance of payments can do is to report the transactions of the residents of the United States with those of other countries as fully and as accurately as possible. Beyond that, the classification of international transactions in the balance of payments, and particularly the distinction between capital flows and settlement items, should be meaningful and reflect the forces that are affecting the world pattern of payments.

By these tests, the balance of payments on an official reserve basis is a more realistic presentation of the impact of the international transactions of the United States on this country and the rest of the world. One may discard at once the fiction in the liquidity balance that it makes any difference in the behavior of foreign monetary authorities whether some of their dollar assets are labelled short-term or long-term, liquid or nonliquid. More important, residents of the United States engage in a variety of financial transactions with banks, business firms, and individuals in all parts of the world. To ignore those financial transactions which involve an inflow of foreign short-term and liquid funds by classifying them as settlement items is to exclude from the U.S. balance of payments that part to which the monetary authorities are most responsive in formulating policy. The liquidity balance in its present form is wholly misleading, and it should be modified or abandoned.

The balance of payments should mirror what is going on in the world economy. Every international transaction goes through the exchange market. It is a contradiction to say that in 1969 the United States had a deficit of $7 billion in the liquidity balance but that the dollar was strong in the exchange market. It is understandable, however, that the dollar was strong in the exchange market because the United States had a surplus of $2.8 billion in the official reserve balance. This surplus compelled foreign monetary authorities to sell gold to the U.S. Treasury, to draw dollars from the International Monetary Fund, and to use their liquid and nonliquid dollar assets to support their currencies in the exchange market. The official reserve balance measures a change in accounts that are important to the monetary authorities—their reserve assets and their reserve liabilities. The liquidity balance measures a change in U.S. reserve assets plus a miscellaneous collection of liabilities, some of which may be the cause rather than the effect of the behavior of the balance of payments.

As this indicates, the inflow of Eurodollars was an integral part of the U.S. balance of payments in 1969. This inflow was a result of the impact of the tight monetary policy on U.S. banks, particularly the money-center banks with foreign branches. The tight monetary policy was undertaken as a means of slowing down the expansion and dampening the inflationary pressures, although the Federal Reserve is never indifferent to the reserve position of the United States and, particularly, to changes in the gold reserves. No informed person assumes that an inflow of foreign funds in response to very high interest rates is a solution to the U.S. payments problem. It does, however, protect the reserves until fiscal and monetary policy becomes effective in halting the inflation and in improving the payments position. Without the inflow of Eurodollars, the United States would have had an enormous deficit on an official reserve basis. No doubt the monetary authorities of some countries would have accumulated more dollars, but there might have been a serious decline in U.S. gold reserves. This would have necessitated radical measures to protect the reserves, completely unsuited to a reserve center and disruptive to the world economy and the international monetary system.

Of course, the United States cannot continue to draw in Eurodollars on the scale of recent years. At the same time, a regular flow of short-term funds and long-term capital to and from the rest of the world is completely normal for the United States as the leading financial center. Such flows, including Eurodollars, are interrelated and they are all capital movements that should be shown in the balance of payments. This will not obviate the need for the United States to have an appropriate payments position suited to its role in world trade and finance. Such a payments position requires a surplus on goods and services sufficiently large to finance our foreign investment and foreign aid, allowance being made for the normal inflow of short-term funds and long-term capital from other countries. The United States is far from having achieved such a payments position. The task is very difficult, but certainly not as great as would be indicated by the inflated and distorted deficit in the liquidity balance in 1969.

VIII

W. EARLE McLAUGHLIN

Mr. McLaughlin was born in Oshawa, Ontario, in 1915. He attended Queen's University, majoring in economics and history. He graduated with an Honors B.A. in 1936, winning the medal in economics.

Immediately after graduation he joined The Royal Bank of Canada as a junior in a Toronto branch, after which he served in various posts in branches in Ontario. Fifteen years after his graduation, Mr. McLaughlin was appointed Manager of the bank's Main Branch in Montreal. Following this, he was appointed Assistant General Manager, Assistant to the President, General Manager (in 1960) and, at the end of that year, President.

Despite the heavy demands of his duties as Chairman and President of the Royal Bank of Canada, Mr. McLaughlin maintains many and varied outside interests. He is a director of a number of important Canadian companies, including the Canadian Pacific Railway Company, Algoma Steel Corporation, GenStar Limited, Power Corporation, Ralston Purina Canada Limited. In the United States he serves on the boards of General Motors Corporation, Metropolitan Life Insurance Company, Standard Brands, Inc., and Ralston Purina Company.

Mr. McLaughlin, a Knight Grace of the Order of St. John, is a Governor of the Royal Victoria Hospital, Montreal; a co-chairman of the Canadian Council of Christians and Jews; and a Trustee of Queen's University.

The Eurodollar Market: A View from Canada

INTRODUCTION

The view from Canada is of a Eurodollar market that exists only outside the boundaries of Canada and the United States. This view prevails because Canadian banks were active in U.S. dollar operations long before the Eurodollar market developed. More recently, the view has been reinforced by the introduction of Canadian guidelines tending to separate U.S. dollar operations in Canada and the United States from those in third countries. However, in keeping with the non-Canadian view of Eurodollars as any U.S. dollar deposit liability of a bank domiciled outside the United States, this chapter will discuss all U.S. dollar deposit operations of the Canadian banks.

U.S. DOLLAR DEPOSITS IN CANADIAN BANKING

U.S. dollar deposits have formed an increasingly significant share of the total liabilities of Canadian chartered banks for many years. Even before the current phenomenon referred to as "the Eurodollar market" really got under way in the late

1950s, U.S. dollar deposits had been attracted to Canada. Total foreign-currency liabilities (held in Canada or abroad) of Canadian chartered banks increased from approximately 10 per cent of total Canadian liabilities in 1955 to approximately $11.6 billion, or 26 per cent of total Canadian liabilities in 1969.

There are 250 branches of Canadian banks abroad which attract foreign-currency deposits from corporations and individuals and employ these funds abroad themselves. As at December 1969, the total of foreign-currency deposits held in Canadian bank branches abroad amounted to $3.9 billion. It is not known what portion of these deposits is in U.S. dollars. In addition, foreign branches spread the names of the Canadian banks abroad and in this way serve to attract foreign-currency deposits to the banks in Canada. At the end of 1969, these deposits on the books in Canada totaled $7.7 billion. U.S. dollars have traditionally formed some 98 per cent of total foreign-currency deposits attracted to Canada with the remainder being mostly sterling.

U.S. DOLLAR DEPOSITS IN CANADA

Of the $7.7 billion of U.S. dollar deposits on the books of the banks in Canada, 40 per cent have been received from Canadian residents, 10 per cent from U.S. residents, and 50 per cent from residents of other areas of the world. Thirty per cent of all U.S. dollar deposits come from banks and 70 per cent from corporations and individuals.

Canadian residents deposit U.S. dollars in Canadian banks for several reasons. They need and acquire U.S. dollar deposits for trade and financial transactions. Since the U.S. dollar is a key world currency and is the main one used in Canadian export trade, Canadian exporters accumulate sizeable amounts of U.S. dollars from large export transactions such as those involving metals and newsprint, pending conversion into Canadian dollars or for use at a later date. The wide branch network of the Canadian banks in Canada assures that U.S. dollar deposit facilities are always easily available to Canadian exporters.

In addition, Canadian corporations, provinces, and municipalities borrow U.S. dollars in the United States and abroad and frequently deposit these funds in Canadian banks until they are required. Balances not required immediately are frequently placed as U.S. dollar term deposits.

Finally, U.S. dollar swapped deposits offer an attractive investment for holders of Canadian dollar balances. U.S. dollar swapped deposits are Canadian funds converted into a U.S. dollar term deposit with a Canadian bank. Simultaneously, the bank has undertaken through a forward-exchange contract with the client to reconvert the U.S. dollars into Canadian funds at maturity. Swapped deposits are a fairly recent money-market phenomenon. Of the present $3.2 billion U.S. dollar deposits owned by Canadian residents, 50 per cent are swapped deposits.

Swapped deposits compete with Canadian dollar term deposits, swaps into U.K. or U.S. treasury bills, and other U.S. dollar denominated money-market instruments on the basis of yield. As U.S. deposit facilities increased, Canadians ceased purchasing the foreign money-market instruments themselves and turned to the swapped-deposit facility provided by Canadian banks. However, swapped deposits are a volatile source of funds for Canadian banks; furthermore, an informal ceiling on their total has been imposed by the Bank of Canada. In July 1969 the Bank of Canada asked each bank to keep its swapped deposits below the total then prevailing, which at that time was $1.7 billion for all banks.[1]

In contrast with the growth in U.S. dollar deposits from Canadians, there has been no growth in the amount of U.S.

[1] At the end of March, 1970 the Bank of Canada removed the ceiling on swapped deposits.

dollar deposits coming from U.S. residents during the past three years. U.S. resident deposits in Canada were quite important ten years ago but now they constitute only a minor part of the total deposits.

U.S. corporations, however, as part of the large U.S. resident-investment interest in Canada, frequently lodge deposits of U.S. dollars in Canada in escrow or to await expenditures for development. In addition, the interest-rate differential between the United States and Canada has in the past attracted deposits from U.S. residents. While generally welcoming these deposits, Canadian banks have not actively solicited them in order to avoid jeopardizing the goodwill of the U.S. banks.

U.S. dollar deposits in Canada from residents of third countries are a more dynamic and growing percentage of the total U.S. dollar deposits in Canada. Deposits from this source have grown from \$1.5 billion in 1966 to \$3.9 billion at the end of November 1969. There are no statistics, however, to show the percentage of these deposits which come to Canada as part of the Eurodollar interbank trading of the Canadian banks. Although deposits from other banks have declined as a percentage of the total since 1966, they still constitute 60 per cent of the total deposits from third countries—more than half from Continental European banks.

U.S. dollar deposits totalling \$1.6 billion are currently received in Canada from individuals and corporations in third countries. The majority of these deposits originate in countries other than the United Kingdom and Continental Europe.

The attraction of U.S. dollar deposits from nonresidents reflects the financial standing of Canadian banks throughout the world. It also reflects the political and economic stability of Canada which has generally caused Canada to be viewed as a suitable "safe haven" by both individual foreign depositors and foreign financial institutions. The latter often distribute their deposits over a wide geographic area as part of a deliberate risk-spreading policy, and Canada has always been regarded as a safe location for these funds.

This motive is reinforced by the higher level of interest rates normally prevailing in Canada relative to those in the United States. Although Canada has one of the highest rates of saving in the world, the opportunities for investment in Canada outrun domestic savings.

In addition, Canadian banks are often able to offer attractive rates for U.S. dollar deposits because of their ability to find profitable outlets for these funds. One important outlet has been the New York money market to which Canadian banks supply advances through their New York agencies.

Canadian banks domiciled outside the United States may pay prevailing market rates to attract U.S. dollar term deposits. Until the late 1950s, banks in the United States were competitive within Regulation Q ceilings on deposit rates. By the late fifties, however, a wider spread developed between the New York prime rate and the rates U.S. banks could pay for deposits.[2] At the same time, the need for U.S. dollar financing in world trade was accelerating and interest rates abroad began to rise. Consequently, banks outside the United States, including Canadian banks, began to attract U.S. dollar deposits by offering rates slightly higher than the maximum rates available from U.S. banks and to use these deposits to provide U.S. dollar trade financing at rates slightly under the New York prime-lending rate.

EMPLOYMENT OF U.S. DOLLAR FUNDS

Before World War II, Canadian banks frequently used the U.S. money market as an outlet for excess Canadian dollar liquidity by means of foreign-exchange swaps. Since the war, the breadth of the Canadian money market has expanded,

[2] Ceilings were removed on short-term CDs of 30–89 days for the first time on June 23, 1970.

enabling it to provide an outlet for most of the Canadian dollar liquidity in Canada. However, Canadian banks have maintained their important contribution to the New York call-loan market by employing part of the proceeds of their U.S. dollar term deposits in that market.

At the present time, 45 per cent of the U.S. dollar funds of the Canadian banks are employed in the United States, 10 per cent in Canada, and 45 per cent abroad. Since 1964, the percentage of these U.S. funds in third countries has increased, while the percentage employed in Canada and the United States has decreased. The large portion of U.S. dollar funds employed abroad and the increase in these assets since 1964 is due in part to the development of the Eurodollar market which produced a demand for U.S. dollar balances in London and on the Continent at rates higher than those available in Canada or the United States.

Traditionally, the banks have been most active in short-term U.S. dollar-trade financing, but they have also expanded their activities into the medium term. In the recent period of rapidly rising interest rates, the banks have continued to finance in the short term, but frequently the interest rates on the medium-term loans are being renegotiated every six months in keeping with the level of the cost of funds.

The need for U.S. dollar-trade financing, particularly in the medium term (one to eight years), has been increasing over the years. In recent periods of rising interest rates the governments of Canadian competitors have continued to subsidize medium-term transactions at rates substantially below those prevailing in the market. Since the Canadian banks could not match these low rates and since there has been no government subsidization for medium-term exports in Canada, Canadian exporters have found it increasingly difficult to compete with foreign exporters on credit terms. At the present time, solutions to this problem are being sought.

The banks have also become more active in long-term export

financing which has been encouraged over the last few years by government participation in large ($100,000 or over) export transactions involving capital goods and related engineering and technical services. By participating with government through the new Export Development Corporation (formerly the Export Credit Insurance Corporation), Canadian banks now expect to become more active in this financing.

Generally speaking, however, most foreign-trade financing in Canada is done in Canadian dollars. Even though a substantial portion of Canadian foreign trade is transacted in U.S. dollars, the financing of foreign trade in U.S. dollars has formed only a small percentage of total foreign trade financing.

TRENDS AND DEVELOPMENTS IN U.S. DOLLAR OPERATIONS

The growth of U.S. dollar liabilities and assets of Canadian chartered banks is now particularly influenced by prevailing tax arrangements and assorted guidelines. Of considerable importance is the exemption of foreign-currency deposits in Canadian chartered banks in Canada from an extension in 1960 of the withholding tax on interest paid to nonresidents.

A withholding tax of 15 per cent on interest paid to nonresidents on Canadian dollar deposits had existed before 1960, but in December of 1960 this tax was extended to interest payments on foreign-currency deposits. When it was proven that this would seriously restrict Canadian chartered banks from competing in the international field for deposits and loans, conditional exemption was granted.

An understanding was reached that the banks would not provide Canadians with loans from nonresident source foreign-currency deposits in order to avoid the withholding tax. In keeping with this understanding, Canadian banks avoid taking part in any arrangement for making what are commonly termed *back-to-back loans*. That is, Canadian banks do not act as "loan brokers" in a foreign currency, receiving requests for loans from Canadian borrowers and seeking the financing by borrowing, say, U.S. funds from nonresidents either to lend these U.S. funds directly, or indirectly by converting to Canadian. Of course, U.S. dollar financing is available to Canadian corporations out of the banks' general pool of U.S. dollar funds subject only to the understanding that total U.S. dollar loans to Canadian residents are not to exceed total U.S. dollar deposits from Canadian residents.

More generally, the 15 per cent Canadian withholding tax on interest paid to nonresidents, and Canadian unfamiliarity with European borrowing arrangements, have more or less excluded Canadian corporations from borrowing in third countries. Also, the general uncertainty about the stability of some European currency values in recent years has deterred some Canadian corporations. However, those corporations, commissions, or associations that are 90 per cent owned by a Canadian province, and all levels of government are exempt from the withholding tax and have borrowed both abroad and in the United States. Tight money in Canada has encouraged this borrowing in recent years.

In May 1968, the Government of Canada sold bonds denominated in Deutsche marks in the German market. Other Canadian borrowers, mainly provincial governments, followed. By the end of 1968, Canadian borrowers had sold the equivalent of about $220 million in bonds denominated in Deutsche marks. Canadian borrowers also tapped the developing European market by selling U.S. dollar bonds in the Eurobond market. In 1968, sales of such issues amounted to over $100 million.

In 1963, the introduction of the Interest Equalization Tax by the U.S. Government proved a significant stimulus to the growth of the Eurodollar market in London and Continental Europe. Consequently, during 1964, the Canadian chartered banks were able to build up their U.S. dollar swapped deposits and other U.S. dollar bank balances from Canadian residents and to increase balances from U.S. residents; these funds were channeled principally into investments in the United Kingdom and Continental Europe.

In February 1965, the first guidelines designed to restrain voluntary short-term capital outflows from the United States were issued to U.S. banks and corporations. Shortly after the U.S. announcement, the Canadian Minister of Finance requested chartered banks to conduct their foreign-currency operations in such a way that the net U.S. dollar-asset position of Head Offices and Canadian branches, vis-à-vis U.S. residents, was not reduced below the position existing at the end of 1964, which was $312 million. As U.S. residents repatriated U.S. dollar funds on deposit in Canada, Canadian banks met only part of the drain by liquidating U.S. dollar investments (assets) in the United States. A large part of the drain ($955 million) was met by liquidating U.S. dollar assets in other countries and increasing liabilities to other countries. Overall, through the medium of the Canadian banking system, there was a net inflow of capital into the United States of $529 million in 1965.

However, the most significant event shaping the U.S. dollar activities of Canadian banks occurred in May 1968. For Canada to qualify for exemption from the U.S. Government's mandatory regulations on foreign direct investment issued in January 1968, the Canadian Government had to ensure that Canada would not be used as a "pass-through" for U.S. funds to Europe, thereby frustrating the purpose of the U.S. balance-of-payments program. On May 3, the Minister of Finance announced three voluntary U.S. dollar guidelines for Canadian chartered banks to supersede that issued in February 1965. They were stated as follows:

> The total of a bank's foreign currency claims on residents of countries other than Canada and the United States should not rise above the level of the end of February 1968 unless the increase is accompanied by an equal

> increase in its total foreign currency liabilities to residents of countries other than Canada and the United States.
>
> If there should be a decline in the total of a bank's foreign currency liabilities to residents of countries other than Canada and the United States from the level at the end of February 1968, the bank should achieve an equal reduction in its total foreign currency claims on residents of countries other than Canada and the United States as quickly as the liquidity of such assets will permit.
>
> Each bank should allow an increase in its U.S. dollar liabilities to residents of the United States from the level at the end of February 1968 only to the extent that the increase is fully matched by the sum of (i) the increase from that date in the bank's U.S. dollar claims on residents of Canada, (ii) the decrease from that date in the bank's U.S. dollar liabilities to residents of Canada, and (iii) the decrease from that date in the bank's own spot position in U.S. dollars.[3]

These three guidelines were extended to financial institutions other than banks on July 24, 1968, and to Canadian incorporated companies other than the financial institutions on September 19, 1968.

The result was to make a distinction between Canada, the United States, and other (third) countries with respect to source and use of funds. This distinction necessitated the adoption of a three-tier interest-rate structure in which residency of the depositor became the criterion which determined the rate the depositor could obtain. Generally, rates

[3] *Annual Report*, Bank of Canada, 1968, p. 70.

offered to third-country residents are highest since the banks have the greatest freedom of action in employing these funds. Rates offered U.S. residents tend to be lowest because the use of these funds is the most restricted.

As a consequence of these guidelines, Canadian banks can no longer accept U.S. dollar deposits from Canadian or U.S. residents to increase their investments in the Eurodollar market abroad; these, however, were minimal when the guidelines were imposed. Furthermore, they cannot increase their total of U.S. dollar deposits from U.S. residents to lend or reinvest in the United States. At the end of December 1969, Canadian banks had only US$0.8 billion in U.S. dollar deposits from U.S. residents while they had investments in the United States of US$3.1 billion.

The guidelines ensure that the only funds that Canadian banks can invest in the Eurodollar market abroad are the funds they attract from abroad. The attraction and investment of these funds now forms a large part of the international business of the Canadian banks.

CONCLUSION

In spite of an increasing number of controls on the sources and uses of their U.S. dollar funds arising from United States efforts to control its balance-of-payments deficits, the Canadian chartered banks have proven their adaptability to changing international conditions. They continue to attract U.S. dollar deposits and to find profitable outlets for these funds in Canada, the United States, and abroad. Now, the Canadian banks are developing ways to direct more U.S. dollar funds into financing in the medium term. As these efforts yield results, the Canadian banks expect to satisfy an increasing demand for U.S. dollar foreign-trade financing in Canada. The Canadian view of the Eurodollar market is one of continued growth in which the Canadian banks expect to remain active participants.

IX

ANDRE de LATTRE

Mr. de Lattre was born in Paris in 1923. After high school studies in Paris, he became Docteur en Droit and Licencié ès-lettres (anglais) of the University of Paris and Diplômé de l'Ecole Libre des Sciences Politiques.

He joined the Ministry of Finance as an Inspecteur des Finances in 1946 and was successively Chargé de Mission at the Cabinet of the Minister (1948), Sub-Director at the Direction des Finances Extérieures (1955), Deputy Director (1957), then Director of the Direction des Finances Extérieures (1962). In 1966 he was appointed Deputy Governor of the Bank of France.

Meanwhile Mr. de Lattre carried out various responsibilities both in France—Financial Counsellor to Général de Gaulle, President of the French Republic (1959), Director of the Cabinet of the Minister of Finance (1960–61—and abroad—Alternate Executive Director of the International Monetary Fund (1954–55) and Adviser to the President of the World Bank for relations with the Government of India (1965–66). Mr. de Lattre has played an active role in the EEC Monetary Committee and the Development Aid Committee of the OECD.

A professor at the Ecole Nationale d'Administration (1955–56), Mr. de Lattre has been since 1959 in charge of the teaching of economic policy at the Institut d'Etudes Politiques de Paris. He is author of two books, Les Finances Extérieures de la France *(P.U.F., 1959) and* Politique Economique de la France *(Sirey, 1966).*

The Eurodollar Market: A French View

The main French banks have been participating in the Eurodollar and Eurocurrency market since its origin, which dates back to the end of the 1950s. According to some learned interpretations, one could even assert that at least one French bank appears among its founders; indeed, the telex address of that bank is said to have suggested the word *Eurodollar* to the first exchange-dealers operating in the market. Such a name is, in many respects, an inappropriate one, but it rapidly spread from the jargon of the people-in-the-know to the cant of bankers, financial editors and, finally, of the economists, until it has become generally accepted.

Since the Bank for International Settlements (BIS) started gathering information in 1963 in Canada, Japan, and eight European countries (West Germany, Belgium-Luxembourg, France, Italy, The Netherlands, United Kingdom, Sweden, Switzerland) on commercial-bank activity in the Eurocurrency market, the French banks[1] have supplied statistical data at the end of each quarter on their position in Eurocurrencies vis-à-

[1] The 30 main banks until December 31, 1967; all French banks since March 31, 1968.

vis their foreign correspondents, i.e., vis-à-vis foreign banks other than U.S. credit institutions.

The comparison of this information with overall statistics published yearly by the BIS gives an accurate view of the role played by French banks in the market and of the evolution of their policy, taking into account the legal frame within which they carry out their Eurocurrency operations.

IMPORTANCE OF FRENCH BANKS IN EURODOLLAR MARKET

A comparison of the amount of Eurodollar assets and liabilities of the French banking system with the overall statistics of the eight reporting European countries shows that the French banks' share in the market has remained practically stable.

Their Eurodollar assets are equal to about 10.5 per cent of the reporting European banks' assets, with very limited fluctuations around this percentage (the minimum having been 8.5 per cent and the maximum 12.5 per cent). Similarly, their liabilities account for about 8.5 per cent of the reporting European banks' (with upper and lower limits of 10.5 per cent and 7 per cent, respectively).

Thus, the role of French banks in the Eurodollar market, although not negligible, is far less important than that of British banks which, during the same period, controlled about half the market (40 to 55 per cent of the liabilities as against 35 to 40 per cent of the assets).

EVOLUTION OF THE EURODOLLAR POSITION OF FRENCH BANKS SINCE 1963

An analysis of the statistical data provided by the French banks suggests three stages in the evolution of their policy and their position since the end of 1963.

Stage 1: Trial and Experimentation

Until the end of 1965, Eurodollar assets and liabilities of the French banking system slowly expanded from roughly $500 million to $1 billion. The net position of the aggregate banks—and even of most of them—remained practically balanced throughout the period.

In other words, it appeared to be the trial and experimentation stage of the system during which the number of the participating French banks somewhat increased. Their approach was still rather cautious, however, and most of them limited their activity to the role of intermediaries in the market, borrowing dollar deposits from banks in various countries, notably Switzerland, to relend to their correspondents in other countries (Great Britain and Italy, for instance) or even to lesser credit institutions of the same country (Germany, Belgium). Let us add that most of their transactions were located in Europe (including Eastern Europe).

Stage 2: Expansion

During the second stage, which roughly includes the following three years (December 30, 1965 to September 30, 1968), the Eurodollar assets and liabilities of the French banks went up at about the same rate as the reporting European banks' overall positions.

However, assets expanded a little more (from $1 to $1.7 billion approximately) than liabilities (from $1 to $1.5 billion). French assets represented around 11 per cent of the eight reporting European banks' overall assets, whereas French liabilities accounted for some 8 per cent. Therefore, during the period, the net Eurodollar position of the French banking system, which had been practically balanced until then, almost steadily showed a surplus averaging $200 million. In the course of the three years, the French banks thus used a bigger fraction of their working balances (owned resources or their depositors) for placements in the Eurodollar rather than the American market, mainly for reasons of profitability. It must be emphasized, too, that the period saw the return to freedom of foreign-exchange transactions and to full convertibility of the French franc.

Geographically, the dollar claims and liabilities of French banks were still largely concentrated in Europe. On the supply side, Germany ranked second to Switzerland and before the Middle East countries. So far as users were concerned, Great Britain kept on absorbing the greatest part of the French banks' Eurodollar placements ($400 million at the end of September 1968 as against $100 million at year-end 1965), far ahead of Eastern Europe and Canada.

Stage 3: On the Defensive

As was true of the evolution in the overall European market, the last period, starting with the fourth quarter of 1968, is characterized by a sharp increase in both Eurodollar claims and liabilities of French banks and by a shift from a net-creditor to a net-borrower position.

In less than a year, between September 30, 1968, and 1969, Eurodollar assets of the French banks increased from $1.7 to $2.7 billion while the liabilities went up from $1.4 to $3.6 billion, the net position thus showing a worsening of $1.2 billion (from +$300 to −$900 million).

Such a shift in the French banks' position resulted from two main factors. On the one side was the reimposition, on November 24, 1968, of drastic exchange controls which prescribed new requirements to the authorized exchange dealers (such as the obligation to balance their foreign-exchange position) and therefore led them to reduce their Eurodollar assets. On the other side, the French branches of U.S. banks, like their British counterparts, strongly increased their borrowings from the Eurodollar market in order to supply their head offices with funds. In this connection, dollar claims of the French banking system upon credit institutions located in the United States have, during the period under review, grown by nearly $500 million, the increase being accounted for by the French branches of American banks alone and reflected in an expansion of the Eurodollar liabilities of the aggregate French banks.

The geographical distribution of the French banks' net claims in Eurodollars was sharply reduced during the period, being circumscribed mainly to the U.K. ($430 million) and to Eastern Europe for a very small balance. By contrast, the liabilities were much better distributed with, however, the greater part still originating from Europe, notably Switzerland ($350 million), Italy ($150 million), West Germany ($150 million), The Netherlands ($100 million), and Belgium ($90 million).

LAWS AND REGULATIONS GOVERNING THE FRENCH BANKS' ACTIVITY ON THE EURODOLLAR MARKET

The legal and regulatory frame within which the French banks carry out their activity in the Eurodollar market has undergone major changes since 1963. A first stage of increasingly mild exchange controls was ended on January 31, 1967 following the implementation of the December 28, 1966 Act restoring freedom on the exchange market and full convertibility of the French franc. Unlimited freedom then prevailed for about one and one-half years, i.e., from January 31, 1967 to May 30, 1968. The "flexible" exchange control, which was instituted for a few months—May 31, 1968 to September 3, 1968—was itself recalled during an even briefer period—September 4, 1968 to November 24, 1968—during which complete freedom again became the rule. Since November 25, 1968, however, drastic exchange controls have been reimposed, severely limiting banking activity in the Eurofield.

Without going into the somewhat tedious details of successive French exchange regulations, it has to be noted that the French banks have always been free to borrow Eurocurrencies for relending either to other correspondents or to their customers, resident or not; similarly, they have always been free to use their foreign-exchange liquid assets, whether their own funds or those of their customers, for placements on the Eurocurrency market.

Only foreign-exchange transactions linked with Eurocurrency lending and borrowing have been submitted to regulations during the periods of exchange controls. Notably, the regulation that prevents the banks from taking up foreign-exchange positions does not authorize them to convert into French francs the foreign currencies borrowed in the Euromarket or vice versa without securing a forward-exchange cover through a reverse transaction (by means of swap or tied operations). However, as only the aggregate exchange position (all foreign currencies together) has been taken into consideration by the control authorities from January 31, 1967 onwards, the French banks can purchase and sell borrowed foreign currencies against others without any forward cover, i.e., they can take up foreign-exchange positions in which the French franc itself is not implied. Similarly, as French residents, particularly the authorized exchange dealers, have since November 24, 1968 been deprived of the possibility of lending French francs to nonresidents, the French banks can no longer borrow foreign currencies against French francs from foreign correspondents through a swap operation although they may still freely act conversely, i.e., swap borrowing French francs against foreign currencies. This freedom is partly theoretical, however, because, given the high level of interest rates prevailing abroad on French-franc deposits on external accounts (which has frequently been above the level of French domestic rates for comparable terms), it was, at least until recently, not profitable to increase liquid assets in French francs in this manner.

It may thus be said that the main function carried out by the French banks in the Eurocurrency market, namely, that of intermediaries between lending and borrowing banks, has never been impeded by any measures of control they were or still are subjected to.

FRENCH BUSINESS ENTERPRISES AND THE EURODOLLAR MARKET

Very few French business enterprises are large enough to take a direct part in Eurodollar transactions, either as lenders or as borrowers.

Moreover, freedom in this respect is restricted in several ways:

1. They must comply with the obligation of repatriating the proceeds of their foreign-currency claims within a more or less limited period of time (one month after collection, according to the present regulations);
2. The banks, acting as authorized exchange dealers, have been given the exclusive right of engaging in foreign exchange transactions;
3. Any borrowing and lending abroad is subject to prior approval.

As a result, French enterprises generally apply to their bankers for their foreign-exchange lending and borrowing operations. Besides, the available statistics show that, as a rule, French banks' advances in foreign currencies to their resident customers are at any time less significant than the foreign-currency assets they hold (for various reasons and more or less temporarily) on behalf of these very customers.

It may thus be observed that, on the whole, the French business enterprises hardly resort to the Eurodollar market to finance their transactions abroad and that, on balance, they are more often lenders of funds to the market.

However, it is worth mentioning that the French banks are sometimes led to borrow from the Eurocurrency market in order to finance local expenditures when French enterprises are engaged in large construction projects in a foreign country.

Last, since foreign-exchange controls have been reimposed, French enterprises have been encouraged by the authorities to finance their foreign investments as often as possible through short-term external borrowing, sometimes consolidated with medium- and long-term loans.

THE FRENCH MONETARY AUTHORITIES AND THE EUROCURRENCY MARKET

While the French monetary authorities have from the outset remained aware of the evolution and the possible implications of the Eurocurrency phenomenon, they have adopted an attitude of "benevolent neutrality" towards the market. Moreover, since the French banks exercised caution in gradually making use of the new facilities available in this market and maintained a somewhat balanced position for so long a time in their dealings thereon, there was no need for any particular intervention on the part of the authorities. The controls set up in November 1968 did indeed restrict the banks' freedom of action in the Eurocurrency market, but such regulations must be regarded as forming part of a comprehensive program to meet the circumstantial need of defending the national currency.

The Bank of France, like other central banks in the major European countries participating in the market, has taken an active part in the studies begun in 1963 on a multilateral basis to get a better knowledge of the market and to try to appreciate its importance. As early as that time the 30 largest French banks, and later the whole banking sector, have been requested to provide the Bank of France with a quarterly detailed report of their sight and short-term Eurocurrency assets and liabilities. These data form the basis for the overall statements which are periodically sent to the Bank for International Settlements, as are similar statements originating from the other reporting countries.

SOME CONCLUDING COMMENTS

The somewhat explosive development pattern of the Eurodollar market in 1968 and 1969 upset not only academic circles but the finance world and central bankers as well and gave rise to many comments about the risks and threats inherent to this market, particularly regarding its power to trigger off speculation.

The Eurocurrency market is indeed a convenient and easily reached shelter for short-term capital flying away from a currency faced with difficulties. Above all, it is a tremendous potential volume of funds ready to flow into a country whose currency is expected to be revalued, as has been the case at times during these last two years, notably at the expense of the pound sterling and the French franc and to the profit of the Deutsche mark. Nevertheless, the Eurocurrency market is not to be blamed for the seesaw movements of short-term money that so badly disturbed the international monetary system. Although undoubtedly responsible for stimulating such movements, it cannot be held responsible for either overvaluation or undervaluation of the referred-to currencies.

It is certain, too, that the velocity of Eurodollar deposits and their current enormous bulk do, at least potentially, threaten the stability of the international monetary system inasmuch as they cannot be actually controlled by the monetary authorities either at the world level or on a national basis. But it would be unfair to ascribe the dollar glut to the Eurodollar market. Such an excess is mainly due not to the multiplier effect of credit upon deposits but to balance-of-payments deficits recorded by the United States and some major industrialized countries, such as Great Britain and France, and also to deliberate policies of some central banks, which make a practice of depositing part of their reserves with this market.

The existence of a world-wide money market working quite freely did obviously promote a certain adjustment of the interest rates prevailing in the various domestic money markets to a level comparable to the leading market, i.e., the one whose size is by far the greatest—the U.S. money market. Therefore, the autonomy of the monetary authorities in the management of their domestic policy is sometimes greatly reduced. But in a world where the various economies are neither coordinated nor integrated and proceed at an uneven pace, the interest-rate adjustment is a direct consequence of currency convertibility, on the one hand, and of the free transferability of short-term funds, on the other hand. In this field, too, the Eurodollar market acts essentially as a transmission medium.

Many people have pointed out the special risks that could be incurred because of the Eurodollar market. Indeed, despite the fact that most Eurocurrency transactions are carried out by the exchange dealers of the banks, it should not be overlooked that such transactions are basically credit operations and, for this reason, involve some built-in dangers which the dealers are neither accustomed to nor, in some cases, able to assess accurately. It is equally true that, in the sometimes long chain of transfers linking the first supplier with the final borrower, no intermediary can measure the risk eventually incurred, and consequently, the credit worthiness of the successive endorsers tends to decrease. But the same thing occurs in all other forms of bank lending; it only matters that each link should be able to assess the risk assumed in relending the deposit borrowed from the prior intermediary and to adjust accordingly the terms and conditions of the transaction.

Eurobanks often bring about a kind of "transformation" by lending at a longer term than they have been borrowing; but this, too, is common banking practice. It belongs to the managers of those institutions participating in the Eurodollar market—generally the biggest ones in each country—to see to it that their exchange dealers do not depart, in their Eurocurrency transactions, from the safety and liquidity rules that they usually comply with in their internal lending operations.

Recently some prominent members of the academic community drew attention to the multiplier or money-creating effect of the Eurodollar market, arguing that such an effect explained the tremendous and dangerous expansion of this market over the last two years. Such an extreme interpretation of the "loans-make-deposits" concept appears to be somewhat exaggerated. Indeed, within the Eurodollar deposit chain, the banks act as financial intermediaries, and the dollars lent are actually transferred, which does not give rise to any artificial creation of Eurocurrency. At the end of the chain, the end-users generally employ the borrowed dollars for making effective payments; as a result, these dollars either get out of the Eurobank system by being transferred to American banks in behalf of U.S. residents or find their way into the central banks' foreign-exchange reserves by being switched into third currencies. Indeed, the most prominent analysts[2] believe that Eurobanks, as a group, can expect to recapture only a relatively small fraction of the proceeds of their Eurodollars loans; consequently, they argue, the multiplier effect must be small in this market and is likely to have acted only as a secondary factor in the Eurodollar-market expansion which took place in 1968 and 1969.

Finally, some others think that the central banks should not merely observe and study the development of the Eurodollar market but should also bring it under effective control by regularly taking a more active part in it. In fact, some central banks have recently influenced this market to at least a marginal extent. Most of their interventions were intended to meet requirements of domestic monetary policy, mainly with a view to regulating bank liquidity. Usually these actions were aimed at either distributing more evenly the official foreign-exchange reserves, financing a balance-of-payments deficit, or investing a payments surplus; very few such transactions were intended

[2] Cf. Fred H. Klopstock, "Money Creation in the Euro-dollar Market," *Monthly Review*, Federal Reserve Bank of New York, January 1970.

to regulate the Eurodollar market itself. Indeed, the usefulness or necessity of a central bank's systematic and permanent participation in the Eurocurrency market has not been proved. One may hope that the monetary authorities will conduct their occasional interventions with caution, in order to keep a free hand in the management of their policies and tactics and not become prisoners of the market.

The advantages offered by this international money market—its flexibility and freedom of access; the way it has adjusted to varying economic conditions; its influence on the level of interest rates of the various domestic-money markets, its adjustment function in private and even public international settlements, notably through the financing of certain countries' temporary balance-of-payments deficits with funds originating from surpluses of creditor nations—should not lead one to overlook the risks it involves or the drawbacks it may incur in some respects.

The Eurocurrency market is an essentially complex mechanism, but its working does meet the needs of its users; like Aesop's tongue, it may become the worst or the best of things, according to the use that is made of it. If, by its nature, it confers a greater fluidity to short-term capital movements and if, by its volume, it sometimes amplifies such movements, it does not engender the basic disequilibria giving rise to these flows of funds and to interest-rate fluctuations. Indeed, because of the outstanding part now played in the Eurocurrency market by the European branches of U.S. banks, the market has tended to become a new extension of the American money market, consequently losing some of its originality and independence.

This evolution, while adding to the special responsibilities of the American monetary authorities in this field, does not reduce the responsibilities of other countries but rather reinforces their mutual interdependence and solidarity. It should normally lead to a higher degree of cooperation among European countries and then between those countries and the United States in order that this international money market should keep on playing a stabilizing rather than a disrupting role on the international monetary scene.

X

FRANZ HEINRICH ULRICH

Mr. Ulrich, born in Hannover in 1910, after university studies took up service with the Deutsche Bank in Berlin in 1936. In 1951 he became a member of the Board of Managing Directors of the Norddeutsche Bank in Hamburg and, in 1957, a member of the Board of Managing Directors of the reunited Deutsche Bank AG, the largest privately owned bank on the European continent. From 1967, Mr. Ulrich was one of the two spokesmen of the Board of Managing Directors of Deutsche Bank; in 1970 he became its sole spokesman.

Mr. Ulrich's main spheres of activity are industrial loans, export financing, investment business, and international relations. For many years he has effectively advanced the concepts of foreign investment by German industry and the purchase of shares by wide circles of the population.

Mr. Ulrich is President of the German Group of the International Chamber of Commerce, Member of the Board of the Bundesverband deutscher Banken, and Chairman of the Supervisory Board of the Deutsche Gesellschaft für wirtschaftliche Zusammenarbeit (Entwicklungsgesellschaft) mbH. He is also chairman, deputy chairman, or a member of the supervisory boards of many renowned West German firms and is one of two German Representatives on the Supervisory Board of the European-American Banking Corporation and European-American Bank & Trust Company.

The Eurodollar Market: A View from the Federal Republic of Germany

INTERNATIONAL-MONEY DEALINGS WITHOUT ADMINISTRATIVE SUPPORT

The freedom of international capital movements is generally regarded as the measure and the acid test of a country's attitude toward international understanding and cooperation. Nevertheless, liberalization in this area is usually at the bottom of the list of priorities for international economic integration. First on the list for further international intensification are transactions in goods and services. Liberalization here does not impinge so decisively on the sovereignty of the countries concerned and has less impact on the specific aims of the various national economic policies.

In view of the expansive development of the Euromoney market the extent to which the European Economic Community (EEC) member states have so far put into practice the treaty directives on the liberalization of long-term capital movements does not appear in a very favorable light. Banks and business firms—and not only those in the EEC countries—

have, to a considerable degree and without administrative support, created over the last few years an efficient Euromarket as an extension to the important national markets. Seen from this angle, the existence of the Euromoney market testifies to a strong will to international understanding and cooperation. Its development is a renaissance of the process of world-wide money market integration which was interrupted during the Second World War.

POSSIBILITIES AND PROBLEMS OF THE EUROMONEY MARKET

Looking at the Euromoney market from the point of view of German banks and business firms means seeing its problems from the point of view of a country which has removed the restrictions on international goods and capital movements more quickly and has taken liberalization further at present than any other country in the world. For banks and business firms, this liberal policy has facilitated and enlarged business possibilities; for the central bank, on the other hand, it has made monetary policy more difficult. The removal of administrative restrictions on transactions with other countries enabled the banks to expand considerably their international business, whereas the Bundesbank has had to watch its traditional instruments become less effective as liberalization in this sphere proceeded.

The emergence of the Euromoney market has very much widened business policy scope for the banks concerned. Transactions on the Euromarket are used mainly for foreign exchange and interest arbitrage, for temporary liquidity adjustments, and for the financing of short-term credit business. Since money-market transactions are possible at any time in both directions on the Euromarket, the banks have additional means of getting a higher return *or* ensuring a greater degree of liquidity. The limited number of those with the means to enter the market gives the Euromarket a wholesale character and enables transactions to take place with much lower interest margins than are usual in other markets. As far as liquidity is concerned, the commercial banks have more room for maneuver as they have recourse to the Euromarket when there is a bottleneck in the domestic money market or when there is a surplus liquidity problem. Surplus liquidity in the banking system can be fed into the Euromarket and funds can be taken up to compensate for a shortage of liquidity at home. As is true for banks in other Western industrial countries, the Euromoney market has actually come to be practically an indispensable instrument of liquidity policy for German commercial banks. It enables them to invest their money more rationally and profitably; nowhere else, neither in the Federal Republic nor in any other country in Europe, is there a money market large enough to allow changing liquidity situations to be balanced out so efficiently.

For many years now, the German banking system has been fully integrated internationally. There can be no doubt that this development, which is the result of a basically outward looking attitude in German economic policy, has benefited every sector of German industry. However, world-wide integration also has its price as events in one country affect all the others. This is also true of the large Euromarket, which is not directly influenced and cannot be directly influenced by any national or supranational body active in the field of monetary policy.

The "External Position" of the Credit Institutions: A Corrective for the Balance of Payments

The short-term external assets and liabilities of the German credit institutions are a particularly important and, at the same time, very flexible link in the financial relations between the domestic economy and economies abroad. They also (and not least of all) indicate the extent to which the Federal Republic is engaged on international money and credit markets. From a monetary policy point of view, the credit institutions' short-term external assets are interesting in two ways. In so far as these are invested funds, they are part of the liquidity reserves of the domestic banking system and are thus affected not only by the prevailing interest differential but also by the liquidity situation at home. But, as foreign assets available at short-term, they are also part of the national exchange reserves, similar to the official reserves held by the Deutsche Bundesbank.

When the balance of payments moves into surplus, the credit institutions markedly increase their external assets. These had remained more or less unchanged from 1962 to 1965 at between DM 4,000 and DM 6,000 million. At the end of 1969, these stood at DM 17,400 million. Hence, the surplus on the basic balance was at times compensated for by an increase in the banks' net external claims. The basis of this export of money was a strong increase in liquid funds available to the credit institutions. This was mainly the immediate result of the high inflow of foreign exchange on current transactions. But since the end of 1966, the growing liquidity of the credit institutions has been due also to repeated reductions in the minimum reserve requirements. Through re-exports of foreign exchange from current transactions, and later through the re-export of speculative funds and through investing liquidity freed at home in foreign money markets, the German banks during this period helped reduce the repercussions on the exchange reserves of foreign countries, caused by the surplus shown by the German balance of goods and services. As France, Italy, Belgium, Holland, Great Britain, and Sweden severely limited or stopped exports of money by banks over the last few years, the flow of funds to the Euromoney market, apart from investment by Middle East countries, was due to an important extent to money exports by banks in the Federal Republic and Switzerland.

The effect of the activities of German banks on the balance of payments with regard to external monetary transactions has a similar significance for the German balance of payments as that of the U.S. banks on the balance of payments of the United States. As is well known, the U.S.A. in 1969 had a balance of payments deficit of $7 billion according to the usual method of calculation on the liquidity basis, which includes almost all dollars used in foreign transactions. Using this method of calculation, the increase in the claims of foreign branches of U.S. banks on their parent banks is entered on the liabilities side. The official settlements method, on the other hand, only includes those dollars which come into the possession of foreign governments and central banks; in other words, it does not include the increase in claims by foreign branches of U.S. banks. Depending on which of these different accounting methods is used, the U.S. balance of payments for 1969 had either a deficit on the liquidity basis of $7.2 billion or a surplus on the official settlements basis of $2.7 billion. It is worth noting that at the end of 1969, the liabilities of American banks towards their foreign branches stood at $13 billion—more than $6 billion higher than at the end of 1968.

A Mirror of Euromoney Market Activity

According to the Bank for International Settlements, *Eurodollars* are those dollars acquired by banks domiciled outside the U.S.A. (including the foreign branches of U.S. banks) and granted as loans to final borrowers either directly in dollars or, after conversion to another currency, perhaps with the inclusion of an intermediary. In general, then, *Eurocurrency* means balances in a convertible currency maintained with foreign banks and lent to other banks or business firms. For this reason, the short-term external assets and liabilities of German credit institutions only partially reflect the German banks' engagement on the Euromoney market. An exact statement of their Euromoney market assets and liabilities would entail a statistical breakdown of the overall position according to debitor and creditor countries and, at the same time, according to different currencies. In principle, assets of

German credit institutions held as U.S. dollar deposits with banks in the U.S.A., pound sterling deposits with English banks, and franc deposits with French banks are not considered part of the Euromoney market until lent out abroad; however, the definition of a particular transaction can certainly be problematic. Nevertheless, the expansion of the German credit institutions' external assets and liabilities does sufficiently reflect their activity on the Euromoney market.

A WIDER RANGE OF INVESTMENT POSSIBILITIES

The increasing relevance of the Euromoney market for German banks is also clear from the longer term development of the structure of the German credit institutions' external assets and liabilities. The acquisition of foreign money market paper by German banks has declined structurally over the last few years. On average for the years 1962 to 1965, this paper accounted for 16 per cent of the banks' total external assets. On average for the years 1966 to 1969, this share dropped to just under 3 per cent. The higher earlier proportion, as far as this represented investment in American treasury bills, was probably due mainly to the fact that, until the spring of 1967, the yield obtainable on these bills was often higher than that for three-month money on the Euromoney market. However, the German banks' withdrawal from the American money market, which can be seen from the decline in the proportion quoted above and which went hand in hand with a strong increase in investment on the Eurodollar market, has structural causes in addition to this.

The demand for credit on the Euromoney market has increased strongly over the last few years. This was due not only to increased demand from Europe but also from the U.S.A., particularly by way of European branches of American banks. The demand for credit by European subsidiaries of American companies has also increased. To satisfy this increased demand, the banks operating on the Eurodollar market increased the range of investment possibilities they were offering; the American branches in Great Britain, for example, introduced marketable certificates of deposit and the English banks introduced similar paper. The range of investment possibilities on the Euromoney market became so finely graded that it was no longer basically different from that available on the American money market. Hence, the German banks to an increasing extent moved over to operating on this market which was, so to speak, on their doorstep. Since the European branches of the big American banks were increasingly acting as intermediaries in money transactions between Europe and the U.S.A., the link with the American money market was also forged without the European banks' having to operate directly in America. Nor did this development prevent the American balance of payments from being eased by the inflow of money from the Federal Republic. The Eurodollar market proved to be a turntable for money exports from European countries to the U.S.A. and, hence, a means of achieving short-term balance of payments equilibrium between the European surplus countries and the deficit U.S.A.

A certain structural change within the whole of the German banking system contributed to the expansion of exports of money by the German banks in the second half of the 1960s. The Central Giro Institutions, who mainly act for the German savings banks on the money market, have since 1966 gained in importance as exporters of money. The tendency on the part of the Central Giro Institutions to become more active in foreign transactions is mainly due to the fact that the domestic money market on occasion proved insufficient to absorb the considerable increase in liquidity in the savings bank sector so that investment abroad was the obvious solution.

SPECULATION OVERRIDES PROFITABILITY CONSIDERATIONS

There is scarcely a sector of the German balance of payments that has not been affected during the last two years firstly by the expectation of revaluation and then by the change in the parity of the DMark. However, revaluation had its greatest repercussions on short-term capital movements. It was only gradually after revaluation on October 27, 1969 and the resultant normalization of the credit institutions' external position that the engagement of German banks on the Euro-money market returned to the basis of profitability and liquidity considerations.

As early as 1968, the deficit on the banks' balance of short-term capital movements was mainly the result of speculation on a revaluation of the DMark and a devaluation of other currencies. It is true that, at the time, the higher degree of liquidity in the Federal Republic was also favoring short-term capital movements abroad. However, the interest differential only occasionally encouraged such movements of capital because fear of parity changes often made forward-cover costs so expensive for German investors that the existing interest advantages were nullified. In fact, foreign investors and lenders were depositing considerable sums at short term in the Federal Republic although these bore little or no interest.

During 1969, speculative movements and countermovements often cancelled out dynamics when on balance, so that the year-end results do not reflect in foreign transactions over the year as a whole. This becomes clear short-term credit transactions by industry before and after revaluation of the DMark are considered together. The inflow of funds to the Federal Republic by the end of September amounted to DM 19,200 million net. The outflow since October came to DM 15,700 million net. Of the inflow of foreign funds, direct deposits with German banks accounted for only DM 3,000 million.

The withdrawal of foreign funds from German credit institutions since revaluation has been more than compensated for by money taken in or held for foreign depositors for nonspeculative reasons. At the end of 1969, the German credit institutions' external short-term assets and liabilities amounted to DM 17,400 million and DM 21,300 million, respectively. At the end of January 1970, the German banks' short-term external liabilities were approximately DM 4,500 million higher than at the end of September 1969. The funds which the banks have taken up abroad have softened the effect on the Bundesbank's official reserves of the outflow of foreign exchange from the industrial sector.

An even stronger mobilization of liquid dollar balances and credits which the Bundesbank had granted to the International Monetary Fund (IMF) and, on condition that premature withdrawal was possible, to foreign monetary authorities in times of a high inflow of foreign exchange could thus at least be partially prevented. But the banks' contribution to covering the foreign-exchange deficit was not very great because the banks continued to stock up their foreign-exchange balances right into the current year. Short-term foreign assets at the end of January 1970 were about DM 700 million higher than before the DMark was floated. A decisive factor which induced the banks to continue stocking up their short-term foreign assets despite a steady reduction of their overall liquid reserves was the higher net yield obtainable on international money markets compared with the interest rates in the Federal Republic.

The fact that the banks did at first continue to invest funds on the Euromoney market after the revaluation of the DM, despite the fact that liquidity was becoming increasingly short, shows to what extent their activity on foreign money markets is, for profitability considerations, dependent on the international interest-rate differential. These money exports slowed down only in the middle of January 1970 when the yield differential, which had reached its peak in mid-December at more than 2 per cent for three months' money between Eurodollars in London and DM in Frankfurt/Main, had dropped to a minimum. Anyhow, the banks had to operate for a long time without official support from the Bundesbank for money exports after the revaluation of the DM.[1]

The development at the beginning of 1970 suited the Bundesbank's considerations. The situation was completely different in 1969, when the bank's attitude to money exports was at times contrary to the Bundesbank's intentions. In May, particularly, it became clear that there was no direct connection between the Bundesbank's swap transactions, with which it aimed to bring about the re-export of the foreign exchange that had flowed in, and the banks' exports of money. The considerable difference between the Bundesbank's swap rates and those on the free market made it lucrative at the time to borrow dollars abroad, have the exchange rate guaranteed for these by forward transactions at the market rate, and convert the borrowed dollars to DMarks. As part of the same transaction, these DMarks were used to acquire Bundesbank dollars which, in turn, were re-invested abroad, whereby the forward cover was obtained at the Bundesbank's rates. The banks were able to obtain a profit on such transactions without using their own liquid funds, and the profit corresponded roughly to the difference between the market forward-discount rates and those of the Bundesbank. Formally, these transactions did fulfill the criterion of money exports, but it was not a question of exporting funds available at home but rather of investing funds which had previously been borrowed abroad. These transactions on the part of the German banks caused the Bundesbank at the time to suspend temporarily its swap trans-

[1] During February and March 1970 the trend towards lower interest rates on the Euromoney market, favored by the development of interest rates in the U.S.A., the lowering of the discount rate in Great Britain, and the rise in the discount and Lombard rates in the Federal Republic of Germany, has at times caused considerable money imports by German banks.

actions in order to put a stop to this kind of "carrousel" business.

FLANK PROTECTION BY CENTRAL BANKS' CONCERTED ACITON

The present Euromoney market may be estimated at approximately $43 billion. There can be no doubt that this market has very much accentuated the international monetary crises of the last few years. According to estimates, the Euromoney market accounted for about two-thirds of the inflow of funds to the Federal Republic between April 28 and May 9, 1969. Central banks accounted for only an estimated 10 per cent of the inflow between September 11 and September 24, 1969. This high proportion and the size of these movements of funds mean that the potency of the Euromoney market with regard to national monetary reserves and the maintenance of the international monetary system should by no means be underestimated. The carrousel transactions and the resultant reaction on the part of the Bundesbank also show, as do analogous measures by other monetary authorities, that the central banks have at least so far succeeded, by a cooperative extension of their monetary policy instruments, in limiting the disruptive influences which can proceed from this market due to the high degree of mobility of the circulating funds.

The market has already survived a whole series of difficult situations, such as the devaluation of the pound, the gold crisis, the flight into the DMark. This is at least an indication of its past efficiency. Cooperative action on the part of the central banks of the countries concerned in fighting the difficulties which can be fostered by the Euromoney market, but certainly do not proceed from it, would be put on a new, positive basis by the implementation of the four-stage plan presently under discussion within the Common Market to complete economic and monetary union.

The "Basic Outline of a Four-Stage Plan" was suggested by the Federal Government on the basis of the decisions taken at the EEC summit conference at The Hague. The fourth stage provides for:

1. An extension of the Committee of Central Bank Governors to a European Central Bank Committee;
2. The introduction of fixed and guaranteed exchange rates between the member states;
3. The introduction of a European currency unit.

This is certainly a very ambitious goal. Its realization would necessitate the solving of many a tricky detail. It would certainly, however, underline the most striking of the three essentials for the Euromoney market—the maintenance of the convertibility of the currencies of the countries concerned and the efficiency of the international monetary system. The creation of a uniform EEC currency and the pooling of the foreign exchange reserves hitherto administered on a national basis would serve like a kind of flank protection as a lasting contribution to the stabilization of this market.

As the Euromoney market is mainly a market between banks, its chief instrument so far has been deposits in foreign currencies. The creation of certificates of deposit was the beginning of specific Euromoney market papers. So far there are no signs that further instruments will be created in the near future. There is no international monetary authority which could regulate for the changing liquidity situation by sales or purchases of this kind of paper in the way a central bank pursues its open-market policy or engages in discount purchases. A further extension of the Euromoney market instruments would of course occur if governments began to cover their short-term need for finance by issuing treasury bonds on the Euromarket. In the interest of an extension of the range of investment possibilities one could finally consider bonded Euroloans, approaching maturity within the context of the international monetary system and monetary policy as they presently exist. Keeping desirable developments in mind, both the ingenuity and the sense of duty of bankers will be needed to further extend what has been up to now the narrow range of investment possibilities on the Euromoney market whose effectiveness will have to be heightened.

It may be attributed to the increased sense of responsibility shown by the banks and companies active in this market that difficulties which arose at the beginning (because the periods for which money was taken up on the one hand and utilized on the other hand did not always coincide) have faded out during the last years. Since the standing of the partners in the market has been improved through qualitative selection, confidence seems justified that, in future, chain reactions will be avoided which, due to the size and flexibility of the market, could lead to quick repercussions.

XI

BANK OF ENGLAND QUARTERLY BULLETIN

[This chapter originally appeared in the March 1970 issue of the Quarterly Bulletin *of The Bank of England. It is the most recent in a series of articles which has reviewed the development of the Eurodollar market, of which London is the acknowledged center.]*

Since June 1964 . . . the foreign-currency liabilities and claims of banks in the United Kingdom have grown at an impressive rate. This growth has been described in the quarterly Commentaries in subsequent issues of the Bulletin, *and has also been touched upon in two recent articles on the U.K. banking sector ["Overseas and Foreign Banks in London: 1962–68,"* Bulletin, *June 1968; "The U.K. Banking Sector: 1952–67,"* Bulletin, *June 1969].*

The present article reviews developments over the past six years as a whole. It brings the earlier material together, and includes some new information about U.K. residents' holdings of nonsterling currencies, and about the maturity pattern of the banks' liabilities and claims in these currencies. The available statistics are summarized in four tables at the end of the chapter, and the sources of the figures are described in an appendix.

The Eurodollar Market: A View from London

INTRODUCTION

In their foreign-currency deposit business, banks in the United Kingdom participate with banks in other centers in what has come to be known as the Eurocurrency market. Eurocurrencies are those other than the domestic currency of the country in which the bank taking the deposit or lending the funds is located. Thus for banks in the United Kingdom—including not only U.K.-registered banks, but also the U.K. offices of overseas banks—Eurocurrency business comprises deposits and lending in currencies other than sterling.[1] The bulk of the business is in U.S. dollars, but the major West European currencies, and occasionally other currencies, are also traded. The term *Eurocurrency* is something of a misnomer in that it implies that the foreign currencies are mainly deposited by, or on-lent to, other countries in Western Europe; in fact, participation in the market is world-wide.

Apart from the additional supplies of dollars generated

[1] In practice, the term applies only to foreign currencies and does not include those of other countries of the sterling area.

mainly by the U.S. and U.K. balance-of-payments deficits, the following are perhaps the most important of the factors contributing to the growth of this business:

a) The market is able, for a number of reasons, to operate on a much smaller margin between borrowing and lending rates than is usual in domestic banking systems. In part, this is because of regulations imposed on domestic business which are not applied to Eurocurrency business. For example, domestic banks are often subject to regulation on interest rates—they may, for example, be limited as to the amount payable on deposits; alternatively, there may be conventions to the same effect. The Eurocurrency market is not restricted in this way. Again, most domestic banking systems have obligatory reserve requirements in one form or another on which the return is at best comparatively low; such requirements do not usually apply to Eurocurrency business and, as this is a time-deposit market in which the maturities of deposits and lending are generally broadly matched, the banks can often work on quite small reserves. There are other reasons for the smaller margins on Eurocurrency business, not connected with monetary regulations. For example, the Eurocurrency market deals only in large amounts whereas, in their domestic business, banks also have to incur the cost of handling far more modest sums.

b) The market itself is not subject to exchange or other controls, although such controls may apply to the suppliers and borrowers of funds in their own countries. In this context, the greater freedom that operators in the principal countries of Western Europe have enjoyed since the move to external convertibility at the end of 1958 has greatly helped the expansion of the market.

c) The existence of the market may allow anonymity, if a holder of a foreign currency prefers not to place it directly with the banking system of the country whose currency is involved.

DEVELOPMENTS IN RECENT YEARS

During the six years from the end of 1963 to the end of 1969, the period covered by this survey, the number of banks and other institutions transacting foreign currency business in the United Kingdom increased from 132 to 193. Their gross foreign-currency liabilities and claims, excluding funds taken from and lent to other banks in London (the interbank market) grew from about £1,300 million to some £12,500 million (*see* Table XI.1). The rate of growth has fluctuated from year to year, but has, on balance, accelerated. Between the end of 1963 and the end of 1965 U.K. banks' gross foreign-currency liabilities to overseas residents increased by over 25 per cent per annum, but in the next three years up to the end of 1968 the average rate of increase climbed to nearly 50 per cent per annum; during 1969 there was an increase of 75 per cent.

The years of greatest growth have been those when tight credit conditions existed in the United States. In 1966 and 1969, for example, some banks in that country borrowed substantial amounts of Eurodollars, mainly through their overseas branches. To a limited extent, the heavy demand from U.S. banks was to offset movements of U.S. funds to the Eurodollar market, to take advantage of the higher interest rate prevailing there. More generally, with demands from other borrowers also growing steadily, the sources of the market's funds broadened to meet the greatly increased requirements.

The increases in London banks' liabilities and claims quoted above were no doubt partly attributable to the redepositing of funds between banks in London and those abroad—perhaps to take advantage of temporary differences in interest rates, or because banks wished to limit the amount of funds they placed directly with individual countries. In any attempt to

TABLE XI.1

NET LIABILITIES/CLAIMS IN NONSTERLING CURRENCIES OF BANKS IN THE UNITED KINGDOM
(In £ Millions)

CLAIMS —	UNITED KINGDOM								
	Banks			*Other*			*Total*		
	Liabil-ities	Claims	Net	Liabil-ities	Claims	Net	Liabil-ities	Claims	Net
End-1963									
Deposit banks	4	56	– 52	21	3	18	25	59	– 34
Accepting houses	76	87	– 11	29	8	21	105	95	10
British overseas and Commonwealth banks	146	137	9	19	5	14	165	142	23
American banks	39	61	– 22	25	4	21	64	65	– 1
Foreign banks and affiliates	77	57	20	1	2	– 1	78	59	19
Other overseas banks	71	24	47	4	5	– 1	75	29	46
Other banks	15	8	7	1	3	– 2	16	11	5
Total	*429*	*429*		*100*	*31*		*529*	*460*	
End-1969									
Deposit banks	128	179	– 51	67	15	52	195	194	1
Accepting houses	375	447	– 72	73	115	– 42	448	562	–114
British overseas and Commonwealth banks	679	1,115	–436	72	188	–116	751	1,303	–552
American banks	2,204	1,527	677	227	174	53	2,431	1,701	730
Foreign banks and affiliates	144	582	–438	18	44	– 26	162	626	–464
Other overseas banks	359	232	127	5	18	– 13	364	250	114
Other banks	549	456	93	31	74	– 43	580	530	50

CLAIMS —	OVERSEAS COUNTRIES								
	Sterling			*Nonsterling*			*Total*		
End-1963	Liabilities	Claims	Net	Liabilities	Claims	Net	Liabilities	Claims	Net
Deposit banks	—	—	—	60	50	10	60	50	10
Accepting houses	14	—	14	202	212	− 10	216	212	4
British overseas and Commonwealth banks	13	2	11	254	221	33	267	223	44
American banks	2	—	2	374	366	8	376	366	10
Foreign banks and affiliates	—	—	—	95	99	− 4	95	99	− 4
Other overseas banks	8	—	8	227	272	− 45	235	272	− 37
Other banks	—	—	—	19	23	− 4	19	23	− 4
Total	*37*	*2*		*1,232*	*1,242**		*1,270*	*1,244*	
End-1969									
Deposit banks	6	2	4	64	105	− 41	69	107	− 38
Accepting houses	87	20	67	753	722	31	840	742	98
British overseas and Commonwealth banks	208	39	169	1,787	1,417	370	1,995	1,456	539
American banks	373	123	250	6,307	7,273	−966	6,680	7,396	−716
Foreign banks and affiliates	19	3	16	1,037	585	452	1,056	588	468
Other overseas banks	157	8	149	495	762	−267	651	770	−119
Other banks	46	28	18	632	707	− 75	678	735	− 57
Total	*896*	*223*		*11,074‡*	*11,570‡*		*11,970*	*11,793*	

TABLE XI.1—(Continued)

CLAIMS —	TOTAL		
	United Kingdom and overseas		
End-1963	Liabil-ities	Claims	Net
Deposit banks	86	108	−22
Accepting houses	321	307	14
British overseas and Commonwealth banks	432	365	67
American banks	440	431	9
Foreign banks and affiliates	174	158	16
Other overseas banks	311	299	12
Other banks	34	34	—
Total	*1,798*	*1,704*	
End-1969			
Deposit banks	265	301	−36
Accepting houses	1,288	1,304	−16
British overseas and Commonwealth banks	2,748	2,761	−13
American banks	9,110	9,097	17
Foreign banks and affiliates	1,219	1,212	7
Other overseas banks	1,014	1,020	− 6
Other banks	1,258	1,265	− 7
Total	*16,902*	*16,959*	

* Of which banks, 1,112; the figure of liabilities to banks is not available.

† Total liabilities to, and claims on, banks in the U.K. should be the same. By the end of 1969, however, a difference had developed between the two sets of figures as reported, and it has not so far been possible to rectify this. There will be compensating differences in other columns of the table, but not in the final totals.

‡ Of which banks, 8,397 and 9,212 respectively.

SOURCE: U.K. Exchange Control.

measure the growth of the Eurocurrency market as a whole, such redeposited funds should, if possible, be omitted to avoid double-counting. The banks themselves, when accepting deposits from banks abroad, cannot distinguish redeposited funds from "new" funds coming into the market—for example, those which the overseas banks are placing on behalf of their customers, or which they have obtained by switching domestic-currency assets into foreign currencies. Similarly, London banks would not know the ultimate destination of funds lent to a bank abroad. The Bank for International Settlements (BIS) has from time to time made estimates of the size of the Eurodollar market, after excluding so far as possible the duplication arising from redepositing between banks; they estimate that the market's gross liabilities on this basis expanded from $9,000 million at the end of 1964 to $25,000 million at the end of 1968.[2]

SOURCES OF FUNDS

Depositors of foreign currencies with banks in the United Kingdom include overseas central banks, commercial banks and similar financial institutions, international companies, smaller traders, and even private individuals. The statistical information about these various categories of holders is limited. At the end of 1969 nearly 70 per cent of the total of these deposits (excluding deposits between U.K. banks) was due to banks abroad, but as already noted this tells little about the origin of the deposits. A further 25 per cent of total deposits was due directly to other overseas residents, and the balance of 5 per cent to U.K. residents other than banks.

A geographical analysis of deposits from overseas (*see* Table XI.2) indicates only the country from which the U.K. bank received the funds and not necessarily the country of

[2] See the thirty-ninth *Annual Report of the Bank for International Settlements, 1968/1969,* p. 149.

TABLE XI.2

GEOGRAPHICAL ANALYSIS OF EXTERNAL LIABILITIES AND CLAIMS OF BANKS IN THE UNITED KINGDOM IN NONSTERLING CURRENCIES
(In £ Millions)

	Liabilities						
End of:	1963	1964	1965	1966	1967	1968	1969
Western Europe							
Austria	81	82	59	99	158	143	142
Belgium and Luxembourg	36	43	61	101	142	306	582
Denmark	5	8	11	21	31	63	102
France	49	97	133	207	309	440	737
Western Germany	36	42	69	82	265	336	441
Italy	77	98	220	282	322	662	988
Netherlands	34	59	49	65	111	215	515
Norway	11	22	52	62	101	157	229
Spain	20	33	34	29	34	79	144
Sweden	10	33	33	34	58	109	90
Switzerland (incl. BIS)	267	305	413	664	824	1,321	2,621
Other	26	28	31	46	58	86	152
Total	*652*	*850*	*1,165*	*1,692*	*2,413*	*3,917*	*6,743*

	LIABILITIES						
End of:	1963	1964	1965	1966	1967	1968	1969
United States	152	204	194	349	588	1,119	1,270
Canada	133	273	170	200	324	505	1,085
Japan	4	7	10	11	16	26	127
Latin America	67	90	100	135	201	276	574
Middle East	132	159	215	234	231	235	286
Overseas sterling area							
Bahamas	9	11	28	46	45	69	188
Bermuda	19	42	59	72	94	109	164
Persian Gulf territories	1	9	16	33	61	174	244
Other	12	20	22	49	98	191	398
Total	*41*	*82*	*125*	*200*	*298*	*543*	*994*
Other non-sterling countries	93	111	116	151	251	405	590
Nonterritorial organizations and unallocated	6	10	27	30	60	105	295
Total	*1,280*	*1,786*	*2,122*	*3,002*	*4,382*	*7,131*	*11,964*
of which:							
U.S. dollars	*1,072*	*1,566*	*1,893*	*2,727*	*4,037*	*6,402*	*10,689*
Deutsche mark	*65*	*83*	*96*	*104*	*128*	*344*	*609*
Swiss francs	*76*	*83*	*72*	*109*	*118*	*242*	*453*
Other nonsterling currencies	*67*	*54*	*61*	*62*	*99*	*143*	*213*

TABLE XI.2—(Continued)

	Claims						
End of:	1963	1964	1965	1966	1967	1968	1969
Western Europe							
Austria	5	11	17	33	65	90	77
Belgium and Luxembourg	92	115	92	124	143	204	423
Denmark	34	40	42	45	83	61	68
France	82	87	89	106	138	243	557
Western Germany	116	182	195	244	216	401	645
Italy	188	171	168	195	191	289	615
Netherlands	34	70	66	97	128	149	203
Norway	29	32	53	76	96	105	129
Spain	11	10	21	27	66	89	113
Sweden	38	36	35	46	64	83	96
Switzerland (incl. BIS)	49	62	97	106	162	289	452
Other	14	24	41	61	100	158	184
Total	*692*	*840*	*916*	*1,160*	*1,452*	*2,161*	*3,562*

	CLAIMS						
End of:	1963	1964	1965	1966	1967	1968	1969
United States	290	435	575	1,244	1,709	3,058	5,613
Canada	37	26	55	98	145	202	267
Japan	127	181	209	249	451	695	675
Latin America	29	30	76	81	177	342	613
Middle East	17	31	42	49	87	124	130
Overseas sterling area							
Bahamas	—	1	3	5	30	49	385
Bermuda	—	—	1	1	6	12	30
Persian Gulf territories	—	—	—	2	3	11	21
Other	3	3	20	31	60	105	113
Total	*3*	*4*	*24*	*39*	*99*	*177*	*549*
Other non-sterling countries	73	79	83	105	247	343	474
Nonterritorial organizations and unallocated	—	—	—	—	7	7	107
Total	*1,268*	*1,626*	*1,980*	*3,020*	*4,374*	*7,109*	*11,990*
of which:							
U.S. dollars	*1,024*	*1,312*	*1,624*	*2,611*	*3,836*	*6,242*	*10,505*
Deutsche mark	*68*	*119*	*162*	*167*	*224*	*439*	*791*
Swiss francs	*71*	*85*	*81*	*94*	*148*	*246*	*487*
Other nonsterling currencies	*105*	*110*	*113*	*148*	*166*	*182*	*207*

TABLE XI.2—(Continued)

End of	Net (Liability —)						
	1963	1964	1965	1966	1967	1968	1969
Western Europe							
Austria	— 75	— 71	— 42	— 66	— 93	— 53	— 65
Belgium and Luxembourg	56	72	31	23	1	— 102	— 159
Denmark	29	32	31	24	59	— 2	— 34
France	33	— 10	— 44	—101	— 171	— 197	— 180
Western Germany	80	140	126	162	— 49	62	204
Italy	111	73	— 52	— 87	— 131	— 373	— 373
Netherlands	—	11	17	32	17	— 6	— 312
Norway	18	10	1	14	— 5	— 52	— 100
Spain	— 9	— 23	— 13	— 2	32	10	— 31
Sweden	28	3	2	12	6	— 26	6
Switzerland (incl. BIS)	—218	—243	—316	—558	— 662	—1,032	—2,169
Other	— 12	— 4	10	15	42	72	32
Total	*40*	*— 10*	*—249*	*—532*	*— 961*	*—1,756*	*—3,181*
United States	138	231	381	895	1,121	1,939	4,343
Canada	— 96	—247	—115	—107	— 179	— 303	— 818
Japan	123	174	199	238	435	669	548
Latin America	— 38	— 60	— 24	— 54	— 24	66	39
Middle East	—115	—128	—173	—185	— 144	— 111	— 156

	Net (Liability —)						
End of	1963	1964	1965	1966	1967	1968	1969
Overseas sterling area							
Bahamas	— 9	— 10	— 25	— 41	— 15	— 20	197
Bermuda	— 19	— 42	— 58	— 71	— 88	— 97	— 134
Persian Gulf territories	— 1	— 9	— 16	— 31	— 58	— 163	— 223
Other	— 9	— 17	— 2	— 18	— 38	— 86	— 285
Total	*— 38*	*— 78*	*—101*	*—161*	*— 199*	*— 366*	*— 445*
Other non-sterling countries	— 20	— 32	— 33	— 46	— 4	— 62	— 116
Nonterritorial organizations and unallocated	— 6	— 10	— 27	— 30	— 53	— 98	— 188
Total	*— 12*	*—160*	*—142*	*18*	*— 8*	*— 22*	*26*
of which:							
U.S. dollars	*— 48*	*—254*	*—269*	*—116*	*— 201*	*— 160*	*— 184*
Deutsche mark	*3*	*36*	*66*	*63*	*96*	*95*	*182*
Swiss francs	*— 5*	*2*	*9*	*— 15*	*30*	*4*	*34*
Other nonsterling currencies	*38*	*56*	*52*	*86*	*67*	*39*	*— 6*

Source: Monthly returns of external liabilities and claims.

beneficial ownership, which may have been masked as a result of redepositing. Bearing this qualification in mind, the pattern of supply seems to have changed remarkably little over the six years to the end of 1969, even though nonresidents' deposits grew nearly tenfold during that time. West European countries have usually provided over half of the London market's overseas deposits, and their proportion of the total was 55 per cent at the end of 1969 against 51 per cent in 1963. Commercial banks in these countries have increasingly found the Eurocurrency market to be a convenient and profitable outlet for the employment of liquid funds; and with the demand for Eurocurrencies very strong and interest rates rising to record levels last year, they were particularly active in placing funds in the market. This was reflected in a rise of over £2,800 million in West European countries' deposits with London banks during 1969, most of which occurred during the first six months. The increase took place in spite of a tightening of monetary policy in many West European countries during the year. In some, measures were adopted to discourage or even reverse the outflow of short-term funds. In several countries, including some that introduced direct measures, official short-term interest rates were raised; whatever the underlying cause of these increases, they lessened the disparity between domestic rates and rising Eurodollar rates. Nevertheless, these measures did not seem to have a significant effect on the supply of Eurocurrencies to the London market; liabilities of banks in the United Kingdom to virtually all countries in Western Europe continued to rise throughout the year. It is possible that this continued rise in liabilities to Western Europe after the imposition of restrictions may have represented other countries' funds being channelled through Europe. In this context, Switzerland, which is the largest source of funds, did not restrict the placing of short-term deposits; it largely operates as an entrepôt centre for funds from elsewhere. (The figures for Switzerland in Table B include deposits by the BIS, which occasionally puts funds in the Eurocurrency market to counter the effect of temporary disturbances such as withdrawals over the end of the year for "window-dressing" purposes.)

Deposits from the United States and Canada both remained reasonably steady in proportionate terms over the six years to the end of 1969, representing around 12 per cent and 10 per cent, respectively, of total deposits. The holdings of overseas sterling area countries rose very steeply over this period—in absolute terms from £41 million to £994 million—mainly because of larger amounts placed by territories in the Persian Gulf and by the West Indies; as a proportion of total deposits, sterling countries' holdings rose from 3 per cent to 8 per cent. Deposits by East European countries (which are included with those of "other nonsterling countries" in Table XIV.2) rose from £57 million at end-1963 to £230 million at end-1969. In proportionate terms, only the deposits of nonsterling Middle Eastern countries showed any significant fall—from 10 per cent to 2 per cent—and even these deposits rose absolutely, from £132 million to £286 million.

U.K. residents also deposit funds in the Eurocurrency market on occasion, provided they have exchange-control permission to hold foreign currencies. Sometimes the deposits represent the temporary employment of foreign currencies borrowed for an approved purpose. For example, much direct investment by U.K. companies in nonsterling countries is now financed by borrowing foreign currencies in London or abroad and, pending investment, the borrowed funds may be redeposited. Similarly, U.K. financial institutions have been allowed to borrow in the Eurocurrency market to finance portfolios of foreign currency securities, and the liquid portion of these portfolios may again be redeposited. There are, of course, other U.K. deposits which do not arise from borrowing. For example, trading and commercial companies with world-wide operations—including insurance, shipping, and oil companies—are permitted, within limits, to hold foreign-currency balances to finance their operations. The proceeds of disinvestment of U.K. residents' portfolios of foreign-currency securities, in addition to those financed by borrowing, are also often held in the Eurocurrency market pending reinvestment. These balances tend to vary according to developments on overseas security markets, and in particular the New York market. In total, U.K. residents' deposits in the Eurocurrency market rose sharply, from just over £200 million in the latter part of 1967 to nearly £500 million at the end of 1969. About one half the latter figure reflected the holdings of trading and commercial companies, especially the substantial holdings of the insurance market, and another third the proceeds of borrowing awaiting investment.

EMPLOYMENT OF FUNDS

In contrast to external liabilities, the pattern of external claims has changed substantially over the years (*see* Table XIV.2). Commercial banks in the United States have found the Eurodollar market an increasingly convenient source of funds, particularly during times of domestic credit stringency, and this has probably been a major cause of growth in the market. (Banks in the United States are not restricted by the Federal Reserve Board as to the rate of interest they may pay on their Eurodollar borrowing from their branches overseas and, until October 1969,[3] such borrowings were also free from the reserve requirements which are imposed by the Federal Reserve Board on other types of deposits.) Foreign currency claims on the United States by banks in London rose from 23 per cent of total external claims at the end of 1963 to 43 per cent at the end of 1968 and 49 per cent—or £5,613 million—at the end of 1969. From late in 1968, banks in the United States experi-

[3] In October, a 10 per cent reserve requirement was imposed on Eurodollar borrowing by banks in the United States from their overseas branches in excess of the average level of borrowing outstanding in May 1969.

enced increasingly tight credit conditions. They lost a substantial volume of deposits in the form of certificates of deposit—the rates for new certificates were subject to regulation by the Federal Reserve Board,[4] and were below market rates—and, at the same time, the domestic demand for loans remained strong. As a result, banks in the United States bid strongly for Eurodollars and rates rose steeply.

Over the six years, U.K. banks' claims on overseas countries other than the United States fell, as a proportion of total claims, from 77 per cent to 51 per cent. The absolute level, however, rose from £978 million to £6,377 million—a broad indication of the growth in the use of Eurocurrencies for trade and investment purposes throughout the rest of the world. In 1969 a considerable part of the growth seems to have been attributable to borrowing, including amounts taken by residents of Western Germany, in order to speculate on a revaluation of the Deutsche mark; but this apart, the countries of Western Europe have been major users of Eurocurrencies. Claims on Japan rose substantially up to the end of 1968, but then changed little; the money was used mainly to support domestic lending to industry. A rise in claims on Latin America was largely attributable to Mexico, whose borrowing rose from £3 million at the end of 1963 to £235 million at the end of 1969. Lending to East European countries (largely in the form of foreign currency bills) rose over the six years by roughly the same amount as their deposits. The rapid rise in lending to the overseas sterling area during 1969 was almost entirely due to the Bahamas, and reflected borrowing by investment companies and similar institutions located there and also by local offices of U.S. banks.

Foreign currency lending by banks in the United Kingdom

[4] The maximum rates of interest payable on deposits were raised on January 21, 1970; the ceiling for deposits of 180 days to one year became 7 per cent, and a new maximum of 7½ per cent was introduced for deposits of one year and over. These rates were still below those ruling in the market at that time.

TABLE XI.3

TOTAL LIABILITIES OF BANKS IN THE UNITED KINGDOM IN NONSTERLING CURRENCIES

(In £ Millions; Percentage of Total in italics)

END OF:	1963		1964		1965		1966		1967		1968		1969	
Deposit banks	86	*5*	93	*4*	105	*4*	131	*3*	177	*3*	245	*3*	265	*2*
Accepting houses	321	*18*	384	*16*	370	*12*	444	*11*	645	*10*	887	*9*	1,288	*8*
British overseas and Commonwealth banks	432	*24*	498	*21*	535	*18*	747	*18*	1,189	*19*	1,559	*16*	2,748	*16*
American banks	440	*24*	712	*30*	1,091	*37*	1,872	*46*	2,847	*45*	4,795	*50*	9,110	*54*
Foreign banks and affiliates	174	*10*	224	*9*	266	*9*	297	*7*	345	*6*	614	*6*	1,219	*7*
Other overseas banks	311	*17*	419	*17*	428	*15*	494	*12*	734	*11*	968	*10*	1,014	*6*
Other banks	34	*2*	76	*3*	135	*5*	132	*3*	392	*6*	564	*6*	1,258	*7*
Total	1,798		2,406		2,930		4,117		6,329		9,632		16,902	
of which:														
U.S. $ certificates of deposit							93	*2*	249	*4*	597	*6*	1,537	*9*
Other U.S. $ liabilities	1,564	*87*	2,157	*90*	2,675	*91*	3,706	*90*	5,681	*90*	8,185	*85*	13,847	*82*
Total U.S. $ liabilities	1,564	*87*	2,157	*90*	2,675	*91*	3,799	*92*	5,930	*94*	8,782	*91*	15,384	*91*

SOURCE: U.K. Exchange Control.

to other U.K. residents, although small, grew very fast after the latter part of 1967. At that time, the total was about £220 million compared with a figure of nearly £630 million at the end of 1969. Some of the purposes for which borrowing may be approved by exchange control have already been mentioned.

Taking the banks' deposits and lending together, there was a very substantial increase in net borrowing by the United States over the six years, to a total of £4,343 million; net borrowing by Japan also rose, but much less steeply. All other areas, taken as groups, were net depositors. In particular West European countries' deposits, less borrowing, grew very sharply, to £3,181 million at the end of 1969. Canada's net deposits also rose substantially, and overseas sterling area countries were other large net depositors.

STRUCTURE OF THE MARKET

At the end of 1963 three groups of banks together accounted for two-thirds of the business done in the London market; these were the American banks and the British overseas and Commonwealth banks (each accounting for about 25 per cent of the total) and the accepting houses (rather less than 20 per cent). More details are given in Table XI.3. With the great increase in the borrowing of Eurodollars by banks in the United States, which has been effected mainly through their branches in London, the share of these branches in the London Eurocurrency market rose substantially over the years to stand at 54 per cent at the end of 1969. Over the same period the number of branches of American banks in London rose from 9 to 29. The share of all other groups of banks fell, and in particular the accepting houses now account for only 8 per cent of the market total.

The Eurocurrency operations of the U.K. deposit banks, comprising primarily the London clearing, Scottish, and Northern Ireland banks, have always been comparatively small. Most of these banks conventionally maintain cash and liquidity reserves in respect of their total deposits, in both sterling and foreign currency; as mentioned in the Introduction, this makes it difficult for them to compete in the Euro-currency market. The deposit banks have surmounted this particular obstacle by operating through their subsidiaries, which are not required to observe the same liquidity conventions. (These subsidiaries are mainly included in the category "other banks" in Tables XI.1 and XI.3.)

At the end of 1963, the liabilities and claims of most groups of banks were nearly in balance for each of the four principal sectors of the market—other banks in the United Kingdom, other U.K. residents, overseas sterling area countries, and nonsterling countries (*see* Table XI.1). The position has, however, changed radically over the years. In particular, the American banks changed from being net lenders of £22 million to the U.K. interbank market at end-1963 to net borrowers of £677 million at end-1969 (*see* Table XI.1). They used these funds, together with others, principally to lend to their head offices. The Japanese banks in London (included among "other overseas banks" in Table XI.1) were also heavy net borrowers from other banks in the United Kingdom, lending the funds to their head offices to support domestic advances. Most other groups of banks borrowed large amounts from overseas and lent the funds to the American and Japanese banks through the interbank market.

Since May 1966, some of the banks in London have issued certificates of deposit denominated in U.S. dollars. The practice was slow to develop at first, but during 1968 and 1969 the rate of growth increased appreciably; by the end of 1969 there were over £1,537 million of certificates of deposit outstanding, representing some 9 per cent of total gross foreign-currency liabilities of the London banks. There is an active secondary market in certificates of deposit now operated by seven institutions (there used to be eight), mostly discount houses. The number of issuing banks has risen to 52, but 10 of these accounted for £1,043 million, or over two-thirds of total certificates outstanding, at the end of 1969.

As mentioned earlier, the great bulk of the Eurocurrency market's business is in U.S. dollars. Since 1965 about 90 per cent of the London market's external liabilities have been in that currency, about 5 per cent in Deutsche mark and 3 per cent in Swiss francs. Much the same pattern emerges on the claims side, although claims in Deutsche mark showed a sharp rise in 1969; this was partly a response to forward covering by customers expecting a revaluation, and partly because of a significant increase in Deutsche mark lending to those prepared to offset the lower interest charges against the possible exchange risk. On balance, banks in the United Kingdom have consistently had net liabilities in U.S. dollars and net assets in other nonsterling currencies apart from Swiss francs (in which the position has varied).

THE MATURITY OF FUNDS IN THE MARKET

The Eurocurrency market is essentially a time-deposit market. The maturity of deposits ranges from call to three years or more. The banks seek broadly to match the maturity of their liabilities and claims in Eurocurrencies although, when assessing their net maturity position, they will concern themselves as well with the quality of their maturing claims.

On two recent occasions the banks have provided a maturity analysis of their assets and liabilities in nonsterling currencies, relating to the end of April 1968 and to the end of July 1969. The results are set out in Table XI.4. For convenience of analysis the market has been divided into three broad groups of banks—British banks (including Commonwealth banks), American banks, and other foreign banks. The liabilities and claims of each group are divided into four broad ranges of maturities and are shown according to whether the transac-

TABLE XI.4

MATURITY ANALYSIS OF LIABILITIES AND CLAIMS IN NONSTERLING CURRENCIES OF BANKS IN THE U.K.: July 1969 *(April 1968 in italics)* (In £ Millions)

LIABILITIES

Liabilities to and claims on:	Sight	Two days to less than three months	Three months up to less than one year	One year and over	Total July 1969	Total *April 1968*
Other U.K. banks:						
British banks*	161	767	459	71	1,458	*777*
American banks	511	1,348	357	10	2,226	*700*
Other foreign banks	17	280	136	16	449	*292*
	689	2,395	952	97	4,133	*1,769*
April 1968	*233*	*1,107*	*368*	*61*	*1,769*	
Other U.K. residents:						
British banks*	96	131	15	—	242	..
American banks	116	74	40	4	234	..
Other foreign banks	3	9	2	—	14	..
	215	214	57	4	490	..
Banks abroad:						
British banks*	327	1,215	556	168	2,266	..
American banks	764	2,893	832	111	4,605	..
Other foreign banks	118	748	290	60	1,216	..
	1,209	4,861	1,678	339	8,087	..

TABLE XI.4—(Continued)

	Sight	Two days to less than three months	Three months up to less than one year	One year and over	Total July 1969	Total *April 1968*
Liabilities						
Other overseas residents:						
British banks*	138	481	290	39	948	. .
American banks	255	922	570	79	1,826	. .
Other foreign banks	32	219	96	25	372	. .
	425	1,622	956	143	3,146	. .
Total liabilities and claims						
British banks*	722	2,594	1,320	278	4,914	*2,543*
American banks	1,646	5,242	1,799	204	8,891	*3,480*
Other foreign banks	170	1,256	524	101	2,051	*1,188*
	2,538	9,092	3,643	583	15,856	*7,211*
April 1968	*1,003*	*4,006*	*1,811*	*331*	*7,211*	
Claims						
Liabilities to and claims on:						
Other U.K. banks:						
British banks*	267	1,321	517	53	2,158	*1,008*
American banks	230	680	290	26	1,226	*489*
Other foreign banks	109	444	180	20	753	*313*
	606	2,445	987	99	4,137	*1,810*
April 1968	*217*	*1,193*	*364*	*36*	*1,810*	

TABLE XI.4—(Continued)

	CLAIMS					
	Sight	Two days to less than three months	Three months up to less than one year	One year and over	Total July 1969	Total *April 1968*
Other U.K. residents:						
British banks*	27	89	94	127	337	..
American banks	10	44	31	68	153	..
Other foreign banks	6	21	13	17	57	..
	43	154	138	212	547	..
Banks abroad:						
British banks*	229	882	395	100	1,606	..
American banks	3,062	2,156	919	82	6,219	..
Other foreign banks	189	529	214	87	1,019	..
	3,480	3,567	1,528	269	8,844	..
Other overseas residents:						
British banks*	66	273	201	322	862	..
American banks	150	485	291	346	1,272	..
Other foreign banks	16	68	44	97	225	..
	232	826	536	765	2,359	..
Total liabilities and claims						
British banks*	589	2,565	1,207	602	4,963	*2,564*
American banks	3,452	3,365	1,531	522	8,870	*3,486*
Other foreign banks	320	1,062	451	221	2,054	*1,174*
	4,361	6,992	3,189	1,345	15,887	*7,224*
April 1968	*1,523*	*3,181*	*1,567*	*953*	*7,224*	

TABLE XI.4—(Continued)

	Net (assets +)					
	Sight	Two days to less than three months	Three months up to less than one year	One year and over	Total July 1969	Total *April 1968*
iabilities to and claims on:						
ther U.K. banks:						
British banks*	+ 106	+ 554	+ 58	− 18	+ 700	*+231*
American banks	− 281	− 668	− 67	+ 16	−1,000	*−211*
Other foreign banks	+ 92	+ 164	+ 44	+ 4	+ 304	*+ 21*
	− 83	+ 50	+ 35	+ 2	+ 4	*+ 41*
April 1968	*− 16*	*+ 86*	*− 5*	*− 24*	*+ 41*	
ther U.K. residents:						
British banks*	− 69	− 42	+ 79	+127	+ 95	..
American banks	− 106	− 30	− 9	+ 64	− 81	..
Other foreign banks	+ 3	+ 12	+ 11	+ 17	+ 43	..
	− 172	− 60	+ 81	+208	+ 57	..
anks abroad:						
British banks*	− 98	− 333	−161	− 68	− 660	..
American banks	+2,298	− 742	+ 87	− 29	+1,614	..
Other foreign banks	+ 71	− 219	− 76	+ 27	− 197	..
	+2,271	−1,294	−150	− 70	+ 757	..
ther overseas residents:						
British banks*	− 72	− 208	− 89	+283	− 86	..
American banks	− 105	− 437	−279	+267	− 554	..
Other foreign banks	− 16	− 151	− 52	+ 72	− 147	..
	− 193	− 796	−420	+622	− 787	..
otal liabilities and claims						
British banks*	− 133	− 29	−113	+324	+ 49	*+ 21*
American banks	+1,806	−1,877	−268	+318	− 21	*+ 6*
Other foreign banks	+ 150	− 194	− 73	+120	+ 3	*− 14*
	+1,823	−2,100	−454	+762	+ 31	*+ 13*
April 1968	*+ 520*	*− 885*	*−244*	*+622*	*+ 13*	

* Including Commonwealth banks.
. Not available.

tions were with other banks, either in the United Kingdom or abroad, or with other domestic or overseas customers.

In total, the banks' positions were broadly matched at the end of July 1969. At sight, their claims exceeded their liabilities by over £1,800 million; this favorable net asset position was almost entirely attributable to the American banks, which had borrowed both in the interbank market and elsewhere at longer term and lent at call to their head offices. Sight liabilities comprise both overnight funds and deposits made originally at longer term which have now run their course and mature the next day; they probably include a large proportion of funds that will not in fact be withdrawn from the banks concerned or, if withdrawn, will be redeposited elsewhere in the system on the same day. Over 25 per cent of the market's assets and liabilities at the end of last July were at sight and a further 45 per cent fell due between two days and three months. Taking the cumulative position from sight up to three months, the banks had net liabilities of just over £270 million, which represented only 2½ per cent of gross liabilities in this maturity range.

Altogether, the market's position was not markedly different at the end of July 1969 from that at the end of April 1968, in spite of the great growth of the market and the intermittent bouts of pressure on the foreign exchanges during the intervening 15 months. Over that period gross liabilities, including liabilities to other London banks, more than doubled, to £15,850 million. The cumulative net position for all maturities up to three months was not very much changed between the two dates—net liabilities of just over £360 million at end-April 1968, compared with just over £270 million at end-July 1969—even though the American banks had greatly increased their sight lending to their head offices; and cumulative net liabilities from sight up to one year increased by only about £120 million, to £730 million.

The net position of British banks, including Commonwealth banks, was much the same at both dates. At end-July 1969 they were almost exactly in balance at sight, an apparent short position of £133 million being largely balanced by holdings of certificates of deposit.[5] Taking the whole range of maturities, this group of banks had, to a marginal extent, borrowed at shorter term to lend longer. Their net position with other banks in the United Kingdom broadly matched their position with banks abroad; but with other customers, and particularly overseas customers, the banks had small net liabilities at the shorter dates and roughly matching net assets at one year and over. This maturity pattern probably occurred because customers other than banks deposited liquid balances at relatively short notice, and borrowed at longer term for investment purposes (including portfolio investment).

The American banks had net sight assets of over £1,800 million at end-July 1969, because their lending to head offices was largely on an overnight basis.[6] The borrowing to finance this lending was mainly for periods up to three months so that, taking the range of maturities from sight to three months, these banks had small net liabilities of £71 million. Like the British group of banks, the American banks in London take short deposits from their overseas customers other than banks and lend to them at longer term; but deposits substantially exceed lending.

The other foreign banks had net sight assets of £150 million, mainly comprising lending by Japanese banks to their head offices and by other banks in this group to the U.K. interbank market. These sight assets were, however, rather

[5] In Table XIV.3, certificates of deposit held by reporting institutions are treated as assets maturing at the due dates; banks themselves, of course, regard certificates of deposits as fully marketable (sight) assets.

[6] Up to that time, it had been advantageous for the U.S. head offices to borrow on an overnight basis, because this had the effect of reducing reserve requirements; the method of calculating these requirements has, however, now been changed.

CHART XI.1

EURODOLLAR RATES COMPARED WITH U.S. INTEREST RATES

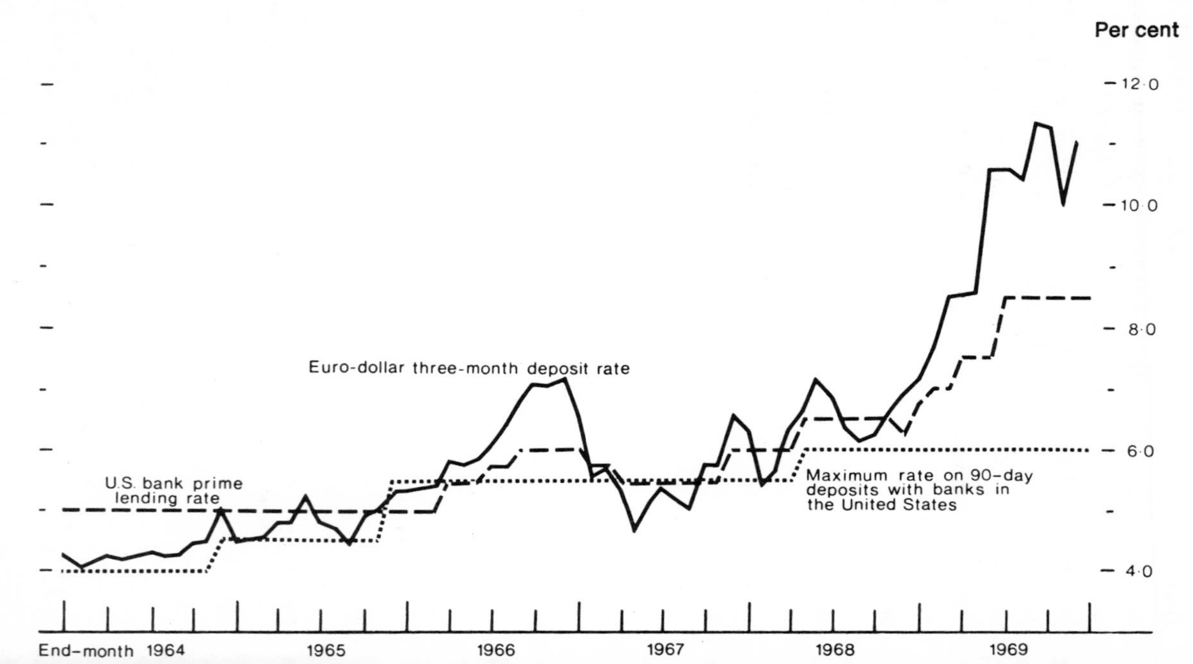

more than offset by net liabilities at longer maturities up to three months.

Many banks are prepared not only to advance foreign currencies but also to make available lines of credit, or stand-by credits, which customers (including other banks) may draw on as they require. Similarly, some banks in the United Kingdom have arranged lines of credit with overseas banks. These stand-by credits are in the nature of contingent assets and liabilities, and so are not included in the figures in the tables.

INTEREST RATES

Since the end of 1963, when the rate for three months' Eurodollar deposits in London stood at 4¼ per cent per annum, interest rates in this market have shown a tendency to rise (*see* Chart XI.1). In the earlier part of the period the Eurodollar rate was generally between the U.S. banks' prime lending rate and the maximum rate which they were permitted to pay on time deposits. However, as credit conditions in the United States became increasingly tight from late 1968 onwards, American banks borrowed Eurodollars heavily to alleviate liquidity shortages. In doing so, they drove rates to much higher levels than those ruling in the United States.[7] From around 6 per cent per annum in August 1968 rates rose to nearly 13 per cent per annum in June 1969; by the end of 1969 the rate had fallen back, but it was still just over 10 per cent per annum.

Eurodollar rates tend to influence domestic interest rates, because differences between them significantly affect the movement of overseas funds into or out of the United Kingdom. Depending mainly upon the state of confidence in ster-

[7] Chart XI.1 suggests that Eurodollar rates had also risen above those ruling in the United States during the credit shortage in 1966. In practice, this was not so. Effective U.S. lending rates are higher than those shown on the chart because borrowers are usually required to leave a proportion of the loan as a noninterest-bearing deposit.

CHART XI.2

COVERED DIFFERENTIAL BETWEEN EURODOLLAR AND U.K. LOCAL AUTHORITY RATES
(3 Months' Deposits)

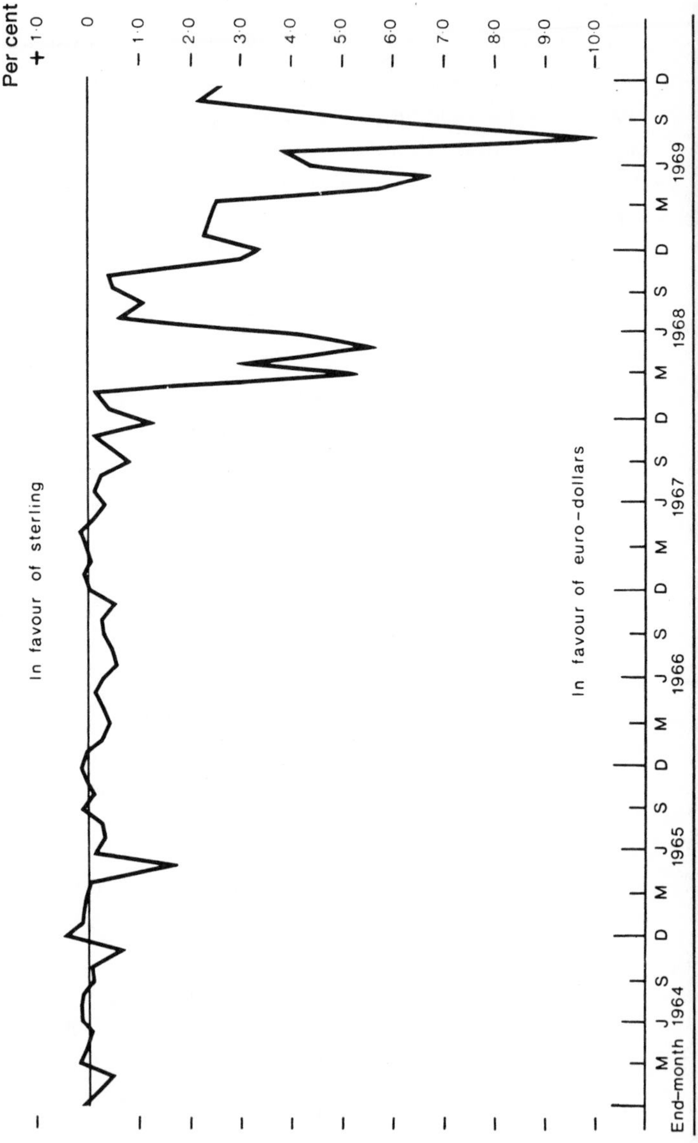

Per cent

+ 1·0
0
− 1·0
− 2·0
− 3·0
− 4·0
− 5·0
− 6·0
− 7·0
− 8·0
− 9·0
−10·0

In favour of sterling

In favour of euro-dollars

End-month M J S D 1964 M J S D 1965 M J S D 1966 M J S D 1967 M J S D 1968 M J S D 1969 ling, the comparison between Eurodollar and domestic rates might often be made after taking account of the cost of forward cover. Various domestic rates might be chosen for this comparison. Those payable in the interbank sterling market would sometimes prove the most suitable, and for some purposes the deposit rates paid by hire-purchase finance houses would be relevant. But the most widely used comparison is with the rates paid for short-term funds by local authorities. A comparison of the three months' Eurodollar rate with the return on U.K. local authority deposits of the same term, adjusted to allow for the cost of forward cover, shows that the yields were nearly the same for most of the time up to the devaluation of sterling in November 1967, save for two short periods around May 1965 and September 1967 (*see* Chart XI.2). This near identity of covered yields was almost entirely attributable to the fact that between November 1964 and devaluation the authorities supported the rate for forward sterling, keeping the discount to a very small figure. Since devaluation the rate for forward sterling has been allowed to find its own level, and has fluctuated a great deal; the cost of three months' cover has ranged between over 8 per cent per annum and, recently, as little as ⅛ per cent per annum. For much of this period, Eurodollar rates have yielded substantially more than local authority deposits, after allowing for the cost of forward cover. Indeed, as a result of the steep rise in Eurodollar rates last year, three months' deposits of Eurodollars have, since May 1969, given a higher return than U.K. local authority deposits even on an uncovered basis.

Banks in the United Kingdom will take account, among other things, of the comparison between Eurodollar rates and the covered return on funds employed in the United Kingdom when judging whether to convert foreign-currency assets into sterling, or to convert back into currency amounts previously switched into sterling. But they have little scope for employing their own funds in the Eurocurrency market because the size of the net currency assets they may hold either uncovered or against forward liabilities is restricted by foreign-exchange limits fixed by exchange control. These limits are very small in relation to the banks' total foreign-currency operations. During 1964 and 1965, the banks consistently employed in sterling part of the foreign currencies deposited with them; the net amount converted into sterling reached a peak of over £300 million during the early months of 1965. The position later changed, however, and at the end of 1969 the banks had net currency assets of nearly £60 million.

CONCLUSION

The Eurocurrency market has expanded greatly over recent years, and in particular during 1969. It has provided some banks in the United States with additional liquidity during times of credit stringency, has allowed surplus funds throughout the world to be utilized profitably, and has accommodated the financial needs of manufacturers, traders, and investors. The market has also enabled short-term capital to be mobilized rapidly within the limits of national exchange-control restrictions. The existence of this market has also led to far closer links between domestic money markets. As a result, interest-rate movements in the Eurocurrency market have been reflected to an increasing extent in domestic markets.

Although periodic disturbances on the foreign exchanges have brought inevitable strains, the Eurocurrency market has weathered these pressures with remarkably little disturbance. The only really noticeable impact has been the adjustment of interest rates, sometimes swift, to match the sudden changes in the supply of and demand for funds. The smoothness with which the market has lived through such times is largely due to its breadth and size.

Appendix

SOURCES OF INFORMATION

There are two regular sources of information available to the Bank of England on the foreign-currency positions of banks in the United Kingdom. Since December 1962 banks and similar institutions transacting foreign currency business in the United Kingdom have completed monthly statistical returns of external liabilities and claims (called E.L.C. returns), giving their customers' and their own external liabilities and claims in U.S. dollars and in other nonsterling currencies, and showing the countries from which deposits have been taken and those to which the funds have been lent. This series of figures has been published quarterly in the *Bulletin* since June 1964.

There are also returns which banks and similar institutions are required to submit monthly to exchange control and which are primarily used to observe and regulate their foreign currency positions. These returns show the positions of banks in nonsterling currencies with both U.K. residents and nonresidents and give an analysis by currencies. This exchange control series is more comprehensive than the E.L.C. returns in that it includes banks' positions with other banks in the United Kingdom and with other U.K. residents.

The two sets of returns are designed for different purposes, and the figures which they show for external liabilities and claims in nonsterling currencies are never exactly the same. One important difference is that, in the E.L.C. series, the reporting banks include the overseas liabilities and claims of their U.K. customers in the form of bills and acceptances deposited with them. In addition, the E.L.C. returns cover all overseas currencies, including currencies of the overseas sterling area; an adjustment is made to exclude such overseas sterling area currencies from the published series.

XII

ALBERTO FERRARI

Managing Director of the Banca Nazionale del Lavoro in Rome since December, 1966, Mr. Ferrari began his career in banking with Banca Commerciale in 1938. Finance expert of the International Reconstruction Committee in 1946–47, Mr. Ferrari later represented Italy for three years in Paris on the Payment Committee of the Organization for Economic Cooperation and Development. In 1951 he was named Secretary General of the Bank for International Settlements in Basel (Switzerland).

Upon his return to Italy, he was named managing director for both the Consorzio di Credito per le Opere Pubbliche and the Istituto di Credito per le Imprese di Pubblica Utilità. Mr. Ferrari was a member of various committees, such as the group of independent experts for the unification of financial markets in the European Economic Community and the Study Group of 32 economists on International Monetary Arrangements.

Alberto Ferrari, with a degree in law from Pisa University and an M.A. in economics from Yale, winner of a graduate scholarship from Bocconi University, professor of economics and finance, has been professor of history of economic thought for five years at the University of Rome. He is the author of various publications, some of which have been translated. He is Vice-Chairman of the Italian Banking Association.

The Eurodollar Market: A View from Italy

Italian participation in the Eurodollar market—and more recently, in the parallel and rapidly expanding Eurobond market—began in the early 1960s and has become increasingly more diversified and complex over the years. Such participation was greatly aided by the process of liberalization of international capital movements initiated when all major currencies were made convertible in 1958.

At first, the monetary authorities allowed Italian banks (in 1959) to keep some liquid balances abroad (or to borrow from their foreign correspondents), as was required to sustain the rapidly expanding foreign trade of that period. Later on, business and individuals, too, were permitted to engage in certain specified foreign financial transactions. Stand-by controls over capital movements have been maintained to this day, but the rules were never too rigidly applied, except for the control of banks' net foreign positions, which was part of reserve-management policies. Banks are still free to keep abroad the volume of short-term assets they wish, as long, however, as they match it by an equal amount of liabilities.

An important element in the expansion of the Eurodollar market during the sixties was the penetration of Europe by large U.S. firms and the spread of international corporations. It is mostly because of this that the effort to insulate Italian monetary trends by the mere management of banks' net foreign-exchange positions began to be seriously impaired.

When monetary policies in the United States became more restrictive and the spread between the Eurodollar rate and money rates in Italy increased sharply, the monetary authorities reacted by requiring banks (in March 1969) to bring their net foreign-exchange position into balance (i.e., to repatriate about $850 million). It was an attempt to defend the domestic interest-rate structure against upward pressures coming from abroad, but the effect of the measure was partly offset by the increased outflow of private capital, which greatly disturbed the existing equilibrium in the financial markets and in the balance of payments, and showed how elusive is the goal of insulating an open economy from monetary pressures originating abroad. The internationalization of monetary conditions was not, however, the result of the existence of the Eurodollar market—which is only a transmitter—but of the rapid liberalization of capital movements, a process which was bound to create a number of problems for Italy.

Needless to say, the conflict between monetary policies needed to further economic development and policies which a country develops as a result of its close ties with more powerful economies can only be solved with time and by strengthening fiscal policies, improving the tax system, and modernizing financial institutions in general.

The Italian experience with the Eurodollar (and Eurobond) market in the 1960s can properly be discussed from three different standpoints: that of *banks*, of *monetary policies*, and of the *repercussions on the economy in general.*

SIGNIFICANCE FOR ITALIAN BANKS

The expansion of Italian banks' money-market business abroad —the bulk of which goes to the Eurodollar market—can be gauged from the rise of the ratio of banks' foreign to total short-term liabilities, from about 6 per cent in December 1961 to 10 per cent in October 1969. Simultaneously, the Italian banks' share in the Eurodollar market—the size of which the Bank for International Settlements places at $37 billion for June 1969—reached a level of about 15 per cent. Their short-term assets and liabilities in convertible currencies amounted in October 1969 to about $5.7 and $5.2 billion, respectively.

It is chiefly the large commercial banks that deal in Eurodollars, though a strong tendency is manifest towards widening the banking base of this profitable business. At the end of 1968, Italy's "big five"[1] accounted for more than 75 per cent of all short-term foreign assets and liabilities of the entire banking system. More than 20 per cent of their short-term loans and 18 per cent of their deposit liabilities were Eurocurrency transactions.

From the viewpoint of Italian banks, at least theoretically, two classes of Eurodollar or Eurocurrency transactions should be distinguished, i.e., (1) *triangular transactions,* in which a deposit placed by a foreign resident with an Italian bank is used to effect a deposit, or make a short-term loan, to a foreign bank or business; or (2) *transfers of funds,* in which a lira deposit of an Italian resident is converted into foreign exchange, deposited with a foreign bank, or lent to a foreign resident, and vice versa. In the latter case, it must be noted, the intervention of the monetary authorities is essential for the

[1] The five largest commercial banks are the Banca Nazionale del Lavoro, the Banca Commerciale Italiana, the Credito Italiano, the Banco di Roma, and the Banco di Napoli.

conversion and often for the provision of forward insurance at specially favorable conditions.

Parallel transactions supplementing the Eurodollar market are: (3) loans to or deposits from, Italian residents, which are denominated in foreign currencies; and (4) forward transactions (swaps) with the central bank.

To give an idea of the position of the Italian banking system at the end of 1968, Table XII.1 shows the amounts outstanding on that date for these four items and for the banking system as a whole.

TABLE XII.1
FOREIGN EXCHANGE ASSETS AND LIABILITIES OF ITALIAN BANKS
(Amounts outstanding on December 31, 1968 in US$ billion)

Description	Assets	Liabilities	Balances*
1. Deposits and short-term loans in convertible currencies, from or to *foreign residents*	4.8	3.8	1.0
2. Deposits and short-term loans in convertible currencies, from or to *Italian residents*	1.7	0.5	1.2
3. Forward cover, from *Bank of Italy*		2.0	−2.0
4. Forward cover, from *the market*		0.2	−0.2
Total position	6.5	6.5	=

* — = net liability

At the end of 1968 the Italian banking system showed on each side of its consolidated balance sheet about $3.8 billion of Eurocurrencies, an amount which grew to $5.2 billion by October 1969. This is the best evidence of the extent and growth of the so-called triangular transactions resulting from constant arbitrage between currencies, over time, and in space. Extraeconomic considerations play a role in determining discrepancies in quotations, as well as expectations and different attitudes toward risk.

The spread (or margin) has now become very thin, thanks to the modern system of information and communication and to the number of efficient brokers operating everywhere. Owing to the large volume of transactions, however, profits can be attractive. The productivity of labor is above average and banks equip their foreign departments with modern computers and other electronic devices to expand this line of business as much as possible. It is interesting to note in this connection that when in March 1969 Italian banks were required to bring their net foreign positions into balance (their net creditor positions then amounted to $1,081 million), they chose to carry out this instruction by increasing their borrowing rather than reducing their lending because, from their viewpoint, it is always convenient to expand the volume of this business.

Banks try to match, as far as feasible, their foreign short-term debts with a similar amount of credits, for each currency and maturity. As a result, these transactions often do not require exchange cover, though Eurocurrency transactions are closely interwoven with parallel exchange transactions in both the spot and forward markets.

In the case of transfers of funds (or of liquidity) from Italy to other countries and vice versa (i.e., for the above-mentioned second category of transactions), conversion and a forward-exchange transaction with the Bank of Italy, or in the market, are necessary to insure against the risk of changes in parity or in the exchange rate within the legally allowed spread.

It must be added that from the banks' viewpoint, foreign-currency denominated loans or deposits of Italian residents are about the same thing as Eurodollar transactions, although it is certainly not so from the standpoint of the balance of payments and of domestic liquidity. Banks also need, therefore, to obtain exchange cover in respect to their net creditor position vis-à-vis their Italian clients (see Table XII.1).

Forward cover is granted by the Bank of Italy at its discretion and generally at a lower cost (for many years the central bank did not charge for this service) than could be obtained in the market. As will be seen later, the monetary authorities have relied on changes in the cost of forward cover as an additional monetary weapon in their armory. The practice of granting foreign-currency denominated loans to Italian residents is chiefly explained by the greater freedom enjoyed from the requirements of the interbank agreement in establishing interest rates.

SIGNIFICANCE FOR MONETARY POLICIES

As already mentioned, the Bank of Italy has relied, from the very beginning of the Eurodollar market, on its power to control banks' foreign-exchange transactions as an efficient tool of overall liquidity and official-reserve management. The central bank carried out its policies, chiefly, by allowing commercial banks to keep a net-creditor or net-debtor position (as the case may be), by carefully regulating its supply of forward-exchange cover (at favorable conditions), and by requiring banks at times to bring their foreign position into balance within a definite time period. But generally, banks were allowed to do this by changing either the level of their gross lending or of their borrowing, or both, according to the bank's preference. It was thus possible to inject or drain off liquidity and, simultaneously, to transfer reserves from the Eurodollar market to the official pool, or vice versa, as circumstances dictated. Needless to say, the success of these policies depended to a large extent upon the existence of an interest-rate differential between Italy and the Eurodollar market which was not in conflict with the policy objectives of the central bank. (For example, in order to drain off liquidity, the Eurodollar interest rate must be above the corresponding rate in Italy.)

It may be of interest to review briefly the policies pursued by the Bank of Italy during the sixties in the use of these particular instruments. At the beginning of the decade, and during the inflationary period from 1959 to 1963, Italian banks were encouraged to import liquidity from the Eurodollar market. Since at that time the interest rate was higher in Italy than in the Eurodollar market, banks took full advantage of the official placet and borrowed heavily. By December 1963 they had brought their net debtor position to a record high of about $1 billion. At the same time the Bank of Italy was able to finance, thanks to this policy, the deficit in the balance of payments without drawing down its official gold and exchange reserves. (Note that banks have brought their foreign accounts into a large debtor position by increasing their liabilities more than their assets.)

In mid-1963 the Government adopted a disinflationary program designed to adjust the balance-of-payments disequilibrium. A cornerstone of this program was the instruction given to banks to bring their foreign positions gradually into balance, which they did, this time by increasing short-term loans to foreign correspondents to the level of their borrowing from them (see Table XII.2). The net debtor position of the banking system thus swung into a net creditor position of $101 million at the end of 1965.

In the following years there was growing monetary tension abroad and Eurodollar interest rates surged to levels high above the corresponding rates in Italy. As a result, Italian banks found it convenient to continue to move funds abroad on a net basis and this they did by increasing by $2.6 billion their lending abroad and by $1.6 billion their borrowings. Simultaneously, lending to Italian residents in foreign cur-

TABLE XII.2

POLICY-INDUCED CHANGES IN THE EXCHANGE POSITION OF ITALIAN BANKS

(Convertible currencies in US$ million)

DESCRIPTION	GROSS ASSETS	GROSS LIABILITIES	NET POSITION
December 1960–	707	707	—
December 1963	1,190	2,155	− 965
Changes	483	1,448	− 965
December 1963–	1,190	2,155	− 965
December 1965	2,312	2,211	+ 101
Changes	1,122	56	+1,066
December 1965–	2,312	2,211	+ 101
March 1969	4,916	3,835	+1,081
Changes	2,604	1,624	+ 980
March 1969–	4,916	3,835	+1,081
October 1969	5,747	5,230	+ 517
Changes	831	1,395	− 564

SOURCE: Bank of Italy, *Statistical Bulletin,* Nov./Dec. 1969, Table 57.

rencies declined, as it had become almost prohibitive because of its cost or of the danger of parity changes.

By March 1969 net lending abroad by Italian banks in convertible currencies (the bulk of which was in the Eurodollar market) amounted to $1,081 million. Though the authorities had, at first, favored the outflow of capital in this form because it helped relieve the strain in the Eurodollar market while alleviating the pressure on the U.S. gold stock, in March 1969 they felt that it was necessary to curb it in consideration of the worsening of the Italian balance-of-payments position. A new directive was thus issued in March 1969 requiring banks to bring their net foreign-exchange positions gradually into balance again.

At the same time, the central bank increased the cost of its swap transactions with banks, and tried in other ways to curb the long-term outflow of private capital through banking channels. For example, Italian banks could no longer act as underwriters for Eurobond issues, except when authorized, and foreign mutual funds were required to obtain a special authorization in order to sell their parts in Italy (the permit was granted only when the foreign funds invested at least 50 per cent of their portfolio in Italian securities).

But controls are now more difficult to enforce as a result of the appearance and development of nonbank financial channels linking Italy with the Eurodollar market and transmitting tensions and strains in a sensitive and very rapid way. Moreover, capital transfers through bank-note remittances (which are illegal) increased so much in the last months of 1969 that they now represent a real threat to the Italian balance of payments and weaken the once-strong position of the national security markets.

SIGNIFICANCE FOR THE ECONOMY

From the standpoint of the Italian economy, the Eurodollar market can be thought of as a delicate and efficient mechanism which helps international trade and financial dealings but which also facilitates the transmission, throughout the Western world, of strains originating anywhere in the system. And this has been particularly true after the Eurodollar market ceased to be the banks' private domain.

Indeed, this new money market provides a highly efficient instrument for "exporting" to the rest of the world the monetary policies that a major country sees fit to adopt.

For all these reasons the market is looked upon in Italy as a sophisticated improvement on the existing international financial institutions, but one which arrived somewhat prematurely, i.e., before the country had a chance to modernize its own institutions, tax system, and budget. In fact, the

Italian economy does not seem quite ready for a situation in which the edge of the independent monetary tools is blunted or perhaps the tools themselves have become ineffective.

Italy was able to keep her monetary policies unchanged (a stable and relatively low long-term interest rate and an expanding money supply) for about a year after the Federal Reserve Bank of the United States took a more restrictive stance. It is only since the last months of 1969 that the authorities have gradually abandoned their support of the quotations of fixed-income securities (adopted several years ago for the purpose of keeping the long-term rate at a suitable level for promoting capital investment, attracting savings, and attaining the economic targets of the 1966–70 Plan).

But the diversion of savings to foreign markets due to the attraction of higher interest rates and other reasons was depriving the government and medium-term banks of much needed resources traditionally obtained in the market for fixed-income securities. International financial integration, which the Italian monetary authorities always supported at heart, ended up, in practice, by one-sidedly stimulating the outflow of savings from a country which, in the field of economic development, still has pressing unfulfilled needs. This situation prompted a series of measures, starting with the gradual withdrawal of Government support from fixed-income security quotations and culminating in a decree of January 1970 which increased from 5 to 6 per cent the interest-rate ceiling on mortgage bonds. New fixed-income security quotations are now (February 1970) competitive with the Eurobond market. Other interest rates are gradually being brought into line with those prevailing in foreign countries. Thus, Italy has been constrained to adopt a policy of high interest rates, perhaps against her better judgment, by the pressure coming from abroad and transmitted through the Eurodollar and Eurobond markets.

If, on the one hand, a relatively low rate of interest is an incentive for business investment but diverts a major portion of Italian savings to foreign countries, a high rate of interest is, on the other hand, likely to reverse the whole situation without perhaps improving the basic climate for investment. It is difficult to say which is the better solution. All that one can state is that the main burden for the achievement of general economic objectives will now fall on fiscal policies.

The Bank of Italy estimates that the proportion of household savings which went abroad rose from 5.7 per cent in 1965 to 15.4 per cent in 1968. According to early indications, this proportion reached 26 per cent in 1969. True, the Italian balance of payments on current account has been strong, showing a surplus of close to $1.7 billion (almost $2.0 billion in 1968). But the overflow of capital was more than enough to offset all the current surplus and there was a loss of monetary reserves of $1.4 billion.

IN SUMMARY

In brief, the development on the European continent of efficient international money and capital markets (Eurocurrencies and Eurobonds) is, strictly from the Italian viewpoint, an event full of lights and shadows.

On the one hand, international financial relations and foreign trade—which are the major elements sustaining growth in Italy—are helped by the existence of these markets; other benefits accrue in the form of financial efficiency and know-how. On the other hand, however, repercussions affecting the pattern of savings and the propensity to invest, although they are difficult to appraise, could hinder the achievement of national goals of economic development, at least until other flexible policy tools have been developed.

XIII

YOSHIZANE IWASA

Mr. Iwasa was born in 1906 in Tokyo. Upon graduation from Tokyo Imperial University in 1928, he entered The Yasuda Bank, Limited, predecessor of The Fuji Bank, Limited, which has been foremost among Japanese commercial banks since 1945. He rose to directorship in 1948, became Deputy Chairman in 1957, and Chairman of the Board and President in 1963.

Because of his broad range of interests and wealth of experience, Mr. Iwasa has held positions of leadership in numerous business and economic groups. He has long been prominent in the financial councils of the Japan Federation of Economic Organizations (Keidanren) and was elected its Vice-President in 1969.

He plays a significant role in developing Japanese finance and also in encouraging fuller Japanese participation in the global economy. He was instrumental in founding the Japan Committee for Economic Development and the Japan Committee of the Business and Industrial Advisory Committee of the Organization for Economic Cooperation and Development. He was also one of the original promoters of the Japan-California Association and the Pacific Basin Economic Cooperation Committee. In February 1969, he was elected Chairman of the Board of Directors of the Private Investment Company for Asia, a newly established multinational private institution.

The Eurodollar Market: A View from Japan

An observer in Japan can view the Eurodollar market from different angles and examine a variety of aspects. The following report will first relate the past connections between Japan and the Eurodollar market and the significance of these relations; then, the future role which the Eurodollar market will be called upon to play on the stage of the world economy will be taken up and its impact on Japan discussed. The views expressed are those of the author as a private citizen. Since there is a great dearth of firm statistical data on Eurodollar transactions, the statistical information given in the text is based almost entirely on estimates.

JAPAN AND THE DEVELOPMENT OF THE EURODOLLAR MARKET

The involvement of Japan in the Eurodollar market began with the acceptance of Eurodollar deposits by the London branches of Japanese banks. This was in 1960, when the Eurodollar market was still in its initial stage. Since then, the market has grown and with it the deposit balances held by the Japanese banks which, in 1968, were estimated at over $1 billion. All through these years, the Japanese banks were active as ultimate borrowers in the Eurodollar market, a wholesale market for funds. The Eurodollars borrowed by the banks were largely short-term funds with a maturity of less than six months; the banks lent these funds, which were partly left in the form of dollars and partly converted into yen, to their customers chiefly for financing short-term foreign-trade transactions.

Eurodollar Transactions of Japanese Banks

Originally, transactions in the Eurodollar market involved short-term deposits but, thanks to the very rapid development of the market, transactions in medium-term deposits with a maturity of two years or longer have also become possible in recent years. Connections with the Eurobond market, which handles medium- and long-term funds, have also become stronger. Furthermore, the issuance of negotiable certificates of deposit for Eurodollars has made transactions in small amounts possible. Generally speaking, the market has gained in stability and its internal transformation has resulted in a gradual diversification of Japan's relations with the market. In 1967, Japanese banks raised medium-term funds in the Eurodollar market to finance the development of overseas raw-material sources.

In the fourth quarter of 1968, interest rates on Eurodollars began to rise, chiefly because of the steep increase in borrowing by American banks; by 1969, these rates had become higher than the Japanese call-money rates. This made it unprofitable for Japanese banks to use Eurodollars for trade financing. Moreover, as one measure for coping with the recent large increase in Japan's foreign-currency holdings, the monetary authorities, in September 1969, supplied the banks with foreign currency out of the official reserves under a swap arrangement and advised the banks to reduce their net borrowing of Eurodollars. The Japanese banks, therefore, began to relend in the Eurodollar market the funds they had borrowed there. In this way, they became normal members of the Eurodollar market.

Eurodollar Transactions of Nonbanking Enterprises

Japanese enterprises satisfied part of their enormous fund requirements by borrowing from foreign banks or by floating foreign bonds. Until the first half of 1963, the principal lenders were American or Canadian banks, and bonds denominated in dollars were issued in the United States.

As a result of the imposition of the Interest Equalization Tax by the U.S. Government in July 1963, the largest part of Japanese dollar debentures were floated in Europe. A portion of the dollar bonds previously issued in the United States had been taken up by European investors, but with the flotation of dollar bonds in Europe, Japan tapped the European capital market directly. The value of Japanese government bonds and corporate debentures denominated in foreign currencies and emitted in Europe amounted to $155 million in 1968 and $261 million in 1969, equivalent to 5 per cent and 10 per cent, respectively, of the total of Eurobond issues in each of these two years.

In 1965, the U.S. Government imposed new restrictions on foreign investment by American corporations; included in those measures was the application of the Interest Equalization Tax to all foreign loans by American banks with a maturity exceeding one year. Hence, American and Canadian banks lent Eurodollars to Japanese firms through their European branches, and Japanese enterprises came to rely more and more on funds borrowed from European banks, thus strengthening Japan's relations with the Eurodollar market. The value of borrowings in foreign currency by Japanese corporations from foreign banks has been estimated at $605 million for 1968 and $456 million for the nine months from

January to September 1969, the largest part of which consisted of Eurodollars.

Eurodollars and Investment in Japanese Securities

Lately, Eurodollars have become an important source of funds for foreign investment in Japanese stocks and other securities. Compared with stock prices in other industrial countries, the Japanese stock-price level is low if the strong growth potential of the Japanese economy is taken into account. Foreign investors, therefore, displayed a growing interest in Japanese stocks which found expression in a great upsurge of stock purchases in 1968. International investment trusts specializing in Japanese stocks were organized, and already existing investment trusts added Japanese stocks to their portfolios. The net increase (purchases minus sales) in the acquisition of Japanese stocks by foreign investors amounted to $220 million in 1968 and $678 million in 1969; the share of European funds in these investments was estimated at $206 million in 1968 and $297 million in 1969, and Eurodollars made up at least part of these funds.

Restrictions on Eurodollar Transactions

Japan, as is generally known, continues to maintain various restrictions on foreign capital transactions, and Eurodollar transactions are no exception. Under the foreign-currency reserve fund system, banks borrowing Eurodollars are obliged to incorporate a certain percentage (at present 15 per cent) into the special foreign-exchange assets. Moreover, the monetary authorities have fixed for each bank a ceiling on borrowings of Eurodollars and other specified short-term foreign-currency funds, and borrowings exceeding this limit are prohibited. The authorities have also placed a ceiling upon the amount of Eurodollars each bank can convert into yen and use for yen financing.

These quantitative restrictions on Eurodollar transactions are apparently related to the following problems inherent in the Eurodollar market. First, Eurodollars are essentially short-term funds of a very volatile nature readily influenced by political uncertainty or changes in interest rates. But interest rates on Eurodollars have usually been lower, and banks can hardly be expected not to make use of these low-cost funds. If, however, outstanding balances of Eurodollar borrowings become too large, foreign-exchange reserves will get an unrealistic boost and foreign-exchange assets as well as liabilities may be affected by the unpredictable and sometimes erratic behavior of these funds. The repayment of Eurodollar debts may have a considerable impact on reserve assets and there is a possibility of disturbances in the foreign-exchange market and even speculation against the yen.

Second, Eurodollar operations are conducted on an international scale and these funds may move into any money market. In a country like Japan, where the authorities rely on credit restraints for adjusting the national economy, the free entry of Eurodollar funds may limit the effectiveness of official policy.

Appraisal

At the end of 1969, 14 Japanese banks, 4 securities companies, and more than 70 other corporations had subsidiaries, branch offices, or representatives in London, the center of the Eurodollar market. Research and gathering of information on Eurodollar transactions and the state of the market is one of the main tasks of these offices.

The Japanese Government does not publish statistics which would show in a comprehensive and definite way Japan's involvement in the Eurodollar market, but the figures given in the 39th Annual Report of the Bank for International Settlements (BIS) may serve as a benchmark. The BIS estimated the size of the Eurodollar market at the end of 1968 at $25 billion and the balance of funds used by Japanese enterprises at $1.7 billion.

Eurodollar transactions of Japanese banks and other enterprises, although limited by official restrictions, contributed in some degree to the growth of Japan's economy. The 1960s were a time of rapid economic expansion and Japanese enterprises needed enormous funds for the enlargement of their activities in production, distribution, and trade. Except for a certain period in 1966, interest rates on Eurodollar funds were lower than those on yen funds until 1968, and Japanese banks as well as other corporations always used Eurodollars to the full extent permitted by the government. The supply of commercially advantageous funds through the Eurodollar market helped to improve the productivity of Japanese enterprises and to strengthen their competitive position so that the market performed a valuable function for the Japanese economy. Until 1968, Japan's reserve assets were hardly sufficient relative to the size of the country's foreign trade and the balance of its foreign liabilities. The Eurodollar borrowings by banks and other enterprises mitigated the drain on Japan's foreign-exchange reserves resulting from the unfavorable balance on current account.

FUTURE PROGRESS OF THE EURODOLLAR MARKET

Two aspects will be decisive for the future development of the Eurodollar market, its continuity and its stability.

The most important reason for the origin and subsequent growth of the Eurodollar market was the accumulation of capital in the form of dollar balances by the European nations after their recovery from the ravages of the Second World War. Since there is no other currency to replace the dollar as an international reserve currency and as a means for international settlements, the European nations will continue to hold dollar balances. The market, therefore, will continue to function, and the mechanism of capital demand and supply will not easily be put out of action. There may be no further increase in the market of the same huge proportions as lately, but the flow of dollars into the market will not come to a complete halt. Profits from Middle East oil contracts are the source of additional funds; interest payments on outstanding loans and sinking-fund repayments already provide sizeable additions to the Eurodollar balances.

Initially, Eurodollars were short-term, extremely volatile funds and, in times of international currency instability, large amounts have been used for gold and exchange speculation. The increase in the size of the market has had the effect not only of augmenting the funds which can be mobilized for speculative purposes but also of making medium-term transactions possible. The diversification of operational instruments, such as the issuance of negotiable certificates of deposit representing Eurodollars, opened the way for drawing small-sized idle funds into the market. Depending on the point of view, the present state of the market can be considered more stable than in the beginning. The Eurodollar market is often regarded with suspicion because it served as a channel for speculative operations and, recently, as a mechanism for spreading high interest rates. But the market is not the cause of gold and currency speculation nor was it originally responsible for the world-wide phenomenon of high interest rates. International cooperation and moderation in economic management will make a further steady expansion of the Eurodollar market possible.

JAPAN AND THE FUTURE OF THE EURODOLLAR MARKET: A CONCLUSION

I want to conclude by briefly stating my personal opinion on the future role of the Eurodollar market and its importance for Japan.

The 1970s have been called the era of internationalization. In the advanced countries, global enterprises, whose activities transcend national boundaries, prepare the ground for the establishment of a postindustrial society based chiefly on information technology; for the progress of the developing countries, assistance in the form of huge amounts of capital secured through international cooperation is required. The Eurodollar and Eurobond markets, which have now reached proportions conterminous with the world, constitute a potent instrument for the international financing of undertakings involving international enterprises or requiring international cooperation.

In this international environment, Japan will hardly have any other choice but to proceed with the liberalization of capital transactions and the internationalization of banks and other enterprises. The present restrictions on Eurodollar transactions will gradually be relaxed and Japan will go into the Eurodollar market not only for raising finance but also for putting temporary capital surpluses to work.

As mentioned previously, the Eurodollar market involves various problems; until now, however, international cooperation has made it possible to overcome occasional crises. The market will continue to grow independently of the factors which brought it into existence and to operate as an international money market indispensable to world trade. Hopefully, the meaning and function of the market will be recognized and the arrangements for international collaboration will make further progress.

In accord with this world-wide trend, Japan will cooperate with all countries in the future development of the market. Recently, Japan was made a member of the Bank for International Settlements; this was a gratifying event in as much as it enables this country to strive with the other advanced nations to maintain the stability of the international money market. The Japanese banks and the entire business community are convinced that the growth of the Eurodollar market will contribute to the progress of the world economy. Cooperating with their partners in the market, conforming to economic principles and the rules of fair play in their competition, and observing self-discipline in their transactions, they will do their best to promote the steady growth of the market.

XIV

E. STOPPER

Dr. Stopper, a Doctor of Economic Science, was educated at the Universities of St. Gall, London, Paris, and Geneva. Following several years of activity in the export trade and in banking, he joined the Commercial Division of the Swiss Federal Department for Economic Affairs in 1939. From 1945 to 1953 he acted as Secretary of the Swiss Association for Trade and Industry and subsequently as a Manager of Nestlé Alimentana Ltd.

In 1953, the Federal Council called Dr. Stopper from private enterprise to assume the post of Delegate for Trade Agreements, entrusting him specially with the cultivation of connections with overseas countries. At the end of 1960, Dr. Stopper was appointed Director of the Swiss Federal Administration of Finance and, one year later, Director for Foreign Trade Relations. At the same time he was a leading counsellor to the Swiss Government in matters relating to general economic policy.

On June 17, 1966, Dr. Stopper was elected President of the Board of General Management of the Swiss National Bank.

For the past 12 years, Dr. Stopper has been Honorary Lecturer in Economics of Basle University.

The Eurodollar Market: A View from Switzerland

THE VOLUME OF SWITZERLAND'S PARTICIPATION

Balances held with foreign banks, as returned by the Swiss banks in their balance sheets at the end of September 1969, exceeded $6,000 million. These—if the comparatively small working balances are disregarded—may be apportioned to the Euromarket. To be added are the investments on trust that do not figure in the balance sheets of the banks; their volume is estimated at $2,000 million. Furthermore, Swiss nonbanks are likely to have placed directly with foreign banks Euromarket investments to the extent of $1,000 million. These estimates add up to about $9,000 million relating to Euromarket investments administered from Switzerland. Liabilities vis-à-vis the Euromarket very likely amount to less than $6,000 million.

THE EXPANSION OF SHORT-TERM BUSINESS

The Swiss economy itself offers only very limited investment opportunities of a profitable nature as far as short-term foreign funds are concerned. This is due partly to the small size of its market and partly to the fact that the savings accruing from Switzerland's economic activity at home and abroad exceed, as a rule, the volume required for the financing of domestic investments.

It was, therefore, primarily the development of a large Euromoney market free of any government restrictions that has enabled the Swiss banks to expand substantially their international short-term banking business. It offers to them a broad scale of opportunities to accept and reinvest short-term funds abroad. The more liquid and more profitable Euromarket investments appear to be, the more favorable are the terms that the big banks are in a position to offer to their foreign depositors. These opportunities have been taken advantage of above all by the big commercial banks whose share in the overall volume of short-term and medium-term foreign business is more than two-thirds.

Largely because of the existence of the Euromarket, the three biggest institutes were able to expand their balance-sheet totals by nearly 80 per cent within the last two years.

The funds accruing to the banks for investments on the Euromarket are likely to originate chiefly from the following sources:

1. Deposits of foreign customers;
2. Deposits of foreign banks;
3. Income on assets administered on behalf of foreign customers, and the conversion of foreign-securities investments originating from such assets into time deposits;
4. Deposits of Swiss customers, or the conversion of Swiss investments in foreign securities into time deposits;
5. The cutting down of domestic liquidity in favor of Euromarket investments.

A part of such funds is exposed to the risk of heavy fluctuations, particularly as far as deposits by foreign banks are concerned. The Swiss banks have made adequate provision against such risks: Their own short-term investments with foreign banks cover more than twice the amount of their liabilities vis-à-vis foreign banks. Short-term Euromarket investments with foreign banks also cover three-fifths of the overall amount of liabilities vis-à-vis foreign nonbanks. The remaining two-fifths of these liabilities are being offset by a much larger amount of claims vis-à-vis foreign nonbanks. If the Euromarket functions normally, the Swiss banks do not depend on the official monetary reserves of Switzerland's central bank to meet their obligations vis-à-vis foreign creditors.

THE EUROMARKET'S INFLUENCE ON SWITZERLAND'S MONEY SUPPLY

The lucrative short-term investment opportunities offered by the Euromarket have led to a significant change in the liquidity policy not only of the banks but also of nonbanks.

The liquidity of the banks held in domestic currency, the percentage of which was high in the past, has been reduced in favor of short-term Euromarket investments yielding high interest. This is clearly manifested by the opposite movement of balances held by the banking system with the central bank and of its short-term liabilities. In the past two years, the balances of the banks maintained with the central bank between quarter-ends have increased very little, although in the same period there has been a very heavy growth in short-term liabilities.

The change in the liquidity policy of nonbanks is reflected in the heavy increase in time balances at the expense of sight balances. From September 1967 to September 1969, time deposits placed with the big commercial banks grew by 115 per cent, sight deposits, on the other hand, by only 34 per cent. In previous years, the movement registered by these two items in the balance sheet was far more parallel. Funds stemming from time deposits being particularly suited for investment on the Euromarket, the banks have been in a position to offer for such funds especially attractive interest rates.

So far, the supply of domestic credit has not been impaired

by the attraction of the Euromarket. The growth in the volume of domestic lendings by the big commercial banks amounted to 8.96 per cent from January 1, 1968 to December 31, 1968, and 23.04 per cent from January 1, 1969 to December 31, 1969.

The fact that domestic lendings have increased so heavily despite the substantially lower interest-rate level in Switzerland (compared with that of the Euromarket) may be attributed chiefly to the banks' competition in trying to secure as great a share as possible in the volume of domestic lendings. In the past few years the banks have offered their domestic customers higher credit ceilings which, since the end of 1968, the customers have made use of to a growing extent as a consequence of the economic boom.

But the attraction of the Euromarket did have an influence on the domestic interest-rate level. However, this influence made itself clearly felt only in the course of 1969, when the peak rate for three-month dollar deposits rose to 12¾ per cent (as compared with 7⅜ per cent in 1968).

Nevertheless, the increase in domestic rates in 1969 was still relatively modest. Compared with the previous year, the major interest rates went up as follows: The major banking group engaging in the domestic credit business raised the rate for current-account advances against collateral security by ¼ to ½ per cent, reaching 6 per cent inclusive of commission charges. With regard to first mortgages, the average interest-rate level rose by about 0.5 per cent and is now moving towards 5¼ per cent. The rates for medium-term bonds issued by the big banks and the cantonal banks went up by ¼ per cent, to 5¼ per cent. The average yield on federal bonds improved by 1 per cent and that on cantonal loans by 0.57 per cent, reaching 5.4 and 5.6 per cent, respectively, by the end of 1969.

Having shown a surplus in savings these past few years along with an appreciable slowing in the pace at which the cost of living increased, Switzerland would probably have experienced falling rather than rising interest rates until the second quarter of 1969 had they not been affected by developments on the Euromarket.

If the interest charge for domestic lendings has shown only a modest rise, this is due to the fact that hitherto the banks have obtained funds at a moderate rate of interest and in a measure sufficiently large to take care of the domestic lending business. However, there are clear signs that henceforth the influence of the high Euromarket interest rates might be felt more strongly. On the one hand, domestic credit expansion has registered a marked acceleration since the end of 1968 and especially since the second quarter of 1969; on the other hand, major Swiss investors have become increasingly inclined to demand from Swiss banks, under the influence of competitive offers from abroad, higher returns on time deposits. In order to prevent such funds from turning to foreign banks, the Swiss banks are prompted increasingly to meet the wishes of their major customers, i.e., in more and more cases to pay interest at rates that exceed those of the present yield on domestic business.

With a simultaneously growing volume of domestic credit grants, the bigger the portion of the banks' resources on which interest at a higher rate is to be paid, the stronger the banks' inclination to raise the interest rates in the domestic lending business as well. The nearer the rates demanded by the major customers are to those of the Euromarket, the more strongly the banks feel prompted to accept the funds only in a trust capacity for Euromarket investments, that is, they carry no commitment in respect to the risk involved. Such funds do not qualify for inclusion in the banks' free-liquidity reservoir which might also be utilized for domestic credit transactions. This, too, may contribute towards a rise in interest rates in the domestic lending business of the banks.

THE EUROMARKET'S INFLUENCE ON MONETARY POLICY

The very vast Euromarket and the considerable size of the Euromarket investments of the Swiss banks have a bearing on the limits and application of Switzerland's monetary policy which, at present, is directed towards slowing down economic activity.

For a small country which is free of any restrictions regarding transactions with foreign countries and which has a banking system closely linked with the Euromarket, this market functions as a reservoir which, according to the interest-rate differential and the economic situation, either absorbs liquidity from the domestic market or furnishes liquidity to the domestic market.

So long as there is an attractive interest margin in favor of the Euromarket, the banks will convert any portion of liquid cash which is not absolutely necessary for their domestic business into short-term Euromarket investments. In the event of the interest margin narrowing appreciably, growing repatriations of funds hitherto invested on the Euromarket would have to be reckoned with if there is a heavy demand for domestic credit and/or liquidity.

In shaping a restrictive monetary policy, the question arises whether an artificial increase in interest rates or a direct limitation of credit expansion would slow down economic activity more effectively. The experience of other countries has shown that in times of an excessive upward trend, characterized by a surplus demand for goods and labor and thus a heavy increase in prices and wages, higher interest charges by themselves produce only a very limited slowing-down effect and this, at best, only after considerable delay. In addition, limits are set on the tightening of the interest screw. As soon as the margin between the domestic interest-rate level and that of the Euromoney market narrows to about 1½ per cent, sizeable repatriations of Euromarket investments can be expected. In that event, any endeavors designed to slow down economic activity by means of interest-rate increases would be doomed. An artificial rise in interest rates would also meet with political opposition and lead to a strong demand for increased government assistance for housing—the area which would be most affected—and thus the move would lose much of its effectiveness. It is for these various reasons that the Swiss monetary authorities have decided to introduce a direct limitation on the admissible volume of credit. They expect that this measure will have a marked slowing-down effect.

Accordingly, the pursuance of an active open-market policy has been renounced so far. In view of the tightness of domestic liquidity, the placing of money-market paper especially created for this purpose would very soon encounter interest-rate competition from the Euromarket. The central bank would have to be prepared to offer for the funds it absorbs interest rates that approach those of the Euromarket. Subsequently, the central bank would be offered funds emanating from liquidations of Euromarket investments. The existing tightness of domestic liquidity would, therefore, hardly be reduced. Moreover, the banks would not be likely to acquire such paper in sufficient amounts to reduce their liquidity potential on the Euromarket to such an extent that they would have to restrict their own domestic lendings. The fact that the central bank offers high rates for open-market paper would, however, accelerate the narrowing of the gap between the domestic interest-rate level and that of the Euromarket, thus facilitating the repatriation of Euromarket investments for the purpose of domestic lendings.

It is for similar reasons that, so far, no minimum reserves have been called in as an anticyclical measure. Such non-interest-bearing minimum reserves would reduce domestic liquidity (which is very tight anyhow) only momentarily, for the amounts called in would immediately be substituted by repatriations of Euromarket money. No doubt the funds first used for that purpose would be the counterpart of those deposits for which the banks pay interest at domestic rates. Accordingly, the volume of the liquidity reservoir, which is primarily employed for the alimentation of the less profitable domestic-credit expansion, would diminish.

With a view to maintaining the liquidity required for their current transactions, the banks would, therefore, increasingly be dependent on the repatriation of Euromarket funds that constitute the counterpart of deposits on which they have to pay interest at rates close to those of the Euromarket. In addition, there would be a loss of earnings on those Euromarket investments that had to be reduced in order to meet minimum reserve requirements. As a result, banks would increase substantially domestic interest rates which would stimulate the repatriation of funds without rapidly reducing the rate of domestic-credit expansion.

On the other hand, direct limitation on the expansion of the volume of domestic credit increases the interest-rate level to a lesser degree. The lower domestic level prevailing at the moment may keep the lendings of the banks more easily within the limits corresponding to the inflow of funds on which the interest payable is governed. The banks would be less dependent on repatriating Euromarket investments in order to meet their domestic liquidity requirements. This is all the more important because a growing portion of these investments is being financed by funds on which the banks themselves have to pay interest at rates influenced by the Euromarket.

Judging from past experience, the restricted volume available for the granting of new credits is not apportioned primarily according to the level of the interest rate offered but is based on qualitative criteria such as solvency of the borrower and the purpose of application. This puts the main emphasis of the measures designed to slow down economic activity on the selective allotment of a reduced volume of new credits and not on an increase in the interest-rate level.

Admittedly, under this system a certain rise in the interest rates as an accompaniment of cyclical overheating is unavoidable. However, the upward trend is of a slower and more moderate nature.

It is also true that a direct-limitation approach allows for the possibility that borrowers who can not be satisfied domestically will turn to the Euromarket; but so long as the margin between domestic interest rates and those of the Euromarket remains relatively wide, such escape operations are not expected to assume considerable proportions. The Euromarket is open only to big firms, and these are less dependent on borrowings. Moreover, short-term Euromarket borrowings are not suited for the financing of long-term investment projects. Such a type of financing would be inconsistent with the tradition of the Swiss business community. Besides, the Swiss banks have undertaken to refrain from assisting in escape operations. The maintenance of the Euromarket's attractive interest margin prevents funds that, properly considered, are of a long-term character but because of the high interest obtainable have been invested by nonbanks on a short-term basis on the Euromarket, from being repatriated and lent to the domestic business community under evasion of the banks.

If, however, under this restrictive system the interest margin in relation to the Euromarket narrows appreciably (for instance, on account of a marked relaxation of the U.S. monetary policy), the direct limitation of credit expansion might also lose part of its effectiveness. In such a situation, it is feared, nonbanks in particular might repatriate appreciable amounts of funds and act as moneylenders outside the banking system.

These explanations show how strongly the existence of the Euromarket influences the shaping of a Swiss monetary policy.

THE EUROMONEY MARKET: AN APPRAISAL

The Euromoney market which, in its substance, is actually a Eurodollar market, serves the purpose of rendering the world more capable of absorbing the short-term indebtedness of the United States. This is particularly true since the restrictive U.S. monetary policy has caused the American business community to pay high interest rates for the funds in question and to make the dollar an instrument yielding interest at attractive rates.

At the same time, it conceals to what extent the international monetary system is based on a dollar which has become greatly susceptible to inflation. Inherent in this are risks that might emerge if and when U.S. monetary policy is relaxed prior to the achievement of a substantial improvement in the U.S. trade balance. A massive relaxation of the restrictive U.S. monetary policy might also lead very quickly to a substantial shrinkage of the market volume. For one thing, the market would have to reckon with the cancellation of the "circular flow," which is not necessarily to be regarded as an unfavorable aspect. However, if interest rates on the Euromarket fall below national interest rates in Europe, this might result in increased conversions of dollars into European currencies, i.e., in an increased accrual of dollars to the European central banks. This further shrinkage of the market might involve disturbances.

In particular, the pursuance of a restrictive monetary policy in the European countries, which is necessary at present because of prevailing inflationary tendencies, could be greatly impeded. Inasmuch as these countries give high priority to the fight against inflation, they would increasingly have to turn to instruments other than monetary policy to maintain control. Adequate strengthening of the fiscal policy over time would encounter difficulties and would lead to results only very slowly. Direct intervention measures for the purpose of slowing down demand—for instance, in the form of a direct limitation on the volume of capital investments, or a wages-and-price ceiling—would be very difficult to carry through and success would be limited. Direct measures might also lead to speculation in anticipation of more frequent changes in the rate of exchange by way of revaluation, which could result in disturbing shifts of Euromarket funds. There would be the danger of the Euromarket having a destabilizing rather than a compensatory effect.

The risk of more frequent changes in the exchange rates would hardly be beneficial to the development of the Euromarket. Stable exchange rates, under present conditions, presuppose that the major countries, from the monetary point of view, are prepared to subject themselves to the influences of the development of the U.S. economy. In the long run, however, this can surely be expected only if the United States succeeds in mastering inflationary influences and if U.S. short-term indebtedness vis-à-vis the remaining world no longer increases in the same measure as registered in recent years. The United States would further have to prove that it is in a position to reduce their present short-term indebtedness. Until such time as this state of affairs is achieved, there are inherent in the Euromarket not only advantages but also risks that are not to be disregarded.

XV

CHARLES P. KINDLEBERGER

Dr. Kindleberger is a professor in the Department of Economics of the Massachusetts Institute of Technology, and the author of numerous books and articles in the field of international economics and economic growth and development.

He was born in New York City in 1910 and educated at the University of Pennsylvania (A.B. 1932) and Columbia University (Ph.D., 1937). At the outset of his career, he served as a research economist for the Federal Reserve Bank of New York, the Bank for International Settlements, and the Board of Governors of the Federal Reserve System. He served with the Office of Strategic Services during World War II and held the rank of Major in the United States Army. Following the war, he entered the Department of State as chief of the Division of German and Austrian Affairs and as Advisor to the European Recovery Program. In 1948, he assumed his present position at MIT.

In 1965–66, Dr. Kindleberger was a member of the President's Advisory Committee on International Monetary Arrangements. In addition, he served in 1966 as Vice-President of the American Economic Association. Among his published works are International Economics, *now in its fourth edition,* Europe and the Dollar, *and* Foreign Trade and the National Economy. *His most recent books are* American Business Abroad *and* Power and Money.

An Economist's View of the Eurodollar Market: Two Puzzles

The division of labor between the student of finance and the economist, as implied by the title assigned to this chapter, is, presumably, that the former explicates what the institution is and how it works and the latter says what it all means and how it fits into economic policy. I have had a try at the second task on another occasion.[1] Here I choose to deal with two narrower topics which present puzzling aspects: one concerns institutional functioning; the other, involving policy implications, concerns how the market will behave in untried circumstances. Specifically the questions are:

1. How does large-scale transfer of dollars from the Euromarket to the United States take place in a short period of time without trouble?
2. Given the large movement from Europe during the last 18 months in response to tight money in the United States, what will happen to the U.S. balance of payments when interest rates are allowed to fall?

---

[1] C. P. Kindleberger, "The Euro-dollar and the Internationalization of United States Monetary Policy," *Quarterly Review*, Banca Nazionale del Lavoro, March 1969, pp. 3–15.

The first of these questions is usefully addressed by reference to the "crunch" of August 1966 when, according to newspaper accounts, United States banks borrowed $2½ billions in the Eurodollar market in one month. The second question notes the inflow of $11 billion in Eurodollars between January 1, 1968, and June 30, 1969, with interest rates in the U.S. bill market of 7 per cent or more. The question is whether this accumulated indebtedness makes it impossible to return to the normal range of interest rates when inflation in the United States has been halted for balance-of-payments reasons.

THE CRUNCH

As is generally known, the crunch in the United States occurred as a consequence of tight-money policies applied by the Federal Reserve System in the spring of 1966, and reached a peak in July and August 1966 when savings and loan associations, especially in California, had difficulty in meeting withdrawals. The pressure spread across the country and, via the Eurodollar market, to Europe and the Middle East. New York banks in particular refused to renew Eurodollar loans and transferred the proceeds of loans as they matured to the United States. At the time, I predicted difficulty along the lines of the traditional nineteenth century banking crises (1847, 1857, 1866, 1890, etc.); Dr. Karl Blessing, retiring president of the Bundesbank, sounds a similar warning today:

> [T]he total turnover in the Euromarket is so big that if anything should go wrong anywhere in the world it could lead to real difficulties. It certainly could happen that a name taking funds in the Euromarket goes broke, creating mistrust in the whole market. So we must go very carefully; to my mind, things in the market have become somewhat overdone.[2]

[2] Karl Blessing, "Currencies, Inflation and Gold," *Euromoney*, January 1970, p. 6.

I confess to somewhat mixed feelings when the IntraBank in Beirut, half-way around the world from Los Angeles where the trouble started, closed its doors in September 1966, after certain rich depositors transferred their funds to Switzerland to take advantage of sharply higher interest rates.

It turns out that the movement did not consist of \$2½ billion in one month, but was more nearly \$1.2 billion in two months.[3] This is still a sizable number, especially when one recalls that \$1.3 billion decline in long-term lending to Europe by the United States between June 1928 and September 1929, which in some analysis played a major role in starting the world depression.[4] Where did it come from?

Dollars borrowed by New York banks from the Eurodollar market have to come from somewhere. They may be created, or they may come from spenders or from capitalists, i.e., owners of dollar balances. The spenders and the owners of dollar balances may be residents of the United States or abroad. But the creators of dollars that United States banks borrow cannot be Europeans—despite Milton Friedman's assertion that Eurodollars have been created by the stroke of a pen[5]—because the act of borrowing dollars created by financial intermediation in Europe is financial disintermediation, which destroys them. Perhaps a word of explanation will be helpful.

The Eurodollar market came into being when foreign and U.S. dollar owners—capitalists, rather than spenders—chose to hold them in Europe rather than in the United States. In the first instance, the bank branches receiving these deposits owed dollars in Europe and owned dollars in the United States. In due course, the Eurodollar banks found that they could make

[3] Liabilities of U.S. banks to foreign branches increased from \$1,951,000,000 on June 29, 1966 to \$2,786,000,000 on July 27 and \$3,134,000,000 on August 31. See *Federal Reserve Bulletin*, December 1969, Table 21, p. 86.

[4] Heywood W. Fleisig, "Long-Term Capital Flows and the Great Depression: the Role of the United States, 1927–1933," unpublished doctoral dissertation, Yale University, 1968.

[5] Milton Friedman, "The Euro-Dollar Market, Some First Principles," reprinted on pp. 273–293 (Chapter XVI).

dollar loans, rather than keep 100 per cent reserves of U.S. dollars against Eurodollars. As some of the proceeds of these loans were redeposited in Europe, Eurodollars were created in the familiar way that banks are understood to "create" money to some multiple of their primary reserves, or perhaps it is more accurate to say that Eurodollar claims were "created" in the familiar way that nonbank financial intermediaries are understood to create near-money assets to some multiple of the primary reserves. Since the proportion of borrowed dollars returned to the Euromarket was relatively low (the rest being used to buy securities, other monies, or goods) the expansion ratio was fairly limited—on the order of 1.4—if one nets out interbank deposits and counts only deposits in the hands of spenders and nonbank investors. When, however, a New York head office borrows Eurodollars from its London branch, disintermediation sets in. Unless the branch can attract more deposits, it must call loans or let them run off. It cannot create more dollars for the purpose of lending to New York since the New York head bank wants dollars in New York, not claims in London.

If we eliminate creation of dollars in London, we have five possible sources of dollars: (1) creation in New York, (2) transfer to London by a United States spender, (3) transfer to London by a New York dollar holder, (4) transfer to London by a foreign spender, and (5) transfer to London by a foreign holder with New York dollars in his portfolio. It is vital to recall that dollars are not substantial things like cotton, wheat, or rubber. Dollars are a claim on someone, and to borrow dollars one must transfer a claim. If the dollars acquired by New York banks from London consisted in currency, it is best not to regard this as a substantial thing but rather as a claim on the U.S. Treasury or the Federal Reserve System which, in the status quo ante, owed a liability to London.

We can eliminate the possibility that New York spenders produced the dollars by a big upsurge of imports, or that foreign spenders produced them by a sudden decline in spending on U.S. exports. The current account does not adjust rapidly, certainly not in a matter of weeks or months. This leaves three possibilities: (1) creation in New York, (2) transfer by New York holders, and (3) transfer by foreign holders. All three took place in the summer of 1966 (and again in the 18 months ending June 30, 1969). They constitute a highly flexible institution which both moves large sums of money about the world and also frustrates the purposes which gave rise to the movement, i.e., application in the United States of independent monetary policy.

United States owner of dollars—As interest rates rise in the Eurodollar market, there is a temptation to take advantage of higher rates than allowed on certificates of deposit, time deposits, etc., in the United States. For companies with direct investment affiliates this would involve violation of the Mandatory Control Program of January 1, 1968. There seems to be little doubt that some owners of dollars nonetheless indulged in the practice, although there is some difference of opinion about the scale. Government officials think the amounts minor.[6] The press suggests somewhat larger numbers,[7] and there are hints the press may be right in, say, the British

[6] See, for example, "Euro-dollars: A Changing Market," *Federal Reserve Bulletin*, October 1969, pp. 768–69: "Some minor part of this borrowing recaptured funds that had flowed to the Euro-dollar market out of the dollar holdings in the United States of U.S. residents or foreign nonbanks. . . ." See also H. David Willey, "Direct Investment Controls and the Balance of Payments," in C. P. Kindleberger, ed. *The International Corporation: A Symposium* (Cambridge, Mass., MIT Press, 1970), pp. 107–108.

[7] E. D. Prinsky, "Hot Money Is Taking Circular Trip in Quest for a Higher Return," *The Wall Street Journal*, March 5, 1969, p. 17; "Americans Flout Euro-dollar Curb," *The New York Times*, December 11, 1969. The latter account quotes a vice-president of the Morgan Guaranty Trust Company in London as having "heard estimates of more than one billion dollars."

data[8] and in the large capital outflow (debit) in Errors and Omissions in the United States balance of payments for 1969.

The European owner of dollars—As interest rates tighten in the Eurodollar market, the European owner is inclined to move dollars held directly in the U.S. to the Euromarket. His ranks are joined by European capitalists, including banks, who are induced to transfer balances from local European monies into Eurodollars, where the absence of restrictions permits. This movement went very far in 1968–69 (though perhaps not in 1966) forcing central banks to lose reserves, tighten domestic credit conditions and, finally, in an effort to limit the pressure on credit, to impose restrictions on domestic purchases of Eurodollars, as occurred in France, Italy, Belgium, The Netherlands, and Canada. The movement of Eurodollars to the United States out of central-bank reserves makes for a surplus in the U.S. balance of payments on the official-settlements basis, while the liquidity balance may be in deficit. As in every other case where the dollars borrowed in Europe ultimately come from the United States, the expansionary effect of new dollars added to the supply is offset by the contractive pressure of old dollars being subtracted.

But the most interesting aspect of the smooth functioning of the short-term capital flows and the Eurodollar market in the summer of 1966 involved not transfers of U.S. dollars to Europe or of foreign, private, or central-bank holdings. It arose from new-dollar creation. The mechanism was roundabout.

In June 1966, a substantial portion of Eurodollar funds had been invested in obligations of British local authorities. These were sterling deposits or paper, which would be bought only

---

[8] See "Euro-dollars a Changing Market," Table 4, p. 773, and discussion, pp. 774–75 in which note is taken of the increased dollar liabilities of banks in the United Kingdom to the United States and Canada. It may be, too, that some portion of the substantial increase of dollar liabilities to Switzerland represents funds owned there by U.S. accounts.

if they could be covered by a forward sale of sterling (purchase of dollars). For the municipal authorities in Britain to be in position to borrow substantial sums from the Eurodollar market, there had to be a substantial offering of forward dollars available to provide the cover. This might have been forthcoming from a large export surplus—except for the fact that the British balance of payments on current account was in deficit. It could only be provided at that time by Bank of England forward operations. In the summer of 1966, the Bank of England had sold dollars to a very substantial amount, well over several billion dollars.[9]

A large short position in forward dollars by the Bank of England could be said to represent a situation in which it, rather than the municipal authorities, had borrowed dollars from the Eurodollar market. When the loans were run off to provide dollars for the New York banks to bring back, the forward contracts had to run off as well. In his early writings on forward exchange, Spraos expressed the view that central banks could borrow foreign exchange through forward operations without limit, rolling over maturing contracts.[10] The crunch provides an interesting test of this proposition, since it was evident that the New York banks were determined to bring back their London funds in order to overcome the credit squeeze to which they each were subject.

The Bank of England appears to have been in no position to have renewed these contracts and was forced to deliver dollars as the contracts matured. Since its reserves were low (ending up negative after subcontracting commitments, it paid

[9] For an ingenious estimate which, however, involves reaching a total by taking a smaller number and blowing it up by a 5:1 ratio, when both the smaller estimate and the ratio are shaky, see John Spraos, "Some Aspects of Sterling in the Decade, 1957–66," in R. Z. Aliber, ed. *The International Market for Foreign Exchange*, (New York; Frederick A. Praeger, 1969), p. 163. The estimate reached is £1,500,000,000 to £2,000,000,000.

[10] See, for example, J. Spraos, "Speculation, Arbitrage and Sterling," *Economic Journal*, March 1959, pp. 1–21. Mr. Spraos repeats this view in the paper cited in note 9 and adds that abandonment of forward selling of foreign exchange (supporting one's own currency in the forward market) is regarded as a sign of weakness. Spraos, "Some Aspects of Sterling . . . ," p. 164.

off its obligation to deliver dollars by drawing on its swap arrangement with the Federal Reserve Bank of New York. The dollars which the New York banks brought back from London were created by the central bank whose action in tightening credit led to the squeeze.

Note that without the swap arrangement, the system might well have been more brittle and given rise to difficulty. The Basle agreement from which the swap facilities evolved is a discounting mechanism which undergirds the system and prevents pressures building up to the point where some major element in the system, in this case the Bank of England, runs into difficulties and proves unable to meet its commitments. The rediscount response to tightness was not taken consciously by the central-bank authorities, who were concentrating on seeking to limit inflation. Its automatic application, however, may well have prevented real difficulty.

THE ULTIMATE RETURN OF NORMAL INTEREST RATES

I was tempted to pose as the second puzzle the apparent anomaly of a strong dollar and a large deficit in the balance of payments.[11] A moment's reflection, however, makes clear that the anomaly is more apparent than real. High rates of interest in the United States attract foreign funds, which means that the dollar is strong. It also means that the balance of payments is weak by the liquidity definition. While the balance of payments was originally designed to throw light on the strength of a currency in the foreign-exchange market, the liquidity definition, which looks ahead to the necessity to repay, converts current strength into future

[11] See, for example, Robert V. Roosa, "Controlling Inflation and the Inflationary Mentality," an address before the Joint Luncheon of the American Economic Association and the American Finance Association, December 29, 1969: "This is not to say . . . that I do not yearn to give you my version of the paradox that the dollar is presently very strong abroad, while the balance of payments deficit as recorded this year will be the worst ever, by twice."

weakness by emphasizing the ultimate repayment. In the case of bank deposits, unlike forward-exchange contracts, such repayment may be postponed indefinitely. When balance-of-payments accounting and the market view of a currency clash, one can look at one or the other.

From 1940 to 1958, the market prevailed. From 1958 to 1968, the shadow of a particular mode of accounting dominated the substance of the foreign-exchange market. Today, the position has returned to that of the 1950s. The dollar has been strong in the foreign-exchange market since the two-tier price system for gold of March 1968, the political and economic crisis of May-June in France, the Soviet occupation of Czechoslovakia in August, the French devaluation of the franc a year later in August 1969, and the German revaluation in September 1969. The deficit in the balance of payments in the second quarter of 1969, which amounted to $13.2 billion at an annual rate, has been virtually ignored, both in the press and in official statements from Washington.

The increase in short-term liabilities of U.S. banks to their branches abroad in the 18 months ended June 30, 1969 amounted to $11.1 billion and brought the outstanding total to $13.3 billion on June 25. From this level it rose to nearly $15 billion on November 26, 1969, despite the requirement on September 4, 1969 of a 10 per cent reserve on the increase in net liabilities to foreign branches above the average daily outstanding amounts of the four weeks ended May 28, 1969 (roughly $9,875,000,000).

The $11.1 billion increase in net liabilities to foreign branches was financed to the extent of $3.3 billions by reduction in foreign central-bank holdings of dollar claims, an increase of $1.2 billion in U.S. official reserve assets (comparable to the swaps of 1966), $1 billion of U.S. nonbank short-term claims on Eurodollar markets, plus some unreported claims which produced an unusually large outflow in errors and omissions.[12] Thus, more than half the increase in indebtedness was the counterpart of opposite short-term outflows. There might be some question whether foreign monetary authorities wanted to keep their official holdings of dollars at the level of $13 billion, which they had reached by the end of 1967. The widespread introduction of restrictions on movements into Eurodollars when official reserves had declined only to $11.6 billion suggests, however, that there was not a burdensome surplus of dollars in the rest of the world when the movement started.

The question of what happens when interest rates start down in the United States can be divided into two parts: First, will the banks want to pay off their liabilities to their foreign branches? Second, if they do want to clear the books, where will the counterpart of the dollars come from?

I do not see any way for an economist to answer the first question. It may be the price-and-quantity type of question that economists can answer. In this case, presumably, whether banks will pay off their liabilities will depend on relative interest rates in New York and in the Eurodollar market. Regarding the much more elusive second question, how strong is the pressure on banks to borrow in Euromarkets when interest rates are higher there than here because of an unwillingness to appear frequently at the Federal Reserve discount window, their inability to cut off valued customers with open lines of credit, and similar long-run considerations which militate against short-run profit calculation?

Raymond F. Mikesell believes that there will not be a rapid repayment of U.S. bank indebtedness.[13] His reasons include the suggestion that as U.S. credit conditions ease, so will those

---

[12] For the overall figures, see "Euro-dollars: A Changing Market," Table 1, p. 768; for errors and omissions, p. 775.

[13] Raymond F. Mikesell, "The Eurodollar Market and the U.S. International Accounts," *Euromoney*, January 1970, p. 45.

in the Eurodollar market so that "there will continue to be an advantage for American banks to obtain funds from the market, at least to the level of their borrowing of May 1969" (below which the 10 per cent reserve requirement does not apply). This implies that Eurodollar rates are now below those in the United States, which is far from the case, or that Eurodollar interest rates will decline faster and further than those in the United States. The latter seems unlikely when it is recalled that Eurodollar rates have always been above New York.

A second reason given is that "the demand for Eurodollar funds from other than U.S. sources is likely to continue to expand and this expansion will be encouraged by a reduction in Eurodollar rates." But growth of demand for Eurodollar funds would seem to encourage New York banks to pay off their indebtedness to their branches, and even to put positive funds abroad for lending out at higher rates.

In my judgment, the question will turn on how the bankers feel about these liabilities—a rather "banking-mystique" type of question which is not answerable in economic terms but about which some clue might be obtained by sampling banking opinion. Much will depend on whether the head office depends on the branch, or the branch on the head office.

There is very little difference in legal form between a loan incurred by the head office to the branch, and a deposit placed by the branch in the head office. The difference in economic behavior may be substantial. When the head office needs money from the branch, the branch cannot expand its loans for fear of losing reserves, considered by the head office as vital. On the other hand, when the head office's liability is regarded not as a necessary loan but as a normal interbank deposit, the branch can expand its loans and the head office can expect some deposit losses. As a rule, these losses will end up elsewhere as other deposits in the New York market.

The conclusion is that it is entirely possible, although hardly predictable, to have "loan liabilities" to the branches converted into reserve claims or interbank deposits of the branches on head office without any substantial rundown as an initial reaction to easier credit.

But the head offices may continue to think of these liabilities as loans, which are a sign of banking weakness, rather than as attracted deposits, which represent strength. In this case, separate banks will try to pay off their liabilities to the Eurodollar market. In the first instance, this will furnish the branch with other dollar claims on New York as a substitute for loans to New York. When the bank lends these to the Eurodollar market, the question is, What becomes of them?

The answer is, of course, the converse of the process of the last few years. Intermediation replaces disintermediation. But not gross. Some U.S.-owned funds return to New York because of the decline in Eurodollar rates. Some funds borrowed in the Eurodollar market end up as foreign bank and nonbank funds held directly in the United States. Some part of the funds borrowed in Eurodollars go directly back into the Euromarket as part of the multiple-expansion process. When Eurodollars are converted to foreign currencies, they may be held in part in private foreign portfolios (as cash increases relative to securities at lower rates of interest), or they may be bought by the central bank in exchange for local monies. The central bank may hold the dollars or convert them into gold, SDRs ("paper" gold representing Special Drawing Rights on the International Monetary Fund), or destroy them by paying off IMF loans or reversing old swaps.

We are back where we started with three ways of getting dollars to borrow by New York. There, three ways of paying off dollar debts to the Eurodollar market are: (1) destroying dollars, (2) paying them to the suppliers of real assets, or (3) transferring them to asset holders in return for other assets. Europe can neither create nor destroy dollars, except as it does so in the United States. U.S. debts to the Eurodollar market can be reduced by a current-account surplus in the longer run, though not in the short; and it is likely that the undoing of the relative inflation of this country in 1966–69 will help in this regard. The current account in the balance of payments remains important.

When it comes to asset holders, however, the only problem is the position of central banks. U.S. holders of Eurodollars may swap them for U.S. dollars, undoing the circular process which has gone some distance to build up our liquidity deficit in recent years. This is economically trivial. Foreigners who give up Eurodollars for dollars held directly in the United States will assist the banks in reducing their indebtedness to their branches, if that relief is desired, but not in any large amount. The major impact seems likely to consist of two strands: Eurodollars borrowed in Europe which end up in the hands of private sellers or asset-holders who are content to hold Eurodollars; and Eurodollars which are sold against local currency to central banks. Only the latter is of possible importance.

Note that the lower interest rates are U.S. rates below those in other financial centers. If other central banks lower their rates at the same pace as the Federal Reserve system, the incentive for transferring out of Eurodollars into European currencies will be reduced. Some transfer will doubtless occur as a signal to European central banks that interest-rate reduction is possible. If inflation persists in Europe longer than in the United States, European monetary policies may work in the direction of maintaining higher interest rates, or reducing them more slowly than in the United States. In these not unlikely circumstances, there is the possibility of a sizable outflow from Eurodollars to European currencies, reversing the sizable opposite movement of the last two years.

The importance of a sizable amount of Eurodollars ending up in central-bank hands is that these banks may choose to convert them into another asset, most effectively gold, SDRs or, in the intermediate position, some other currency—sterling, Deutsche marks, French francs, lire, etc. This latter action would transfer the choice between dollars and gold or SDRs to the central bank whose currency was chosen. However, it is hardly likely that in the next few years, within which time we shall want to be in position to lower interest rates, these other currencies will gain the strength to challenge the dollar as a reserve asset. The Deutsche mark looked especially strong prior to its revaluation on September 28, 1969, but the more than $6 billion of capital which has flowed out of Germany, as profit-taking on exchange speculation, has made the Bundesbank lose gold and turn to the IMF to borrow foreign currencies. If the dollar bears a long-run flaw in the inflation of 1966–69 and a weak current account, every other possible challenger has a short-run disability. The failure of the Republic of South Africa and France to succeed in raising the gold price, and the decline of the free-market price below $35, suggests little pressure to convert dollars into gold in large volume.

Lower interest rates will thus worsen the position of the dollar in the foreign-exchange market, as either New York banks press dollars on their branches to repay debt and/or the branches expand their dollar lending at lower rates of interest, and sizable amounts of dollars end up in central-bank hands. The liquidity measure of balance-of-payments deficit is unlikely to show much improvement, as Eurodollar interest rates will probably remain above those in New York and there will be some incentive for Americans, Canadians, etc., to hold dollars through London. But I venture to predict that those who contemplate disaster for the United States when it comes time to reduce interest rates again will find themselves in the same position as those who predicted Armageddon brought on by a shortage of liquidity. And the Eurodollar market, with its complications, will have played a major role in falsifying both predictions.

XVI

MILTON FRIEDMAN

Dr. Friedman is Paul Snowden Russell Distinguished Service Professor of Economics at the University of Chicago, a member of the research staff of the National Bureau of Economic Research, and a columnist for NEWSWEEK *magazine. He is also a leading world authority on money and monetary policy.*

Dr. Friedman received the A.B. degree from Rutgers University (1932), the M.A. from the University of Chicago (1933), and the Ph.D. from Columbia University (1946).

During 1967 he served as president of the American Economic Association. Dr. Friedman is a fellow of the American Statistical Association, the Econometric Society, and the Institute of Mathematical Economics; on the Board of Editors of Econometrica; *on the advisory board of the American Enterprise Institute; a member of the American Philosophical Society; and vice-president of the Mont Pelerin Society.*

Considered classics in the study of economics, his books include Essays in Positive Economics *(1953);* A Theory of the Consumption Function *(1957);* A Program for Monetary Stability *(1959);* Capitalism and Freedom *(1962);* A Monetary History of the United States *(1963);* Dollars and Deficits *(1968);* The Optimum Quantity of Money and Other Essays *(1969); and with Anna J. Schwartz,* Monetary Statistics of the United States *(1970).*

The Eurodollar Market: Some First Principles

The Eurodollar market is the latest example of the mystifying quality of money creation to even the most sophisticated bankers, let alone other businessmen. Recently, I heard a high official of an international financial organization discuss the Eurodollar market before a collection of high-powered international bankers. He estimated that Eurodollar deposits totaled some $30 billion. He was then asked: "What is the source of these deposits?" His answer was: partly, U.S. balance-of-payments deficits; partly, dollar reserves of non-U.S. central banks; partly, the proceeds from the sale of Eurodollar bonds.

This answer is almost complete nonsense. Balance-of-payments deficits do provide foreigners with claims on U.S. dollars. But there is nothing to assure that such claims will be held in the form of Eurodollars. In any event, U.S. deficits, worldwide, have totaled less than $9 billion for the past five

---

This chapter originally appeared as an article in the *Morgan Guaranty Survey* (October 1969, pp. 4–14), a publication of the Morgan Guaranty Trust Company of New York, and subsequently was published as Paper No. 34 in the Selected Papers of the Graduate School of Business, University of Chicago. Reprinted here by permission.

years, on a liquidity basis. Dollar holdings of non-U.S. central banks have fallen during the period of rapid rise in Eurodollar deposits, but by less than $5 billion. The dollars paid for Eurobonds had themselves to come from somewhere and do not constitute an independent source. No matter how you try, you cannot get $30 billion from these sources. The answer given is precisely parallel to saying that the source of the $400 billion of deposits in U.S. banks (or for that matter the much larger total of all outstanding short-term claims) is the $60 billion of Federal Reserve credit outstanding.

The correct answer for both Eurodollars and liabilities of U.S. banks is that their major source is a bookkeeper's pen.[1] The purpose of this article is to explain this statement. The purpose is purely expository. I shall restrict myself essentially to principle and shall not attempt either an empirical evaluation of the Eurodollar market or a normative judgment of its desirability.

Another striking example of the confusion about Eurodollars is the discussion, in even the most sophisticated financial papers, of the use of the Eurodollar market by U.S. commercial banks "to evade tight money," as it is generally phrased. U.S. banks, one reads in a leading financial paper, "have been willing to pay extremely high interest rates . . . to borrow back huge sums of U.S. dollars that have piled up abroad." The image conveyed is that of piles of dollar bills being bundled up and shipped across the ocean on planes and ships—the way New York literally did drain gold from Europe in the bad—or good—old days at times of financial panic. Yet, the more dol-

[1] The similarity between credit creation in the U.S. fractional reserve banking system and in the Eurodollar market has of course often been noted. For example, see Fred H. Klopstock, "The Euro-Dollar Market, Some Unresolved Issues," in *Essays in International Finance*, No. 65 (Princeton University, March 1968), p. 6. A recent excellent analysis is given in an article by Joseph G. Kvasnicka, "Euro-Dollars—an Important Source of Funds for American Banks," *Business Conditions*, Federal Reserve Bank of Chicago, June 1969. A useful but analytically less satisfactory examination of the Eurodollar market is Jane Sneddon Little, "The Euro-Dollar Market: Its Nature and Impact," *New England Economic Review*, Federal Reserve Bank of Boston, May/June 1969.

lars U.S. banks "borrow back" the more Eurodollar deposits go up! How come? The answer is that it is purely figurative language to speak of "piled up" dollars being "borrowed back." Again, the bookkeeper's pen is at work.

WHAT ARE EURODOLLARS?

Just what are Eurodollars? They are deposit liabilities, denominated in dollars, of banks outside the United States. Engaged in Eurodollar business, for example, are foreign commercial banks such as the Bank of London and South America, Ltd., merchant banks such as Morgan Grenfell and Co., Ltd., and many of the foreign branches of U.S. commercial banks. Funds placed with these institutions may be owned by anyone—U.S. or foreign residents or citizens, individuals or corporations or governments. Eurodollars have two basic characteristics: first, they are short-term obligations to pay dollars; second, they are obligations of banking offices located outside the U.S. In principle, there is no hard and fast line between Eurodollars and other dollar-denominated claims on non-U.S. institutions—just as there is none between claims in the U.S. that we call "money" and other short-term claims. The precise line drawn in practice depends on the exact interpretation given to *short-term* and to *banks.* Nothing essential in this article is affected by the precise point at which the line is drawn.

A homely parallel to Eurodollars is to be found in the dollar-deposit liabilities of bank offices located in the city of Chicago —which could similarly be called *Chicago dollars.* Like Eurodollars, Chicago dollars consist of obligations to pay dollars by a collection of banking offices located in a particular geographic area. Again, like Eurodollars, they may be owned by anyone—residents or nonresidents of the geographic area in question.

The location of the banks is important primarily because it affects the regulations under which the banks operate and hence the way that they can do business. Those Chicago banks that are members of the Federal Reserve System must comply with the System's requirements about reserves, maximum interest rates payable on deposits, and so on; and in addition, of course, with the requirements of the Comptroller of the Currency if they are national banks, and of the Illinois State Banking Commission, if they are state banks.

Eurodollar banks are subject to the regulations of the relevant banking authorities in the country in which they operate. In practice, however, such banks have been subject neither to required reserves on Eurodollar deposits nor to maximum ceilings on the rates of interest they are permitted to pay on such deposits.

REGULATION AND EURODOLLARS

The difference in regulation has played a key role in the development of the Eurodollar market. No doubt there were minor precursors, but the initial substantial Eurodollar deposits in the post-World War II period originated with the Russians, who wanted dollar balances but recalled that their dollar holdings in the U.S. had been impounded by the Alien Property Custodian in World War II. Hence they wanted dollar claims not subject to U.S. governmental control.

The most important regulation that has stimulated the development of the Eurodollar market has been Regulation Q, under which the Federal Reserve has fixed maximum interest rates that member banks could pay on time deposits. Whenever these ceilings became effective, Eurodollar deposits, paying a higher interest rate, became more attractive than U.S. deposits, and the Eurodollar market expanded. U.S. banks then borrowed from the Eurodollar market to replace the withdrawn time deposits.

A third major force has been the direct and indirect exchange controls imposed by the U.S. for "balance-of-payments" purposes—the interest-equalization tax, the "voluntary" controls on bank lending abroad and on foreign investment, and, finally, the compulsory controls instituted by President Johnson in January 1968. Without Regulation Q and the exchange controls—all of which, in my opinion, are both unnecessary and undesirable—the Eurodollar market, though it might still have existed, would not have reached anything like its present dimensions.

FRACTIONAL RESERVES

Eurodollar deposits, like Chicago deposits, are in principle obligations to pay literal dollars—i.e., currency (or coin), all of which consists, at present, of government-issued fiat (Federal Reserve notes, U.S. notes, a few other similar issues, and fractional coinage). In practice, even Chicago banks are called on to discharge only an insignificant part of their deposit obligations by paying out currency. Eurodollar banks are called on to discharge a negligible part in this form. Deposit obligations are typically discharged by providing a credit or deposit at another bank—as when you draw a check on your bank which the recipient "deposits" in his.

To meet their obligations to pay cash, banks keep a "reserve" of cash on hand. But, of course, since they are continuously receiving as well as paying cash and since in any interval they will be called on to redeem only a small fraction of their obligations in cash, they need on the average keep only a very small part of their assets in cash for this purpose. For Chicago banks, this cash serves also to meet legal reserve requirements. For Eurodollar banks, the amount of literal cash they hold is negligible.

To meet their obligations to provide a credit at another bank, when a check or similar instrument is used, banks keep deposits at other banks. For Chicago banks, these deposits (which in addition to facilitating the transfer of funds between banks serve to meet legal reserve requirements) are held primarily at Federal Reserve banks. In addition, however, Chicago banks may also keep balances at correspondent banks in other cities.

Like cash, deposits at other banks need be only a small fraction of assets. Banks are continuously receiving funds from other banks, as well as transferring funds to them, so they need reserves only to provide for temporary discrepancies between payments and receipts or sudden unanticipated demands. For Chicago banks, such "prudential" reserves are clearly far smaller than the reserves that they are legally required to keep.

Eurodollar banks are not subject to legal reserve requirements but, like Chicago banks, they must keep a prudential reserve in order to be prepared to meet withdrawals of deposits when they are demanded or when they mature. An individual bank will regard as a prudential reserve readily realizable funds both in the Eurodollar market itself (e.g., Eurodollar call money) and in the U.S. But for the Eurodollar system as a whole, Eurodollar funds cancel, and the prudential reserves available to meet demands for U.S. dollars consist entirely of deposits at banks in New York or other cities in the U.S. and U.S. money market assets that can be liquidated promptly without loss.

The amount of prudential reserves that a Eurodollar bank will wish to hold—like the amount that a Chicago bank will wish to hold—will depend on its particular mix of demand and time obligations. Time deposits generally require smaller reserves than demand deposits—and in some instances almost zero reserves if the bank can match closely the maturities of its dollar-denominated liabilities and its dollar-denominated loans and investments. Although a precise estimate is difficult to make because of the incompleteness and ambiguity of the available data, prudential reserves of Eurodollar institutions are clearly a small fraction of total dollar-denominated obligations.

This point—that Eurodollar institutions, like Chicago banks, are part of a fractional reserve banking system—is the key to understanding the Eurodollar market. The failure to recognize it is the chief source of misunderstanding about the Eurodollar market. Most journalistic discussions of the Eurodollar market proceed as if a Eurodollar bank held a dollar in the form of cash or of deposits at a U.S. bank corresponding to each dollar of deposit liability. That is the source of such images as "piling up," "borrowing back," "withdrawing," etc. But this is not the case. If it were, a Eurodollar bank could hardly afford to pay 10 per cent or more on its deposit liabilities.

A HYPOTHETICAL EXAMPLE

A Eurodollar bank typically has total dollar assets roughly equal to its dollar liabilities.[2] But these assets are not in currency or bank deposits. In highly simplified form, the balance sheet of such a bank—or the part of the balance sheet corresponding to its Eurodollar operations—must look something like that shown in the adjoining column (the numbers in this and later balance sheets are solely for illustrative purposes).

It is the earnings on the $9,500,000 of loans and investments that enable it to pay interest on the $10,000,000 of deposits.

Where did the $10,000,000 of deposits come from? One can say that $700,000 (cash assets minus due to other banks) came from *primary deposits,* i.e., is the counterpart to a literal deposit of cash or transfer of funds from other banks.[3] The other $9,300,000 is "created" by the magic of fractional reserve banking—this is the bookkeeper's pen at work.

[2] Which is why it is not subject to any special foreign-exchange risk simply by operating in the Eurodollar market. The balance sheet of its Eurodollar operations balances in dollars; if it is, for example, a British bank, the balance sheet of its pound sterling operations balances in pounds. It is operating in two currencies but need not take a speculative position in either. Of course, it may take a speculative position, whether or not it operates in the Eurodollar market.

[3] Note that even this is an overstatement, since most of the deposits at New York banks are themselves ultimately "created" rather than "primary" deposits. These are primary deposits only vis-à-vis the Eurodollar market separately.

EURODOLLAR BANK H OF LONDON

Assets		Liabilities	
Cash assets*	$1,000,000	Deposits	$10,000,000
Dollar-denominated loans	7,000,000	Due to other banks	300,000
Dollar-denominated bonds	2,500,000	Capital accounts	200,000
Total assets	$10,500,000	Total liabilities	$10,500,000

* Includes U.S. currency, deposits in New York and other banks, and other assets immediately realizable in U.S. funds.

Let us look at the process more closely. Suppose an Arab Sheik opens up a new deposit account in London at Bank H (H for hypothetical) by depositing a check for $1,000,000 drawn on the Sheik's demand-deposit account at the head office of, say, Morgan Guaranty Trust Company. Let us suppose that Bank H also keeps its New York account at Morgan Guaranty and also as demand deposits. At the first stage, this will add $1,000,000 to the deposit liabilities of Bank H, and the same amount to its assets in the form of deposits due from New York banks. At Morgan Guaranty, the transfer of deposits from the Sheik to Bank H will cause no change in total deposit liabilities.

But Bank H now has excess funds available to lend. It has been keeping cash assets equal to 10 per cent of deposits—not because it was required to do so but because it deemed it prudent to do so. It now has cash equal to 18 per cent ($2/11$) of deposits. Because of the $1,000,000 of new deposits from the Sheik, it will want to add, say, $100,000 to its balance in New York. This leaves Bank H with $900,000 available to add to its loans and investments. Assume that it makes a loan of $900,000 to, say, UK Ltd., a British corporation engaged in trade with the U.S., giving corporation UK Ltd. a check on Morgan Guaranty. Bank H's balance sheet will now look as follows after the check has cleared:

Assets		Liabilities	
Cash assets	$1,100,000	Deposits	$11,000,000
Dollar-denominated loans	7,900,000	Due to other banks	300,000
Dollar-denominated bonds	2,500,000	Capital accounts	200,000
Total assets	$11,500,000	Total liabilities	$11,500,000

We now must ask what UK Ltd. does with the $900,000 check. To cut short and simplify the process, let us assume that UK Ltd. incurred the loan because it had been repeatedly troubled by a shortage of funds in New York and wanted to maintain a higher average level of bank balances in New York. Further assume that it also keeps its account at Morgan Guaranty, so that it simply deposits the check in its demand-deposit account.

This particular cycle is therefore terminated and we can examine its effect. First, the position of Morgan Guaranty is fundamentally unchanged: it had a deposit liability of $1,000,000 to the Sheik. It now has a deposit liability of $100,000 to Bank H and one of $900,000 to UK Ltd.

Second, the calculated money supply of the U.S. and the demand-deposit component thereof are unchanged. That money supply excludes from "adjusted demand deposits" the deposits of U.S. commercial banks at other U.S. commercial banks but it includes deposits of both foreign banks and other foreigners. Therefore, the Sheik's deposit was included before. The deposits of Bank H and UK Ltd. are included now.

Third, the example was set up so that the money supply owned by residents of the U.S. is also unchanged. As a practical matter, the financial statistics gathered and published by the Federal Reserve do not contain sufficient data to permit calculation of the U.S.-owned money supply—a total which would exclude from the money supply as now calculated currency and deposits at U.S. banks owned by nonresidents and include dollar deposits at non-U.S. banks owned by residents. But the hypothetical transactions clearly leave this total unaffected.

Fourth, Eurodollar deposits are $1,000,000 higher.

However, fifth, the total world supply of dollars held by *nonbanks*—dollars in the U.S. plus dollars outside the U.S.—is $900,000 not $1,000,000 higher. The reason is that interbank deposits are now higher by $100,000, thanks to the additional deposits of Bank H at Morgan Guaranty. This amount of deposits was formerly an asset of a nonbank (the Arab Sheik); now it is an asset of Bank H. In this way, Bank H has created $900,000 of Eurodollar deposits. The other $100,000 of Eurodollar deposits has been transferred from the U.S. to the Eurodollar area.

Sixth, the balance of payments of the U.S. is unaffected, whether calculated on a liquidity basis or on an official settlements basis. On a liquidity basis, the Arab Sheik's transfer is recorded as a reduction of $1,000,000 in short-term liquid claims on the U.S. but the increased deposits of Bank H and UK Ltd. at Morgan Guaranty are a precisely offsetting increase. On an official settlements basis, the series of transactions has not affected the dollar holdings of any central bank or official institution.[4]

[4] It is interesting to contrast these effects with those that would have occurred if we substitute a Chicago bank for Bank H of London, i.e., suppose that the Arab Sheik had transferred his funds to a Chicago bank, say, Continental Illinois, and Continental Illinois had made the loan to UK Ltd., which UK Ltd. again added to its balances at Morgan Guaranty. To simplify matters, assume that the reserve requirements for Continental Illinois and Morgan Guaranty are the same flat 10 per cent that we assumed Bank H of London kept in the form of cash assets (because, let us say, all deposit changes consist of the appropriate mix of demand and time deposits).

First, the position of Morgan Guaranty is now fundamentally changed. Continental Illinois keeps its reserves as deposits at the Federal Reserve Bank of Chicago, not at Morgan Guaranty. Hence it will deposit its net claim of $100,000 on Morgan Guaranty at the Chicago Federal Reserve to meet the reserves required for the Sheik's deposit. This will result in a reduction of $100,000 in Morgan Guaranty's reserve balance at the New York Federal Reserve Bank. Its deposits have gone down only $100,000 (thanks to the $900,000 deposit by UK Ltd.) so that if it had no excess reserves before it now has deficient reserves. This will set in train a multiple contraction of deposits at Morgan Guaranty and other banks which will end when the $1,000,000 gain in deposits by Continental Illinois is completely offset by a $1,000,000 decline in deposits at Morgan Guaranty and other banks.

Clearly, there is no meaningful sense in which we can say that the $900,000 of created Eurodollar deposits is derived from a U.S. balance-of-payments deficit, or from dollars held by central banks, or from the proceeds of Eurodollar bond sales.

SOME COMPLICATIONS

Many complications of this example are possible. They will change the numbers but not in any way the essential principles. But it may help to consider one or two.

(a) Suppose UK Ltd. used the dollar loan to purchase timber from Russia, and Russia wished to hold the proceeds as a dollar deposit at, say, Bank R in London. Then, another round is started—precisely like the one that began when the Sheik transferred funds from Morgan Guaranty to Bank H. Bank R now has $900,000 extra deposit liabilities, matched by $900,000 extra deposits in New York. If it also follows the practice of maintaining cash assets equal to 10 per cent of deposits, it can make a dollar loan of $810,000. If the recipient of the loan keeps it as a demand deposit at Morgan Guaranty, or transfers it to someone who does, the process comes to an end. The result is that total Eurodollar deposits are up by $1,900,000. Of that total, $1,710,000 is held by nonbanks, with

Second, the calculated money supply of the U.S. and the demand-deposit component thereof are still unchanged.

However, third, the money supply owned by the residents of the U.S. is reduced by the $900,000 increase in the deposits of UK Ltd.

Fourth, there is no change in Eurodollar deposits.

Fifth, there is no change in the total world supply of dollars.

Sixth, the balance of payments of the U.S. is affected if it is calculated on a liquidity basis but not if it is calculated on an official-settlements basis. On a liquidity basis, the deficit would be increased by $900,000 because the loan by Continental Illinois to UK Ltd. would be recorded as a capital outflow but UK Ltd.'s deposit at Morgan Guaranty would be regarded as an increase in U.S. liquid liabilities to foreigners, which are treated as financing the deficit. This enlargement of the deficit on a liquidity basis is highly misleading. It suggests, of course, a worsening of the U.S. payments problem whereas, in fact, all that is involved is a worsening of the statistics. The additional dollars that UK Ltd. has in its demand-deposit account cannot meaningfully be regarded as a potential claim on U.S. reserve assets. UK Ltd. not only needs them for transactions purposes; it must regard them as tied or matched to its own dollar indebtedness. On an official-settlements basis, the series of transactions does not affect the dollar holdings of any central bank or official institution.

the other $190,000 being additional deposits of banks (the $100,000 extra of Bank H at Morgan Guaranty plus the $90,000 extra of Bank R at Morgan Guaranty).

If the recipient of the loan transfers it to someone who wants to hold it as a Eurodollar deposit at a third bank, the process continues on its merry way. If, in the extreme, at every stage the whole of the proceeds of the loan were to end up as Eurodollar deposits, it is obvious that the total increase in Eurodollar deposits would be: $1,000,000 + $900,000 + $810,000 + $729,000 + $........... = $10,000,000. At the end of the process, Eurodollar deposits would be $10,000,000 higher; deposits of Eurodollar banks at New York banks, $1,000,000 higher; and the total world supply of dollars held by nonbanks, $9,000,000 higher.

This example perhaps makes it clear why bankers in the Eurodollar market keep insisting that they do not "create" dollars but only transfer them, and why they sincerely believe that all Eurodollars come from the U.S. *To each banker separately in the chain described, his additional Eurodollar deposit came in the form of a check on Morgan Guaranty Trust Company of New York!* How are the bankers to know that the $10,000,000 of checks on Morgan Guaranty all constitute repeated claims on the same initial $1,000,000 of deposits? Appearances are deceiving.

This example (involving successive loan extensions by a series of banks) brings out the difference between two concepts that have produced much confusion: Eurodollar creation and the Eurodollar multiplier. In both the simple example and the example involving successive loan extensions, the fraction of Eurodollars outstanding that has been created is nine-tenths or, put differently, 10 Eurodollars exist for every U.S. dollar held as a cash asset in New York by Eurodollar banks. However, in the simple example, the Eurodollar multiplier (the ratio of the increase in Eurodollar deposits to the initial "primary" deposit) is unity; in the second example, it is 10. That is, in the simple example, the total amount of Eurodollars goes up by $1 for every $1 of U.S. deposits initially transferred to Eurodollar banks; in the second example, it goes up by $10 for every $1 of U.S. deposits initially transferred. The difference is that in the simple example there is maximum "leakage" from the Eurodollar system; in the second example, zero "leakage."

The distinction between Eurodollar creation and the Eurodollar multiplier makes it clear why there is a definite limit to the amount of Eurodollars that can be created no matter how low are the prudential reserves that banks hold. For example, if Eurodollar banks held zero prudential reserves—as it is sometimes claimed that they do against time deposits—100 per cent of the outstanding deposits would be created deposits and the potential multiplier would be infinite. Yet the actual multiplier would be close to unity because only a small part of the funds acquired by borrowers from Eurodollar banks would end up as additional time deposits in such banks.[5]

(b) Suppose Bank H does not have sufficient demand for dollar loans to use profitably the whole $900,000 of excess dollar funds. Suppose, simultaneously, it is experiencing a heavy demand for sterling loans. It might go to the Bank of England and use the $900,000 to buy sterling. Bank of England deposits at Morgan Guaranty would now go up. But since the Bank of England typically holds its deposits at the New York Federal Reserve Bank, the funds would fairly quickly disappear from Morgan Guaranty's books and show up instead on the Federal Reserve's. This, in the first instance, would reduce the reserves of Morgan Guaranty and thus threaten to produce much more extensive monetary effects than any of our other

[5] This is precisely comparable to the situation of savings and loan associations and mutual savings banks in the U.S.

examples. However, the Bank of England typically holds most of its dollar reserves as treasury bills or the equivalent, not as noninterest earning deposits at the Federal Reserve. It would therefore instruct the Federal Reserve to buy, say, bills for its account. This would restore the reserves to the banking system and, except for details, we would be back to where we were in the other examples.

THE KEY POINTS

Needless to say, this is far from a comprehensive survey of all the possible complications. But perhaps it suffices to show that the complications do not affect the fundamental points brought out by the simple example, namely:

1. Eurodollars, like *Chicago dollars*, are mostly the product of the bookkeeper's pen—that is, the result of fractional-reserve banking.
2. The amount of Eurodollars outstanding, like the amount of Chicago dollars, depends on the desire of owners of wealth to hold the liabilities of the corresponding group of banks.
3. The ultimate increase in the amount of Eurodollars from an initial transfer of deposits from other banks to Eurodollar banks depends on:
   (a) The amount of their dollar assets Eurodollar banks choose to hold in the form of cash assets in the U.S., and
   (b) The "leakages" from the system—i.e., the final disposition of the funds borrowed from Eurodollar banks (or acquired by the sale of bonds or other investments to them). The larger the fraction of such funds held as Eurodollar deposits, the larger the increase in Eurodollars in total.
4. The existence of the Eurodollar market increases the total

amount of dollar balances available to be held by non-banks throughout the world for any given amount of money (currency plus deposits at Federal Reserve Banks) created by the Federal Reserve System. It does so by permitting a greater pyramiding on this base by the use of deposits at U.S. banks as prudential reserves for Eurodollar deposits.

5. The existence of the Eurodollar market may also create a greater demand for dollars to be held by making dollar balances available in a more convenient form. The net effect of the Eurodollar market on our balance-of-payments problem (as distinct from our statistical position) depends on whether demand is raised more or less than supply. (My own conjecture—which is based on much too little evidence for me to have much confidence in it—is that demand is raised less than supply and hence that the growth of the Eurodollar market has on the whole made our balance-of-payments problem more difficult.)
6. Whether my conjecture on this score is right or wrong, the Eurodollar market has almost surely raised the world's nominal money supply (expressed in dollar equivalents) and has thus made the world price level (expressed in dollar equivalents) higher than it would otherwise be. Alternatively, if it is desired to define the money supply exclusive of Eurodollar deposits, the same effect can be described in terms of a rise in the velocity of the world's money supply. However, this effect, while clear in direction, must be extremely small in magnitude.

USE OF EURODOLLARS BY U.S. BANKS

Let us now turn from this general question of the source of Eurodollars to the special issue raised at the outset: the effect of Regulation Q and "tight money" on the use of the Eurodollar market by U.S. banks.

To set the stage, let us suppose, in the framework of our simple example, that Eurodollar Bank H of London loans the $900,000 excess funds that it has as a result of the initial deposit by the Arab Sheik to the head office of Morgan Guaranty, i.e., gives Morgan Guaranty (New York) a check for $900,000 on itself in return for an IOU from Morgan Guaranty. This kind of borrowing from foreign banks is one of the means by which American banks have blunted the impact of certificate of deposit (CD) losses. The combined effect will be to leave total liabilities of Morgan Guaranty unchanged but to alter their composition: deposit liabilities are now down $900,000 (instead of the $1,000,000 deposit liability it formerly had to the Sheik it now has a deposit liability of $100,000 to Bank H) and other liabilities ("funds borrowed from foreign banks") are up $900,000.

Until very recently, such a change in the form of a bank's liabilities—from deposits to borrowings—had an important effect on its reserve position. Specifically, it freed reserves. With $1,000,000 of demand-deposit liabilities to the Arab Sheik, Morgan Guaranty was required to keep in cash or as deposits at the Federal Reserve Bank of New York $175,000 (or $60,000 if, as is more realistic, the Sheik kept his $1,000,000 in the form of a time deposit). With the shift of the funds to Bank H, however, and completion of the $900,000 loan by Bank H to Morgan Guaranty, Morgan Guaranty's reserve requirements at the Federal Reserve fell appreciably. Before the issuance of new regulations that became effective on September 4, 1969, Morgan Guaranty was not required to keep any reserve for the liability in the form of the IOU. Its only obligation was to keep $17,500 corresponding to the demand deposit of Bank H. The change in the form of its liabilities would therefore have reduced its reserve requirements by $157,500 (or by $42,500 for a time deposit) without any change in its total liabilities or its total assets, or in the composition of its assets; hence, it would have had this much more available to lend.

What the Federal Reserve did effective September 4 was to make borrowings subject to reserve requirements as well. Morgan Guaranty must now keep a reserve against the IOU, the exact percentage depending on the total amount of borrowings by Morgan Guaranty from foreign banks.[6] The new regulations make it impossible to generalize about reserve effects. A U.S. bank losing deposits to a Eurobank and then recouping funds by giving its IOU may or may not have additional amounts available to lend as a result of transactions of the kind described.

If Bank H made the loan to Chase instead of to Morgan Guaranty, the latter would lose reserves and Chase would gain them. To Chase it would look as if it were getting additional funds from abroad but, to both together, the effect would be the same as before—the possible release of required reserves with no change in available reserves.

The bookkeeping character of these transactions, and how they can be stimulated, can perhaps be seen more clearly if we introduce an additional feature of the actual Eurodollar market, which was not essential heretofore, namely, the role of overseas branches of U.S. banks. In addition, for realism, we shall express our example in terms of time deposits.

Let us start from scratch and consider the head office of Morgan Guaranty in New York and its London branch. Let us look at hypothetical initial balance sheets of both. We shall treat the London branch as if it had just started and had neither assets nor liabilities, and shall restrict the balance sheet for the head office to the part relevant to its CD operations. This set of circumstances gives us the following situation:

[6] The required reserve is 3 per cent of such borrowings so long as they do not exceed 4 per cent of total deposits subject to reserves. On borrowings in excess of that level the required reserve is 10 per cent.

NEW YORK HEAD OFFICE

ASSETS		LIABILITIES	
Deposits at Fed. Res. Bank of N.Y.	$ 6,000,000	Time certificates of deposit	$100,000,000
Other cash assets	4,000,000		
Loans	76,000,000		
Bonds	14,000,000		
Total assets	$100,000,000	Total liabilities	$100,000,000

(Note: Required reserves, $6,000,000)

LONDON OFFICE

ASSETS		LIABILITIES	
$	0	$	0

Now suppose a foreign corporation (perhaps the Arab Sheik's oil company) which holds a long-term maturing CD of $10,000,000 at Morgan Guaranty refuses to renew it because the 6¼ per cent interest it is receiving seems too low. Morgan Guaranty agrees that the return should be greater, but explains it is prohibited by law from paying more. It notes, however, that its London branch is not. Accordingly, the corporation acquires a time deposit at the London office for $10,000,000 "by depositing" the check for $10,000,000 on the New York office it receives in return for the maturing CD —or, more realistically, by transfers on the books in New York and London. Let us look at the balance sheets:

NEW YORK HEAD OFFICE

ASSETS		LIABILITIES	
Deposits at Fed. Res. Bank of N.Y.	$ 6,000,000	Time certificates of deposit	$ 90,000,000
Other cash assets	4,000,000		
Loans	76,000,000	Due to London branch	10,000,000
Bonds	14,000,000		
Total assets	$100,000,000	Total liabilities	$100,000,000

(Note: Required reserves, before issuance of new regulations, $5,-400,000; since issuance of new regulations, between $5,400,000 and $6,400,000).

LONDON OFFICE

Assets		Liabilities	
Due from N.Y. office	$10,000,000	Time certificates of deposit	$10,000,000

Clearly, if we consolidate the branch and the head office, the books are completely unchanged. Yet these bookkeeping transactions: (1) enabled Morgan Guaranty to pay a rate in London higher than 6¼ per cent on some certificates of deposit; and (2) reduced its required reserves by $600,000 prior to the recent modification of Regulation M. The reduction in required reserves arose because until recently U.S. banks were not required to keep a reserve against liabilities to their foreign branches. With the amendment of Regulation M, any further reduction of reserves by this route has been eliminated since the Federal Reserve now requires a reserve of 10 per cent on the amount due to branch offices in excess of the amount due on average during May.[7]

HYPOCRISY AND WINDOW DRESSING

This example has been expressed in terms of a *foreign* corporation because the story is a bit more complicated for a U.S. corporation, though the end result is the same. First, a U.S. corporation that transfers its funds from a certificate of deposit at a U.S. bank to a deposit at a bank abroad—whether a foreign bank or an overseas branch of a U.S. bank—is deemed by the Department of Commerce to have made a foreign investment. It may do so only if it is within its quota under the direct control over foreign investment with which we are still unfortunately saddled. Second, under pressure from the Federal Reserve, commercial banks will not facilitate direct transfers by the U.S. corporations—indeed, many will not ac-

[7] An amendment to Regulation M effective September 4, 1969, established a 10 per cent reserve requirement on head office liabilities to overseas branches on that portion of such liabilities in excess of the average amount on the books in the four-week period ending May 28, 1969.

cept time deposits from U.S. corporations at their overseas branches, whether their own customers or not, unless the corporation can demonstrate that the deposit is being made for an "international" purpose. However, precisely the same results can be accomplished by a U.S. holder of a CD making a deposit in a foreign bank and the foreign bank in turn making a deposit in, or a loan to, the overseas branch of a U.S. bank. As always, this kind of moral suasion does not prevent profitable transactions. It simply produces hypocrisy and window dressing—in this case, by unnecessarily giving business to competitors of U.S. banks!

The final effect is precisely the same as in the simple example of the foreign corporation. That example shows, in highly simplified form, the main way U.S. banks have used the Eurodollar market and explains why it is that the more they "borrow" or "bring back" from the Eurodollar market, the higher Eurodollar deposits mount. In our example, borrowing went up $10,000,000, and so did deposits.

From January 1, 1969, to July 31, 1969, CD deposit liabilities of U.S. banks went down $9.3 billion, and U.S. banks' indebtedness to their own overseas branches went up $8.6 billion. The closeness of these two numbers is not coincidental.

These bookkeeping operations have affected the statistics far more than the realities. The run-off in CDs in the U.S., and the accompanying decline in total commercial bank deposits (which the Federal Reserve uses as its "bank credit proxy") have been interpreted as signs of extreme monetary tightness. Money has been tight, but these figures greatly overstate the degree of tightness. The holders of CDs on U.S. banks who replaced them by Eurodollar deposits did not have their liquidity squeezed. The banks that substituted "due to branches" for "due to depositors on time certificates of deposit" did not have their lending power reduced. The Federal Reserve's insistence on keeping Regulation Q ceilings at levels below market rates has simply imposed enormous structural adjustments and shifts of funds on the commercial banking system for no social gain whatsoever.

CORRECTING A MISUNDERSTANDING

A column that appeared in a leading financial paper just prior to the Federal Reserve's revision of reserve requirements encapsules the widespread misunderstanding about the Eurodollar market. The Eurodollar market, the column noted, has:

> . . . ballooned as U.S. banks have discovered that they can ease the squeeze placed on them by the Federal Reserve Board by borrowing back these foreign-deposited dollars that were pumped out largely through U.S. balance-of-payments deficits. Of this pool of $30 billion, U.S. banks as of last week had soaked up $13 billion. . . .
>
> Thanks to this system, it takes only seconds to transmit money—and money troubles—between the U.S. and Europe. . . . The Federal Reserve's pending proposal to make Eurodollar borrowing more costly to U.S. banks might make their future demands a shade less voracious, but this doesn't reduce concern about whether there will be strains in repaying the massive amounts already borrowed.

Strains there may be, but they will reflect features of the Eurodollar market other than those stressed by this newspaper comment. The use of the Eurodollar market by commercial banks to offset the decline in CDs was primarily a bookkeeping operation. The reverse process—a rise in CDs and a matching decline in Eurodollar borrowings—will also require little more than a bookkeeping operation.

XVII

ALEXANDER K. SWOBODA

Dr. Swoboda, a Swiss national, is Professor of International Economics at the Graduate Institute of International Studies, Geneva, Switzerland. He studied economics at Yale University where he received his B.A., M.A., and Ph.D. (1966). He was Post-Doctoral Fellow in Political Economy at the University of Chicago in 1966–67 and a visiting assistant professor at the Graduate School of Business of the University of Chicago in 1967–68. He has been Visiting Professor in Economics at the Johns Hopkins School for Advanced International Studies in Bologna and is a visitor at the London School of Economics and Political Science, where he teaches international monetary economics.

Dr. Swoboda was rapporteur of the Chicago Conference on International Monetary Problems and of the Ditchley Conference on the Foreign Exchange Market. His published work includes The Euro-Dollar Market: an Interpretation, *Princeton Essay in International Finance, No. 68 (February 1968) and he was co-editor with Robert A. Mundell of* Monetary Problems of the International Economy *(Chicago: University of Chicago Press, 1969). In addition he has written several papers on the theory of international adjustment and on international finance.*

The Eurodollar Market: An Economist's Point of View

INTRODUCTION

The Eurodollar market is many things to many people. To the banker it is a potential for profits; to the statistician, a source of frustration; to monetary authorities, a cause of much worry; to the layman, a fascinating and mysterious game. For some economists, it represents the irritating intrusion of a complicated real-world phenomenon into the models of standard international monetary theory; for others, an institution that can and should be studied quite apart from the received analytical framework.

Yet, in many respects, the Eurodollar market can be analyzed with the standard tools of economic analysis. Though there are some important differences, Eurodollar and other types of capital flows have much in common. Among the differences, the role of banks and of dollar denomination as well

Portions of this chapter are based on a talk entitled "Should the Eurodollar Market be Controlled?" delivered by the author before the American Management Association's briefing on American Business and the Future of the International Monetary System, in December, 1969.

as the process of credit creation are worth singling out. The growth of the Eurodollar market clearly has implications for the efficiency, equity, and stability of the international financial system; these implications, together with the need and possibilities for control, are again amenable to elementary economic analysis. A more speculative, but perhaps also more interesting, question concerns the role of the market in the evolution of the international monetary system as a whole.

Similarities and differences between Eurodollar and other capital flows, credit creation, equity and efficiency, stability and control, and the broader international monetary perspective are the five themes we will touch upon.

EURODOLLAR AND OTHER CAPITAL FLOWS

One of the functions of the Eurodollar market and instrument is to facilitate the transfer of short-term capital from one country to another. This function, of course, can be and is performed by many other financial institutions. The determinants and consequences of capital flows through the Eurodollar market are, in many respects, similar to those of other types of capital flows. To illustrate this obvious point, compare the effects of two alternative ways for capital to flow from, say, Italy to Germany.

Suppose that interest rates in Germany rise relative to those in Italy. An Italian corporation sells some Italian commercial paper, converts the proceeds into Deutsche marks, and acquires a short-term claim on a German corporation. This transaction—after various effects have been traced through and under the appropriate set of assumptions—will tend to result in a gain of foreign-exchange reserves and a multiple expansion of money and credit in Germany and in a loss of reserves and multiple contraction of credit in Italy. Suppose now that, as a consequence of the rise in German interest rates, a United Kingdom bank finds it profitable to make a dollar loan to the

German corporation (which converts the proceeds into Deutsche marks to make payments to domestic suppliers) and to "accept" a dollar deposit from the Italian corporation, the source of which is the sale of Italian commercial paper. The end result of this Eurodollar operation in terms of reserve and credit changes in Germany and Italy is the same as before.

Although this example illustrates the similarities between Eurodollar and other types of capital flows, it also helps draw attention to four important features specific to the Eurodollar system: first, the dollar denomination of transactions (particularly interbank transactions); second, the holding of dollar balances and the incurring of dollar liabilities by non-United States residents, especially nonbanks; third, the holding of these balances at—and the dollar indebtedness to—non-United States banks; fourth, the important role played by banks in the Eurodollar system.

A combination of specific institutional factors and general economic motivations account for both this preference for dollar denomination and holdings, and the role of European and other non-U.S. banks in dollar transactions. Among institutional factors, official regulation and private agreements have played a particularly important role. Thus, foreign-currency transactions sometimes escape the scope of gentleman's agreements concerning domestic-currency transactions; the foreign-currency liabilities of banks are not always subject to the same reserve requirements as their domestic-currency liabilities; and the interest-rate ceilings imposed by regulation Q have, at times, put American banks at a disadvantage vis-à-vis European banks in competing for dollar deposits. This last factor (regulation Q) can help explain partly why dollar balances have been held at European rather than U.S. banks and some of the recent massive borrowings of United States banks in the Eurodollar market; it does not account for the overall growth of foreign-currency denomination of transactions, of foreign-currency holdings, and of foreign-currency liabilities owed by nonbanks; nor does it account for the predominant role of the dollar in these transactions and holdings.

An analysis of the rationale for specific currency preferences on the part of economic agents, and of the reasons for the choice of a specific vehicle currency, is needed as a supplement to particular historical and institutional factors in explaining the role of the dollar in international financial markets. The basic proposition that emerges from a theory of currency preferences is that substantial economies in transactions costs as well as increases in the interest return on working balances can be obtained by denominating all transactions, and holding all working balances, in one and the same currency.[1] That the dollar should be chosen as the "vehicle currency" that performs this function is not surprising. The sheer size of United States markets for both goods and services and financial assets, the preponderance of the United States in world trade, the role of the dollar as reserve and intervention currency, and the efficiency of the United States financial system all contribute to greater liquidity of dollar balances and lower asset-exchange costs on dollar transactions. In addition, the growth in the use of a currency as a vehicle for transactions between third countries constitutes a self-reinforcing process: use of a currency as vehicle, by enlarging its transactions domain, results in economies of scale and information that further enhance its usefulness and attraction.

The motivation for European bank participation in the Eurodollar market derives simply from a desire and ability to share in the profits of the expanding dollar business that goes with the dollar's status in private financial markets. European banks have been able to break, profitably, the American bank

[1] For a more rigorous development of a theory of currency preferences, an analysis of the role and choice of vehicle currencies, and the application of these principles to the Eurodollar market, see A. K. Swoboda, "The Euro-dollar Market: An Interpretation," *Essays in International Finance*, No. 64 (Princeton University, February 1968).

monoply on the provision of dollar loans and deposits for a variety of reasons including, as mentioned previously, special factors such as regulation Q and differences in reserve requirements. More generally, however, Eurobanks have been able to operate profitably because dollar deposits in Europe and dollar loans from a European bank are not perfect substitutes for deposits in, and loans from, United States banks (because of location, business hours, knowledge of clients, and so on, on the one hand, and because of the scope for economies of scale and information inherent in the specialization of the functions of wholesaler, broker, and retailer in the highly efficient Eurodollar market, on the other).[2]

CREDIT CREATION

In the example of one chain of Eurodollar transactions given at the beginning of the preceding section, dollar assets and liabilities were created through the intermediation of a Eurobank; however, no net credit creation took place: credit expanded in Germany and contracted in Italy. Instead of a single chain of transactions, consider now the network of Eurobanks taken as a whole; it constitutes a banking system—the Eurodollar banking system—and as such is capable of multiple deposit and credit creation.[3]

In discussing credit creation in the Eurodollar market, it will be useful to define, first, what it is that is being created and, second, to make some initial simplifying assumptions in order to focus on the forest rather than on the trees. Credit creation in the Eurodollar market refers to the creation of

[2] One of the consequences of this specialization is the possibility for several intermediary banks to operate on the spread between the rate paid to the original depositor and that charged to the final borrower.

[3] The issue of credit creation was discussed in some analytical detail in my "The Euro-Dollar Market: An Interpretation," esp. pp. 30–34 and appendix. A more recent discussion can be found in Milton Friedman, "The Eurodollar Market: Some First Principles," reprinted on pp. 273–293 (Chapter XVI). For a critical view of Friedman's empirical assumptions, see Fred H. Klopstock, "Money Creation in the Euro-Dollar Market—A Note on Professor Friedman's Views," *Monthly Review*, Federal Reserve Bank of New York, January 1970, pp. 12–15.

credit to (and deposits by) nonbanks, not to the piling up of interbank assets and liabilities that would wash out in a consolidated balance sheet for the Eurodollar system as a whole. Furthermore, creation of Eurodollar assets and liabilities held by nonbanks must be distinguished from multiple credit creation within the Eurodollar system. In the imaginary Eurodollar operation involving the Italian lender and the German borrower, no additional amount of credit is made available in the world as a whole even though a Eurodollar deposit and a Eurodollar loan have been "created." It is also relevant to ask whether multiple credit creation in the Eurodollar market may not lead to multiple credit contraction in some other part of the world banking sysem.

Finally, the reader must adopt the following initial simplifying assumptions (some of these will be relaxed later, the consequences of relaxing others may easily be worked out): banks in all countries are fully loaned up; reserve requirements and money and credit multipliers are the same in all *national* banking systems; and the sale of one currency for another in the foreign-exchange market leads to a reserve loss and credit contraction in the country whose currency is sold, a reserve gain and credit expansion in the other country. This is a gold-standard type assumption that enables us to abstract, for the moment, from asymmetries introduced by holdings of dollars as official reserves and associated special policies.

The mechanism of multiple credit creation in the Eurodollar banking system can be illustrated with the help of a simple example. Suppose the owner of a dollar deposit in New York transfers it to Eurobank 1, that the deposit is re-lent to Eurobank 2, who then extends a dollar loan to a German borrower; suppose that, instead of converting the dollars into Deutsche marks, the German borrower uses the dollars to extinguish a debt to a Dutch supplier who in turn re-deposits the dollars with Eurobank 3. The latter may now lend dollars to an Italian borrower, and so on. The re-deposit of the original dollar deposit with Eurobank 3 has started a new chain of Eurodollar transactions and thus is part of a process of multiple expansion of deposits and credit in the Eurodollar market. As long as the process of re-depositing with Eurobanks continues, the flow of credit and the stock of money in national banking systems need not be affected:[4] the deposit originally transferred to the Eurodollar market remains also as a deposit with the United States banking system.

Re-depositing with Eurobanks gives rise to multiple deposit creation in the Eurodollar market, while the fact that Eurobanks keep their reserves in the United States explains why this process need not occur at the expense of credit creation elsewhere. Eurobanks taken together constitute a private banking system that keeps as reserves, deposits with another private banking system—that of the United States. In one sense, therefore, the Eurodollar system, as has sometimes been pointed out, bears certain similarities to the nonmember bank system in the United States. The transfer of a dollar deposit from a member to a nonmember bank provides the latter with excess reserves that can serve as the basis for a multiple expansion of deposits and credit in the nonmember bank system; as nonmember banks keep their reserves in the form of deposits with member banks, no credit contraction need occur in the member-bank system.

The size of the Eurodollar deposit multiplier is inversely related to the leakages from successive rounds of re-lending in the market. Dollar reserves kept by Eurobanks against dollar deposits diminish the amount re-lent on each successive round of lending; so do any leakages from the re-depositing process into the acquisition of other than Eurodollar deposits, that is, principally, into dollar deposits in New York and into foreign-

[4] I abstract here, of course, from changes in interest rates, income and price levels, and other economic variables that would accompany the multiple credit expansion process and would induce substitutions between Eurodollar and other types of loans and between Eurodollar and other types of deposits.

currency assets. In brief, the size of the Eurodollar deposit multiplier is directly related to the system's loan-retention ratio and inversely related to the Eurobanks' reserve ratio.

While the overall ratio of leakages to re-deposits determines the size of the Eurodollar multiplier, the particular form that these leakages take determines the changes in money stocks and credit flows that take place elsewhere in the world economy. Assume still that the source of the initial Eurodollar deposit is an existing dollar deposit in the United States. First, when dollar reserves held in the United States by Eurobanks constitute the only leakage from the Eurodollar system, no multiple expansion or contraction of credit need occur in any national banking system: total dollar deposits in the United States remain unchanged and no deposit flow to or from any other country need take place. Second, when instead of being re-deposited in the Eurodollar market, the proceeds of a Eurodollar loan are deposited in the United States, further credit expansion in the Eurodollar market is halted, but nothing else need happen. Third, when the dollar deposit acquired from a Eurodollar borrower, instead of being re-deposited in the market, is converted into foreign exchange, multiple credit creation in the Eurodollar market again stops but, in addition, based on our initial assumptions, an equal contraction and expansion of credit take place in the United States and Europe, respectively. Had we assumed that the central bank that acquires the dollars decides to keep those on deposit with a United States bank, no contraction of credit need take place in the United States.[5]

So far, the source of the initial Eurodollar deposit has been assumed to be a dollar deposit already held in the United States. The analysis of deposit and credit creation within the Eurodollar market need not be modified if the initial deposit

[5] Such contraction could still take place if American monetary authorities react to an increase in liabilities to foreign official holders by reducing the United States money supply.

was acquired in the foreign-exchange market. The implications for credit creation and contraction in national banking systems, however, are different. Under our assumptions, the initial acquisition of a dollar deposit in the foreign-exchange market leads to a multiple expansion of credit in the United States and contraction abroad. This conclusion can be appropriately modified if it is assumed that the dollar deposit is acquired from a foreign central bank that previously held it at a United States bank.[6] The remainder of the analysis follows as in the preceding examples.

Conceptually, then, it is clear that multiple credit creation can take place in the Eurodollar market and that this need not be matched by credit contraction elsewhere. The interesting question concerns the extent to which expansion of the Eurodollar market actually can be attributed to multiple credit and deposit expansion as contrasted with initial transfers to the market. Unfortunately, available statistical evidence cannot be used to answer this question. It may be possible (though difficult) to estimate the ratio of net Eurodollar liabilities to dollar deposits held in New York by Eurobanks. That ratio, however, may be the result of straightforward intermediation as well as of credit creation. Suppose that dollar liabilities of Eurobanks stood at $40 billion and their dollar deposits in New York at $5 billion. These figures are consistent with either the transfer of $40 billion to the Eurodollar market and the conversion of $35 billion into foreign currencies, or the transfer of $5 billion to the Eurodollar market serving as the basis for a total Eurodollar deposit expansion of $40 billion; they are thus consistent with a Eurodollar deposit multiplier ranging anywhere from 1 to 8.

However, a rough guess at the possible magnitude of the

[6] The consequence may be that credit does not expand in the United States; therefore, no net addition to credit in the world occurs. However, credit contraction abroad may not take place either if, as is likely, the dollar deposit is acquired with bank *excess* reserves.

Eurodollar deposit multiplier can be made by guessing at the likely magnitudes of the market's loan-retention ratio and the banks' customary or required reserve ratio. There is fairly general agreement that reserves kept against dollar liabilities by Eurobanks are quite low, say, somewhere between 5 and 20 per cent. On the other hand, the proportion of dollar deposits that are re-deposited in the market is very difficult to estimate. To the extent that Eurodollar loans are made to corporations and individuals engaged in international trade invoiced in dollars, Eurodollar deposits may serve as means of payments or near-money and the proportion re-deposited (and, hence, the loan-retention ratio) may be fairly high. On the other hand, any New York deposit obtained through the Eurodollar market that is converted into foreign exchange—as would be the case when Eurodollar borrowings are used to finance, as is frequently done, a foreign domestic-credit expansion—or that is held directly in the United States would escape the Eurodollar pool. On the whole, leakages from the Eurodollar system are probably substantial. Hypothetical values of the Eurodollar deposit multiplier can be obtained by combining alternative assumptions concerning the sizes of reserve and redeposit (or loan-retention) ratios. Some such values are given in Table XVII.1.[7] A multiplier value of 1 in Table XVII.1 indicates that no multiple deposit creation takes place; a multiplier of 2.5, that an initial deposit of $100 generates $150 of additional deposits. Based on reasonable guesses of the proportion of re-deposit (say, somewhere between 20

[7] Entries in Table XVII.1 are calculated from the formula $k = 1/1 - (1 - a)d$, where k is the multiplier, a the reserve ratio, and d the proposition re-deposited or loan-retention ratio within the Eurodollar market. If m intermediations take place along one Eurodollar "lending-borrowing" chain, the multiplier formula must be rewritten as $k = 1/1 - (1 - a)^m d$. To take into account this possibility for several intermediaries, say, two, to operate on the lending-borrowing spread, re-interpret the reserve ratios in Table XX.1 as being equal to $1 - (1 - a)^2$; thus if each intermediary keeps a reserve ratio of .134, the effective reserve ratio along one chain is approximately 25 per cent. For derivation of the formula for k, see "The Euro-Dollar Market: An Interpretation," p. 41.

TABLE XVII.1
HYPOTHETICAL DEPOSIT MULTIPLIERS

Proportion Re-Deposited	Reserve Ratio 0	5%	10%	25%
100%	∞	20	10	4
75%	4	3.48	3.08	2.29
50%	2	1.90	1.82	1.60
33%	1.5	1.46	1.43	1.33
25%	1.33	1.31	1.29	1.23
0%	1	1	1	1

and 45 per cent) and of reserve ratio (say, somewhere between 5 and 25 per cent), one would estimate the deposit multiplier in the Eurodollar market to lie somewhere between 1.25 and 1.75—and in any case, not above 2.

Systematic re-channeling of dollar reserves to the Eurodollar market by foreign central banks, however, could significantly raise the value of the Eurodollar deposit multiplier. Suppose, for instance, that all leakages from the Eurodollar market result in the acquisition of dollar deposits by foreign central banks and that the latter always re-deposit 50 per cent of increases in their dollar reserves in the market. Incorporating this re-depositing process in our multiplier formula would result in doubling the multiplier values given in Table XVII.1; more generally, the value of the deposit multiplier must be multiplied by $1/(1–R)$, where R is the proportion of gains in dollar reserves re-deposited by foreign central banks. However, whether depositing of foreign-exchange reserves by central banks should be incorporated in the multiplier or counted as a source of primary deposits is a matter of choice that depends partly on the purpose for which the multiplier is to be used and partly on the stability of the "leakage to foreign central banks" ratio and of the central bank re-deposit ratio.

EFFICIENCY AND EQUITY

If there exists some disagreement as to the importance, let alone the possibility, of multiple deposit creation in the Eurodollar market, there is little doubt that the market has contributed, at least in a limited sense, to a more efficient international allocation of short-term capital. This contribution has taken several forms. The development of a rapid and international communications network, the convenience of the Eurodollar instrument, and similar factors have significantly increased the responsiveness of capital to differences in national interest rates, thus making it easier to transfer capital from areas where its productivity is (presumably) low to those where it is high. The specialization of the functions of wholesaler and retailer, the quality of the names of the main participants, the possibility of borrowing large amounts without exerting too depressing an influence on a single small market have made it possible to realize significant economies of scale in lending and borrowing. These economies, together with the increased competition among financial and nonfinancial institutions that has accompanied the market's development, have made it possible to increase the return to lenders and reduce the cost to borrowers. In other words, the efficiency of financial intermediation has been spurred by the market's development with beneficial effects on the overall rate of capital accumulation and the allocation of saving to alternative uses.

This picture of the contribution of the Eurodollar market to economic efficiency is subject to at least three qualifications. In the first place, increased efficiency in one part of the economy may also increase the undesirable impact on economic welfare of remaining distortions; this is, of course, the central proposition of the so-called theory of second best. Second, increased efficiency may bring in its wake increased instability. Third, increased efficiency may be accompanied by changes in the distribution of income and profits that society deems to be undesirable or, in the economist's jargon, "inequitable."

In the present context, the "equity" issue—how the gains from the Eurodollar market's growth have been distributed—can be put overly simply as follows: Have certain groups within a country or certain countries within the market benefitted more than others—or even at the expense of others—from the market's growth? No precise answer to this question is available; nevertheless, three general remarks may be worth making. First, large institutions (for instance, large United States banks with branches abroad) have benefitted, at least directly, more than, and sometimes at the expense of, small ones (though smaller institutions have begun to react to this problem by sponsoring various forms of joint ventures into the Eurocurrency area). Second, the market can be said to have contributed to a more equitable distribution of the gains from international investment by breaking the monopoly of U.S. banks on dollar financing. Third, some of the inequities that do exist are the product of disparities in national regulations concerning residents' participation in external capital-account transactions. For instance, reserve requirements against net foreign liabilities (liabilities minus assets) of German banks have, at times, put these banks at a disadvantage vis-à-vis their foreign competitors who are not subject to similar reserve requirements. Such inequities may be exacerbated by increased efficiency in Eurodollar transactions: the higher the interest sensitivity of capital flows, the larger the flows of funds and the changes in the distribution of profits that would result from differential regulation of banks in various countries.

STABILITY AND CONTROL

The Eurodollar market has sometimes been said to constitute a major source of instability of the international monetary system. This, at best, is a highly misleading argument, although it does contain an important (if badly stated) grain of truth: instability, whatever its cause, will tend to spread more rapidly when capital is highly mobile internationally, as in the Eurodollar market. Nevertheless, it is not the Eurodollar market that causes currency crises, but currency crises that have given rise to unsettled conditions in the Eurocurrency market. It is not the Eurodollar market that causes balance-of-payments deficits, but rather payments imbalances that have been reflected in capital outflows to the Eurodollar and other money markets. It is not the existence of an international money market that has caused a steep rise in interest rates over the past year; rather, generally high levels of interest rates, due partly to world—and particularly U.S.—inflation, have resulted in high interest rates on the Eurodollar market.

To come back to the grain of truth referred to above, wide use of the Eurodollar instrument has contributed to the integration of national money markets and to a high sensitivity of capital flows to changes in expected yield differentials. As the problems for stabilization policy posed by the existence of the Eurodollar market have been discussed elsewhere,[8] only a few general remarks on this topic need be made here.

The basic problem that capital mobility—as embodied, for instance, in Eurodollar flows—poses for an individual country's stabilization policy is that it sharpens the conflict between internal and external balance when only monetary policy instruments are available. The greater the interest sensitivity of capital flows, the greater the payments imbalances that result from gearing monetary policy to internal balance in inflation-surplus or deflation-deficit situations. The reserve loss (gain) per unit of time, and the consequent rate of neutralization operations required to keep the money supply at a level consistent with internal balance but above (below) the level

[8] See, for instance, "The Euro-Dollar Market: An Interpretation," pp. 35–38; and Fred H. Klopstock, "The Eurodollar Market: Some Unresolved Issues," *Essays in International Finance*, No. 65 (Princeton University, March 1968).

required for external balance, is an increasing function of the interest sensitivity of capital flows. In the extreme case, where this sensitivity becomes very high, open-market operations will hardly succeed in affecting the money supply at all since capital flows and attendant reserve flows tend to return the money supply to the level consistent with external balance almost at once. In practical terms, this means that as the central bank expands domestic credit and domestic interest rates tend to fall, capital flows out to, say, the Eurodollar market, the central bank loses foreign-exchange reserves, and the money supply tends to return to its original level.

One lesson for policy is that to break the general rule which says that monetary policy must be used for external balance under fixed exchange rates results in reserve flows that frustrate the offending policymaker's aims all the more rapidly when capital is highly mobile. Another lesson is that payments imbalances *can* be rapidly corrected under fixed exchange rates when capital mobility is high *if* monetary policy is geared to external balance. Fiscal policy can then be used for internal balance.[9]

Countries have used a variety of devices to try and prevent Eurodollar flows from frustrating the pursuit of domestic objectives through monetary policy. These devices have included explicit or implicit exchange controls, for example, outright prohibition of Eurodollar transactions by residents; regulations affecting the cost and extent of bank participation in the market, such as the imposition of special reserve requirements on foreign-currency liabilities or the request that banks keep a specified maximum or minimum net liability position in the market; and forward-market intervention (either general or limited to swaps with commercial banks) to

[9] This is, of course, the pairing of instruments to targets proposed by Mundell. See, for instance, Robert A. Mundell, "The Appropriate Use of Monetary and Fiscal Policy under Fixed Exchange Rates," *IMF Staff Papers,* 9(March 1962): 70–79.

affect the cost of conversion of dollars into and out of local currencies.[10]

Short of generalized exchange controls, however, these measures offer only a partial escape from potential conflicts between internal and external balance. Capital mobility is not limited to Eurodollar flows. Intervention margins put limits on achievable forward discounts or premia, at least if no parity change is expected. Reserve requirements would have to be raised continuously to achieve a rising level of interest rates and this poses familiar problems of equity and feasibility. More basically, there is no escape in the long run from the necessity of gearing monetary policy to the balance of payments if a system of fixed exchange rates is to be run properly.

Problems of stability and control of the Eurodollar market also arise at the global level. For instance, a case can be made for intervention designed to moderate undue seasonal and speculative strains on the Eurodollar market, strains that, if left unchecked, could bring in their wake brutal disruptions of national money markets and the exacerbation of confidence crises. Smoothing out such temporary disturbances requires coordinated intergovernmental intervention in the market for, in its absence, control of the Eurodollar market is limited to control of the access of individual countries to the market's facilities. Cooperation among central banks to temper temporary disturbances has developed on informal lines and has, on the whole, been quite successful in moderating abrupt short-

[10] Even the United States has felt the need to impose reserve requirements on Eurodollar borrowings by United States banks to counteract the influence of these borrowings on bank liquidity. It is true that these borrowings were partly due to the discriminatory impact of regulation Q; this has led Professor Friedman to speak of a "statistical artifact" in connection with these borrowings (see Milton Friedman, *op. cit.*). However, part of the increase in Eurodollar borrowings by U.S. banks over the past two years found its source in the conversion of foreign-currency into dollar balances and represents a net capital inflow that would not have taken place in the absence of rising United States interest rates even if regulation Q had not been in force. Moreover, the fact that a capital inflow into the United States may result in the transfer of a foreign central bank deposit to private nonbanks, thus leaving total deposits and reserves unchanged, applies to most flows of capital into the United States and not just to Eurodollar flows.

term changes in the general level of Eurodollar rates by channeling or re-channeling to the market substantial amounts of short-term capital. There has emerged a central bank club that, in cooperation with the Bank for International Settlements now deals almost routinely at year-end, half-year, and even quarterly, with seasonal stringencies in the market. Less routinely, it also cooperates in alleviating the disruptive effects of speculative crises.[11]

On balance, informal cooperation among central banks "to alleviate undesirable strains on the market," in Charles Coombs's words, has proved quite useful in providing a service comparable to the "maintenance of orderly conditions" in domestic markets by national banks. However, such cooperation, or isolated intervention for that matter, when limited to intervention in the Eurodollar market, does not strike at the cause of monetary instability but rather at the symptoms that may manifest themselves in the Eurodollar market. Neither can it answer more fundamental questions such as, Who is responsible for setting the world or Eurodollar level of interest rates?

A BROADER PERSPECTIVE

The level of Eurodollar rates can be taken as a real-world approximation to the theoretical concept of a world level of interest rates. In practice, of course, national interest rates can and will diverge from Eurodollar rates; however, as has been argued previously, the extent of the divergence is limited in a world of fixed exchange rates, currency convertibility, and capital mobility. In such a world one may well ask, Who is—and who should be—responsible for setting the world level of interest rates?

It is, of course, the demand and supply for deposits and loans that set the level of Eurodollar rates; as these demands

[11] For a more detailed and informative description of central bank cooperation in this area, see the quarterly reports of Charles Coombs in the *Monthly Bulletin*, Federal Reserve Bank of New York.

and supplies originate in a variety of countries, no single country entirely controls the rate level. Moreover, in a world made up of a large number of countries of equal size, no single country could exercise a predominant influence on that level. If one country is significantly larger than the others, however, its monetary policy will play an important role in setting the world level of interest rates.[12] Let us illustrate this point. Suppose the world to be divided into two parts, the United States and Europe, the latter being made up of some ten countries of roughly equal size. Suppose, further, that capital is perfectly mobile internationally (there cannot be any lasting differences between national interest rates) and that the United States represents 50 per cent of the world economy in terms of income, money supply, and so forth. Now let the United States increase its money supply by 10 per cent; this results in a 5 per cent increase in the world money supply (and a corresponding downward pressure on interest rates, other things being equal). However, a 10 per cent increase in the money supply of an isolated European country would only result in a ½ per cent increase in the world money supply.[13] Alternatively, suppose that the rate of increase of the money supply in the United States is 10 per cent per annum and that money supplies are kept fixed in Europe. Abstracting from the effect of economic growth and assuming an income elasticity of the demand for money equal to 1 in every country, this will result, in equilibrium, in a rate of world inflation of 5 per cent and a

[12] These conclusions about interest rate levels could and should be extended to price-level changes and rates of inflation.

[13] It can be demonstrated, within both classical and Keynesian models of the world economy, that the relevant magnitude in determining changes in world interest rates (or price levels) under perfect capital mobility is, other things being equal, changes in the world money supply. Reserve changes, but not interest-rate changes, depend on the national origin of the change in the world money supply. Moreover, it can be shown that, when capital is immobile internationally, equilibrium interest-rate *differentials* are invariant to changes in money supplies which again influence interest rate *levels*. Capital mobility does make a difference, however; it shortens significantly the length of time that elapses before the effects of policy changes are fully felt.

corresponding increase of money over real rates of interest. Had one of the European countries been adopting a 10 per cent rate of monetary expansion, the world rate of inflation would have been only ½ per cent.[14]

These hypothetical examples point to the importance of the size of nations in determining world trends in economic activity. They would hold even if there was no Eurodollar market. The latter's role in this context is to provide the institutional channel through which changes in United States interest rates are speedily transmitted to European (and other) national money markets. The predominance of United States economic policy in determining world economic trends (in particular, price and interest-rate trends) in the absence of coordinated policies in the rest of the world constitutes one aspect—the control aspect—of what has been referred to as "the dollar standard."[15]

A second aspect of the dollar standard resides in the ability of the United States to finance deficits through the issue of dollar liabilities to foreign monetary authorities. To illustrate the point in an oversimplified way, a 5 per cent (anticipated) rate of world inflation stemming from a 10 per cent rate of monetary expansion in the United States will create a flow demand for nominal balances in the rest of the world to maintain the value of real balances; in the absence of domestic credit expansion in "Europe," this desire for additional money balances can be satisfied through a European balance-of-payments surplus that results in a 5 per cent per annum expansion of the European money supply. If the world were on a gold standard, this process would fairly rapidly exhaust the United

[14] For a two-country "monetarist" model incorporating growth rates, inflation rates, and the balance of payments, see Robert A. Mundell, "Politique monétaire américaine et européenne," *Economie Appliquée,* Tome XXIII, No. 1, 1970.

[15] This control aspect, incidentally, is independent of the fact that the world is on some version of the gold-exchange standard. It would hold even if the world were on a gold standard!

States gold stock; to the extent that a dollar standard prevails, the process can continue as long as European central banks are willing (have to) accumulate international reserves in the form of dollar balances.[16] This is the "liquidity-issue aspect" of the dollar standard which is closely related to the so-called seigniorage problem.[17]

A third aspect of the dollar standard concerns the extent to which the dollar is used as a unit of account and settlement, medium of exchange, and store of value in private transactions, that is, within the domain of the dollar-transactions area. I have argued here and elsewhere that the growth of the Eurodollar market is in part a reflection of the expanding role of the dollar as an international private-vehicle currency, of a broadening of the domain of transactions denominated in dollars. In that sense, the Eurodollar market represents an institutional counterpart to the vehicle-currency aspect of the dollar standard.

Put in this broader perspective, then, the growth of the Eurodollar market can be viewed as part of the evolution of the international monetary system towards a (far from pure) dollar standard. The role of the Eurodollar market in this evolution, however, is fraught with paradoxes. In the first place, part of the development of the market can be attributed to an attack on the monopoly position of United States banks in accepting dollar deposits and making dollar loans: the Eurodollar market enables non-American banks to participate in dollar-denominated transactions. In the process of compet-

---

[16] Note that this does not mean that European surpluses are always the counterpart of inflation-caused American deficits. Suppose that the demand for liquidity expands rapidly in Europe as a result, say, of rapid economic growth. The consequence will be, ceteris paribus, a United States deficit (as conventionally measured) as European central banks acquire the dollar balances required to serve as a base for monetary expansion in Europe.

[17] For a discussion of the seigniorage problem in general, see Herbert G. Grubel, "The Distribution of Seigniorage from International Liquidity Creation," and Harry G. Johnson, "A Note on Seigniorage and the Social Saving from Substituting Credit for Commodity Money," in Robert A. Mundell and Alexander K. Swoboda (Eds.) *Monetary Problems of the International Economy* (Chicago: University of Chicago Press, 1969).

ing with United States banks for the profits generated by such transactions, European (and other non-American) banks bid away some of the dollar-denomination rents accruing to United States banks and some of the seigniorage accruing to the United States from the vehicle-currency use of the dollar.[18] Paradoxically, the very success of European banks in entering the dollar-business industry serves to broaden the transactions domain of the dollar.

The Eurodollar market has become, at least to some people, a symbol of the dollar standard (one prominent French economist has gone so far as to call the market "un scandale"). As such, its growth has contributed to the call for the creation of a European currency as a counter to the hegemony of the dollar. Ironically, if the Eurodollar market acts as a stimulus for such proposals it also makes it more difficult for any existing currency, or any new European currency, to displace the dollar as the world's most important vehicle currency.

[18] For a more detailed analysis of the seigniorage and denomination rents arising from the vehicle-currency role of the dollar, see "The Eurodollar Market: An Interpretation," esp. pp. 11–14.

XVIII

ROBERT L. GENILLARD

Mr. Genillard was born in Lausanne, Switzerland, 40 years ago. He studied at Lausanne College and University, holds an M.A. in economics, and did graduate work in economics, business administration and finance at Columbia and New York universities. He joined White, Weld & Co. in New York in 1953 and became a General Partner in 1958. He is a member of the firm's management committee and is in charge of its international operations.

White, Weld & Co., one of the leading international investment banking firms, has played a key role in the creation and growth of the Eurobond market. Mr. Genillard, who actually coined the term Eurobond, *is considered one of the principal authorities on the subject. His activities have been described in many publications, notably in a December 1967* Fortune *article entitled "Our First Real International Bankers."*

Mr. Genillard has frequently written and spoken on the international capital market under the sponsorship of various institutions, including The Royal Institute of International Affairs, The Federal Trust, the American Bankers Association's 16th Monetary Conference, Chambre Nationale des Conseillers Financiers, Centre de Recherches et d'Etudes de Chefs d'Enterprises, the American Petroleum Institute, the Stanford Research Institute, and the Economic Club of Chicago.

The Eurobond Market

AN EMERGING MULTINATIONAL CAPITAL MARKET

Internationalization of business, multinational corporations, world industries, supranational markets—these terms, which have become commonplace, underscore one of the principal concerns of business today: how to adapt in a fast changing and shrinking world. The growth of world trade and investment has been among the main economic stimulants in the postwar era. Political and especially social conditions have committed all governments to economic policies of growth which, when matched with technological stimuli, give business fundamental reasons to pursue an expansionary strategy quite apart from competitive considerations. These same policies have led to strains in the international monetary system. We now face the paradox whereby governments vitally interested in increasing the international competitive position of their key industries are often forced to make it more difficult for those industries to finance their foreign expansion. According to various prophecies, in 20 years some 600 huge international companies will be responsible for the bulk of the free world's industrial activity. The economic and social impact of such global companies will substantially influence the rate and manner of development in the countries in which they operate, requiring a departure from the limitations of a strictly regional approach to capital financing.

In the past, international financing took place within the context of national markets, as an extension of such markets. London in the last century and, until recently, New York were the major centers and proved in normal periods able to cope with all reasonable requirements of public and private borrowers.

Even if the international monetary scene should revert to a climate of complete stability and confidence, it is unlikely that any single capital market will, in the future, be in a position to supply alone a major portion of the fast growing international long-term capital requirements. Historically, governments have actively encouraged foreign access to their capital markets only when internal needs were readily satisfied and it was in the national interest to export capital. In any case, only the United States could in such a situation make a reasonably major contribution to world-wide needs. This is an unlikely occurrence for at least the next few years, and other capital markets are, individually, too small or structurally unable to make more than marginal contributions to total requirements. In addition, some multinational companies happen to be headquartered in small countries with capital markets geared primarily to the requirements of the smaller national companies.

Money may, therefore, indeed prove the root of all evil as far as international capital investment is concerned, unless the availability of exportable long-term capital keeps pace with the growth in international investment. The strains which the international monetary system has been undergoing in recent years make this unlikely in the short run, and structural problems make it difficult in the long run. Fortunately, the challenge of monetary adversity has given birth to the forerunner of an international capital market which has a truly multinational character and is being tacitly accepted, if not already sanctioned, as such by many monetary authorities.

At the moment, it is most often referred to as the Eurobond market. It is not, strictly speaking, the European capital market, as none exists, but is an international bond market functioning at the moment primarily in Europe, still heavily dependent on U.S. currency as its unit of account. The funds which it taps are at this time more importantly European, but the contribution made by investors in other parts of the world is quite substantial. For the year 1969, internationally syndicated issues reached $2.7 billion. By way of comparison, foreign public-bond offerings in convertible currencies which took place in national markets during the ten-year period 1959–69, barely exceeded some $2 billion.

A HISTORICAL EXPLANATION OF THE MARKET

The best way to delineate the Eurobond market may be to retrace its history.

The era following World War II can be divided roughly into three monetary periods: The first such period was characterized by the famous "Dollar Gap" which less than ten years ago was still described by many economists as a structural and chronic problem. During that time, for evident reasons, the New York capital market was the principal center for raising long-term finance for foreign borrowers. Issues offered in the United States must be registered under the 1933 Securities and Exchange Act, which had the practical effect of limiting borrowers primarily to government institutions since most semiprivate and private entities found these requirements too cumbersome or incompatible with their own standards. The management of such issues was almost entirely dominated by a small number of United States investment banking firms with historical ties to the foreign borrowers involved. If one excludes issues of the World Bank and, subsequently, of the Interamerican Bank, flotations amounted only to $150 million in 1955, $395 million in 1960, and in 1962 (the year prior to the Interest Equalization Tax) to $553 million. If both Canada and all international institutions are excluded, the figures dwindle to $48 million in 1955, $95 million in 1960, and $336 million in 1962.

At the time it was generally not appreciated that while New York was the clearing place for such operations and the dollar was the currency in which the issues were expressed, the securities were bought largely by nonresidents of the United States, in spite of the fact that they were offered at rates substantially higher than those available on internal American issues. This remark must be qualified with the statement that, while the bulk of these securities was indeed sold outside of the United States, the preference of American investors varied widely among different borrowers. Some issues of European governments were sold to the extent of 90 per cent to nonresidents, while some other issues, such as those of Australia, found a much larger acceptance among resident investors in the United States.

The second monetary postwar period may be described as one during which the dollar shortage in the world started receding as European recovery gained momentum and a climate of economic liberalization began to prevail. Controls on purchases of foreign securities by residents of various European countries were eased but, in general, the controls on internal capital markets remained stringent. This contrast is quite important because it leads to the introduction of an important postulate. The asymmetry between loose controls on the purchase of foreign securities by residents of countries with stringent and diverse controls or regulations governing their internal capital markets has tended, historically, to give rise to a parallel international market or to make an existing one grow. Yet the market which functioned in New York was already, in a nontechnical sense, a parallel market while the climate in Europe was beginning to favor a similar development here.

Only isolated attempts were made in Europe at floating issues across borders. Of course, internal capital markets were becoming more hospitable to foreign borrowers and foreign issues were being floated in increasing numbers in Switzerland, Holland, and England, to name the active markets. But those were foreign issues in local currency, without international syndication or planned international distribution. This is, by the way, a very important distinction which most statistics on international bond flotations do not always take into account; too frequently foreign issues floated internally without a conscious effort to distribute them world-wide are lumped with those which are internationally syndicated and sold simultaneously in many countries. The task is of course complex because foreign issues made in an internal market are not necessarily bought by residents of that market alone.

Nevertheless we can and, for the purpose of this dissertation, must divide foreign issues into two broad groups: (1) internationally syndicated (excluding Canadian, World Bank, and Interamerican Bank issues floated in the United States) and (2) nationally floated.

Now we can turn to the third monetary period of the postwar era characterized by a reversal in the United States balance-of-payments position and which culminated with the introduction of the Interest Equalization Tax and the subsequent direct-investment guidelines. This marked the first major setback in the postwar process of monetary liberalization which, ironically, was suffered by the United States, the country which had done so much to promote European economic unification and liberalization.

While the Interest Equalization Tax effectively barred U.S. residents from purchasing foreign-bond issues, thus confining the market for such issues to nonresident purchasers, the imposition of the tax did not require the creation of an entirely new source of demand for so-called foreign-dollar bonds because, as we saw earlier, such issues were already being sold largely to nonresidents of the United States. Nevertheless, this development did require a change in marketing techniques to facilitate the syndication and offering of dollar issues entirely outside of the United States.

One of the major paradoxes resulting from the Interest Equalization Tax was that it caused Europe to discover that a substantial international market could function here in which European bankers could play a leading role, in spite of the severe handicaps under which they often had to labor in their internal markets. Favorable conditions already existed for such a development, but it really took the American tax to force an internationalization of investment banking in this field, which in turn materially helped to broaden the international capital market. We have seen how modest the volume of internationally syndicated issues was until 1962 by present standards. By 1964, it had climbed to $980 million and reached nearly $1.2 billion in 1965. The highest volume so far was registered in 1968 with $3.1 billion. In 1962, such issues in dollars were floated by syndicates almost exclusively managed and comanaged by a handful of U.S. investment banking firms. However, using the traditional American system of ranking firms by the volume of issues managed or comanaged, we find in 1969 that, among the first 20 firms, only four were American and the balance European. (*See* statistical appendix, Table XVIII.6.)

No statistics are available on the volume of underwriting contracted by the various firms in the field but here, without doubt, the balance is now overwhelmingly in favor of European firms.

Another favorable development which can be ascribed to the Interest Equalization Tax is the advent of substantial borrowings by private corporations. When the market functioned primarily from a New York base, governmental borrowers dominated the scene. The imposition of the voluntary guidelines on direct foreign investment in the United States paradoxically again helped the Eurobond market to grow, through diversification. Top United States companies well-known to international investors made their appearance in the Eurobond market and many of the issues they floated received a highly enthusiastic response. While it is undeniable that the flotations by American companies did at the outset displace a number of other borrowers, this proved a temporary phenomenon. (*See* statistical appendix, Table XVIII.4.) The lasting effect is that major European companies are finding it easier to borrow in the broadened Eurobond market.

This review of the antecedents of the Eurobond market has hopefully placed it in proper focus and differentiated it from the foreign issues floated in internal capital markets in local currency under the internal laws and regulations of each such market. A definition which emerges from the foregoing is that the Eurobond market is one in which investors deal in bonds which represent for most of them foreign assets and where the final primary claim on the borrower is almost always to be made outside of the legal jurisdiction of the holder of the bond. We shall see later how the foregoing can logically evolve in a truly multinational and permanent institution.

STRUCTURE OF THE EUROBOND MARKET

Article 67 of the Treaty of Rome envisages the development of a unified "European" capital market. While the problems involved are now receiving active consideration from many sides, it is fair to say that practical achievements towards this aim remain few. On the other hand, there now functions in Europe a very substantial international capital market in fixed-income securities—the Eurobond market—which has developed without any official assistance. It has made important financial history and set precedents which will endure. The divergent trends between the international market and the national ones deserve analysis.

Divergent National and International Trends

The recent history of national capital markets is a matter of public record. It may therefore be sufficient to look at their present condition. No generalizations can be made, as each of the national capital markets is a virtually unique collection of public, semipublic, and private institutions operating under a variety of laws, regulations, and self-imposed practices which developed in response to their own set of historic circumstances. The qualitative differences are therefore as great as the quantitative ones. Some markets, such as the British and, to a lesser extent, the Swiss and Dutch, can be described as well-developed, accepting (at least as far as the British market is concerned) a free-market mechanism which relies on sensitive prices as an indispensible component for efficient allocation of capital. This qualification should apply to Germany also, because its regulatory climate is liberal, but the development of its market has been at times impeded by structural problems.

Although evolutionary changes are being made in several of the other capital markets, one has the impression that the changes already made or under discussion are the result primarily of domestic-policy considerations. Preoccupation with future internationalization of internal markets, or at least their technical alignment with other more advanced markets, is no more than a secondary motive. Inertia in such matters has been the rule historically, and steps are rarely taken in this direction except when the national interest calls for a deliberate effort to export long-term capital.

The development of international trade and industrial integration has progressed much faster in Europe than the development of national capital markets, leaving a wide gap between the long-term financing needs of companies with international commitments and the possibilities offered by national markets.

No single continental capital market today enjoys the kind of technical position or size that would permit it to open its doors indiscriminately to foreign borrowers. The British and American capital markets, the largest and best organized in the world, are closed for the majority of foreign borrowers. Therefore, however much we may wish to see the market mechanism function as the prime regulator of the amounts to be taken up from national markets by domestic and foreign borrowers alike, it is rather unrealistic to hope that governments can be persuaded in the short run to materially ease controls over such matters.

So far regulations regarding the purchase of foreign securities by residents of various European countries have undergone greater liberalization than those governing foreign-capital flotations in the national market or even the ability of national borrowers to borrow internationally. As we have seen, this dichotomy has speeded the development of a parallel international market. In fact, in the age of the telex, many governments continue to take a provincial view of their own national capital markets. The question now is whether, in the present protectionist climate, governments will have the wisdom or even the possibility of letting the international capital market continue to develop freely.

Sources of Funds

The original source of funds for the Eurobond market remains one of the closely guarded professional secrets. Those engaged in the management of international issues need an accurate knowledge of the true placement potential of each member of their syndicates and a pretty good idea of the ultimate destination of the merchandise. A frequent question asked by bankers trying to enter this field or by government officials, who tend to be naturally suspicious, is "Where did the $2.7 billion raised in 1969 come from, and would it otherwise have gone into local capital markets?" Unfortunately, this is not a subject for polite conversation, at least among bankers. One can only offer the assurance that the bulk of the funds represent bona fide long-term money from investors who dispose of reserves outside their countries of residence and who wish to keep them in a different jurisdiction.

In any event, the Eurobond market has reached the impressive size of over one-tenth of the volume of new domestic and foreign issues from the public and private sectors which are being floated internally in the countries of the European Economic Community, plus Switzerland and the United Kingdom. While institutional interest in such securities has been growing considerably, the larger portion of straight-debt issues is still taken up by wealthy individuals whose funds are traditionally administered by bankers in countries such as Switzerland, Belgium, Holland, Great Britain, and the United States. These wealthy individuals are not only Europeans, but also South Americans and Middle and Far Easterners who fear inflation or political risks in their own countries and want a fair return on their money combined with freedom from taxation.

As the market has broadened, more institutions have been attracted to it, and not only to invest off-shore funds without immediate taxation. Insurance companies, investment trusts, pension funds, and the like are increasingly coming into the picture. Convertible bonds have helped considerably to diversify the source of funds. Of course, with the market stretching from Hong Kong to Zurich via Beirut and Caracas, the problem of good distribution is a most delicate one, and a number of issues have shown how easy it is to misjudge not only the size of the market but also the mood of investors.

Mechanics of Distribution

Turning to the organization of the market, we find that in the first place the Eurobond market is mainly a placement market. There is no active attempt to sell the bonds directly and on a competitively open basis to the general investment public. In other words, the issues are placed before the loan is advertised publicly and the publicity in the press is merely informative and not an invitation to the public to subscribe. General public investment is of course possible in the secondary market. The comparative but abstract pricing judgment which we can make in a well-established internal capital market, with all its familiar points of reference, is not possible in the Eurobond market. The managing underwriter cannot leave the merchandising of the issue to third parties without having conducted a prior market study and tested ultimate demand himself.

The pattern of Eurobond syndicates has now become fairly well established. It is the orthodox three-tier structure with a manager, an underwriting group, and a selling group; syndication techniques follow closely those of the U.S. market. However, because many investment bankers in Europe are also commercial bankers with a great deal of correspondent relationship with bankers in other lands, the composition of syndicates has tended to include many institutions which lack direct placement power. At the same time, other bankers, such as the Swiss (who are very important placers), can participate in only a limited way because of government policies and regulations in their country.

A certain number of Swiss banks have now resorted to forming foreign affiliates which act as underwriters of these issues. The bulk of Swiss banks active in the placement of Eurobond issues do not act as underwriters, however. On the other hand, many banks in other countries with less natural outlets for Eurobonds appear in practically every issue. This dichotomy between underwriters and distributors has functioned successfully in some internal markets, notably the British, but is basically against the traditional method of operating in the international bond market. This situation has been improving markedly as managers of Eurobond issues have gained better knowledge of the ultimate potential of members of their underwriting syndicates. The reliance on Swiss buying has considerably decreased as underwriters and selling-group members of other nationalities have striven to develop their own distribution. In fact, some issues have been placed largely outside of Swiss banks which, because of their fiduciary responsibilities, often act with great selectivity.

There are still deficiencies in syndication of Eurobond issues and these have given support to those who favor some form of regulation of this new market. However, many of the critics have confused the symptoms of the illness with its causes. The concrete achievement is that financial institutions which only a few years ago operated in their isolated national markets have now learned to work together in international syndicates which often comprise over 100 underwriters flanked by as many or more selling-group members located in some 15 different countries.

The Listing of Issues and the Vital Secondary Market

Another interesting technical aspect of the Eurobond market is the listing of its issues. Here we must revert to some history. When the market was functioning in New York, even though the issues were registered with the Securities and Exchange Commission and listed on the New York Stock Exchange, the bulk of the turnover in the after-market took place outside of the stock exchange in the so-called over-the-counter market. The Eurobond market is likely to remain an over-the-counter one simply because investors reside in so many different places that resident brokers will never be able to compete with the specialized trading organizations which are able to cover simultaneously many countries and even different continents; nor will they be able to foil international institutions which are not members of the various stock exchanges where such bonds might be listed, wishing to deal directly with one another and save brokerage commissions.

An analogy may be found in foreign-exchange trading. If, say, it was decided to list all currencies on stock exchanges and have brokers deal in them at set commission rates, it would be impossible to stop banks in most countries from dealing with one another at net prices simply because foreign exchange, like the Eurobond market, is in essence international. Why then list Eurobond issues at all? Well, there are many reasons. A listing is frequently required for an issue to be eligible as an investment for certain types of institutional investors. More importantly, in the case of major exchanges, listing requirements are a guarantee of proper and continuing disclosure of financial information to investors.

One of the most important contributions of the Eurobond market has been in the realm of secondary market dealings. In view of the wide geographical distribution of the market and the inability of any local stock exchange to prove a common denominator to all the investors and other factors involved, a new form of secondary market had to be devised. The latter is probably the most important single ingredient of the Eurobond market and, for that matter, of any future multinational or supranational capital markets. Such a development could not have taken place without instant communications, initially through telex connections, supplemented today by the fast-spreading international direct dial telephone.

Even though the institutional segment is growing, we have seen that individual investors still make up a large part of the Eurobond market. However, they themselves deal through institutions which often originate investment decisions on their behalf and are simultaneously prepared to act for a number of other clients in large amounts. The growth in primary offerings (which from the inception of the Eurobond market has risen from issues typically of $15 to $20 million up to $100 million) could not have taken place without a parallel increase in the size of dealings in the secondary market. Fortunately, a number of international firms able to operate simultaneously in several geographical locations and willing to commit large financial means to maintaining an inventory in Eurobonds and the accompanying administrative infrastructure have made this development possible.

Today the liquidity of the Eurobond market compares favorably with that of markets in major national financial centers, and there have even been times when its liquidity proved superior. Admittedly these were rather exceptional times when spiraling interest rates caused a major breakdown in the mechanisms of those national bond markets which, under normal circumstances, remain larger than the Eurobond market. However, it is gratifying to note that the degree of organization of the Eurobond market and the commitment of financial firms to it is sufficient to permit it to operate with reasonable continuity even in times of monetary stress.

The complexity of such international dealings, and particularly of the settlement procedures, are considerable. A typical transaction may involve a buyer in one country, a seller in a second country, the delivery of the bonds in a third country, and the corresponding payment in a fourth. Lack of uniform practices has led at times to administrative problems. However, the recently formed International Bond Dealers' Association, comprising nearly 200 firms in 15 countries, has taken upon itself the task of establishing uniform standards and procedures which should greatly facilitate orderly and continued growth of the secondary market. Also, a number of banking organizations have established multinational clearing facilities to speed and ease settlements of Eurobond trades. The current volume of dealings in the secondary Eurobond market is not an official record but can be estimated to range daily between $20 and $40 million. This is more than twice the volume of transactions in fixed-income securities of all types on the Paris Bourse, on which all trades in the French market must, by regulation, be recorded.

"Guest Currencies"

In spite of the recent monetary turmoil, the dollar remains the most acceptable common denominator in the Eurobond market. However, it is fair to say that at times, investors have accorded their preference to other currencies such as Deutsche marks (DM), the European unit of account (EUA), and even, at one point, Eurofrancs. (*See* statistical appendix, Table XVIII.2.) In any case, this is a desirable development. It broadens the base of long-term holdings in Eurocurrencies other than dollars, thus widening their acceptance and increasing possibilities for additional future flotations in these currencies which would attract a new class of borrowers and investors to the market.

The unit of account was an interesting attempt to create a composite vehicle of all the European currencies in order to create a currency which would have the widest possible acceptance and insure the holder against devaluation risks. However, the complexity of the formula, and the fact that it has not always met with an enthusiastic response from the monetary authorities, has not permitted it so far to emerge as the ideal forerunner of a common European currency.

The Swiss franc would unquestionably have proved a highly desirable vehicle. Swiss monetary authorities have, however, consistently resisted any attempt to cast the Swiss franc in the role of an international reserve currency on the perfectly legitimate contention that the flow and size of the monetary movements which would thereby arise would adversely affect the domestic credit and internal interest-rate structures.

While the Deutsche mark is not an international reserve currency, it came to play an important role in the Eurobond market, partly because of the ingenuity of German bankers and partly because of the strength of this currency. One drawback is that a great deal of the recent investment in DM bonds was based on a short-term currency preference by investors in spite of a lower return, leading to potential liquidity problems in case of quick disinvestment. The problem, of course, pertains not only to the DM, since loss of confidence in any one of the "guest" currencies in which Eurobonds are expressed would have serious consequences. It would seem, therefore, that currency stability is essential to an orderly international capital market.

A second fundamental observation is that no currency has been able to substitute for the dollar on a large scale. This is likely to remain the case for a long time, barring a real breakdown of the international monetary system. No individual European currency offers the scope the market now needs, and no unified European currency is likely to emerge for quite some time. The Common Market might evolve a "common market unit of account," but greater political unification would be necessary to ensure its wide acceptance. And should the deficits in the U.S. balance of payments be eliminated, the propensity of investors to hold dollars will increase greatly so that the role of this currency as an international unit of account would increase further simply because the interrelationships of present-day trade and investment call for a common international monetary denominator. None exists officially and, as we have seen, none can be arbitrarily created and imposed.

Types of Borrowers and Size of Issues

Today, the Eurobond market is open to any borrower of sufficient standing to attract the interest of internationally minded investors. This translates into a very wide spectrum, ranging from governments and top multinational companies down to small and newer growth companies prepared to offer the investor an equity participation through conversion on other similar privileges.

There has also been wider diversification in the term of issues offered, and a departure from the conventional 15- to 20-year maturities, with a sinking fund starting after five years or more. Under the world-wide pressure of rising interest rates and a growing volume of offerings, it has been necessary to offer intermediate maturities with early sinking funds, short-term notes, and a number of other variations to attract new buyers. In fact, with the introduction of Eurodollar certificates of deposit we have a fairly complete spectrum of maturities from very short to very long. (*See* statistical appendix, Table XVIII.3.)

With regard to the size of issues, the expansion of the market has been equally remarkable. The freedom which bankers have enjoyed to tailor terms of issues to the changing moods of the market and the requirements of new borrowers has permitted progresively more ambitious offerings. So far, issues have reached maximum sizes of $50 million for straight debt issues, $75 million for debt issues with warrants attached, and $100 million for convertibles.

The same widening of the market and of the investors' interest in it should enable the Eurobond market also to accommodate increasingly smaller corporate borrowers, especially if the use of convertible issues can be broadened. Legislation is under consideration in a number of countries to facilitate the issuance of convertible issues or warrants, which would give many European companies a fine new tool with which to compete in terms of international financing with their American counterparts. The lower limit in size of an individual issue is of the order of $5 to $10 million, but smaller issues have been placed privately. However, to insure optimum distribution and liquidity in the secondary market, an issue should normally be for at least $15 million.

Regulation

While the market has often tended to pay more attention to the name of a borrower than to his balance-sheet ratios, it has nevertheless shown a remarkable ability at self-regulation by excluding borrowers of insufficient standing. This is primarily because placement and much of the preselling is done not with individuals, but with institutions which manage private funds and bear the responsibility of bad judgment. Such professional investment managers are readily aware of the quality of the merchandise shown to them, and an unsatisfactory name can simply not be syndicated.

One of the contributions of the Eurobond market is that standards of disclosure are generally higher than those prevailing in most domestic markets in Europe. The pioneering role of U.S. and British firms accounts for this since they were compelled to export their own higher standards. An interesting consequence is that many European corporations which borrowed in the Eurobond market have raised substantially their domestic standards of disclosure in order to meet those of the Eurobond market.

Essentially the Eurobond market remains self-regulated. We live in an era in which anything not subject to some form of control is almost automatically suspicious. Yet, the Eurobond market demonstrates that freedom and sharp competition do give rise to ingenious new techniques which, in this case, have led to the raising of very substantial capital, most of which, by the way, whether borrowed by American or European companies, has been invested in Europe, while a substantial portion of the funds come from non-European sources. It had been proposed that a queue system be instituted to regulate access to the market and avoid bottlenecks and oversupply. The idea certainly has merit, but its implementation is fraught with danger and in many national markets has failed or distorted supply/demand relationships. If the Eurobond market has prospered, it is because it is a free market. If mistakes have been made, they are not mistakes of morality but of judgment, and controls neither improve the good judgment of bankers nor correct their vision when inaccurate.

Taxation

The subject of taxation is both fascinating and painful. The feature which Eurobonds have in common is that interest is paid to the holder free of any withholding tax. This has led some critics to describe the market as a tax dodgers' market. This is an unfair allegation. Paying interest free of any deduction is an indispensable feature simply because in any international market there cannot be any other common denominator between all the diverse tax treatments suffered by participating investors, not even making allowance for double-taxation treaties. As to the differences between countries in the local tax treatment of foreign withholding taxes, we enter an area of infinite permutations. Therefore, even if there were no tax evaders in the world, freedom from withholding taxes would be a prerequisite in the international bond market, as it is in the Eurodollar short-term market.

Rate Structure

Since the Eurobond market is a completely free market, it is axiomatic that the pattern of its interest rates is a purer reflection of supply and demand than is that of any other capital market. Nevertheless, while the Eurobond market may seem to the uninitiated to operate in the "ether," it is directly related to comparative investment opportunities available to those investors in a position to employ their funds freely across borders. As far as supply is concerned, the relative terms and availability of financing in national markets determine the types of borrowers who address themselves to this market and the frequency with which they make use of it.

Obviously the number of variables involved in the supply and demand equation is considerable. One can say in general terms that, given the structural factors which operate in favor of a continuous expansion of this market and given a reasonable degree of external convertibility in the world, the fluidity and diversity of the Eurobond market should cause its rates to align themselves increasingly with those of major national capital markets, particularly those corresponding to the "guest currencies" used by the Eurobond market. The dollar is the primary currency, as we saw, and the Deutsche mark the next most important. In fact, in 1969 we witnessed at one point a complete closing of the yield gap between Eurobonds of U.S. companies (whether expressed in dollars or marks) and the yields of equivalent securities in the domestic bond markets of the U.S. and Germany.

The Eurodollar-deposit market and, in general, the Eurocurrency-deposit market are not the primary sources of funds for the Eurobond market, as we have seen, although funds awaiting investment in Eurobonds or the proceeds of such issues often find temporary employment in Eurocurrency deposits. Nevertheless, the freely operating Eurocurrency-money market is a primary point of reference for investors and borrowers in appraising the terms on the longer-term maturities in the Eurobond market. A short list showing current terms and yields on representative Eurobond issues, among the several hundred presently outstanding, is shown in the statistical appendix (Table XVIII.7).

THE FUTURE OF THE EUROBOND MARKET

"The history of humanity has been one of constant movement from the realm of necessity towards the realm of freedom." We owe this thought—which applies so well to the international capital market—to Mao Tse Tung. In spite of the numerous hindrances which stand in the way of a free flow of capital internationally, we stand at an important crossroad in financial markets. If the opportunities at hand are used constructively, we may well move a few steps closer to the realm of freedom which, in the context of financial markets, means the reign of the market mechanism, with self-regulation helped, when needed, by sophisticated controls but without direct interference in the allocation of resources. The reason why optimism is not unwarranted is simply because a good deal of organized thinking is now taking place on ways and means to broaden capital markets. Governments and the private sector presently share a desire to improve financial mechanisms, and the Eurobond market offers them an unusual opportunity to make pragmatic progress in this area.

Because of the political and social situation in today's world, no one considers deflation as a valid tool of economic management. Most discussions center currently around maintaining inflation at a controlled rate sufficiently low to permit credit and capital mechanisms to function, but sufficiently high to permit solving development problems at an acceptable pace. The monetary-depreciation factor may well become a constant structural component of interest rates. They will thus necessarily have to remain higher than we have been accustomed to, but in such a context should not prove an impediment to the proper functioning of national or international capital markets.

The Eurobond market, being an across-border institution functioning in "guest currencies," faces some problems which are peculiar to it. If disagreement over monetary reform persists or if the shock waves of American disinflation cause an outbreak of monetary nationalism and a retaliatory climate, then the Eurobond market could be in difficulty. It is not subject to regulatory authority but to impediments from the various national restrictions and exchange controls of the countries which participate in the market as borrowers, underwriters, traders, and investors. We have recently witnessed one major creditor nation take restrictive measures against both the Eurocurrency-deposit market and the Eurobond market. It is a sign of the times, although the justification as far as the Eurobond market is concerned is questionable. The two markets are forever being lumped together. While the Eurocurrency market serves as the most logical point of reference for the Eurobond market regarding the level of free interest rates, it is not its source; in fact, the Eurobond market could exist without it. If governments appreciate the foregoing and the long-term necessity of evolving a permanent multinational capital market, then the market should be kept free of political interference.

Economically, one of the market's main idiosyncrasies is its dependence on the "guest currencies" in which it operates. The availability of an acceptable currency in which to denominate fixed-income securities in the Eurobond market is thus a key factor. We will not dismiss the problem by citing Professor Friedman's view that the world is on a dollar standard anyway. However, in 1967 the GNP of the U.S. did amount to 32.8 per cent of that of the free world. Part of our present troubles may well stem from a rather belated recognition by the U.S. of the need to bring its financial house in order as an indispensable complement to reform of the international monetary system.

The other part of these difficulties is the result of the very measures which have been taken in the U.S. and for which the rest of the world has been clamoring. However painful they may prove in the interim, they are a substantial guarantee that an outright catastrophy will be averted. Thus, if the U.S. does succeed in reducing its inflation to an acceptable rate, the dollar should remain the most acceptable unit of account in the international capital market. A better balance in the external accounts of the U.S. will curtail the supply of funds in the Eurodollar-deposit market. However, this is not the primary source of funds for Eurobonds. Such a development will also reduce the need for U.S. companies to raise money in the Eurobond market. But as an offset, the propensity of investors to hold their savings in dollars would increase.

We have seen in recent times that European companies are making growing use of the Eurobond market, raising funds on competitive terms vis-à-vis U.S. borrowers and often on more favorable conditions than in their national markets. In addition, many governments will revert to the market as the climate for floating fixed-income instruments improves. Even if many U.S. corporations no longer find it to their advantage to tap this market, a number of them will continue doing so because, if the tendency for world long-term rates to equalize continues, it will enable many U.S. multinational companies to increase the international ownership of their securities without cost disadvantages. This is an increasing political necessity.

The foregoing is a chapter in itself; we can only say here that the Eurobond market, if allowed to progress, will continue giving rise to new forms of securities fostering greater international ownership. We have recently witnessed interesting derivations such as sterling loans convertible into shares of U.S. companies as well as the primary and secondary across-border distribution of shares of international corporations handled with Eurobond syndication techniques and christened "Euroequities." Furthermore, a natural extension of the market has already taken place in the medium and shorter maturities with the emergence of five-year notes and London-dollar certificates of deposit. Other such projects are afoot and should prosper given reasonable confidence in the "guest currencies."

There are momentous political obstacles to unification of capital markets, even within an organization such as the Common Market. Unification requires, if not a common currency, at least a common denominator such as a unit of account resting on strong legal foundations. Taxes must likewise be harmonized. Progress will be made in this direction so that an increase in international links and flows may eventually take place, especially once the international monetary house is put in order. But it is doubtful that in the next decade such unification in continental Europe will become the cornerstone of international financing.

As to the other two major capital markets in the world, American and British, unification seems even more distant, if not downright unlikely, and the ability of these markets to regain their dominant international positions is open to question. The British market is unlikely to be reopened to non-sterling-area borrowers for a long time to come, possibly until the sterling area is dismantled. By that time, the scope of the British market will be determined only by the long-term capital exporting capacity of the British economy as it will then stand. As to the U.S. market, it is important to recall that since restrictions were introduced, the volume of internationally syndicated issues expressed in U.S. currency has more than quadrupled. It is highly unlikely that the U.S. market will be able, when it reopens, to accommodate a sizeable portion of world requirements quite apart from severe and often prohibitive U.S. regulatory and fiscal problems for non-U.S. borrowers. This is not because of any chronic weakness in the U.S. economy or its monetary system. It is simply because it would take some cataclysm such as World War II to restore an imbalance in financial resources between Europe and America of the magnitude that existed in, say, 1945.

Meanwhile, of course, the numbers in the game of trade and international investment have multiplied frantically.

The Eurobond market has offered a vivid demonstration of the capacity of the international private sector to organize, on a complex and multinational basis, the raising of substantial amounts of capital, both for private and public needs. If we accept that no single capital market can take its place and that unification of existing markets will be slow and will offer only a partial solution, it would seem in the interest of governments to encourage a gradually increasing overlap of the Eurobond market with their national capital markets. Such a course would give pragmatic recognition to the structural changes that are taking place in international long-term financing and the growing limitations of national markets. It would avoid the risk of future clashes between existing national markets and the international one which, given reasonable monetary stability and convertibility, should thus emerge as a highly needed, permanent, multinational institution.

Statistical Appendix

TABLE XVIII.1

EUROBOND ISSUES BY TYPE OF BORROWER

	1965	1966	1967	1968	1969
		(U.S.$ MILLION EQUIVALENT)			
Central governments	212.5	95.1	254.7	224.4	239.7
Government guaranteed and agencies	222.0	133.6	380.1	354.6	506.3
Municipalities	60.5	35.0	62.0	116.3	287.0
International and European agencies	142.5	101.0	155.0	25.0	40.0
Industrial and financial companies:					
straight debt	269.4	470.5	817.7	599.8	589.6
straight debt with warrants	—	20.0	20.0	82.5	250.0
convertibles	110.0	222.0	227.0	1727.5	823.5
	1016.9	1077.2	1916.5	3130.1	2736.1

TABLE XVIII.2

EUROBOND ISSUES BY CURRENCY

	1965	1966	1967	1968	1969
		(U.S.$ MILLION EQUIVALENT)			
Dollars	702.5	837.2	1716.3	2361.5	1622.5
Deutsche marks	250.0	146.3	148.8	662.5	1053.6
EUA	—	74.1	19.0	57.0	60.0
£/DM	64.4	19.6	20.2	28.8	—
French francs	—	—	12.2	20.3	—
	1016.9	1077.2	1916.5	3130.1	2736.1

TABLE XVIII.3
ANALYSIS OF STRAIGHT-DEBT EUROBOND ISSUES BY MATURITY

Maturity	1965	1966	1967	1968	1969
	(U.S.$ million equivalent)				
0– 5 years	20.0	183.0	230.0	272.5	87.0
6–10 years	—	162.1	182.0	86.4	115.0
11–15 years	471.9	260.6	958.7	876.2	1370.6
16–20 years	415.0	229.5	298.8	85.0	90.0
	906.9	835.2	1669.5	1320.1	1662.6

TABLE XVIII.4
ANALYSIS OF EUROBOND ISSUES IN 1968 AND 1969, SHOWING BREAKDOWN BETWEEN STRAIGHT DEBT AND CONVERTIBLE ISSUES WITH THEIR RESPECTIVE CURRENCIES

	Straight Debt		Convertible Debt*		Total Issues	
	(U.S.$ million equivalent)					
	Calendar Year					
Currencies	*1969*	*1968*	*1969*	*1968*	*1969*	*1968*
U.S. $	549.0	551.5	1073.5	1810.0	1622.5	2361.5
DM †	1053.6	662.5	—	—	1053.6	662.5
£/DM	—	28.8	—	—	—	28.8
EUA	60.0	57.0	—	—	60.0	57.0
FF	—	20.3	—	—	—	20.3
Total	1662.6	1320.1	1073.5	1810.0	2736.1	3130.1
Issuers						
American issuers	399.1	378.8	519.5	1545.0	918.6	1923.8
All others	1263.5	941.3	554.0	265.0	1817.5	1206.3
Total	1662.6	1320.1	1073.5	1810.0	2736.1	3130.1

* Includes debt issues with warrants: 1969—$250.0 million and 1968—$ 82.5 million.

† DM issues offered subsequent to October 20, 1969 have been included on the basis U.S.$1 = DM 3.66.

TABLE XVIII.5
LONDON DOLLAR CERTIFICATE OF DEPOSIT MARKET

	CDs Outstanding (U.S.$ million)	Quarterly Secondary Market Turnover (U.S.$ million)
December 1966	225.40	N/A
December 1967	597.12	N/A
March 1968	769.92	503.6
June 1968	941.04	435.5
September 1968	1362.96	862.3
December 1968	1432.80	785.7
March 1969	1811.04	1006.0
June 1969	2461.00	1010.4
September 1969	3133.70	1042.4

TABLE XVIII.6

LEADING MANAGERS AND COMANAGERS OF INTERNATIONALLY SYNDICATED ISSUES IN 1969

Name	$	DM	EUA	Total	No. of Issues
	(U.S.$	million	equivalent)		
1. Deutsche Bank A.G.	424.0	588.3	—	1012.3	30
2. Morgan & Cie International SA	455.0	—	—	455.0	12
3. White, Weld & Co. Limited	367.0	77.3	8.0	452.3	17
4. S. G. Warburg & Co. Limited	242.0	194.8	15.0	451.8	19
5. N. M. Rothschild & Sons	290.0	107.5	—	397.5	14
6. Westdeutsche Landesbank Girozentrale	20.0	309.1	48.0	377.1	15
7. Banca Commerciale Italiana	316.0	50.0	—	366.0	13
8. Commerzbank A.G.	80.0	214.8	—	294.8	11
9. Dresdner Bank A.G.	75.0	217.3	—	292.3	14
10. Lehman Brothers	257.0	25.0	—	282.0	12
11. Crédit Commercial de France	100.0	118.5	48.0	266.5	13
12. Kuhn, Loeb & Co. International	236.0	25.0	—	261.0	9
13. Banque Lambert S.C.S.	110.0	128.6	15.0	253.6	10
14. Algemene Bank Nederland N.V.	130.0	41.0	48.0	219.0	10
15. Banque de Paris et des Pays-Bas	159.0	50.0	—	209.0	8
16. Deutsche Girozentrale –Deutsche Kommunalbank–	—	204.9	—	204.9	7
17. Kredietbank S.A. Luxembourgeoise	52.5	91.0	60.0	203.5	11
18. Crédit Suisse (Bahamas) Limited	185.0	—	—	185.0	5
19. Hill Samuel & Co. Limited	—	167.8	15.0	182.8	6
20. Pierson, Heldring & Pierson	160.0	—	—	160.0	6

TABLE XVIII.7

CROSS SECTION OF OUTSTANDING EUROBOND ISSUES TO ILLUSTRATE DIVERSITY OF ORIGIN AND TERMS

STRAIGHT-DEBT BONDS (ORIGINAL OFFERING)

Amount and currency		*Year*	*Security*	*Country of borrower or guarantor*	*Coupon*	*Maturity*	*Middle price*	*Yield to maturity*
DM	150	1969	Commonwealth of Australia	Australia	7¼%	1984	93¾	8.00
$	15	1966	Brenner Autobahn	Austria	7 %	1971	100¾	6.53
$	20	1969	Quebec Hydro Electric Commission	Canada	8 %	1974	97⅝	8.71
$	25	1967	Kingdom of Denmark	Denmark	6¾%	1982	89⅞	8.05
$	25	1967	European Coal & Steel Authority	Int. Instit.	6½%	1987	88	7.79
DM	60	1969	Mortgage Bank of Finland	Finland	6¾%	1984	88¾	8.10
$	30	1967	Electricité de France	France	6½%	1979	84¾	9.02
FF	60	1967	Roussel-Uclaf	France	7 %	1979	83	9.74
$	75	1969	Bayer Int. Finance, with warrants	Germany	6 %	1981	100¾	5.90
$	30	1967	Philips International Finance	Holland	6½%	1979	93⅛	7.54
$	20	1969	Aer Lingus	Ireland	8¼%	1981	92⅜	9.37
$	50	1969	Ente Nazionale Idrocarburi—ENI	Italy	7 %	1981	95	7.64
$	20	1965	Japan Development Bank	Japan	6½%	1980	88¼	8.15
$	12	1964	Sumitomo Chemical	Japan	6¾%	1979	87½	8.65
$	20	1969	Société Financière Européenne	Luxembourg	7 %	1974	94¾	8.58
$	25	1967	United Mexican States	Mexico	7 %	1982	87¼	8.71
EUA	15	1968	Comisión Federal de Electricidad	Mexico	7¼%	1978	92¾	8.43
$	20	1967	Government of New Zealand	New Zealand	6¾%	1979	97	7.19
$	30	1965	Kingdom of Norway	Norway	5½%	1985	77¾	8.06

$	20	1965	Republic of Portugal	Portugal	5¾%	1985	84⅞	7.43
DM	100	1969	Republic of South Africa	South Africa	6¾%	1984	87½	8.27
$	25	1968	Argentine Republic	Argentina	7¼%	1973	88½	11.02
$	20	1967	Autopistas Españolas S.A.	Spain	7 %	1987	84¾	8.73
$	20	1966	Ericsson Telephone	Sweden	6½%	1986	87	7.94
DM	200	1969	Gas Council	U.K.	6¾%	1984	90½	7.88
$	30	1967	ICI Imper. Chem. Ind.	U.K.	6½%	1982	86¼	8.33
$	25	1969	Chrysler Overseas	U.S.A.	7 %	1984	90½	8.14
$	20	1965	Cyanamid International	U.S.A.	5¾%	1980	86¼	7.66
DM	100	1965	Du Pont Europa S.A.	U.S.A.	6 %	1980	91⅛	7.20
£/DM	10	1965	Mobil Oil Holdings	U.S.A.	5¾%	1980	84	8.04
$	30	1969	Transocean Gulf Oil	U.S.A.	7 %	1981	89¼	8.52

CONVERTIBLE BONDS (ORIGINAL OFFERING)

Amount and currency		*Year*	*Security*	*Country of borrower or guarantor*	*Coupon*	*Maturity*	*Middle price*	*Conversion premium*
$	60	1969	Swiss Aluminium Co.	Switzerland	4¾%	1987	95½	20.77
$	15	1966	Beecham International	U.K.	5½%	1981	181	13.81
$	54	1970	Michelin International	France	6 %	1985	95¼	.23
$	100	1968	Philips Lamps	Holland	4¾%	1983	106	.70
$	30	1965	Hitachi Ltd.	Japan	6¼%	1984	96½	20.63
$	20	1966	Bankers International	U.S.A.	5 %	1986	105	5.08
$	25	1969	Chesebrough Pond	U.S.A.	6¼%	1984	95½	1.17
$	8	1968	Dictaphone International	U.S.A.	5½%	1988	95	20.16
$	50	1967	Gillette International	U.S.A.	4¾%	1982	84½	8.64
$	30	1968	Honeywell Overseas	U.S.A.	5 %	1983	133½	2.59

XIX

MILTON GILBERT and WARREN McCLAM

Dr. Gilbert, born in Philadelphia in 1909, holds M.A. and Ph.D. degrees from the University of Pennsylvania. He began his career with the U.S. Department of Commerce, serving as Editor of the Survey of Current Business from 1939 to 1941 and as Chief of the National Income Division from 1941 to 1951, the period when the national income accounts system of the U.S. was developed. From 1951 to 1960 he was Director of Economics and Statistics of the OEEC (later OECD) in Paris.

Since 1960, Dr. Gilbert has been the Economic Adviser of the Bank for International Settlements and a regular participant in the deliberations of Working Party No. 3 of the OECD and of the Group of Ten.

His recent major research studies include The Problem of Rising Prices *(1961), and* The Gold-Dollar System: Conditions of Equilibrium and the Price of Gold *(1968).*

Dr. McClam, born in Florence, S.C. in 1920, obtained his B.S. and Ph.D. degrees from the University of California, Berkeley. He also did graduate study as a Fulbright Scholar at the University of Leeds, England, and as a Teaching Fellow at Harvard University. From 1952–54, Dr. McClam was an economist in the Foreign Research Department of the Federal Reserve Bank of New York. Since that time he has been an economist in the Monetary and Economic Department of the Bank for International Settlements in Basle.

Regulations and Policies Relating to the Eurocurrency Market

The conditions governing the participation of countries in the Eurocurrency market are quite diverse and change from one time to another. In the first place, policy attitudes with respect to borrowing in foreign currencies for purposes of relending abroad are not everywhere the same. Second, policies differ with regard to the possibilities for resident banks and nonbanks to take up external positions in foreign and domestic currency. Third, participation in Eurocurrency transactions is to some extent the result of technical—even accidental—differences in regulations and policies as they relate to the treatment of foreign versus domestic currency instruments, residents versus nonresidents, and banks versus nonbanks.

The object of this chapter is to survey present regulations, policies, and banking practices as they impinge on Eurocurrency activity. Attention is directed mainly to exchange-control regulations and selective control techniques but also, where they seem pertinent, to interest-rate regulations and conventions, reserve requirements, and fiscal considerations. The chapter begins with a comparative summary along broad lines and follows with a detailed description of the conditions prevailing in individual countries.

COMPARATIVE SUMMARY

Exchange Control over Nonbank Residents

For residents other than banks, participation in Eurocurrency activity is governed largely by exchange control. Borrowing from, lending to, and the holding of short-term claims against nonresidents are subject to exchange restrictions in Austria, Denmark, France, Italy, the Netherlands, Norway, Sweden, the United Kingdom (outside the sterling area), and Japan. Nonbank residents of these countries are not normally permitted to hold liquid foreign-currency assets in excess of commercial requirements, and authorized holdings must generally be placed with approved domestic banks.

In Italy and the Netherlands residents have somewhat wider scope to borrow from or lend to domestic banks in foreign currency. All these activities are freely permitted, with minor qualifications, in Canada, Germany, Switzerland and, through the free-exchange market, Belgium. In France, where virtually free convertibility had been established in January 1967, exchange controls were temporarily reimposed between May and September 1968 and again as from November 1968, so that at the present time resident nonbank borrowing and lending and the holding of balances abroad remain subject to comprehensive controls.

Over the past year or so various steps to strengthen existing exchange controls in these respects have been taken in Belgium (where since August 1969 transactions on the controlled market have been subjected to greater scrutiny), Denmark (where advance debt repayment and most import prepayments were prohibited in May 1969), Norway, and Sweden. Earlier, in 1967, on the other hand, both Italy and the Netherlands raised considerably the maximum size of individual transactions not subject to supervision. Exchange controls generally have been progressively liberalized in Japan, but short-term capital transactions remain subject to close supervision.

The conclusion of forward-exchange transactions is regulated in various ways in certain countries (*see* pages 358–59). Moreover, some countries have also at times introduced provisions to prevent resident holders of foreign exchange from benefiting from currency-parity changes.

Although in the United States residents other than banks are, in a formal sense, free to lend to foreigners and to place dollars in the Euromarket, the balance-of-payments program has for the time being put an end to such activity as far as nonbank financial institutions and business corporations with direct-investment affiliates are concerned. (Placements in Canada, however, are unrestricted.) The program has also given companies a strong incentive to borrow abroad for terms over a year, while the short-term investment of funds raised through U.S. company issues abroad has added to supply on the Eurodollar market. The program has had the further effect of leading foreign affiliates to borrow more heavily in European markets, including the Eurodollar market. Following Canada's exemption from the U.S. balance-of-payments program, guidelines were issued to Canadian banks, other financial institutions, and business corporations.

Borrowing and Re-lending in Foreign Currency by Banks

With regard to banks, a large part of Eurocurrency business in most countries is of an intermediary nature—borrowing in foreign currency for purposes of relending in foreign currency, often ultimately to nonresidents. In the United Kingdom, in particular, such activity has been encouraged as a purely banking function, and international competition of this kind has spread, particularly through the overseas branches of U.S. banks, to most continental countries as well. For even where exchange controls are intensive, they are usually permissive with regard to "offshore" banking transactions in foreign currencies. In most cases, moreover, where selective techniques or guidelines have been used to regulate the banks' net foreign position (Canada, Denmark, France, Italy, the Netherlands, Sweden and, on occasion, Austria and Switzerland), the banks are left free to adjust their gross positions as they wish. Furthermore, foreign-currency deposits are usually exempted from reserve requirements and are not covered by regulatory and conventional interest-rate limitations.

Only in one or two countries do the regulations in force tend to impede purely external banking activities. In Germany liabilities to nonresidents are generally subject to reserve requirements. During most of 1969, borrowing in the Euro-currency markets even for purposes of relending abroad was particularly discouraged by a prohibition of interest payment on deposits of nonresidents and by 100 per cent reserve requirement against the growth of liabilities to foreigners. These regulations were abolished after the revolution of the Deutsche mark in October 1969, but a marginal reserve requirement of 30 per cent against foreign liabilities was introduced in April 1970.

Direct Regulation of Outflows Via the Banks

In Austria, Germany, the Netherlands, and Switzerland, banks are virtually free to switch out of domestic currency and to increase their foreign positions in any currency. But ceilings on banks' total net foreign assets at present exist to restrict any outflows of short-term funds, including switched funds in Denmark (in force since February 1969), Italy (since March 1969), and Sweden (since August 1969). In Canada, the guidelines issued to banks following Canada's exemption from the U.S. balance-of-payments controls in effect require banks to avoid increasing their foreign-currency position vis-à-vis residents of foreign countries other than the United States, while for the United States the ceiling on bank credit to foreigners puts a limit on the expansion of all claims whether denominated in dollars or foreign currencies.

In France, banks' foreign-currency positions must be in balance or deficit and may not exceed the January 1969 levels. (The banks' French franc claims against nonresidents are also subject to a ceiling.) In Belgium, a ceiling was fixed in April 1969 for (1) bank spot positions in currencies drawn from the controlled foreign-exchange market plus (2) their advances in Belgian francs to foreigners on convertible accounts. As from October 1, 1969, separate ceilings were applied to each of these two categories and at a lower total level than before. Also tending to inhibit outward switching are the regulations in the United Kingdom which place quantitative limits on the banks' open-exchange positions and on their spot claims against forward liabilities. In Norway, the credit guidelines for 1969 recommended that, instead of increasing their net foreign assets, banks should place idle funds in Norwegian bonds.

Direct Regulation of Inflows Via the Banks

Domestic employment of Eurocurrency funds and inward switching are currently subject to important disincentives in Germany and Japan. Recently, certain restrictive measures have been taken in the United States, and possibilities for more effective control, should it be required, have been created in Austria and Switzerland. Various controls have been applied in the past in other countries; some remain in force, but generally without great current significance.

In Germany, inflows through the banking system are discouraged by the 30 per cent reserve requirement against increases in nonresident deposits above the level of March 1970. (On the other hand, there is little to deter borrowing abroad by nonbanks.) Prohibitions on interest payments on nonresident deposits have at various times been applied in Germany and, for domestic-currency deposits only, in France and Switzerland, but these regulations are not at present in force. Marginal reserve requirements have also recently been introduced in the United States, in relation to dollar funds passing through the banking system from abroad, as described below.

In Japan the inflow of short-term funds via the banks is allowed, but borrowing from the Eurocurrency markets is subject to ceilings fixed for individual banks and the requirements that banks hold a reserve in foreign assets amounting to at least 15 per cent of certain of their foreign liabilities.

Measures designed to limit the growth of net foreign liabilities have been introduced at times, but subsequently discontinued, in various countries. Still in force are rules in Italy and the Netherlands that generally prevent banks from incurring a net liability position abroad and in Denmark that require banks to deposit the full equivalent of any net liability position beyond a certain level with the Nationalbank. In Switzerland, too, capital inflows have at times been countered by requiring banks to hold reserves with the central bank. In Norway, the annual credit guidelines have often included provisions restricting increases in banks' foreign currency liabilities abroad, frequently only in so far as such funds were used for lending to domestic nonbanks.

In Sweden banks are not permitted to incur a net liability position in any individual foreign currency. In France the exchange controls introduced in 1968 restrict banks in transactions which involve simply borrowing foreign exchange for sale against francs on the exchange market. Inward switching is permitted in relation to authorized transactions, provided it is covered forward. In the United Kingdom inward switching is freely permitted on condition that conversions by banks into domestic currency are covered forward. Inward switching is allowed in Belgium but has, in practice, occurred only to a limited extent in connection with treasury financing. In Canada inward switching by banks has remained virtually free.

The Role of Reserve Requirements

Reserve requirements, as they concern foreign-currency borrowing and borrowing from nonresidents, provide in most countries little impediment, and often a positive incentive, to borrowing in foreign currencies for relending abroad. But they also frequently encourage borrowing in foreign currencies either from nonresidents or, where exchange controls permit, residents to finance, after switching, domestic lending. Banks' foreign-currency liabilities are at present subject to reserve requirements only in Germany, Norway, Sweden and, for the clearing banks only, the United Kingdom.

In Germany reserve requirements apply to the level, and occasionally to the growth, of liabilities to nonresidents, irrespective of currency. The ratio may be set higher than that for liabilities to residents, as occurred recently, and under existing legislation may be raised to 100 per cent. (Liabilities to foreign banks are exempt from reserve requirements only under certain conditions. In the United Kingdom the cash-reserve ratio applies to the deposit liabilities of the clearing, Scottish, and Northern Ireland banks but not to liabilities of other banks. Special deposits which must be held with the Bank of England in proportion to total deposit liabilities also relate at present only to the clearing, Scottish, and Northern Ireland banks; the provision in a 1968 arrangement for extending these to other banks is not yet operative. (In most other countries reserve requirements cover virtually all resident banks.)

In Austria recent legislation permits the imposition of reserve requirements against both the level (up to a maximum rate of 25 per cent) and the growth (up to a further 50 per cent) of *net* foreign-currency liabilities, while in Switzerland a reserve requirement against the increase in *net* foreign positions (which could rise to double the level applied to liabilities to residents) is provided for in a new agreement. Neither country has to date imposed such requirements. In Denmark banks are required to lodge with the Nationalbank the full equivalent of increases over early 1965 levels in a *net* foreign-liability position. Thus, in Austria, Denmark, and Switzerland, reserve requirements would not affect borrowing abroad for re-lending abroad (irrespective of currency).

Furthermore, in Canada, France, Italy, Japan, and the United States, the reserve requirements in force relate only to domestic-currency liabilities, and the requirements which could potentially be brought into force in Belgium and the Netherlands are of the same type. (In France a 10 per cent reserve requirement was applied to residents' foreign-currency deposits between July and September 1968.)

In the United States, reserve requirements had until recently the effect of reducing the cost to U.S. banks of funds obtained from abroad relative to the cost of domestic deposits. Funds borrowed by home offices from their foreign branches had not been subject to the usual reserve requirements applied to domestic and nonresident deposits, but have recently been subjected to a 10 per cent marginal-reserve ratio. In addition, special reserve requirements have been imposed on borrowings from foreign banks other than a bank's own branches.

One should not, of course, exaggerate the significance of the absence of reserve requirements on foreign-currency liabilities or on certain domestic-currency liabilities to foreigners. For even where no formal requirements exist, banks no doubt take care to maintain liquid reserves against such liabilities, though probably on a limited scale. In fact, little is known about the banks' liquidity practices in this respect.

Even where exchange controls or rules on external positions are tight, rises in reserve requirements on domestic-currency deposits, such as have occurred during 1969 in Denmark, Japan, and Norway, may induce banks to restrict placements on the Eurocurrency market. Variable reserve requirements also exist in France, Italy, and the United States and are provided for, but are not at present in force, in Belgium, the Netherlands, and Switzerland.[1] In Canada, Sweden and the United Kingdom (for the clearing, Scottish and Northern Ireland banks only), reserve requirements are fixed. (In Canada there is a variable secondary reserve requirement.) In Austria, Denmark, Germany, the Netherlands, and Switzerland, in particular, banks normally appear to hold a significant proportion of their total liquidity in foreign currency and to employ changes in these assets as a regular method of adjustment to domestic conditions. In Denmark and Sweden, net foreign assets count at least in part towards the satisfaction of minimum reserve requirements, but steps have recently been taken with the effect of reducing their eligibility for this purpose.

Terms of Credit from the Central Bank

Changes in the terms of credit from the central bank (including basic interest rates), penalties for excessive borrowing, restrictions on the eligibility of particular types of security or reductions in borrowing ceilings are also important externally as well as internally. In Japan, excessive conversion of foreign currency into local currency has expressly been taken into account in fixing rediscount ceilings. The same was true earlier in Germany. Even in Canada, the Netherlands, and the United Kingdom, where banks do not normally borrow extensively from the central bank, changes in discount rates retain an important indirect influence; however, as in the United States, other techniques of general domestic monetary policy (such as open-market operations) also assume considerable importance in directing international flows of short-term funds between currencies and countries.

[1] Reserve requirements were terminated in Belgium in July 1965 and in the Netherlands in September 1963 in order to avoid inflows of funds, possibly unstable, which might result from variations in the ratio. The provisions have not subsequently been reactivated.

Quantitative Ceilings on Bank Lending

The incentives to inward switching may be considerably reduced by quantitative limits on the permissible rate of domestic bank-credit expansion. Such limits are at present in effect in Belgium, France, the Netherlands, Sweden, Switzerland, and informally the United Kingdom. In Italy the scope for quantitative restraint comes to much the same thing because bank loans above a certain modest size are subject to central-bank approval. In Japan, too, bank-credit expansion has at times been regulated by quantitative ceilings, but these are not in force at present.

Policies Relating to Forward Exchange

In certain countries, measures to influence the availability and cost of forward-exchange cover to banks have been a significant influence in switching. In Germany, the Netherlands, and Switzerland, the authorities have, as a matter of domestic-liquidity control, offered swap facilities at special rates to encourage banks to place or keep short-term funds abroad. In Italy swap facilities at par have also been made available, but in recent years only to banks in a net debit position vis-à-vis foreigners. Banks are frequently subject to regulations limiting or preventing the incurring of uncovered positions in foreign currencies (e.g., France, Italy, Japan, and the United Kingdom) or requiring that they cover inward switches (e.g., France and the United Kingdom).

Official intervention in the forward market has been undertaken from time to time, or regularly over certain periods, in Denmark, Italy, the Netherlands, Norway, and the United Kingdom but has seldom or never been undertaken in Belgium, Canada, France, Japan, or Sweden. Conditions in the forward market, of course, affect the attractiveness of switching not only to domestic banks but also to nonbank residents (in so far as exchange controls permit) and nonresidents. In certain countries the scope for the conclusion of forward contracts—especially by nonbank residents—has been restricted by the authorities in respect to either the type of transaction which may be covered (e.g., trade or current transactions, as in Austria, Norway, Sweden, and—for particular goods only—France) or the maximum duration of the contract (1 to 3 months for certain goods in France, 6 months in Austria, Italy and, in certain cases, Japan, 12 months in Denmark, and —depending on the nature of the transaction—6, 12, or 24 months in Sweden). In other countries the possibilities of concluding forward transactions are often limited by the narrowness of the market (e.g., Belgium and Norway). Frequently, nonbank residents may conclude forward contracts only with domestic banks.

Interest Rate Controls and Conventions

Limitations on the interest payable on deposits are, of course, one of the basic factors determining the scope for Eurocurrency activity. Such limitations, often in the form of ceilings, may act as an inducement to residents and nonresidents alike to hold a given currency with a foreign bank. In the United States the maximum rates are officially determined under Regulation Q and apply virtually to the whole banking system. Much the same is true in France, where the ceiling rates are laid down by the National Credit Council, though only for sight deposits and for term deposits of up to one year and of less than Fr.fr. 100,000. In Japan, too, maximum rates are set by the authorities.

In Italy maximum deposit rates were for some years, governed by an interbank cartel agreement, but in 1969 it was not renewed. In the United Kingdom the interbank agreement linking the time-deposit rate to the Bank rate is valid only for the London clearing, Scottish, and Northern Ireland banks. In Sweden and Denmark deposit rates of all banks are conventionally linked closely to the discount rate, while in Switzerland the maximum rates are determined by a convention among the big banks only, rates paid by other banks being influenced by competitive market conditions. In Belgium most Belgian franc-deposit rates are determined by interbank agreement, subject to official influence. Rates on deposits of B.fr. 10 million or over are fixed freely by the banks. In Germany interest rates on residents' deposits were freed from controls in April 1967. In the Netherlands time-deposit rates are freely determined under conditions of strong competition.

Frequently special rules or practices relate to deposits from nonresidents or from banks. Thus, in Germany nonresident sight and time deposits have been subject to a ban on interest payments. In Sweden, under an interbank agreement, no interest is paid on nonresident krona accounts. In France and Switzerland the payment of interest on nonresident domestic-currency deposits has at times been prohibited. Time deposits placed with U.S. banks by foreign monetary authorities and certain foreign institutions are exempt from Regulation Q ceilings.

Withholding Taxes

Withholding taxes on interest from deposits also influence Eurocurrency activity. Where such a tax exists, and where at the same time residents are free to place deposits abroad, they may choose to hold deposits with foreign banks in order to avoid this taxation. There is a withholding tax on interest income of usually 20 per cent in Japan, 20 per cent in Belgium, 25 per cent in France, and 30 per cent in Switzerland. In Belgium and Switzerland, but not in France or Japan, residents are free to hold deposits abroad. Apart from these four countries, there are no withholding arrangements on interest income in the countries under consideration. In Italy there is a special tax of 35 per cent on interest income on deposits deductible at source, but the banks themselves make the tax payment and quote deposit rates free of tax.

Nonresidents other than banks are generally subject to the withholding arrangements mentioned above, except in Belgium, where they are specifically exempt.

In no country except Japan[2] are nonresident banks subject to withholding taxes on interest income from deposits. In Belgium they are, like foreign nonbanks, specifically exempted. In Switzerland foreign banks' deposits of up to one year's duration are exempted as interbank deposits. In France nonresident banks could, under existing legislation, be made to pay withholding taxes, but they are exempted on the grounds that such deposits are mainly working balances. In Italy foreign banks' deposits are treated as interbank balances and are not subjected to taxation. Generally speaking, the absence of withholding taxes on nonresident banks' deposits is a factor that widens the scope for Eurocurrency activity.

INDIVIDUAL COUNTRIES

United States

The recent strength of demand on the Eurodollar market owes much not only to the existence of maximum rates payable on time deposits by U.S. domestic banks under Regulation Q but also to the incentives to employing foreign funds domestically which are associated with monetary restraint in the United States. Moreover, the U.S. balance-of-payments controls have tended to increase both demand and supply on the Eurodollar market from U.S. nonbanks and from nonresidents (including U.S. corporate affiliates abroad), who might otherwise have been borrowers from U.S. banks.

Foreign branches of U.S. banks are not subject to Regulation Q and may bid for dollar deposits at rates higher than the ceilings which this regulation stipulates in respect to deposits with domestic banks. In April 1968, Regulation Q ceiling rates for single-maturity deposits of $100,000 or more, at over 60 days,

[2] The Japanese tax does not apply, however, to yen and foreign-currency deposits held with Japanese banks abroad.

were adjusted upwards—progressively according to maturity—to a maximum of 6¼ per cent in the case of deposits at 180 days and over. But ceiling rates on other types of time and savings deposits remained unchanged. Subsequently, in January 1970, Regulation Q rates were increased across the board, those on simple maturity deposits of $100,000 or more, for example, rising from 5½ to 6¼ per cent on 30- to 59-day deposits and from 6¼ to 7½ per cent on deposits of 360 days or more. Moreover, the rate on passbook savings was raised, for the first time since 1964, from 4 to 4½ per cent. No interest may be paid on deposits for less than 30 days, all of which are classed as "demand deposits." (By way of comparison, the three-month treasury bill rate, discount basis, after falling below 4 per cent in the spring of 1967, rose to a level of about 5¾ per cent in the spring of 1968; it then moved irregularly to a level of 7¾ per cent in January 1970.) To inhibit circumvention of Regulation Q, the Federal Reserve Board warned banks in June 1969 not to solicit or accept deposits at foreign branches (including those in U.S. external territories) from U.S. residents for purposes unconnected with foreign or international transactions.

When severe monetary restraint is applied in the United States, banks are faced with a sharp reduction in domestic time deposits (particularly negotiable certificates of deposit) as interest rates on competing instruments rise relative to Regulation Q ceilings. Considered in terms of their demand for funds, moreover, the banks' prime lending rate bears no direct relationship with Regulation Q ceilings. Rather it broadly reflects supply/demand relationships for bank credit and, in practice, changes are frequently associated with movements of Federal Reserve discount rates. Thus the prime rate, which had been increased from 6¼ per cent in November 1968 to a record 8½ per cent by June 1969, has since late March 1970 stood at 8 per cent. Banks have therefore been willing to pay rates much above the Regulation Q ceilings in order to continue expanding their loans if possible, or in any case to avoid the need for sudden withdrawal of accommodation from established customers or to make short-term reserve adjustments.

Available sources have included the interbank Federal funds market and the Eurodollar market; in addition, various other nondepositary sources have been exploited this year, but a series of changes in regulations (some put into effect and some announced as proposals for comment) have closed off these other sources, or threaten to do so. (These changes in regulations relate to sales under repurchase agreements of assets other than U.S. Government securities, to Federal fund borrowings from nonbanks, and to the obtaining of funds through the issue of short-term promissory notes by bank affiliates.)

In June 1970, in a move of considerable importance to Eurocurrency markets, the Federal Reserve Board suspended Regulation Q ceilings for single-maturity time deposits of $100,000 or more with maturities of 30–89 days. However, no change was made in the ceilings applying to other types of time and saving deposits.

Over a long period, the incentive for banks to borrow from the Eurodollar market via branches abroad was enhanced by the fact that home offices did not have to keep compulsory reserves against advances or loans from their overseas branches, or against deposits held at the branches. Advances from branches to the head office could be treated by the home offices as "miscellaneous" liabilities and not as interbank deposits, which would have been subject on a net basis to reserve requirements. Effective as of September 1969, the Federal Reserve Board amended its Regulation M (governing banks' foreign activities) to establish a 10 per cent reserve requirement on increases over May 1969 levels in the total of net balances due from domestic offices of U.S. banks to their foreign branches plus outstanding assets (with certain exceptions for loans to nonresidents) bought from the domestic offices by foreign branches. A new reserve-free base is to be established at the current level of borrowings from foreign branches when, in any reserve period, this falls below the original base. (To reduce inequities, borrowings from branches not exceeding 3 per cent of total deposits normally subject to reserve requirements remain reserve-free for any bank with a foreign branch, irrespective of its previous use of foreign funds.)

A 10 per cent reserve requirement was also placed on increases over either end-June or average May outstandings in foreign branch loans to U.S. residents. For borrowings amounting to less than 4 per cent of aggregate deposits, the reserve requirement is only 3 per cent. At a 10 per cent level of interest rates, the 10 per cent marginal-reserve requirement increases the cost of Eurodollar funds to U.S. banks by more than 1 percentage point per annum. (The reserve requirement on domestic savings deposits and time deposits up to a total of $5 million per bank was lowered to 3 per cent in March 1967, but that on time deposits in excess of $5 million has remained at 6 per cent since September 1966. Reserve requirements on demand deposits were raised in January 1968, and again in April 1969 to 17 per cent on deposits up to $5 million at a reserve city bank and 17½ per cent on deposits over $5 million.)

Parallel with its changes in Regulation M, the Federal Reserve Board amended Regulation D to establish a 10 per cent reserve requirement on borrowings by member banks from foreign banks other than their own branches. (Borrowings not exceeding 4 per cent of a bank's total deposits normally subject to reserve requirements carry only the 3 per cent statutory minimum reserve requirement.) Such borrowings from foreign banks remain exempt from Regulation Q ceilings on interest rates. It may be noted that liabilities of agencies or branches in the United States (which are not Federal Reserve member banks) to banks abroad (including their head offices) are not subject to any reserve requirements. The foreign agencies and branches have been asked to observe moderation in their lending to member banks.

Earlier, effective July 1969, the Federal Reserve Board revised its Regulation D (governing banks' reserves) to prevent a bank from reducing its ordinary domestic reserve requirement through the use of "London checks" and "bills-payable checks" in the settlement of Eurodollar deposit repayments and other transactions involving foreign branches. Previously these checks could, while in process of collection, be deducted by the recipient bank from its demand deposits for reserve-requirement computations. The amendment ensured that the bank issuing the check would include it, like other cashiers' checks, in gross-demand deposits subject to reserve requirements. The effect was to reduce the profitability to banks of using Eurodollar funds in overnight and weekend adjustment of reserve positions.

Funds drawn by home offices from their overseas branches and deposits at the branches remain exempt from the insurance charges that must normally be paid to the Federal Deposit Insurance Corporation on bank deposits.

It is noteworthy that time deposits placed with U.S. banks by foreign governments and certain foreign institutions are exempt from Regulation Q ceilings. In view of the substantial volume of such deposits, this exemption has served, if anything, to limit the volume of dollars passing through the Eurodollar market. Instead, official holdings of dollars, if not placed in U.S. Treasury bills and other government obligations, tend to be offered directly to U.S. domestic banks at rates which are at times appreciably above the Regulation Q ceilings. In October 1968 this exemption was clarified by officially permitting the payment of above-ceiling interest rates on certificates of deposit of up to two years which were originally issued to an exempt depositor but subsequently transferred to a nonexempt depositor, for the period during which the certificate is held by an exempt depositor.

The fact that there is no withholding tax on interest from bank deposits and bankers' acceptances also facilitates direct placement of dollars in the United States by foreigners. However, interest on government securities, including treasury bills, is subject to withholding arrangements, except for foreign governments and central banks.

Given the marginal and highly competitive character of Euroloan business, foreign banks (including U.S. banks' branches abroad) have at times been prepared to offer better terms on dollar lending than U.S. domestic banks. In particular, foreign banks do not generally request the holding of compensating balances such as domestic banks usually require even of foreign borrowers in amounts, depending on monetary conditions, ranging up to the equivalent of 20 per cent of the sum borrowed.

Whenever monetary conditions become easier in the United States, U.S. banks' home offices may have an incentive to repay some part of their present large borrowings from their overseas branches, thereby enabling the latter to repay deposits or relend in the Eurodollar market. The automatic reduction of the reserve-free base under Regulation M that would occur when a bank's borrowings from branches go below their May 1969 level would be the only influence provided by the present regulations to deter such repayments.

Recourse by foreigners (including foreign subsidiaries of U.S. firms) to the Eurodollar market is to some extent a substitute for loans obtained directly from U.S. domestic banks. Under the balance-of-payments program announced on January 1, 1968, the ceiling on bank credit to foreigners was reduced from 109 to 103 per cent of the end-1964 base. Bank-term loans to continental Western European countries were not to be renewed upon maturity, or the proceeds re-lent to these countries except for export credits; short-term credits to these countries were to be reduced by 40 per cent in the course of 1968. Moreover, the drop in such credits was to be matched by a further reduction in the ceiling. A revision of the guidelines in April 1969 permitted banks to select an amount equal to 1.5 per cent of total assets as of the end of 1968 as an alternative limit on the extension of foreign credits. Recently, however, to the extent that foreign-credit demand has been diverted to the Eurodollar market, this reflects not so much the impact of the ceiling as such but rather the fact that tight monetary conditions in the United States led banks to give priority to domestic customers.

For the nonbank financial institutions, the January 1968 program limited holdings of specified foreign assets to 95 per cent of end-1967 levels and stipulated that liquid funds held abroad be reduced to zero or to minimum working balances. In April 1969 the ceiling on foreign assets was raised from 95 to 100 per cent of the end-1967 base.

As it relates to nonfinancial business firms, the U.S. balance-of-payments program impinges significantly on Eurocurrency markets.

Under the existing mandatory controls, the outflow of new direct investments to countries of continental Western Europe (except Greece and Finland) was prohibited, and annual net investment abroad of foreign earnings there was restricted to 35 per cent of the annual average of total direct investment (transfers and re-invested earnings) in that area in the base years 1965 and 1966. As of January 1968, total annual direct investment (transfers and retained earnings) in most other developed countries was limited to 65 per cent, and in developing countries to 110 per cent, of the 1965–66 average. In April 1969 companies were given the option of employing the equivalent of 30 per cent of foreign earnings in 1968 as an alternative ceiling for 1969 without regard to area. Moreover, in all cases the proportion of foreign earnings repatriated was to at least equal the 1964–66 average, and holdings of short-term assets abroad were to be reduced to the 1965–66 average levels. Subsequent minor modifications permitted transfers of quotas between countries in different groups to a limited extent and the carry-over of unused quotas to subsequent years. Canada was exempted from the provisions of the program in March 1968.

Insofar as direct investment is financed by funds raised abroad, whether by capital issues or by borrowing in the Eurocurrency markets or on domestic credit markets of other countries, it is not subject to the limitations imposed by the balance-of-payments program. It is primarily for this reason that U.S. business firms and their financial subsidiaries incorporated in the United States or abroad have turned on a major scale to flotations of international issues. As some of this borrowing has taken place in anticipation of need, the proceeds have frequently been channelled to the Eurocurrency markets. The mandatory controls on direct investors restrict their placements of liquid funds abroad (except in Canada) other than the temporary investment of proceeds of securities issued abroad to finance direct investments. To what extent subscriptions to international issues by U.S. and other borrowers have been made with funds withdrawn from the Eurocurrency market, or even directly from other U.S. investments, is an open question. It may be noted that in most continental countries, with the exception of France and the Scandinavian countries, residents are generally free to convert domestic currencies for portfolio investments abroad. And, except in the United Kingdom and Canada, there is little to impede switching out of existing holdings of foreign securities, including dollar ones. The U.S. program also tends to encourage borrowing on the Eurocurrency markets by U.S. firms and their subsidiaries.

The U.S. Interest-Equalization Tax has also had important implications for financial markets abroad, including the Euro-currency markets. The tax applies to U.S. residents' and citizens' acquisitions of foreign shares and debt claims, including loans by domestic banks (except to finance U.S. exports) with a maturity of one year or more. The tax also applies to U.S. residents' and citizens' acquisitions of securities issued abroad by U.S. corporations organized for the purpose of obtaining foreign financing for direct investment. Foreign currency loans and, as of February 1967, dollar loans to foreign borrowers by overseas branches of U.S. banks are exempt.

Under discretionary authority granted by Congress in 1967, the President can vary the effective annual rate of the tax from zero to 1½ per cent. In April 1969, as part of the balance-of-payments announcement at that time, it was proposed to extend the tax until the end of 1970 but, partly in recognition of the reduced differential between U.S. and foreign interest rates, the rates of the tax were cut from those established in August 1967. The reductions were from 18¾ to 11¼ per cent for shares and, in terms of annual interest equivalent, from 1¼ to ¾ per cent for debt obligations.

In November, legislation was passed extending the tax until the end of March 1971, with a new provision allowing more flexibility in setting tax rates for newly issued securities. Issues of the less-developed countries are exempt, as are those by Canadian and (up to $100 million per annum) Japanese borrowers. Another major exemption is direct investment, including the acquisition of shares of companies in developed countries. Purchases of foreign shares and debt obligations are exempt from the tax only if made from the existing holdings of other U.S. citizens.

The Interest-Equalization Tax has served to limit new issues in the United States by borrowers in developed countries, mainly those of Western Europe. Such borrowers have turned in part to flotations of international issues and, to some extent, to shorter-term accommodation in the Eurocurrency markets. The tax has also tended to impede U.S. purchases of securities in secondary markets.

United Kingdom

Residents other than authorized banks may not borrow outside the sterling area, either in foreign currency or external sterling, without express permission.[3] This regulation applies, inter alia, to local authorities and financial institutions not authorized to deal in foreign exchange. If the borrowing is for an acceptable purpose, either at home or abroad, permission is granted. It is not granted for low-priority purposes—for example, for loans from abroad to finance the compulsory deposits required in respect to certain imports since December 1968. Lending outside the sterling area by residents other than authorized banks is not normally permitted.

The foreign-currency holdings of nonbank residents mainly comprise: essential working balances of companies with international business, particularly insurance, oil and shipping; funds borrowed to finance outward direct and portfolio investment held in liquid form pending investment; and investment currency balances derived from the sale of foreign currency securities held pending reinvestment. Finally, nonbank residents are not permitted to switch out of sterling for purposes of interest arbitrage.

Resident banks authorized to deal in foreign exchange may borrow foreign currencies without limit for purposes of

[3] This is, more precisely, a direct effect of U.K. exchange-control legislation. The regulations relate to foreign exchange or sterling payments to countries outside the sterling area, and permission would, therefore, be required to repay, or pay interest on, a borrowing from outside the sterling area. In addition, permission is needed to borrow or to retain foreign currency. Permission is also required to accept loans in sterling from nonresidents where the transactions involve the entry in the books of the borrower of a credit in favor of the lender.

re-lending abroad. Most of the banks' activities in the Eurocurrency markets are of this intermediary nature. However, U.K. banks' sterling lending to nonresidents is restricted; in particular, in October 1968 the authority under which U.K. banks provided sterling-usance credits to finance trade between nonsterling-area countries was withdrawn. This had the effect of preventing U.K. banks from financing such trade in sterling, but they may still conduct such business in foreign currencies.

Foreign-currency deposit business is largely the province of London banks other than the clearing banks (i.e., mainly the merchant banks, British overseas banks, and the foreign banks). In competing for deposits, both foreign currency and sterling, these banks have an advantage over the London clearing banks. The latter are obliged to maintain a cash-reserve ratio of at least 8 per cent and a minimum liquid-assets ratio of 28 per cent, both of which apply to deposits in sterling and foreign currencies alike. It is the 8 per cent noninterest-bearing cash ratio which mainly discourages the clearing banks from taking Eurocurrency deposits. Moreover, the foreign banks and merchant banks are not bound, as are the London clearing banks, to an interbank agreement with regard to maximum rates on time deposits in sterling. Under this agreement the clearing banks fix the rate on seven-day sterling deposits at 2 per cent below Bank rate.

In addition, the convention with respect to lending rates, according to which the banks charge private borrowers a minimum of 1 per cent above Bank rate, is a practice of the London clearing and Scottish banks only. Moreover, since 1960 the clearing banks have also been obliged to lodge special deposits with the Bank of England to the equivalent, since April 1970, of 2½ per cent of total gross deposits. In June 1969 interest payable on these deposits, until then equivalent to the previous week's treasury bill tender rate, was halved as a temporary penalty measure designed to induce banks to reduce their domestic lending to the official ceiling.[4] Provision was made in 1968 for banks other than clearing, Scottish, and Northern Ireland banks to lodge deposits with the Bank of England in relation to all or part of their sterling deposits and also foreign-currency deposits to the extent that they may have been switched into sterling. The ratio would normally (but not necessarily) be the same for all the banks affected, and the deposits would normally bear interest equivalent to the current yield on treasury bills, though lower rates could, if necessary, be applied. This scheme has not yet been implemented.

Banks authorized to deal in foreign exchange may switch foreign currencies into sterling for domestic use without limit, provided they cover spot sales of foreign exchange by forward purchases. As a rule the funds drawn from the Euro-currency markets by local authorities and hire-purchase finance companies are the sterling counterpart of foreign-currency deposits placed with resident banks authorized to deal in foreign exchange. While the clearing banks do not place funds with the local authorities and finance houses, they may grant advances to them.

Indirectly, inward switching tends to be limited by various quantitative restrictions on domestic-credit expansion. First, banks' lending to residents in foreign currencies is closely controlled and the clearing and Scottish banks' advances in sterling were until recently subject to a ceiling, which from November 1968 onward was fixed at 98 per cent of loans outstanding as of November 1967. This ceiling was amended several times over the past few years. After November 1968, it referred to all sterling lending (including purchases of com-

[4] The special deposit scheme also applies to the Scottish banks, currently at the rate of 1¼ per cent of their total gross deposits. The Scottish banks were not subject to the penalty measure applied to the clearing banks (withdrawn in April 1970).

mercial bills) to the nonbank private sector and to the overseas sector (other than fixed interest-rate lending under special arrangements for exports and shipbuilding). The sterling lending of most other banks in the United Kingdom was subject to a similar ceiling, which was fixed in November 1968 at 102 per cent of the level of such lending in November 1967. In April 1970 the ceilings on bank credit expansion were replaced by guidelines envisaging a rise during 1970–71 of 5 per cent for the London clearing and Scottish banks and finance houses and 7 per cent for other banks in sterling lending other than special rate lending for exports and shipbuilding. Second, it is an objective of policy to limit the growth of local authority short-term debt, with a view to bringing down its share in total local authority debt. Moreover, there is a global restriction in effect inasmuch as the local authorities can borrow only for approved projects. Third, the restrictions on hire-purchase terms, which were tightened in November 1967 and again in November 1968, also tend to curtail the outlets for switched funds.

With regard to official policy attitudes, the authorities consider that any attempt to regulate inward switching by means of direct quantitative restrictions would be ineffective and therefore pointless. If, for instance, such switching were made subject to a ceiling, the switching operations could be carried out by a foreign bank which could then place sterling deposits with banks in the United Kingdom. Moreover, if sterling liabilities to nonsterling-area residents were subjected to interest-rate limitations, their funds could still come in indirectly via sterling-area countries.

On the other hand, the authorities do put quantitative limits on the banks' outward switching of sterling. In the first place, the banks may maintain only small open (uncovered) positions in foreign exchange, up to limits determined for each bank. Second, limits are also laid down as to the amount of spot exchange they may buy and hold against forward liabilities. In August 1966 these limits were reduced, particularly those for the larger dealers in foreign exchange.

Eurocurrency activity may, to some extent, be affected by the voluntary restraint program with respect to investment in the developed countries in the overseas sterling area, i.e., Australia, New Zealand, the Republic of Ireland, and South Africa. The request to companies and institutional investors, issued in May 1966, to delay direct and portfolio investment in these countries has probably diverted some borrowing by these countries out of sterling in London into other currencies and to other sources, including the Eurocurrency market.

The pound sterling is used as a Eurocurrency, although on a considerably smaller scale than is the dollar. In the first place, there is no officially determined limit, comparable to Regulation Q in the United States, on the rates that may be offered for sterling time deposits. Second, the foreign banks and the merchant banks in London are in a favorable position to compete for nonresidents' sterling deposits because they are bound neither to the clearing banks' conventions with respect to creditor and debtor interest rates nor to the 8 per cent cash and 28 per cent liquid-assets ratios. Third, residents are prohibited under exchange-control regulations from placing sterling with banks in countries outside the sterling area.

Austria

Nonbank residents must apply for licenses for borrowing and lending abroad at short and medium-term, but the licenses are normally granted on a liberal basis. Residents are permitted to take up from nonresidents loans with maturities of five years or more for investment purposes, loans to enterprises in which the nonresidents participate, loans for prefinancing of exports, and loans for a period of up to five years to be used abroad for definite merchandise transactions. However, residents other than banks are not generally permitted to accumulate liquid funds abroad. Foreign-currency export earnings earmarked for import payments need not be surrendered but must be held with authorized Austrian banks.

With regard to authorized banks, a general license issued by the National Bank permits them (1) to employ or invest for periods of up to five years their foreign exchange held abroad in countries settling with Austria in convertible currencies, and (2) to incur liabilities by accepting foreign funds for periods of up to five years. In doing so, these institutions are also exempted from the generally applicable limit of six months for forward transactions.

Moreover, most Austrian credit institutions are authorized to keep accounts denominated in foreign currency with banks abroad, and to undertake foreign-currency conversions and forward transactions at not more than six months.

The credit institutions are allowed to show a net debtor position vis-à-vis nonresidents. From September 1964 until June 1965 they undertook, under an agreement with the National Bank, to avoid the repatriation of foreign assets. Subsequently, excessive creation of domestic liquidity through inflows from abroad was limited by changes in compulsory minimum-reserve requirements. At the present time no formal guidelines are in force.

Banks can be required to hold minimum reserves with the National Bank up to a maximum of 25 per cent for sight deposits and of 15 per cent for time and savings deposits. In October 1969 the requirements then in effect were increased for the larger credit institutions to 9½ per cent for sight liabilities and to 7½ per cent for time- and savings-deposit liabilities of less than one year and 6½ per cent for those of more than one year.

Interbank liabilities in Austria are not subject to minimum-reserve requirements. Under the amended National Bank Law passed in 1969, the banks' liabilities to nonresidents (to both banks and nonbanks and in both domestic and foreign currency), together with foreign-currency liabilities to residents, can be subjected to minimum-reserve requirements, but only in so far as they exceed foreign assets. In the case of net foreign liabilities, the maximum rates are fixed at 25 per cent of their level and can also be imposed at up to a further 50 per cent of their growth.

Banks are also committed under agreement with the National Bank to hold, in relation to their total schilling liabilities (domestic and foreign), a liquid reserve of 10 per cent in the form of cash and net assets with the central banks and the postal savings bank, and a further 30 per cent, which may be held in a variety of forms, including net balances with banks abroad. (Between July 1965 and June 1966 it was specified that at least 5 of the latter 30 per cent had to be held in the form of net assets abroad, BIS notes and money-market treasury bills.) The agreements, which cover nearly all types of credit institution, also restrict credit-granting in Austrian schillings to 75 per cent of banks' own funds and 70 per cent of schilling deposits. For the credit system as a whole, both the liquidity and credit-ceiling requirements appear to have been consistently met with comfortable margins.

No distinctions are made between residents and nonresidents insofar as fiscal considerations or interest rates are concerned. Maximum-deposit rates for schilling deposits by nonbanks are fixed by agreement. Rates for the time and savings deposits at over 12 months were raised or newly introduced in April 1969; other rates have remained unchanged since July 1955.

Belgium

Exports of short-term financial capital, whether by banks or nonbanks, are subject to the provision that they must take place by way of the "free" (as distinct from the "controlled") exchange market. To ensure stricter observance of this rule, banks were requested in May 1969 to effect payments in foreign exchange only where documents are available to prove that the transfer is in respect of payment for imported goods. Since August 1969 documentation of exchange operations on the controlled market involving amounts exceeding B.fr. 10 million must be submitted by the banks to the Exchange Institute. Moreover, since August 1969 no interest may be paid on foreign-exchange holdings resulting from exporting and, in the case of currency-parity changes, such holdings must be used for payment abroad or surrendered to authorized banks within 30 days, any resultant profits having to be surrendered to the Treasury.

Imports of short-term capital may take place via either the free or the controlled market. In practice, however, all operations are carried out through the free market, for there is no point in investors importing capital via the controlled market when they will subsequently be able to export it only via the free market.

Provided conversions take place on the free market, there is little to prevent banks and nonbanks from freely taking positions in foreign currencies. The approved banks may also make short-term investments with funds obtained on the controlled market, subject to a ceiling imposed in April 1969 on banks' spot positions in foreign currency drawn from the controlled foreign-exchange market plus their advances in Belgian francs in convertible accounts to foreigners. This ceiling, which excludes authorized advances to foreigners with respect to Benelux Economic Union imports and exports, was designed to reduce the banks' foreign balances as from end-June 1969 to a level in line with authorized operations. As of October 1, separate ceilings were placed on banks' foreign-currency positions drawn from the controlled market and on their Belgian-franc advances on convertible accounts. Moreover, the total of these ceilings was lower than that fixed in April.

In the free market, the National Bank is under no obligation to intervene, although at times it may find it expedient to do so. Except at times of unusual external strain, the rate on the free market has been only marginally above that on the controlled market.

As a rule, the National Bank does not engage in forward-exchange transactions with the banks for purposes of influencing private short-term capital movements. On occasion it has done so, however, in order to facilitate Treasury financing by means of short-term borrowing abroad via the Belgian banking system. Thus the Belgian banks have borrowed foreign currencies, partly from the Eurocurrency markets, and switched them into Belgian francs for re-lending to the Treasury, with the National Bank providing forward cover for the banks; alternatively, the Treasury has placed paper denominated in foreign currency with the banks, which have financed it partly by borrowing from abroad and partly by resales to foreign correspondents. In the latter case the Treasury sells the foreign exchange to the central bank, which may provide forward cover to the Treasury itself.

Belgian banks are permitted to engage in inward switching for purposes of relending to the private economy. It has never been their practice to do so, however, partly because of the difficulties of obtaining cover through Belgium's narrow forward market. Moreover, increases in their domestic credit-granting (in Belgian francs and foreign currency, except certain investment credits and acceptance export credit) has often been restricted by ceilings, while liquidity could readily be obtained through central-bank rediscount facilities. At the end of April 1969 a ceiling permitting an expansion of 14 per cent (reduced in the autumn to 11.2 per cent) for 1969 as a whole was placed on bank credit to enterprises and individuals. In addition, the National Bank limited rediscounting by individual banks to 16 per cent of their average resources in 1968.

Although the monetary authorities may lay down a reserve requirement in relation to Belgian franc liabilities of up to 20 per cent for sight deposits and liabilities up to one month, and of up to 7 per cent for savings deposits and liabilities exceeding one month, the ratio has not been used since July 1965. But as of June 1969, as a temporary measure lasting until June 1970, banks were required to observe a ratio between their readily negotiable assets in Belgian francs—mainly discountable trade bills, bank acceptances, and bonds issued by the public sector—and their short-term liabilities in Belgian francs. Moreover, the banks' access to central-bank credit was reduced by a lowering in August 1969 of the ceiling on rediscounting with the National Bank from 16 to 14 per cent of the 12-month average level of Belgian franc liabilities. Moreover, this ratio was to be reduced to 12 per cent as of the end of 1969 and then gradually to 9 per cent effective September 1970. In March 1970 the existing ceilings on bank credit to the economy were replaced by a new system limiting the increase in credit lines utilized during the first nine months of 1970 to 5.5 per cent for each bank, subject to reductions in rediscount ceiling to the extent of any excess lending.

The banks' foreign positions can be influenced to some extent through changes in the rates paid on time deposits in Belgian francs. In practice, the chief form of short-term investment in Belgian francs is a time deposit with a bank. Neither nonresident nor the nonfinancial private sector may acquire treasury certificates in Belgian francs. Interest rates on Belgian franc deposits with banks are fixed under an interbank agreement subject to prior consultations on changes between the National Bank and the Belgian Bankers Association. Time-deposit rates were reduced twice in 1968, but increased five times in 1969. Changes depend upon monetary conditions, the balance of payments, and economic developments. Since 1964, when they were freed of control, relatively higher rates have been paid on deposits of B.fr. of 10 million or more.

A withholding tax of 20 per cent is in force on interest income from bank deposits except for certain savings accounts. The tax applies to residents' holdings of both domestic and foreign-currency deposits. Nonresidents, both banks and others irrespective of currency, are exempt.

The Belgian franc is little used as a Eurocurrency. In principle, however, it is possible for nonresident holdings of francs obtained either through the controlled or through the free market to be placed with foreign banks for relending. Moreover, residents may deposit Belgian francs with foreign banks by going through the free market.

Denmark

Transfers abroad of a capital nature by residents generally require permision from the Nationalbank, and short-term lending is permitted only in connection with commercial transactions. Residents also have an obligation to repatriate proceeds from the sale or liquidation of assets abroad. Except for amounts not exceeding D.kr. 40,000 which are to be used within three months to meet certain commercial expenses, export proceeds and foreign exchange derived from invisibles must be transferred to Denmark without delay, unless the Nationalbank permits otherwise, and offered for sale to the central bank or an authorized exchange dealer. Nonresidents may grant credits within certain limits to residents to finance current transactions. Under a liberalization measure instituted in July 1968, Danish nonbank residents were permitted to take up abroad foreign-currency loans of between D.kr. 100,000 and D.kr. 1 million a year to finance domestic productive activity except building and construction, provided these loans have a life of at least five years. On the other hand, regulations introduced in May 1969 prohibit advance repayment of foreign debts and subject prepayment for imports to licensing.

The duration of forward-exchange contracts is limited to 12 months. Otherwise there are no restrictions on the forward-exchange transactions of resident banks. For nonbank residents, forward transactions may be concluded only to cover payments due within two years for goods and services or on authorized loans and credits. Intervention by the authorities in the forward-exchange market is confined mainly to periods of international currency crises. Though the market is narrow, there is no difficulty, thanks partly to the official intervention, in concluding authorized transactions.

Under an agreement concluded with the Nationalbank in February 1965, the banks are obliged to apply the full equivalent of any increase in their net foreign liabilities beyond the January 1965 level and also a certain percentage of any increase in their domestic deposit liabilities (other than to banks) either to making deposits of cash or bonds with the Nationalbank or to improving their net foreign positions. Interest-rate considerations have induced them to fulfill this commitment largely by placing funds abroad. The special placement commitment was reduced from 20 to 10 per cent of domestic deposit growth as from October 1968. But this reduction was reversed with retroactive effect in May 1969 and, at the same time, a commitment of 30 per cent was established in respect to deposit growth as from May 1969. Also effective May 1969, the banks could satisfy the reserve-requirement obligation by placing funds abroad only if they were reducing a net foreign deficit to a balanced position abroad. Whereas, for a Danish bank, increases in net foreign liabilities may be subject to a 100 per cent reserve requirement, no corresponding obligation applies to a reduction of a net positive asset position abroad.

In February 1969 the banks were asked to reduce their foreign position to early 1968 levels (or by about one-fifth) and not to exceed this level until further notice.

Bank lending rates are fixed in relation to the discount rate by convention and bank borrowing rates are determined by interbank agreement.

There is no withholding tax on interest income from nonresident deposits.

France

At the end of January 1967 the French Government introduced a system which, in principle, established virtually full convertibility on capital account for residents and nonresidents alike. The exceptions related mainly to long-term capital transactions and the principal remaining restriction on borrowing abroad, other than for commercial purposes, was that nonbank residents had to obtain authorization for foreign loans in excess of Fr.fr. 2 million, while projected borrowing operations of an investment nature of under Fr.fr. 2 million were subject to possible deferment. Residents were permitted to deal directly with foreign banks and, as before January 1967, nonresidents could open accounts in France with any bank whatever.

With the re-establishment of exchange controls in May 1968, it was laid down that all exchange transactions between France and foreign countries, or in France between residents and nonresidents, had to pass through officially recognized intermediaries. Prior authorization was required for operations of residents resulting in the establishment of balances abroad, exports of foreign exchange and foreign securities, and for all settlements and transfers that were not current or normal payments carried out by residents vis-à-vis foreigners or (in France) nonresidents. The controls were lifted on September 4, 1968, but they were re-imposed in November 1968 in a stricter form. Inter alia, noncurrent payments to foreign countries now required prior authorization, and all import and export transactions of a resident had to be domiciled with one authorized intermediary.

The controls in effect as of November 1968 required residents to encash all income and proceeds from claims abroad and to repatriate and sell on the exchange market any foreign currency obtained within one month. Forward purchases of foreign exchange are restricted to requirements with respect to certain types of imports and are limited to between one and three months, depending on the type of goods.

All borrowing abroad by residents other than banks requires authorization, with the exception of loans of less than Fr.fr. 2 million contracted "at a normal rate."

Under the 1967 legislation, banks were completely free in their transactions in both francs and foreign currencies. They could take up positions in foreign exchange, both spot and forward, and borrow from and lend to nonresidents without restriction, as well as switch out of or into foreign currencies for their own account at will.

Outward switching (notably in the form of foreign-exchange swaps) was generally prohibited by the exchange controls in force between May and September 1968 and again beginning November 1968.

In May 1968 banks were instructed not to increase their net positive exchange position (including that vis-à-vis residents). Later, in December 1968, they were told to reduce by the end of 1968 both their net positive-exchange position and their French franc claims against nonresidents to early September 1968 levels. Subsequently, in January 1969, the Bank of France required banks with a net surplus position in foreign currencies to bring it into deficit or at least into balance by the end of that month and banks already in a net deficit position to avoid reducing it. Banks failing to comply were obliged to make dollar deposits with the Bank of France at market interest rates in amounts equivalent initially to one-third, and as of March 25 to the whole, of their net foreign position. In April 1970 the banks' compulsory dollar deposits were reduced from 100 to 50 per cent of the excess of their net positive exchange positions, and as from July such deposits were no longer required.

In November 1968 the expansion of bank credit was made subject to quantitative limitations. The ceilings, which are fixed separately for each month, cover short-term credits and those medium and long-term credits which are not rediscountable with the central bank and special credit institutions. In June 1970 the restrictions were extended until the end of 1970. The extension of medium-term mobilizable credits has long been subject to the prior supervision of the central bank, but since October 1969 also to a fixed ceiling. The ceilings could provide a limit on the extent of inward switching in circumstances where other incentives were such as to encourage it.

Reserve requirements against residents' foreign-currency deposits with banks were introduced in July 1968 at the maximum permissible rate of 10 per cent. The banks could satisfy the requirement only by making noninterest-bearing deposits with the Bank of France. Although this requirement was lifted in September 1968, the banks' French franc liabilities to both residents and nonresidents remained subject to the cash-reserve ratio introduced in January 1967, under which the banks must keep reserves in noninterest-bearing deposits with the Bank of France. The requirements do not apply to domestic interbank deposits, but they do cover franc deposits made by foreign banks or correspondents. In July 1970 the ratio with respect to sight deposits was 6½ to 7½ per cent, and that for time deposits (including cash bonds and deposits at less than three years) and for savings deposits, from 1½ to 2½ per cent. The highest level to which reserve requirements may be raised by the Bank of France is laid down by the National Credit Council and is currently 10 per cent for both classes of deposits.

For a transitional period following the abolition of the "coefficient de trésorerie" in January 1967, banks must observe a specified minimum ratio in respect of rediscountable medium-term paper. This is defined in terms of the same French franc liabilities as come under the cash-reserve requirements, except that the deposits of foreign banks and correspondents are excluded. The ratio was initially fixed at

20 per cent and was to be gradually reduced to nil in the course of four years. (It will be recalled that, effective January 1, 1966, the availability of rediscount facilities for most types of medium-term credits was restricted to credits having at the most three years to run and, as from November 1969, two years.) Credit-policy considerations have generally played a part in the timing of reductions; in November 1968, as a restraint measure, the ratio, which by then had been gradually reduced to 13 per cent, was restored to 14 per cent. In October 1969 the ratio was increased to 15 per cent and again in April 1970 to 16 per cent.

In France the terms and conditions for recourse by the banks to the central bank are frequently varied in detail when the basic discount rate is changed and also at other times. While these measures are generally designed principally to influence the rate of particular types of domestic credit-granting, they may also indirectly influence the banks' possibilities and incentives for inward and outward switching, as well as their French franc transactions with nonresidents.

Interest payable on nonresident accounts with French banks has been the same as that payable to residents since November 1966. Time deposits of over two years' duration or of over Fr.fr. 250,000 were freed from interest-rate controls in July 1967; beginning May 1968, only sight deposits and term deposits at up to one year, in amounts of less than Fr.fr. 100,000, remain subject to interest-rate ceilings.

Interest earnings on both resident and nonresident franc accounts are subject to a 25 per cent withholding tax, as also are those on resident foreign-currency deposits. Residents, however, may choose between this rate and the normal graduated income tax. Foreigners have the possibility of recovering withheld interest income when a double taxation agreement is in force. Exempt from the withholding tax are nonresidents' foreign-currency deposits and also franc deposits used by nonresident banks as working balances.

In France loan operations are generally subject to an indirect tax (*taxe sur les prestations de services*) on a value-added basis. In December 1965, however, loans granted by French banks to firms abroad, whether in foreign currency or francs, were exempted from the tax insofar as the funds in question are for use outside France. Nor does the tax apply to loans made by foreign banks to French firms.

The French franc is used to a limited extent as a Euro-currency.

Germany

German exchange policy makes no distinction between external positions in Deutsche mark and those in foreign currencies. Both are treated on exactly the same basis.

German nonbank residents are free to borrow and lend abroad in Deutsche mark as well as in other currencies. Banks' money exports are free from exchange control, as are their money imports. Between late November 1968 and late February 1969, however, the acceptance of foreign deposits (including savings deposits) and the raising of loans aboard by German banks were subject to Bundesbank authorization. Permits to accept within global limits foreign payments for deposit were allotted to the banks on an individual basis. Transactions necessary for the proper handling of goods, services, and capital movements remained exempt from these restrictions. Loans at maturities of four years or more were exempted from the restrictions on loan-taking. Subsequently the banks' money imports were again freed from these controls. The Bundesbank has sought to exert an active influence on the banks' foreign positions by means of various policy instruments. Among the most important of these has been the selective use of reserve requirements. Not only are liabilities to nonresidents (including foreign banks) subject to reserve requirements similar to those on the banks' liabilities to domestic nonbanks (a wider range of liabilities to nonresidents than of liabilities to residents is subject to reserve requirements) but the ratios may be changed independently of those applying to liabilities towards residents. Moreover, differential reserve ratios may be applied against increases in liabilities to nonresidents as of a particular date.

Reserve ratios against domestic and foreign deposits were equal from February 1967 until the end of November 1968, when reserve requirements with respect to the increase in liabilities to nonresidents were raised to 100 per cent. In June 1969 basic reserve requirements against liabilities to nonresidents (amounts outstanding in April 1969) were raised by 50 per cent, while reserve requirements with respect to domestic liabilities were raised by only 15 per cent.

In July 1969 the Federal Bank Law was amended to authorize the imposition of a reserve requirement of up to 100 per cent against existing foreign liabilities. It allowed the reserve ratios with respect to the banks' foreign liabilities to be fixed without reference to the ceilings applicable to the reserve ratios for domestic liabilities. This statutory authorization was incorporated in the Bundesbank's regulations which became effective September 1, 1969. (Previously, the marginal ratios applied to foreign liabilities on condition that, for a given credit institution, the average reserve ratios for the individual types of domestic and foreign liabilities subject to reserve requirements did not exceed 30 per cent in the case of sight liabilities, 20 per cent in the case of time liabilities, and 10 per cent in the case of saving deposits—"Massgaberegelung.") Shortly afterwards, reserve requirements were raised by 10 per cent for resident and nonresident deposits alike. But in November 1969, after the revaluation of the Deutsche mark, the 100 per cent reserve requirement on increases in the banks' foreign liabilities was abolished. At the same time, reserve requirements against existing foreign liabilities were adjusted to the lower rates applying for domestic liabilities. Moreover, an overall 10 per cent reduction of reserve requirements was implemented. Subsequently, in early March 1970, when the official discount rate was raised from 6 to 7½ per cent, the reserve requirements against net new nonresident liabilities were raised by 30 per cent in order to discourage renewed inflows of funds. This move was followed in July by a 15 per cent across-the-board increase in reserve requirements.

Variations in reserve requirements have also been used to encourage short-term capital exports by banks. Thus, between May 1961 and the end of 1966, the banks were permitted to deduct certain of their money placements abroad (but not their loans to foreign customers) in calculating their reserve obligations. Since the beginning of 1969, except for the period August to December of that year, liabilities arising from certain interest-arbitrage transactions of banks with nonresidents have been free of minimum-reserve requirements.

Another policy instrument used by the Bundesbank concerned the banks' rediscount quotas with the central bank which, effective July 1964, were subject to reduction by an amount equivalent to any increase in the banks' gross foreign liabilities due to credits taken up abroad in excess of the average in a reference period. This rule did not apply insofar as such an increase was connected with primary financing transactions relating to import and transit operations. This regulation remained in force until June 1967.

A third instrument of German exchange policy is the ban on interest payments on deposits made by nonresidents with German financial institutions. It has been imposed with respect to sight and time deposits at several times since 1957. In 1961 this instrument became part of the Foreign Trade Regulation (Aussenwirtschaftsverordnung).[5] To underpin its effectiveness, this measure was accompanied at the outset by a prohibition on those types of short-term capital transactions that might

[5] Since February 1962 German credit institutions may obtain permission to pay interest on nonresident credit balances that serve as cover for letters of credit.

have enabled it to be circumvented. Bans have thus been imposed, for instance, on sales by the banks of German money-market paper or DM bills of exchange to foreigners[6] and on the conclusion with foreigners of "pension" transactions in domestic securities.[7] In December 1969 the existing regulations prohibiting interest payments on nonresidents' deposits (including the supporting restrictions intended to prevent circumvention) were abolished. (Resident deposits had been freed from interest-rate controls in April 1967.) But in May 1970 the Bundesbank announced it would cut rediscount quotas insofar as banks used pension and other operations to evade reserve requirements on foreign liabilities.

In this context mention may also be made of the 25 per cent withholding tax announced in March 1964 on interest from foreign holdings of German fixed-interest securities.

Finally, a rather flexible instrument used by the Bundesbank to encourage money exports, which again assumed considerable importance in 1969, is the dollar-swap facility. The Bundesbank offers the banks forward cover for dollar placements abroad at more favorable rates than those obtainable in the forward-exchange market. It may be mentioned that this facility, which really amounts to an interest-rate subsidy on foreign-currency holdings, is the only instrument which, by definition, applies only to external positions in foreign currencies. Following a period beginning in July 1964 when the swap rates offered by the Bundesbank to the banks for purchases of U.S. treasury bills became unattractive in relation to Eurodollar interest rates, the effectiveness of the facility was restored in November 1967; in September 1968 it was extended to cover 30-day deposits in addition to 60- to 90-day deposits

[6] This does not apply to DM balances of foreign central banks employed in German money-market paper through the intermediation of the Bundesbank.

[7] However, such pension transactions can be effected with all types of foreign assets, including DM bonds issued by foreigners, and also with domestic assets other than long-term bonds (e.g., with certain types of Schuldscheindarlehen). These operations normally involve the sale of fixed-interest-bearing securities based on a repurchase agreement.

previously covered. Rates offered may be varied frequently in response to changes in interest rates and the desired volume of capital flows. At the end of September 1969, when the Deutsche mark was set free to float, the Bundesbank ceased to offer privileged swap rates.

The deterrents to foreign borrowing by banks were designed to protect internal monetary policies from external disturbances rather than to influence the Eurocurrency markets. But they would seem to have the side-effect of discouraging banks from borrowing in the Eurocurrency markets.

Outward switching has at times been indirectly influenced by changes in the cost and availability of central-bank credit. Not only the discount rate but also the cost and availability of particular types of central-bank credit to banks, as well as borrowing ceilings, have been varied as a method of domestic-liquidity control. Thus, in March 1969, bank rediscount quotas were reduced by 20 per cent and the lombard rate (the rate for advances against securities) was raised. For a few days in September, supplements to the lombard rate were introduced for cases of excessive utilization of this facility. Since March 1970 the lombard rate has stood at 9½ per cent, or 2 percentage points above the discount rate.

The Deutsche mark is used to a considerable extent as a Eurocurrency.

Italy

Under existing exchange-control regulations, short-term capital transactions are almost completely free when they are connected with current transactions, but subjected to controls and limitations when they are of a financial nature. Up to Lit. 1 million of foreign exchange can be bought or sold without formality. As far as the financial movement of funds is concerned, borrowing and lending abroad as well as the holding of accounts with foreign banks by nonbank residents require official authorization. Exempt from this requirement are credits from or to European Economic Community countries of up to five years for amounts not exceeding Lit. 50 million (or of between one and five years if not exceeding Lit. 250 million) and long-term loans to or from residents of Organization for Economic Cooperation and Development countries (other than loans by financial institutions to nonresidents) for the purpose of establishing or maintaining lasting economic relationships.

Residents engaged in import activities can incur short-term foreign-exchange debts with Italian banks for current transactions. Export proceeds must be placed on account at an authorized Italian bank within 30 days, but may be held for up to six months for use in authorized transactions or for sale, after which any remaining funds must be surrendered to the official Exchange Office at the lowest rate ruling during the six-month period. In general, Italian regulations provide for foreign-exchange financing only to importers and exporters and for a period usually of three months. This normally occurs whenever interest rates in a given foreign currency are lower than rates prevailing for lira credits.

Authorized banks are allowed to engage in forward exchange transactions up to 180 days. They are not permitted to take an open position in foreign currency. The monetary authorities may intervene in the forward-exchange market from time to time; otherwise, forward premiums and discounts are left to the interplay of market forces.

Italian banks may open accounts for nonresidents in either foreign currency or lire. They are free, moreover, to contract short-term foreign debts on their own initiative by accepting deposits or by utilizing credit lines opened to them by correspondents abroad.

On the lending side, the Italian banks are permitted to keep various kinds of deposit accounts in convertible foreign currencies with banks abroad and to invest in foreign money-market assets. They may also open credit lines for foreign clients for the purpose of financing commercial transactions, whether or not an Italian resident is involved. Finally, they may grant foreign-currency credits to domestic nonbank customers. For commercial purposes, therefore, the banks enjoy wide latitude in borrowing and lending in foreign currencies.

Mention may also be made of several general factors that condition the participation of Italian banks in the Eurocurrency market. First, the reserve requirement, at present 22½ per cent of total deposits with the principal banks, applies to lira liabilities only (including those to nonresidents) and not to foreign-currency liabilities. Second, there is a tax of about 35 per cent on interest income from both lira and foreign-currency deposits with Italian banks, whether held by residents or nonresidents. The Italian banks quote deposit rates free of tax, making the withholding payments themselves. However, their foreign-currency deposit liabilities to banks abroad are treated as interbank deposits and are not subject to the tax. Third, banking cartel arrangements governing maximum-deposit rates and minimum-loan charges on lira business existed up to 1969 but have since been discontinued. Cartel arrangements with respect to foreign-currency lending to residents are still effective, but these rules are limited in scope and not very binding.

In regulating the banks' net foreign position (in exchange and lire) vis-à-vis nonresidents, the authorities sometimes issue instructions with respect to the net (not gross) position at which the banks should aim. In addition, the Exchange Office may make foreign exchange available, by means of swaps, subject to a ceiling for each bank.

As of January 1966, the Exchange Office made available forward cover at par only until a bank had reached a balanced position abroad. Thereafter, if a bank wished to move to a net credit position, it had to bear the cost of forward cover obtained either through the market or, alternatively, from the Exchange Office at a premium approximating the market cost of the swap. From the same date, so as to preserve their external balance, the banks were not permitted to draw upon their sight assets abroad unless these assets exceeded liabilities. Foreign-exchange lending to residents by banks with a balanced or negative foreign-currency position abroad had therefore generally to be financed either by foreign-currency swaps at the premium rate with the Exchange Office or in the market.

In December 1966 and again at the end of 1967, in order to prevent a major reduction in the banks' foreign positions for end-year purposes, the authorities were generally not prepared to permit swaps with the Exchange Office to be temporarily run down and instead provided short-term lira credits to tide the banks over. By March 1969, however, the banks' net foreign assets had reached some Lit. 500 milliard; to stem the outflow of funds associated with high interest rates abroad, as well as to help stimulate domestic-credit expansion, the banks were instructed to reduce their net foreign assets and to achieve a balanced position by June 30. In April 1970 the banks were informed that, as an exception to the 1969 guidelines, they could incur net debt abroad provided the purpose was to finance exports.

Specifically with a view to limiting short-term capital outflows, the terms applicable to bank borrowing at the central bank have been modified recently. In March 1969 a supplement of up to 1½ per cent on the interest rate charged on short-term advances against security was introduced for each case of renewed borrowing by any one bank within a six-month period. Beginning in June, the penalty margin of up to 1½ per cent was also applied for any bank whose rediscounting exceeded one-twentieth of its required reserves in the preceding six months.

A nonbank resident who has borrowed foreign exchange from an Italian bank to pay for imports cannot convert the foreign exchange into domestic lire. If, however, the foreign-currency credit has been granted to an exporter, then the foreign exchange can be converted into lire, given the exporter's commitment to deliver foreign exchange from export proceeds at a future date.

The role of the lira as a Eurocurrency has not been very important.

The Netherlands

Foreign-exchange controls were liberalized during 1967. Nonbank residents were permitted to lend to, and to borrow from, nonresidents up to Fl. 100,000 (formerly Fl. 10,000) for each resident in a calendar year. The general permission to lend was limited to loans to nonbanks, but licenses to keep accounts with foreign banks and to pay money into them are freely granted. Nonbank residents are not allowed by general license to hold foreign money-market paper.

Dutch banks have been allowed to accept deposits in foreign currency or florins since December 1967 at any maturity, from both residents and nonresidents. In the granting of credits to foreign banks and in transactions in foreign money markets, the banks are also completely free. Moreover, they may grant short-term credits to foreign nonbanks. They may also buy from and sell to residents and nonresidents any amount in foreign currency, spot or forward, without limit as to the period of delivery. These regulations allow the Dutch banks a high degree of freedom in their Eurocurrency transactions.

In recent years the Dutch banks have typically had a strong positive net foreign position, reflecting the fact that they keep part of their liquidity abroad. They may draw as necessary upon their foreign liquid assets or, alternatively, increase their indebtedness to the Eurocurrency markets. The banks are generally expected by the monetary authorities to remain free of indebtedness to the central bank, except for possible month-end or other temporary needs. For the most part and under normal circumstances, the banks regulate their local liquidity through the dollar. When the banks are net sellers or buyers of dollars, the Nederlandsche Bank's direct role, apart from smoothing operations, is usually passive. In the spring of 1969, however, it actively intervened in the forward-exchange market with a view to insulating to some extent domestic interest rates from the rising trend in rates abroad.

A regulation effective August 1964 stipulates that a bank's foreign liabilities (in both foreign and domestic currency) may not, without specific approval, exceed its foreign claims. In observing this regulation, each bank has a leeway of Fl. 5 million. But banks authorized to deal in foreign exchange were subject to no limit as to the size of their positive net foreign positions until July 1969, when the Nederlandsche Bank requested them not to increase their net foreign assets and to reduce them by the end of 1969 by 10 per cent compared with either the end-May level or the average March–April level, according to the individual bank's choice. The economic situation changed again in October when, as a consequence of the appreciation of the Deutsche mark, an inflow of funds took place and conditions on the local money market improved. As a result, each individual bank's ceiling under this regulation was increased in November to 125 per cent of the optional base periods mentioned above. In April 1970 the ceilings were abolished altogether.

In regulating the banks' liquidity, the monetary authorities have the possibility of applying a cash-reserve requirement, variable within a range of zero to 15 per cent. Over a period of several years, beginning in the summer of 1961, this ratio was progressively lowered from 10 per cent to zero, the object being to reduce the banks' incentive to repatriate funds held abroad. The ratio has not been employed since 1963.

In order to regulate domestic liquidity, the Nederlandsche Bank has on occasion engaged in swap operations with the banks at relatively favorable rates. The main purpose of these swaps has been to encourage the re-export of funds repatriated during periods of unsettled market conditions or to meet seasonal needs.

A ceiling is in force limiting the permissible rate of expansion of short-term bank credit to the domestic private sector, while the increase in longer term bank lending is restricted to the increase in long-term liabilities. There is no prohibition on foreign-currency bank loans to residents, but such loans would be subject to these overall ceilings and, in practice, the banks do not make foreign-currency loans to residents. The banks are also subject to a regulation limiting their total credit-granting (including lending to nonbanks abroad) to five times their own funds. At times of strong domestic demand for credit this has tended to limit the available outlets for funds borrowed abroad.

In the Netherlands there are no withholding taxes on interest income from deposits.

The florin finds fairly wide use as a Eurocurrency. In this connection, however, it may be noted that time-deposit rates in the Netherlands are competitively determined. The banks' rates for domestic lending in florins are normally 1½ to 2½ per cent above the official discount rate.

Norway

Residents other than banks require the prior approval of Norges Bank or the Department of Commerce before raising loans abroad. Outward capital transfers also have to be authorized, and portfolio investment abroad is approved only in exceptional cases. All foreign exchange accruing from exports and receipts from invisibles must be surrendered.

Forward-exchange transactions with residents must have a commercial basis. Forward premiums and discounts are generally left to the play of market forces, but Norges Bank has in a few cases intervened in the forward market, especially in the period following the devaluation of sterling in November 1967, when the principal object was to maintain confidence in the parity of the Norwegian krone.

In the National Budget submitted to Parliament each year,

the government presents guidelines on monetary and credit policy. In accordance with these guidelines, Norges Bank prescribes rules for the banks' foreign borrowing and lending operations. The annual guidelines have generally included provisions restricting increases in banks' foreign-currency liabilities abroad, sometimes referring specifically to loans and credits raised abroad and foreign-currency deposits of nonresidents. Often the restriction has applied only insofar as such funds were used for the financing of lending to domestic nonbanks, whether in Norwegian krone or in foreign currencies (i.e., to net positions). On several occasions in the past, the banks have been asked to avoid reducing their foreign-currency balances with banks abroad; for 1969, however, the banks were asked not to increase further their net foreign-currency assets (which had shown a strong increase during 1968). Under the Monetary and Credit Act, banks may be required to maintain special central-bank deposits against foreign liabilities calculated on the basis of the increase in deposits and loans from foreign depositors and lenders. The rate may be set differently for deposits and loans with a term exceeding twelve months and for deposits and loans with a shorter term.

Banks were specifically requested in July 1969 to refrain from approving any applications for credit which made possible either the postponement of repatriation of foreign-exchange earnings or the acceleration of foreign settlements.

Banks are required to maintain liquid reserves in the form of cash, current-account deposits at Norges Bank, postal transfer-account deposits, treasury bills, and government or government-guaranteed bonds, against total liabilities (with the exception only of documentary credits and assessed but unpaid taxes). In contrast to the situation in Denmark and Sweden, no part of banks' foreign position counts as liquid assets for the purpose of satisfying this requirement. As laid down in the Monetary and Credit Act, the maximum ratio to which the liquidity requirements may be raised is 25 per cent. As a special measure, in force from September 1966 until March 1967, banks were required to make special deposits with Norges Bank in proportion to increases in their lending in excess of certain limits. This was designed to reduce the rate of domestic lending, and banks' foreign lending was excluded from the computation.

Most bank interest rates are fixed by agreement or convention in relation to the discount rate and have remained at low levels by international standards. Banks have an obligation to consult with Norges Bank before making interest-rate changes. These conventions cover interbank demand deposits but not nonresident or foreign-currency deposits.

Sweden

The depositing or lending of funds abroad by residents is subject to restrictions. In principle, residents may buy foreign currency only when needed in connection with the execution of current foreign payments or authorized capital payments. For the purpose of financing current external-trade payments, importers and exporters are allowed to use credit facilities abroad. Exporters are also generally allowed to receive advance payments from their buyers. Foreign-owned companies in Sweden are usually permitted to borrow from the parent companies but otherwise loans from nonresidents to residents for financing economic activity in Sweden are generally not permitted. Receipts in foreign currencies by residents may either be sold to a Swedish bank against kronor or kept in a foreign-currency account with a Swedish bank and used by the holder to make authorized payments abroad. Since September 1969 no interest may be paid on such foreign-currency accounts. Short-term borrowing abroad of kinds other than those mentioned above is restricted.

Swedish banks are free to incur foreign-currency liabilities.

However, they may not allow their assets in any individual currency to fall below their liabilities in that currency. They are not allowed to borrow abroad for relending in Sweden or in order to sell the proceeds against kronor in the market, even for relending abroad in kronor. They are usually permitted to make foreign currency loans to nonresidents for financing certain specified Swedish import and export transactions. Such credits must conform with normal commercial practice. Payment of interest on nonresident foreign-currency deposits is permitted.

Authorized banks may conclude with residents other than banks forward-exchange transactions covering current payments and authorized payments for periods not exceeding 24 months with respect to receipts for exports, freight, and charter services; 12 months with respect to payments for imports, freight, and charter services; and 6 months with respect to other receipts and payments. Authorized banks may conclude forward transactions for a period not exceeding 12 months with other authorized banks and, under certain conditions, foreign banks. Such transactions between banks may, however, be for longer periods if made to cover forward deals with residents. Forward-market rates are left to the play of market forces.

As of August 1969, ceilings on banks' total net assets abroad were introduced.

Since March 1969 the Swedish system of liquidity-reserve requirements has been placed on a statutory basis. The bigger banks are required to hold the equivalent of 30 per cent of their total deposits, plus certain other short-term liabilities, as a reserve in the form of cash, checks and bankers' drafts, net claims on domestic and foreign banks, foreign bills, treasury bills, and government and mortgage institutions' bonds. Deposits in foreign currency by residents and nonresidents are in general included. Interbank deposits are, however, calculated on a net basis in the numerator. A penalty of 4 per cent per annum is applied to any shortfall. Previously the requirements were based on agreements between the banks and the Riksbank, and infringements by any bank were penalized only by a surcharge on the interest cost of its borrowings from the Riksbank. This sanction is still in force and is applied to the statutory requirement. Beginning in December 1967, banks could count only half (previously all) of their net foreign assets towards satisfying the requirement, while in implementing the March 1969 legislation the Riksbank laid down that net foreign-currency claims on foreign banks may be counted only to the extent of 1½ per cent of the denominator (i.e., total liabilities less a few items such as own funds).

Also on a statutory basis is the power whereby commercial banks may also be required to hold on noninterest-bearing account at the Riksbank amounts fixed in relation to the denominator used for the liquidity-reserve requirement calculation. Recourse was had to this power in January–February 1968, when the ratio was set at 2 per cent for the larger banks and 1 per cent for the smaller ones, and again in August 1969, when it was 1 per cent for all banks.

In addition to the use of these liquidity and special-deposit requirements to help restrain capital outflows, ceilings were fixed in August 1969 on the borrowings of each individual bank from the central bank, with the same objective in view. At the end of April 1970 the Riksbank concluded an agreement with the commercial banks under which credit-granting other than for housing was to be subject to monthly ceilings limiting the increase by December 1970 to 4 per cent of the end-1969 level.

The Riksbank does not generally make use of forward operations in the exchange markets as an instrument of policy.

The creation by foreigners of krona holdings with Swedish commercial banks must not result in abnormal balances. Furthermore, banks may grant only normal overdrafts to nonresidents. With regard to interest payments, there are no withholding-tax arrangements in Sweden, either for foreign or domestic currency liabilities. However, krona balances held by foreigners with Swedish commercial banks do not, except for minor amounts, bear interest. This is not a matter of exchange control but rather of an interbank agreement dating from before the war.

Switzerland

Nonbank residents enjoy full freedom in borrowing, holding, and lending foreign currencies.

In general, the regime of full convertibility also applies to the banks. They may incur foreign-currency liabilities, using the proceeds either for relending abroad or for switching into Swiss francs. Nor is there any restriction on their converting francs into foreign currencies for purposes of placing funds abroad. The only exception is that bank loans to nonresidents of at least Sw.fr. 10 million and of at least one year's duration are subject to the approval of the National Bank. This control is exercised primarily with regard to the situation on the domestic money and capital markets. It is not used to check on the quality of the borrowers or the borrowing country. Permission for such loans is usually granted in a very liberal manner.

Several measures have been employed in recent years to limit the growth of deposit liabilities to nonresidents. However, these measures have related not to deposits in foreign currency but rather to those in Swiss francs, the primary object being to discourage the inflow of flight money from abroad insofar as it was inflating domestic money and credit. Thus between 1964 and March 1967, the payment of interest on nonresident Swiss franc deposits was prohibited, and any increase in a bank's Swiss franc liabilities to nonresidents that was not offset by a rise in its *net* foreign-currency assets abroad had to be placed on special noninterest-bearing deposit with the National Bank. Under the Swiss Constitution such legal measures are allowed on an emergency basis for a limited period of time only, but they could be renewed.

Mention may also be made of the ceilings on domestic (ordinary and mortgage) credit expansion employed between 1962 and 1966 which, though liberally applied, indirectly served to discourage the banks from drawing upon liquidity from abroad, and also of the National Bank's recommendation for 1967 that bank lending should not increase by more than a certain percentage. In 1961, also to offset inflows, commercial-bank funds were blocked in giro accounts at the National Bank. These funds were released in two stages in April and December 1967.

Proposals for revisions to the National Bank Law, presented to Parliament in August 1968, envisaged empowering the National Bank to call, after consultations with the banks, for minimum deposits from the banks in the event of too rapid an expansion in the volume of money and credit. Minimum reserves would be related to the increase in the banks' total liabilities, with maximum limits set at 40 per cent with respect to domestic sight-deposit liabilities and 10 to 30 per cent for domestic time deposits, while for increases in net foreign liabilities the rate could in principle be double that applicable to domestic liabilities. It was also proposed that the National Bank be empowered to limit the growth of credit for not more than two years if this objective cannot be obtained by other policy instruments or by agreement with the banks. In September 1969, provisions along these lines for minimum reserves and for a ceiling on domestic credit expansion were embodied in a formal five-year agreement between the National Bank and the credit institutions, which will serve as an alternative to statutory controls. Simultaneously, a ceiling was imposed on total domestic lending, with the range, depending on the individual bank's previous rate of lending activity, being initially set at 9–11.5 per cent per annum and subsequently reduced in January 1970 to 7.65–9.75 per cent.

As in Germany, Italy, and the Netherlands, the Swiss monetary authorities have at times carried out swap operations with the banks. The primary object of such operations has always been to absorb excess domestic bank liquidity, usually at times when there has been an exceptional inflow of foreign funds, by providing the banks with opportunities to invest funds abroad. The terms offered to the banks have normally been closely in line with market conditions. At year-end and sometimes at quarter-ends, the Swiss National Bank has engaged in dollar/franc swaps with the banks, making liquid funds available to them for tiding-over purposes. By accepting treasury bills or promissory notes, the commercial banks have contributed to the financing of Roosa bonds taken over by the Bank for International Settlements (BIS). Also, swap transactions have been effected with the commercial banks to cover the exchange risk of the Federal Government on its investments in foreign currencies resulting from budget surpluses.

In Switzerland there is a withholding tax of 30 per cent on interest income, inter alia from deposits (other than interbank deposits), both resident and nonresident, whether in Swiss francs or in foreign currencies. A resident may reclaim the tax when filing an income-tax return, but the right of a nonresident to do so depends upon whether his country has a double-taxation agreement with Switzerland. To some extent, therefore, the tax may act as a deterrent to the placement of deposits by nonresidents other than banks. The Swiss banks' foreign-currency liabilities to banks abroad are treated as interbank deposits and are therefore not subject to the withholding tax. If such deposits extend beyond one year, however, they become subject to withholding. Moreover, if from the outset they are placed as deposits at more than one year, they are subject, in addition, to a stamp duty of 1.2 per mille per year.

The Swiss franc is used fairly extensively as a Eurocurrency. This is partly because, by interbank agreement, the larger banks set a limit to the rate that they offer for time deposits, which is at the present time 5 per cent for three-month deposits. Lending rates, on the other hand, are freely determined and, by international standards, are relatively low.

Canada

There have been no formal exchange controls of any kind since 1951. Resident banks and nonbanks are generally free to hold assets and to borrow and lend in foreign currencies. However, certain official requests aiming directly at banks' foreign-currency positions have been issued in recent years. Moreover, nonbank residents' freedom to invest abroad is restricted by a request designed to avoid a pass-through of funds resulting from Canada's exemption from the U.S. balance-of-payments controls. Thus, in September 1968 the government asked Canadian companies not to embark on new investment programs in Western Europe involving a transfer of capital funds, to exercise restraint in other new investment outside Canada and the United States, and to give priority to investment contributing to improvement in Canada's trade and payments.

In seeking to influence residents' external positions in foreign and domestic currencies, the authorities rely principally on general monetary measures designed to affect interest differentials, at both short and long term. Operations in the forward-exchange market have not generally been an important instrument of policy.

Measures directed towards the external, including Eurocurrency, side of the banks' business have been confined to specific requests designed either to limit sharp capital outflows, particularly in the period immediately following the devaluation of sterling, or to fulfill international commitments. Thus, in January 1968 the banks were requested to discourage the use of bank credit by Canadian subsidiaries of foreign companies either to facilitate abnormal transfers of funds abroad to meet financial requirements in Canada which had in the past been met by parent companies. By August this request had become redundant because of the decline in demand for such loans and it was withdrawn.

In early March 1968, as a move specifically designed to prevent an outflow of funds and to loosen the link between domestic and Eurodollar interest rates, chartered banks were called upon not to enter into or renew agreements with their customers swapping Canadian-dollar deposits into foreign-currency deposits. At the same time, banks and other financial institutions were asked not to place, or facilitate the placement of, swapped short-term funds abroad. These requests were withdrawn in June 1968; subsequently in July 1969, in quite different circumstances chartered banks were asked to avoid increasing swap deposits beyond the current level. (Chartered banks' swap transactions are undertaken at the initiative of residents who give up Canadian dollars in exchange for foreign-currency deposits, usually U.S. dollars, subject to reversal of the transaction at a later date. The banks thus provide forward cover for liabilities to residents in foreign currencies; as a counterpart, the banks buy in the market equivalent amounts of foreign exchange, some of which may be placed in the Eurocurrency markets.) At the end of March 1970, after a decline in interest rates abroad, the Bank of Canada removed the ceiling on swap-deposit transactions.

In line with undertakings at the time of Canada's exemption from the U.S. balance-of-payments controls, guidelines for banks designed to prevent the pass-through of funds to third countries were announced in May 1968. These provided, first, that Canadian banks' foreign-currency loans and investments in countries other than the United States and Canada should not exceed end-February 1968 levels, except to the extent of any increase in deposits from residents of third countries. Second, any withdrawal of funds by residents of third countries was to be matched as soon as possible by a reduction in foreign-currency assets outside North America. And finally, Canadian banks were asked not to accept U.S. dollar deposits from U.S. residents for reinvestment in the United States (such transactions increase the U.S. balance-of-payments deficit measured on a liquidity basis). In July 1968 these principles were extended to other financial institutions.

Some of the regulations and conditions relating to domestic banking practices also have a bearing on the banks' Euro-dollar business.

Reserve requirements provide a limited incentive to banks to incur debt in foreign currencies vis-à-vis both residents and nonresidents. Under the new Bank Act of May 1967, banks are required to maintain a cash reserve in noninterest-bearing deposits with the Bank of Canada and vault cash amounting to 12 per cent against demand and 4 per cent against time deposits. By comparison with the former uniform 8 per cent minimum-reserve requirement against both demand and time deposits, this provision widened the scope for competition for domestic time deposits. Nonetheless, some incentive to engage in swap transactions with residents and to borrow foreign currency from nonresidents remained, since foreign-currency liabilities, whether to residents or nonresidents, are subject only to the provision that "adequate and appropriate assets" be held against them. Against their Canadian-dollar deposit liabilities, moreover, banks are obliged to hold secondary reserves in the form of treasury bills, day-to-day loans to investment dealers, and notes of and deposits with the central bank in excess of minimum cash-reserve requirements. This secondary reserve requirement was placed on a statutory basis in January 1968 and the ratio was increased from 7 to 8 per cent, beginning June 1969.

The 1967 Bank Act replaced the former 6 per cent interest-rate ceiling on domestic lending (whether in Canadian dollars or foreign currency) with a ceiling fixed for 1967 at 1¾ per cent above the average market yield on short-term government bonds (with the provision that the ceiling ceases to operate when this yield falls below 5 per cent). By raising the ceiling and increasing its flexibility, this change reduced the banks' potential incentive, in the absence of guidelines, to shift funds to Eurocurrency markets when interest rates on Eurocurrency loans rise sharply. Indirectly, the higher ceiling also made it possible for the banks to offer higher rates for time deposits. Subsequently, as provided for in the 1967 Act, the interest ceiling was completely removed at the beginning of 1968.

New Canadian issues (but not trading in existing issues) are exempted from the U.S. Interest-Equalization Tax (IET). In this connection, a request was issued in March 1966 to all Canadian investors, including financial institutions, not to purchase securities denominated in Canadian or U.S. dollars which are issued by U.S. corporations and their non-Canadian subsidiaries and which would be subject to the U.S. Interest-Equalization Tax if purchased by U.S. residents. This guideline serves to discourage purchases which, through their effect on domestic monetary conditions, could indirectly give rise to a larger volume of issues on the U.S. capital market, and also to switching out of U.S. securities. In December 1968 it was agreed with the United States that the exemption from IET does not require that Canada's monetary reserves be limited to any particular figure (though Canada would continue to avoid increasing its reserves through borrowing in the United States).

Interest on Canadian-dollar investments held by nonresidents in the form of bonds or short-term paper issued by corporations and Canadian-dollar bank deposits in Canada is subject to a 15 per cent withholding tax, which does not, however, apply to interest on federal, provincial, or municipal security issues.

The use of the Canadian dollar as a Euro-currency has been negligible.

Japan

Foreign-currency loans from foreign banks do play an important role in financing external trade; however, nonbank residents require approval before raising funds abroad or making outward capital transfers.

Export proceeds must be surrendered within ten days of the date of acquisition, except that resident Japanese trading concerns may be permitted to hold foreign-currency deposit accounts with authorized banks in which they may keep their proceeds from exports and invisibles for a maximum of 20 days, during which time they may be used for approved payments for imports and invisibles.

Nonbank residents may freely enter into forward contracts based on actual requirements with banks located in Japan but not with banks located abroad. Authorized exchange banks may freely enter into forward contracts for other than speculative purposes except that the duration of forward contracts with banks located abroad (excluding foreign branches of Japanese banks) may not exceed six months. There has been no official intervention in the forward-exchange market.

Since nonbanks are subject to restrictions regarding their external transactions, the banking system has been the main channel through which short-term funds have moved. Control over such flows has, therefore, been aimed chiefly at the commercial banks. Of their short-term external transactions, those relating to foreign-trade finance are, in principle, freely permitted as long as they are considered normal practice.

Several different instruments have been used to control capital flows. The 12 Japanese banks authorized to engage in ordinary foreign-exchange business are required to hold foreign-currency assets equivalent since April 1966 to at least 15 per cent of certain of their foreign liabilities. These liabilities are foreign-currency deposits, call money, loans from foreign banks, nonresident free yen deposits, etc. This obligation is quite distinct from the normal reserve-requirement system under which commercial banks are required to deposit with the Bank of Japan an amount equivalent to a given proportion of their yen-deposit liabilities to both residents and nonresidents alike. At present, the normal reserve requirements are quite low. Those against the sight deposits of the larger commercial banks (banks with deposits in excess of Yen 100 milliard) were raised from 1 to 1½ per cent in September 1969, but requirements against time deposits for these banks have remained unchanged at 0.5 per cent since November 1962.

For banks authorized to deal in foreign exchange, total open positions, spot and forward combined, carried in any foreign currencies are subject to maximum limits.

Between July 1961 and July 1966 the authorities restricted the rates of interest paid on Eurocurrency borrowing by ceilings, based on rates prevailing in the London market. In July 1966 these ceilings were removed but guidance is still exercised to ensure that interest rates paid by the Japanese banks will not be excessive in relation to rates prevailing in the London market.

The authorities have since July 1964 prescribed the maximum amount of short-term borrowing from Eurocurrency markets for each of 12 banks. The total permissible maximum is first calculated so as not to weaken the overall external position of the commercial banks for a given period, then the total is divided among the banks. This guideline has been used as a check to capital inflows, but it has not been used to influence outflows.

As of October 1967, with a view to stabilizing Eurocurrency

borrowings, the authorized exchange banks were permitted to borrow Eurodollar funds at medium and long-term and to lend at medium and long term in foreign currency for approved investment abroad. Funds borrowed abroad which are relent abroad in this way may, at the request of the bank, be exempted from the ceilings on bank overseas borrowing fixed under the guideline. In February 1968, mainly to counter expected difficulties in raising funds in the United States, the borrowing ceilings under the guidelines were raised substantially, but the guideline ceilings were increased only slightly in April 1968, and again operated quite restrictively.

To prevent excessive switching from foreign currency into yen when the limits on bank Eurodollar borrowing were raised in the context of tight domestic-monetary policy, Japanese banks were instructed in February 1968 to avoid any increase in the level of their foreign liabilities converted into yen.

Since April 1969 the Bank of Japan has, in the course of providing guidance to the banks on their domestic-liquidity positions, been prepared to take into account, in a flexible way, any deterioration in the domestic-liquidity positions of the exchange banks which was attributable to borrowings of yen call-money for the purpose of repaying Eurodollar or other foreign borrowings.

In September 1969 new measures were taken, in view of recent trends in the balance of payments and in domestic and foreign interest rates, to induce the exchange banks to improve their external positions. Thus, from September to December 1969, the Bank of Japan supplied yen funds to the authorized exchange banks at call-money rates by purchasing securities under a three-month (renewable) repurchase agreement. Concurrently, the Foreign Exchange Special Account supplied the foreign-exchange banks with the dollar funds necessary for repayment of Eurodollar and other foreign borrowings or for Eurodollar lending by means of three-month (renewable) yen/dollar swaps. The same exchange rate was applied for both the spot and the forward transactions, i.e., the interbank spot rate on the Tokyo foreign-exchange market on the day prior to the transaction.

On occasion, as a measure to control inward switching, relatively low central-bank credit ceilings have been imposed on commercial banks which have carried out large yen conversions, though this is only one of the many factors taken into account in setting such ceilings. Beyond these limits, the penalty rate, which is 4 per cent higher than the discount rate (3.65 per cent higher until the end of August 1969), may be applied to loans and rediscounts from the central bank.

There is a withholding tax generally of 20 per cent on interest income from yen and foreign-currency deposits of nonresidents, including foreign banks. (There are reduced rates of 10 or 15 per cent for payments to residents of certain countries.) The tax does not apply, however, to any deposit balance with Japanese banks abroad. Otherwise, interest payments on interbank or nonresident deposits with Japanese banks are subject to the same conditions as resident deposits.

INDEX

PRINTED IN U.S.A.